Trends and Cycles in Economic Activity

Trends and Cycles

AN INTRODUCTION TO

HOLT, RINEHART AND WINSTON   •   New York

WILLIAM FELLNER / Yale University

John

in Economic Activity

PROBLEMS OF ECONOMIC GROWTH

"No point of view, once expressed, ever seems wholly
to die; and in periods of transition like the present, our
ears are full of the whisperings of dead men."

SIR ALEXANDER GRAY

22776-0116

Printed in the United States of America

Preface

While this book was written for readers interested in studying the general area of dynamic economics, the writer also incorporated into the book the product of some of his more recent research efforts (perhaps primarily in Chapter 8 and in the Appendix to Part 3, but also in Part 2). However, all along he was aware of the danger that uncontrolled inclinations of this type might impair the generality of the discussion, and he tried his best to minimize this danger.

The dual problem of the qualitative adequacy and of the quantitative sufficiency of technological and organizational improvements has, to some extent, been placed in the foreground of the argument. In the author's thinking, at least, this dual problem has stayed in the foreground. By qualitatively adequate improvements we shall here mean improvements the laborsaving, capital-saving, and land-saving, effects of which stand in a desirable relation to one another. Sustained economic growth requires qualitative adequacy as well as quantitative sufficiency of technological and organizational improvements, that is, of new skills. This may be considered the main theme of the book (although we shall not lose sight of the price-behavior requirements and the resource-mobility requirements of sustained growth).

An attempt will also be made to gauge the ability of improvements to offset the consequences of differential factor supplies (relative scarcities in factors of production). The criteria for this appraisal will be developed in Chapter 8, and quantitative materials will be presented in the Appendix to Part 3. The data relate chiefly to trends in the average productivity of capital, in distributive shares and in the rate of return from investment.

The central analytical structure of the book is first sketched in Part 2, and is further elaborated subsequently. Part 1 is mainly concerned with research methods and with empirical findings that have resulted from these, but it includes also interpretation and appraisal. Discussions and appraisals of research methods will, however, be found in later sections of the book, too (*e.g.,* in Chapter 12).

v

Methodologically, the present volume springs from the conviction that much can be said for presenting the elements and the main content of economic dynamics in terms of long-run tendencies, and thus for analytically subordinating the problem of fluctuations to that of secular growth. Readers who wish to engage in a more detailed analysis of cyclical disturbances have at present no difficulty finding books that serve them well. Nor do they have difficulty supplementing these books with articles on specific aspects of the business-cycle problem. All will agree that the study of cyclical fluctuations should be combined with a discussion of what may be called trend forces. Indeed, no widely used text in business cycles overlooks this. But readers might agree that in addition to the usual trend-supplemented treatment of cycles we also need a type of analysis which places long-run tendencies in the center and works the problem of business cycles into that theme. This is the methodological conviction which motivated the present writer.

The primarily growth-oriented, or trend-oriented, attitude to dynamic economics has now been in the air for some time. As one important contributor, Evsey D. Domar, has said, it may be preferable to call this a recent *revival* of an attitude.[1] In the contemporary circumstances, the attitude in question is certain to leave its mark on monetary and fiscal policy as well as on economic theory. Throughout the area of Western civilization governments will make a substantial effort to prevent the recurrence of major depressions. In the United States, and perhaps in most other Western countries, this effort is likely to be fairly successful, and there exists no good reason for believing that it will prove incompatible with the essentials of the private enterprise system. If this view turns out to be justified, then, in the economies in which long-run growth rates are satisfactory, we shall probably experience a weakening of one type of radicalism, namely, of the pressure toward radical "redistribution." A primarily trend-conscious, rather than cycle-conscious, population is very unlikely to press toward a risky course in matters relating to the division of a given pie. This could fail to be true only if, aside from deliberate redistributional policies, the relative share of the lower income groups tended to diminish in the course of growth process. But, at least for advanced industrial nations (and perhaps for rapidly growing economies in general), such an hypothesis would seem to be unrealistic.

---

[1] See Evsey D. Domar, "Economic Growth: An Econometric Approach," *American Economic Review, Papers and Proceedings* (May 1952), pp. 479-495.

While, therefore, the analysis in this book is primarily oriented toward growth problems, we shall not lose sight of the fact that the trend is a statistical abstraction and is not "real" in the sense in which the cycle is. Growth trends express themselves in the real world in the rising tendency of observable cyclical movements. They cannot be understood without studying the cycle. Much of the presentation in this book will therefore be concerned with the problem of the cycle, as part of the problem of economic growth.

The following kindly gave permission for the use of numerical and graphic materials: The Staples Press Limited, London (as successor of King and Son, publishers of Augustus Sauerbeck's 1908 volume on English commodity prices); *The Statist; The Manchester School; The Review of Economics and Statistics;* The National Bureau of Economic Research; The McGraw-Hill Book Company, as publisher of the late Professor Schumpeter's book on business cycles, a graph from which, along with materials of a different sort, underlies Figure 6 on page 44 *infra*. The courtesy of these periodicals and publishers is appreciated. So is that of Mr. Raymond W. Goldsmith, who kindly approved the use of data which he submitted to a conference of the National Bureau of Economic Research.

The author had the benefit of Mr. Leland L. Johnson's assistance in the research that led to this book. Mr. Johnson also prepared the index. Mrs. Jerome H. Logan helped all along not only by typing successive drafts of the manuscript but also by giving advice in matters of presentation.

Professor Gottfried Haberler discussed the completed manuscript with the author and made valuable suggestions. Professors James Tobin and Henry C. Wallich read parts of the manuscript and their comments, too, were very helpful.

To all these, the author expresses his gratitude.

W. F.

New Haven, Conn.
November 15, 1955

Contents

Part 1—General View of Growth with Interruptions

PART 1/

General View of Growth with Interruptions

Introductory Remarks on Trends, Cycles and Paths of Dynamic Equilibrium

1. The problem of the Chapter.

The forces determining the upward *trend* of an economy may be studied with the aid of theoretical systems in which the economy is represented as moving on a path of uninterrupted growth. Such a path we shall call one of "dynamic equilibrium." Interruptions of the growth process—cyclical disturbances—may then be regarded as being caused by violations of the conditions of dynamic equilibrium.

This suggestion is useful for some purposes, but it requires clarification. What is the relationship between an upward-sloping trend line, such as is characteristic of growing economies, and a path of dynamic equilibrium? After all, "the trend" which cuts through the ups and downs of an economy is a somewhat arbitrary statistical concept, and paths of dynamic equilibrium (or of uninterrupted growth) are hypothetical paths.

In the present Chapter we shall briefly discuss the concept of the trend and that of cyclical disturbances, and we shall relate these to the concept of dynamic equilibrium. The discussion will be merely illustrative: only a minimum of factual information will be used here, and research techniques will not be explored in any detail. We are merely trying to prepare the ground for the subsequent analysis in Chapter 2.

2. The common sense of drifts and trends.

As we look back at several decades, much of the economic history of industrialized countries can be told in terms of trends. These trends disregard the ups and downs of short-term development. They are devices for

3

summing up a story by means of averaging or finding representative values. There exists no unique method of trend fitting which would be logically superior to other methods, just as there exists no unique, objectively superior method of summing up the essentials of the life history of an individual. A story can never be fully told, only more or less fully. Whether a method of summarizing and of thereby neglecting details, a method of representing a movement as if it had proceeded from its point of departure to its terminal point without detours, is satisfactory or misleading depends on the nature of one's interest. This interest, which intuitively exists prior to the development of a technique, determines whether we are willing to view a specific condensed account as containing, for our purposes, the essentials of reality.

When we wish to take a long-run point of view, we are expressing an interest in the *general drift* of events over a longer period. This should not suggest that when a development is completed its general drift is its only significant characteristic over longer periods. It is true of a completed century, as well as of a completed month, that in one direction or another events were constantly deviating from their general drift. These deviations remain significant characteristics of the development during the period as a whole. In one sense, they could be said to stay significant in the long run. However, ambiguous words, such as that of the long run, frequently acquire specific meaning through common usage, and an interest in the long run has come to mean an interest in the general drift of events over longer periods.

The trend lines with which we are concerned here express the general drift of time series, that is, of time sequences of numerical data. They disregard the detours.

3. An illustration.

In industrialized or industrializing economies, most significant time series show a steep upward drift. For example, the aggregate output of the United States, measured in constant prices (in the prices of 1929), rose about fivefold from the eighteen-nineties to the nineteen-forties.[1] If we compare the average yearly output of the successive decades with each other, the percentage increase from one decade to the next is, of course,

---

[1] F. C. Mills, *Productivity and Economic Progress* (New York, 1952), p. 2. We are here using gross rather than net national product for illustrating trends in "aggregate output." It should be mentioned that depreciation charges (capital consumption allowances), of which the difference between gross and net consists, showed an increase as a percentage of the total output during the period under consideration.

not always the same. While averaging for decades smooths out much of the cyclical instability, the decade-averages remain noticeably influenced by the somewhat depressed character of the decade of the eighteen-nineties as a whole, by the significantly depressed character of the nineteen-thirties as a whole, and by the war and postwar prosperity of the entire decade of the nineteen-forties. The rate of increase of output is comparatively small when we move into decades of generally depressed character, and it is comparatively great when we move out of these, especially if we move into very prosperous ones. But the data give the impression of a basic tendency toward a proportionate rate of increase of between 30 percent and 40 percent per decade. This rate of increase appears to be typical of the transition from one "normal" decade to the next, and when two successive decades are "abnormal" in opposite directions as the nineteen-thirties and the nineteen-forties, the tendency asserts itself for a twenty-year period. Similarly, the decade-to-decade increase in output divided by man-hours performed (the rise in so-called man-hour output) tended to be somewhat in excess of 20 percent, with an especially significant increase for the transition into the nineteen-twenties, and a relatively small increase from the 'twenties to the 'thirties.

Trends aim at disclosing tendencies of this sort. Both Simon Kuznets and Frederick C. Mills have made effective use of decade averages for the characterization of the main properties of long-run drifts or "trends."

4. Some technical problems raised by the illustration.

In graphic presentation it would be awkward to express the trend of the American aggregate output series for the period just considered by showing merely the decade averages for the eighteen-nineties, for the next decade, and so on. This would mean substituting for all observed values (say, yearly values) during the eighteen-nineties the decade average for that period, and substituting for the observed values during the other decades *their* decade averages. If such a representation of the drift were charted, we would obtain a succession of straight lines or horizontal stretches with steplike vertical rises between the successive horizontal stretches. By such a method we would be introducing into our graphic representation sharp discontinuities at arbitrarily chosen dates, namely, on January 1 of the first year of each decade. We have to find some smoother method of expressing the general drift of a time series. In the first approximation it is plausible to interpret the average yearly output of a decade as characteristic of the center date of that decade, and, having thus obtained one point for the center-date of each decade, to fit a continuously rising line to these points. But if yearly data, or data for even shorter periods, are available, it is also possible to obtain a continuous trend representation by direct tracing of the drift of a fluctuating series.

Assume, for example, that the observed data are those of successive years, or of quarters of years, and that all data lie along the fluctuating

FIGURE I

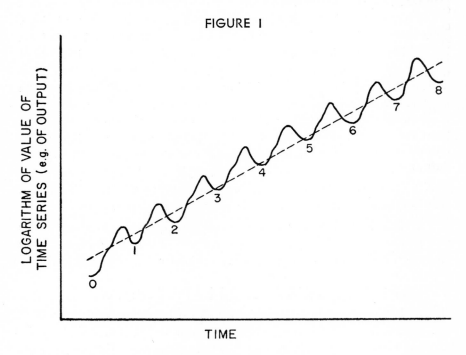

curve of Figure 1. If the original data relate to periods shorter than a year, then it is necessary to eliminate from them the so-called seasonal variations because the increased sales of the Christmas season and similar variations form no part of the problem with which we are dealing here. Let us assume that the "seasonal" has been eliminated. We now have before us a path reflecting the nonseasonal ups and downs of a time series, and we wish to obtain a smooth or continuous graphic expression of the general drift of such a complex movement. In Figure 1 the trend line is drawn freehand in such a way that, for the period as a whole, the above-trend and the below-trend values should be of approximately equal weight. The trend here is supposed to be logarithmically linear, expressing a tendency of the time series to rise at a constant *proportionate* rate

(that is, at a steeply increasing, so-called "exponential," *absolute* rate) .²
We have seen that the trend line which fits the American output series
from the eighteen-nineties to the nineteen-forties may be interpreted as
suggesting logarithmic linearity, with a proportionate rate of increase
of about 35 percent per decade. Aside from logarithmic linearity of the
trend, the data of Figure 1 are invented merely for the purpose of exposition.

Figure 1 happens to have been drawn in such a way that it would have
been possible to represent the trend of the time series alternatively by a
curved line, on a logarithmic scale, rather than by a straight line. This is
because, of the eight cycles appearing in the graph, the first and the third
(two rather early ones) point to a steeper trend slope, and the sixth and
the eighth (two rather late ones) point to a reduced trend slope.³
Whether or not it is useful to express this detail in the shape of the trend
unfortunately depends partly on what is going to happen in the next
periods of comparable duration. In other words, we do not know whether

---

² If, for example, the yearly rate of proportionate increase along the trend line is
constant (say 3 percent) , then the size of the absolute rate of increase per period is
getting bigger at this same rate (3 percent per year). At the moment when the value
of the time series was 100, the absolute rate of increase was 3 per year, assuming for the
sake of simplicity that the series at that moment moved along its trend; later, when
the value was 200, the absolute rate of increase would be 6 per year. With the value of
the trend measured on the vertical axis and time on the horizontal, this gives an exponential function. With the *logarithm* of the trend value on the vertical axis and
time on the horizontal, the function becomes a straight line. Logarithmic slopes
measure proportionate rates of increase. This is because $d \log y = dy/y$.
A simple, nontechnical illustration will make it clear that a constant absolute rate of
increase in the logarithm of a magnitude corresponds to a constant proportionate rate
of increase in the magnitude itself. While it is convenient for many purposes to use
logarithmic systems with a base that is a specially defined number, we shall use for the
present illustration logarithms the base of which is the number 10. Then the logarithm
of 10 is the number *1* because 10 is the *first* power of 10; the logarithm of 100 is the
number *2,* because 100 is the *second* power of 10; and the logarithm of 1000 is the
number *3,* because 1000 is the *third* power of 10. Consequently, when the logarithm of
a magnitude rises from 1 to 2, the magnitude itself increases tenfold, namely, from 10
to 100; and when the logarithm of a magnitude increases from 2 to 3, then the magnitude itself again increases tenfold, namely, from 100 to 1000. It follows that a constant
proportionate rate of increase of a magnitude (in our case, a tenfold increase from 10
to 100 and then from 100 to 1000) expresses itself in a constant absolute increase in its
logarithms (from 1 to 2 and then from 2 to 3) . When the logarithms increase at a
constant absolute rate, say, by one unit in each period, the magnitude of which they
are the logarithms increases in a constant *proportion*.
³ The difference between the height of the terminal trough and that of the initial
trough is appreciable for the first and the third cycle. This difference is very small for
the sixth and the eighth cycle. For the other cycles, this difference is about the same as
it is for the average of the eight cycles. To make this clearly discernible, the slope of
the trend has been exaggerated (the logarithm of output appears to rise about fourfold
in the course of eight cycles) .

the trend line drawn in the chart is more, or less, "adequate" than would be a curved line such as tends to flatten out and to look like the rising range of a parabola nearing its maximum point. If in the next longer period by and large the same eight cycles repeat themselves, then the linear trend representation in the chart does not prove misleading, because in this case it is not misleading to offset in one's averaging the more steeply rising tendency of some subperiods by the less steeply rising tendency of others. On the other hand, the experience during the subsequent span comprising a similar number of cycles may prove that the drift shows a definite tendency toward flattening, and that it would therefore have been more appropriate to emphasize the steeper drift for the early part of our period and the reduced upward tendency for the late part. This could have been done by fitting to the chart a curvilinear (in this case parabolic) trend which pays more attention to the sequence of events during the constituent parts of the period as a whole. Moreover, even if approximately the same course of events should repeat itself in the next span, and hence the trend line of Figure 1 should prove appropriate, it would be possible here to add valuable information by stating that the subperiod trend ("secondary trend" or intermediate trend) for the early part of our eight-cycle periods is steeper than the primary trend for our eight-cycle periods as a whole, while the secondary trend for the later part of the entire period is less steep.

To state that there occurs an alternation of steeper and of less steep intermediate (or secondary) trends around the secular (or primary) trend is tantamount to saying that we can distinguish in our time series not only business cycles in the usual sense but also longer waves. To stress the analogy with business cycles, these longer waves are sometimes called long cycles or trend cycles. This terminology can become misleading because there is usually *even less* regularity in the alternations of trend slopes than in the business cycle proper.

Nowadays it is somewhat more usual to fit trend lines by mathematical methods than by freehand drawing. This, however, does not make it possible to avoid the arbitrary methodological decisions to which attention was called. It remains necessary to make a decision about the length of the period which for trend fitting is considered a unit. Also, it remains necessary to make a decision on the method by which the above-trend section of the chart is made to be of equal weight (in some sense) with the below-trend section.

Once the trend is found, it can be technically separated from business cycles. This is done by *plotting the deviations from the trend,* that is, by expressing the value of the time series, not relatively to the zero level which serves as the horizontal axis in Figure 1, but relatively to the height of the trend line for the date in question. For example, after removal (or "extraction") of the trend, a value of plus fifty or of minus fifty will mean that the time series at a certain date exceeded its trend value, or fell short of its trend value, by this number of the stated units of measurement.

It is frequently useful to express deviations from the trend by percentage differences between the value of the time series and the trend value, rather than by absolute differences. Representation in terms of percentage deviations reduces an absolute deviation of, say, 20 units, when the trend value is 200, to the same significance as that which an absolute deviation of 10 units has when the trend value is 100. We are interested in proportions more frequently than in absolute magnitudes.

Logarithmic plotting automatically shows percentage deviations from trend. On the other hand, arithmetic plotting shows absolute deviations from which percentage deviations may be computed subsequently. The decision to represent a drift logarithmically, in terms of proportionate rates of changes in the time series, or arithmetically, in terms of absolute rates of change, is, of course, a mere decision of convenience.

A time series such as that for sugar production, or for new buildings started, or for the value of bank clearings during a specified period, can be measured either in natural units (tons or dollars) *or* in index numbers. A series for a statistical composite, such as that for aggregate output, must be measured in index numbers or in money units.

5. Unrealistic features of the simplified illustration.

Figure 1 serves expository purposes and therefore makes the problem appear simpler than it is. We shall make a few comments on the relationship of this illustration to reality.

The logarithmic linearity of the trend line (in contrast to its slope) [4] is perhaps not particularly unrealistic with respect to the American aggregate output series, although it might be argued that some amount of flattening is observable if our period of investigation starts further back than in the eighteen-nineties. For some other countries this flattening of the logarithmic or proportionate (percentage) rate of increase is

---

[4] As for the exaggerated steepness of the slope, see Footnote 3, Page 7.

more pronounced. Even for the United States we do get a very marked flattening of the trend if we examine time series for certain individual industries or groups of industries rather than for aggregate output. For many individual sectors of the economy, the trend line seems to have been rising at first at an increasing and subsequently at a more or less constant or at a significantly decreasing rate. This does not show to any appreciable extent in the aggregate output series because, when one sector arrives in the later stages of its development, a new development frequently starts in another sector.

Whether the secondary or intermediate trends (subperiod trends) which are distinguishable around the long-run secular trends do or do not alternate with a fair degree of regularity is a controversial question about which much has been written. For some series a moderate regularity of this sort does appear to exist, and in these cases the concept of long cycles (trend cycles) may possess relevance. In many cases no simple or observable regularity in the alternation of secondary trend slopes exists.

However, it should be borne in mind that the business cycle itself shows but a moderate degree of regularity with respect to (a) the duration of successive movements and (b) the rough coincidence, in time, of movements in different series (or even with respect to rough coincidence, in time, after introduction of some simple "lead-lag" hypothesis for the various series). Figure 1 strongly oversimplifies the properties of business cycles, that is, of the eight units lying between points 0, 1, 2, etc. of the graph. It is sufficient to glance briefly at the time series in Figure 3, on Page 20 to convince oneself of the high degree of simplification involved in the illustrative chart of Figure 1.

In what respects does Figure 1 present an oversimplified picture?

In our chart it is very easy to identify the number of cycles and the peaks and troughs, with or without removal of the trend. Cyclical expansion and contraction mean expansion and contraction relative to a hypothetical movement along the trend, while the raw contours of a series give us the sequence of absolute rises and drops. Our chart is drawn in such a way that trend removal would probably displace each peak and trough merely by a small distance. This, in itself, is not a particularly unrealistic feature because in many cases it is true in practice, too, that reasonable methods of trend elimination do not appreciably shift a turning-point chronology or "rhythm" which is observable in the con-

tours of the series from the outset.[5] However, in actual practice the identification of cycles in time series calls for certain arbitrary decisions, quite
aside from the trend decision.

In our chart it would be clearly unreasonable to interpret any of the
eight cycles as consisting of two or more minor ones. It would be equally
unreasonable to maintain that the business cycle in the relevant sense is
not one of the easily distinguishable units of the chart but a multiple of
such a unit. In real time series such problems do, however, frequently
arise. Periods of expansion and of contraction are almost always interrupted by episodic countermovements of short duration, and we therefore cannot identify a cycle unless we adopt a convention by which the
cycle, to be recognized as such, must have some minimum duration. Some
investigators accept one year as the minimum duration, while others
treat this question with more flexibility. In computing duration some investigators count from trough to trough, while others count from the middle of the upswing (which they consider a relatively "normal" period)
to the next such phase, or from peak to peak.

Also, in real time series the question sometimes arises of whether two
or more cycles that do have the required minimum duration should not
at the same time be interpreted as expressing episodic interruptions of
a movement that describes also a longer cycle.

For example, in many American time series a cycle is distinguishable
which extends from an initial trough (upturn) in 1921, through a peak
in 1923, to a terminal trough (upturn of the next cycle) in 1924; another cycle of this sort is distinguishable which extends from 1924
through a peak in 1926, to a terminal trough in 1927; and a third cycle
can be added which starts with the initial trough of 1927, leads through
a peak in 1929 and ends with a trough in 1933. Cycles in this sense usually have a duration of a few years. They possess an *average* duration of
between forty and fifty months over long periods in the United States.

On the other hand, it is possible to interpret the American data for
the nineteen-twenties and the early 'thirties as pointing to a single and
more significant cycle, extending from the 1921 trough of the postwar
depression, through a peak in 1929, to a terminal trough in 1932 or in
1933. On this interpretation, the expansion phase of the twelve-year
cycle in question, that is, the upswing from 1921 to the peak of 1929,
was interrupted merely by episodic countermovements in 1923-1924 and

---

[5] Amplitudes and some other characteristics of cyclical fluctuations are, however,
significantly influenced by trend elimination.

again in 1926-1927. The cycle from 1921 to 1932 or to 1933 (eleven to twelve years from trough to trough [6]) is more significant than the shorter ones, because it ended not with a minor recession but with a major depression, which in this case happens to be the worst depression in modern economic history. Until 1937, cycles, in the sense of periods lying between major depressions, have had a typical duration in the order of ten years, mostly seven to eleven years. The 1937 depression came about eight years after that of 1929, and it came after a recovery period which in the United States was very incomplete, but which it is usual to interpret as not having been interrupted by minor downturns. Since 1937, we have had no major cyclical downturn but merely minor recessions.

Earlier cycle chronologies were frequently limited to the "seven-to-eleven-year cycle" ending on major depressions, but nowadays most investigators recognize the shorter variety of cycle as well. Some recognize only the shorter variety because they feel that the distinction between the two varieties is not meaningful in a sufficient number of cases to warrant defining the seven-to-eleven-year cycle as a unit. However, even if we decide to define the shorter fluctuation as *the* business cycle, and do not wish to speak of a second and more severe type of oscillation which has produced seven-to-eleven-year cycles in addition to the shorter ones, we should still add that some downturns have been recorded as very much more serious disturbances than others.

To summarize: when we are confronted with real time series, the problem of identifying cycles calls for definite methodological decisions, the difficulties of which are hidden by the extreme simplicity of our chart.

We should add that in the real world, in contrast to the chart, the duration of successive cycles may be very different. Regardless of the rules which we adopt for identifying cycles, we shall find some that are very much longer than others.

The chart by-passes, of course, the question of how the cycles in the various lines of activity are related to one another. Here we may limit ourselves to the statement that the peaks and troughs (turning points) of the aggregate output series, as well as those of some other representative series,[7] fall in months or quarters around which the turning points of a great number of specific series are clustered. However, these turning points do not, of course, strictly coincide, and there always exist many

---

[6] The peak-to-peak duration of this cycle was nine years (1920-1929).

[7] These representative series may be statistical composites, such as aggregate output or they may be individual series relating to especially significant lines of activity.

"exceptional" series that do not follow the typical pattern. Some of these series have behaved irregularly on only a few occasions, while others, like many agricultural output series, do not even tend to follow a cyclical pattern.

In spite of the crudity of the illustration, we did make an attempt to express in the shape of the cycle diagram some typical properties of real cycles. The downswing or contraction is usually steeper in the beginning, shortly after the downturn, than at the end. The upswing or expansion tends to be less steep toward the middle than before or after the middle range. The upswing tends to be somewhat longer than the downswing or contraction. However, there are exceptions to these rules.

6. Trend and dynamic equilibrium.

The techniques which we have considered imply a proposition that has strong common-sense foundations. When someone asks us about the long-run performance of an economy, he takes it for granted that the typical long-run tendency was disturbed by forces producing ups and downs. On the other hand, when we are asked about the character and the causes of the ups and downs in business activity, it is taken for granted that population increase, savings, and inventions would result in economic growth, aside from *what is meant* by ups and downs. Conceptually, the general, long-run "up" is no part of the ups and downs, that is, of the boom-bust or prosperity-depression problem about which the person is inquiring.

This can also be stated in such a way that it should lead more directly into a basic problem of dynamic economics. In spite of some lost arts, it is reasonable to state that our technological and organizational skills are *continuously* increasing. Population has also been continuously increasing, and additions have been made to the real capital stock of Western economies whenever their resources were reasonably fully utilized. These fundamentals might lead one to expect that output should also be continuously rising, sometimes rapidly and sometimes more slowly, except in periods of specifically identifiable disaster which would have to show in a loss of basic resources or skills. We are interested in the forces producing the long-run movements which express themselves in the slopes of observable trends; at the same time, we would like to know why economic activity is not continuously rising at the rate of its trend slope. One would not, of course, expect it to rise all the time at the rate of a trend slope which is as simple as the trend fitted to the cycles of Figure 1. While our skills and resources may be said to rise continuously, they do not rise at a constant proportionate rate. But if economic activity moved in strict accordance with changes in our skills and in our fundamental resource position, then output would have to rise all the time, approximately at the rate of secondary trend slopes (alternating trend slopes for successive subperiods). The secondary trends in question surround the long-run secular trend of Figure 1.

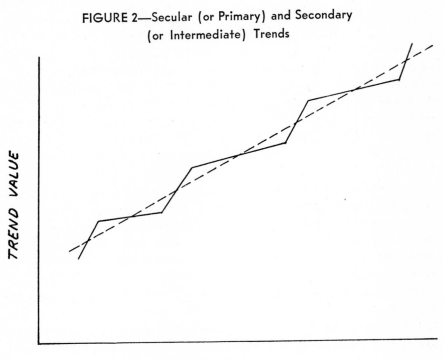

FIGURE 2—Secular (or Primary) and Secondary (or Intermediate) Trends

The relationship between the secular trend and the secondary or intermediate trends surrounding it is illustrated in Figure 2. There exists, of course, no reason to assume that even in relatively short periods the economy would be moving on a strictly linear path, involving constant proportionate rates of growth. The statistical methods, by which secondary trends are usually derived, are methods smoothing out the edges observable in Figure 2 and thus giving the visual impression of a long wave around the primary trend line.

Why does economic activity not rise all the time, approximately at the rate of such trend slopes? Asking the question in this fashion brings out clearly an important contrast between modern industrial economies and systems of a more primitive kind. Primitive economies, with no significant upward trend, also have good and bad times, but in these economies a diminution of output is usually explainable by a loss of resources. Bad harvests, wars, and epidemics may lead to the destruction of resources, and therefore to a diminution of output. Events of this kind reduce the stock of available resources, but they need not reduce the ability of an economy to use *existing* resources. In the modern world growth interruptions and contractions result mainly from temporary inability to use existing resources.

For example, in 1929 neither resources nor skills were destroyed, but there nevertheless started a world-wide contraction of economic activity which was very sharp, lasted very long, and led to political and social consequences of great significance. What prevents modern industrial economies from moving upward continuously in accordance with their resources position and their skills? What prevents them from progressing *all the time,* sometimes very rapidly and sometimes more slowly?

The problem can be approached by inquiring into the conditions of smooth (uninterrupted) growth or *dynamic equilibrium.* As will be seen, smooth growth would assume that in each subperiod much of the tendency toward diminishing returns should be offset. Also, smooth growth would require sufficient mobility of resources to assure, all the time, the adjustability of the structure of output to the structure of demand; and it would require, all the time, the adjustability of the money and credit supply to the needs of a growing economy. In reality, these conditions have not been satisfied all the time, and an economy, the technological structure and saving habits of which are geared to growth, will *contract* whenever it cannot grow at a sufficient rate. Thus the interruptions of the growth process have presumably lowered the statistically observable trend lines as compared to what would have been genuine paths of dynamic equilibrium. The effect of the oscillations is highly unpredictable, and part of the investment of each period turns out to be ill-conceived ("malinvestment").

We shall now turn to a brief discussion of the methods by which economists have obtained information about trends and cycles, and we shall explore the analytical implications of these methods. One of these implications, obviously, is that it is worth while to distinguish trend forces or growth factors from factors producing cyclical disturbances.

However, it will be necessary to remember that there is interaction between these two sets of forces. The observable trends are influenced by the cyclical disturbances. A hypothetical economy, growing with no cyclical disturbances, would stay on a path of dynamic equilibrium. Such a path would presumably move at a higher level than do the statistically observable trend paths. In a cyclically disturbed economy, trend lines may be interpreted as lowered paths of dynamic equilibrium.

Finding Trends and Cycles:
Methods and Their Analytical Implications

A discussion of various methods of approach, all of which have merit as well as limitations, is apt to leave the reader somewhat in the dark concerning the author's own preferences. While the choice of a single method among many reasonable ones must, of course, depend on the specific research objectives of the economist, we may at this point make a few brief statements about the general methodological implications of the later analysis in this volume. How do the methods to be discussed in the present Chapter bear on the analysis in which we shall engage later on?

Generally speaking, it will be possible to interpret the "cycles" and "trends" of our later analysis as having been identified by the kind of method which Warren M. Persons has described (see Section 1, below). But as will be explained in the present Chapter (especially in Section 3), we feel that reasonable use of this method should give results concerning turning-point chronologies and also some other characteristics of fluctuations, similar to those obtainable by the so-called National Bureau method. Also, we feel that the main properties of a trend that is discovered either by a reasonable use of the Persons method, or by the National Bureau method for finding intercycle trends, can be illustrated effectively and in a simple fashion by numerically listing the sequence of average values of a time series for successive ten-year periods (as, for example, Simon Kuznets does).[1] These presentations frequently give indications also with respect to variations in the steepness of trends for successive subperiods of a long span.

---

[1] See Page 62, *supra.*

What has been said so far suggests that in our later analysis "the cycle" will consist of relatively short fluctuations, such as those identified by the National Bureau of Economic Research. This is true, and it implies that a "cycle" can end either with a minor recession or with a major depression. But we shall take account of the fact that for some purposes it is important to draw a distinction between minor recessions and major depressions, and that the time interval between successive major depressions has typically been longer than the "cycle" in the foregoing sense.

1. The Persons method.

Warren M. Persons gave a detailed description of a method for separating trend from cyclical fluctuations in specific time series, such as pig-iron production, bank clearings, stock prices, etc. The method includes a procedure for discovering whether the time series in question shows seasonal variations and, if so, for eliminating these (that is, for separating these, too, from the cyclical movements). The Persons method was described in 1919.[2] But it is a specific application of a general idea which has a long past and which has been used extensively for distinguishing trends from cycles (thus for implicitly *defining* these concepts). The general idea is simple. It is the idea implied in our preliminary illustration of trend and cycle identification in Section 4, Chapter 1.

A simple type of function (frequently, but not always, a straight line) is selected for representing the long-run drift of a "fluctuating" time series. The trend line in question is made to cut through the time series in such a way that, by some mathematical criterion, the above-trend values of the series should possess the same weight as the below-trend values. This means that, by the criterion in question, the line fits the series as well as a simple line of the chosen type (*e.g.,* a straight line) is capable of fitting it.

The time series, with time measured along the horizontal axis and the value of the series vertically, consists of many points, each of which relates to a specific month (or quarter, or year). These points can be connected with each other on a diagram, and the connecting lines can be smoothed out, to obtain a continuous diagram of the fluctuating time series. This is not, however, essential to the method. What is essential is the choice of the *general type of trend line* or function which, for the period in question, seems to fit the points of the time series reasonably

---

[2] W. M. Persons, "An Index of General Business Conditions," *Review of Economic Statistics* (April 1919), pp. 111-211.

well;[3] and it is essential to choose a technique for discovering which *specific line* falling in that general type fits best.[4] The "least squares" method is one of the techniques frequently used for this latter purpose, and it is the technique that Persons uses. Assuming that seasonal variations have been removed from the time series,[5] the deviations of the original points of the time series from the trend line express the "cyclical movement," the turning points and the amplitudes of which are to be examined. Mostly, it is preferable to use percentage deviations (relative deviations) rather than absolute deviations from the trend; and some investigators (including Persons) prefer to express the relative deviations in terms of units of standard deviation, rather than simply in terms of percentages.[6]

Figure 3 shows the fitting of a linear trend to a fluctuating series. This time we are faced with an actually observed series, not with one that was invented for illustration. When the trend is extracted, that is, when only deviations from the trend are plotted, the upward drift disappears and the base around which the fluctuations occur appears to be horizontal.

This method and its variants relate directly to specific time series, not to "business in general." However, some specific time series are reasonably satisfactory indicators of the course of "general business activity." Unfortunately, the best of these (national product in constant prices) is not available for successive short intervals for a sufficiently long period back. At any rate, the Persons method is not *directly* applicable to the problem of dating business cycles "in general." Synthetic measures, relating to general economic conditions, can be obtained here merely by the use of an *ad hoc* selected time series. For this purpose, some investigators have

---

[3] A straight line, for example, is a "general type" in this sense.

[4] This determines what the slope of a straight line should be and what should be its intersection point with the vertical axis (assuming that we have decided to fit a straight line).

[5] There exist various techniques for discovering and removing the seasonal. Essentially, these aim at discovering the typical deviation, during the period as a whole, of values for January, February, March, etc., from yearly average values.

[6] Measuring relative deviations in units of standard deviation facilitates the comparison of the size of specific cyclical swings (that is, of the so-called *amplitude* of specific swings) in different time series. For if, at the peak, one cycle rises 20 percent beyond the trend, while another series rises 40 percent beyond *its* trend, then we shall not wish to say that the specific upswing in question was more extreme in the second than in the first time series, *provided that* deviations are typically twice as great in the second as in the first series. If the standard deviation in the second series is twice as great as in the first, then measuring the deviations in units of standard deviation makes the amplitude of the upswing in question appear to be identical in the two series. For certain purposes this is an advantage. On the other hand, the procedure hides from the eye the generally greater instability of the second series.

FIGURE 3—Persons' Least Squares Trend Line and Cyclical Fluctuations.

Monthly Bank Clearings in New York City, 1903-1918

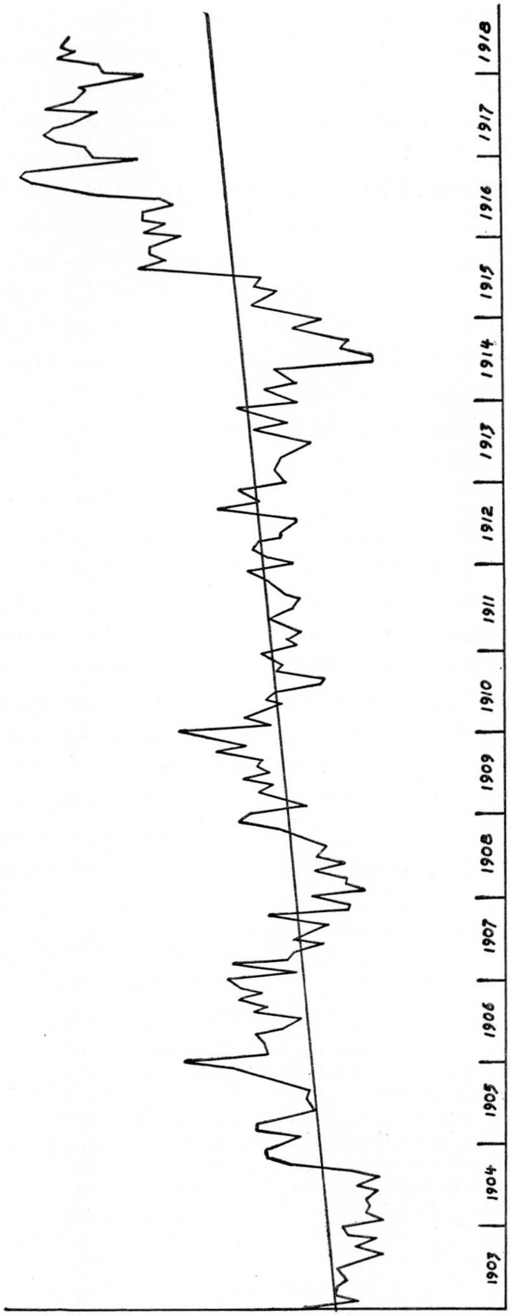

used composite index numbers, put together from various important time series (usually with some attempt to weight these). Others, including Persons himself, have used several composites, where each composite applies merely to one major type of economic activity.

2. The National Bureau method.

The work which Wesley C. Mitchell and Arthur F. Burns have directed at the National Bureau of Economic Research has resulted in the so-called National Bureau method of dating the turning points of the "reference cycle" (business cycle in general), as well as of "specific cycles" in the individual time series.[7] A very significant number of specific time series was examined and, after the elimination of the seasonal variations,[8] the dates (months) were found *around which the cyclical turning points of the individual series may be said to cluster.*[9] The convention was adopted that each up-and-down movement in the specific time series must have a minimum duration of more than one year (from trough to trough as well as from peak to peak)[10] to qualify as a complete cycle. Ups and downs of shorter duration are viewed as episodic interruptions of an expansion or of a contraction phase which jointly make up a complete cycle. Of the ups and downs qualifying by this criterion, the National Bureau selects the shortest in each specific time series, usually insisting, however, that the amplitude of the fluctuation should be greater than the amplitude of those episodic movements which were disregarded as a consequence of the minimum-duration rule.[11]

In addition to examining the clustering dates of the turning points of specific cycles, the National Bureau has consulted business annals prepared by Willard L. Thorp on the basis of past commentaries. The annals disclose views of the changing state of general business conditions during past periods. Using the information provided by the clustering tendencies of the turning points in specific time series, and also by the annals, the

---

[7] A. F. Burns and W. C. Mitchell, *Measuring Business Cycles* (New York, 1946).

[8] See Footnote 5, Page 19.

[9] No trend elimination is undertaken at this point.

[10] The rule used in most of the work of the Bureau seems to be that "more than one year" means a minimum of fifteen months.

[11] But at any rate the National Bureau method sets the upper limit of the duration at ten to twelve years. Consequently, if in some twelve-year period they should find no fluctuation the amplitude of which markedly exceeds that of the episodic oscillations (such as are disregarded because they do not qualify by the minimum-duration rule), then they might have to "accept" a cycle which has no greater amplitude than the episodic oscillations. However, the method is obviously based on the idea that such a situation would be very exceptional.

National Bureau was able to "date" the lower turning points (upturns or troughs) and the upper turning points (downturns or peaks) of the so-called reference cycle, that is, of the *general* business cycle.

Reference cycle patterns (general business cycle calendars) have been prepared for several countries. The dates for the United States are reprinted here in Table 1. The average duration of the American reference cycles is about forty-seven months, a shorter period than that found for the European countries. However, for the successive cycles the variation of cycle durations around the average duration is considerable in all countries.

Table I—Monthly Reference Dates of Cycles in the United States (1854-1950)

Peak	Trough
—	Dec. 1854
June 1857	Dec. 1858
Oct. 1860	June 1861
Apr. 1865	Dec. 1867
June 1869	Dec. 1870
Oct. 1873	Mar. 1879
Mar. 1882	May 1885
Mar. 1887	Apr. 1888
July 1890	May 1891
Jan. 1893	June 1894
Dec. 1895	June 1897
June 1899	Dec. 1900
Sep. 1902	Aug. 1904
May 1907	June 1908
Jan. 1910	Jan. 1912
Jan. 1913	Dec. 1914
Aug. 1918	Apr. 1919
Jan. 1920	July 1921
May 1923	July 1924
Oct. 1926	Nov. 1927
June 1929	Mar. 1933
May 1937	June 1938
Feb. 1945	Oct. 1945
Nov. 1948	Oct. 1949

SOURCE: A. F. Burns and W. C. Mitchell, *Measuring Business Cycles* (New York, 1946), p. 78. Some dates were revised by the Bureau in 1951 and in these cases we have listed the revised dates.

The information available on reference cycles consists, of course, merely of dates. The reference cycle in general business activity has no "amplitude": it is meaningless to ask how much higher a given *reference-cycle* peak is than a given reference-cycle trough. This question can be asked concerning the cycles in the specific time series, that is, in connection with the so-called *specific cycles* of the National Bureau. The same question can also be asked in connection with statistical composites put together from individual time series by some method of weighing the constituents. The movements of these, too, are in the nature of specific cycles in that they have "body." They fluctuate with an observable amplitude. The reference cycle in general business activity consists merely of a chronology.

We now turn from the reference-cycle dates to the more detailed treatment of specific cycles. As was said before, the dating of the turning points of specific time series, relating, for example, to the production of coal or of pig iron, or to interest rates, bank clearings, etc., was undertaken from each specific series after the elimination of seasonal variations (if such variations were found). However, it is necessary to add here that in defining and identifying specific cycles the National Bureau treats the problem of the secular trend differently from other investigators.

The National Bureau locates the turning points of the specific cycles in the individual time series *without* eliminating any portion of the trend, and when this has been done, the average value (average "standing") of the time series for *each* of the successive cycles (successive trough-to-trough intervals) is called "one hundred." With this average value of each cycle as the index-number base, the values of the time series are found for nine dates or time points (so-called stages) during each of the successive cycles, that is, during each of the successive trough-to-trough intervals in the series under consideration. The first of these points (or stages) coincides with the *initial trough* of the specific time series in question, the second with the center date of the first third of the expansion,[12] the third with the center date of the second third of the expansion, the fourth with the center date of the last third of the expansion, the fifth with the *peak*, the sixth, seventh, and eighth with the center dates of the three successive thirds of the contraction, and the ninth with the *terminal*

---

[12] The expansion is, of course, the trough-to-peak interval, and the contraction the peak-to-trough interval.

trough (which is identical with the initial trough of the next cycle).[13]
Lines connecting the points, that express the values of the series at the
nine selected dates ("stages"), give specific-cycle diagrams for each time
series—a separate diagram for each of the successive cycles or trough-to-
trough intervals in the chronology of the specific time series in question.
For some purposes, it is instructive to derive, by averaging, a single
specific-cycle diagram for, say, twenty successive pig-iron cycles, but aside
from such operations the specific-cycle diagrams here described are final
products.

By plotting a specific cycle in a framework which shows the standing
of that specific time series at all nine stages of its own specific-cycle
chronology, *and also at all nine stages of the reference-cycle chronology*,[14]
it is possible to compare certain characteristics of the individual "specific
cycles" with the behavior of the "business cycle in general." Such comparisons relate mainly to leads and lags and to trough-to-trough durations. These comparisons also show that, for example, a series which
"leads"—that is turns earlier than business in general—may have expanded by 50 percent from its own trough level to its own peak level
but by only 40 percent from the (later) trough of the reference cycle[15]
to the (later) peak of the reference cycle.[16] This is illustrated by Figure 4.

The procedure by which specific cycles are identified implies that the so-
called *intercycle portion* of the secular trend—the portion that lies *between*
the successive cycles or successive trough-to-trough intervals—is eliminated.

---

[13] The values of the time series (in terms of index numbers, with the average value
of the series during that specific trough-to-trough interval as 100) are computed as
follows: for the initial and the terminal troughs and the peak, that is, for the first,
fifth, and ninth stages, the average value during the three months surrounding the
turning point in question is determined; for the other stages, the average value during
the corresponding third of the expansion or contraction is determined. It follows from
the stage dating described in the text that the time interval elapsing from the first to
the second stage and that from the fourth to the fifth stage are half as long as the
other two inter-stage spans of the expansion. Also, the interval from the fifth to the
sixth stage and that from the eighth to the ninth stage are half as long as the time
intervals lying between the other stages of the contraction.

[14] To plot a specific series in the framework of the reference-cycle chronology, the
interval between the reference-cycle troughs and peaks, and between the peaks and
troughs, is divided into "thirds" in the same fashion as the trough-to-peak and the
peak-to-trough intervals in the specific cycles. This gives nine "stages" in both the
specific-cycle and the reference-cycle chronologies. But the stages of the reference-cycle
chronology do not usually coincide in time with the stages of the specific-cycle chronology. Usually, there are leads and lags.

[15] At the reference-cycle trough, the specific series in question has already risen to
some extent. This is because we are assuming a "lead" here.

[16] At the reference-cycle peak, the specific series in question has already declined to
some extent. This is because we are assuming a lead here at both turning points.

The average value of *each* of the successive complete cycles in the chronology is treated as 100, even though in a series with a rising trend the second cycle usually occurs on a higher level than the first. This rise in the level does not show in the processed data and in the diagrams of the National Bureau. Consequently, the procedure implies elimination of the inter-cycle portion of the trend. But the National Bureau method does not eliminate the *intracycle portion* of the trend. The value observed for the terminal trough (ninth point) is typically higher than the value observed for the initial trough (first point). This *does* show in the processed data and in the diagrams. The intracycle trend is not removed.

FIGURE 4—Time Series Plotted for Stages of Reference Cycle (—)
and of Specific Cycle (- - -)

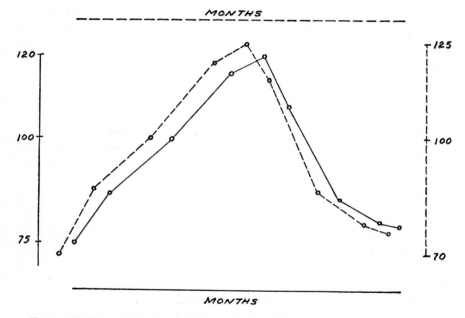

For example, with the average value of the time series called "100," we might find in one trough-to-trough interval a value of 75 at the initial trough (first point), a value of 120 at the peak (fifth point), and a value of about 85 at the terminal trough (ninth point). The difference between 85 and 75 expresses, in this case, the intracycle portion of the trend. But when, in the diagram applying to the next cycle, the previous terminal trough changes its role and becomes an initial trough, it might there well be assigned the value of 75. This is because, while the terminal trough of the first cycle was only 15 percent lower than the average value of the series during the first cycle, the same trough may very well be 25 percent lower than the average value of the series during the next cycle, for which the trough in question is "initial" rather than "terminal." Indeed, some such statement is typically valid for time series with rising trends. What eliminates the intercycle portion of the trend is precisely the practice of assigning to the terminal trough of the *nth* cycle a lower value *qua* the initial trough of the $(n - 1)$ *th* cycle than *qua* the terminal trough of the *nth*. One always starts anew, with the average value of the time series during the next cycle again regarded as "100," even though the average value of the series during the next cycle is really higher.

The idea underlying the method is that each trough-to-trough interval (cycle) is a meaningful unit of experience in the annals of the economy and that the account given of that unit should not be doctored by defining away the upward tilt from the initial to the terminal point. That is to say, the intracycle portion of the trend should not be eliminated. At the same time, it is postulated that the successive pieces of experience recorded by the annals (and corroborated by the clustering of specific-cycle turning points around certain dates) are members of one family of experiences: they are all business cycles. In treating them as if they had occurred around the same average level (around "100"), we emphasize their belonging together as cycles, and we thus separate the cycle problem from another problem—the problem of the *intercycle trend* expressing itself in the fact that "really" each of these cycles was discovered around a different average level (namely, around increasingly high levels). But we do not eliminate the intracycle portion of the trend because, after having put each unit on the same level, we try to describe the true behavior of the cyclical movement, including its climbing tendency. In series with an upward trend the terminal troughs are higher than the initial troughs.

This method has been used by many authors. F. C. Mills used it to represent the average behavior of sixty-four time series in the course of twenty successive reference cycles, or trough-to-trough intervals in the reference-cycle chronology, during the period 1858-1938.[17] However, many of his individual series were not available for all these successive cycles. Mills' chart, which we reproduce in Figure 5, reflects *average behavior* in two senses. For *any one series,* the data pertaining to the successive twenty (or fewer) cycles of the chronology are averaged; and these aver-

---

[17] F. C. Mills, *Price-Quantity Interactions in Business Cycles* (New York, 1946).

ages for the various specific time series are averaged again into an over-
all pattern for the *sixty-four series.* To take an unrealistic but simple
illustration, if the standing of a time series at the initial trough of the
reference-cycle chronology were 80 in 50 percent of the successive trough-
to-trough intervals and 90 in the other 50 percent, then the average
standing of that series at the initial trough would be represented as 85.
This is the first kind of averaging involved in the procedure. Further, if
for 50 percent of Mills' time series 85 were the average standing at the
initial trough of the reference-cycle chronology, and for the other 50 percent of his time series 75 were the average standing at the initial trough,
then, at the initial trough, 80 would be *the* standing shown in a composite chart such as is reproduced here. In his composite Mills included

FIGURE 5—Cyclical Behavior of Time Series Studied by F. C. Mills

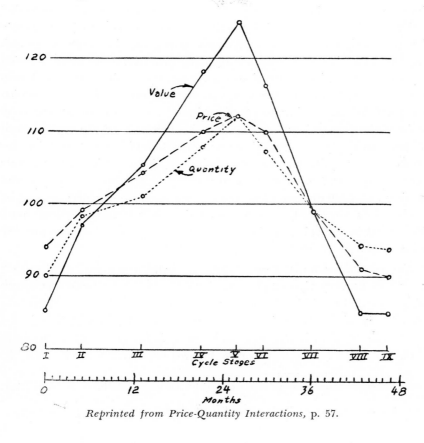

Reprinted from Price-Quantity Interactions, p. 57.

sixteen commodity groups, such as producer goods, consumer goods, durable goods, metals, foods, etc. Mills' quantity indexes and price indexes are charted separately in Figure 5, and a third diagram in the same figure shows "value" in the sense of price times quantity. However, we do not here reproduce the behavior of the constituent series (producer goods, consumer goods, etc.) separately. These, too, are statistical composites, although less inclusive than the one which we have reproduced from Mills' work.

Generally speaking, by the National Bureau method it is possible to compare the behavior of individual time series with one another as to leads and lags, duration of expansion and contraction, amplitudes of fluctuation, etc. It is also possible to discover leads and lags of the turning points of individual series, relative to the reference-cycle turning points, and to compare the duration of the expansion and contraction phases of individual series with the duration of reference-cycle expansions and contractions. However, as we have seen, the "reference-cycle" —the cycle in general business activity—consists merely of dates. Only the specific time series can be represented as possessing different "standings" for the nine stages of their own specific-cycle chronologies (which are marked by their own turning points) or as possessing different "standings" for the analogous stages of the reference-cycle chronology (which is marked by the turning points of business in general). By using a composite series, as well as investigating the behavior of the constituents, Mills could apply the method to an aggregate which is intermediate between specific cycles and general business activity. This aggregate does have "body," and it enables us to arrive at tentative conclusions concerning the more or less rapid increase and decrease of prices, quantities produced or consumed, and the algebraic products of prices and quantities (that is, of "values"), in successive stages of the expansion and the contraction.

We see, for example, from Figure 5, that the expansion of output tended to be very vigorous in the earliest stage and that it was rather mild toward the middle, before experiencing renewed acceleration (and exceedingly slight slackening at the very end). The contraction tended to be much sharper in the early and especially in the middle stages than later.[18] Toward the end, it usually became exceedingly mild. After the

---

[18] All these statements are valid for quantities and values (prices times quantities), but they are not valid in all respects for prices viewed separately. For example, the price fall tends to be very mild in the earliest phase of the contraction.

contraction business activity frequently stayed at an approximately stable and low level for some time. It may be added that the consumption-goods series tended to lead the producer-goods series on the upturn, but no clearcut lead-lag tendency emerges for these two series on the downturn.

The representativeness of the arithmetic averages on which the National Bureau method in general, and Mills' version of it in particular, must rely, is of course questionable. Yet some such difficulty arises in connection with any attempt to express the "typical" behavior of economic data. While each individual instance is influenced by certain unique events, we are interested in properties which these individual instances share.

3. Frickey's technique and some further suggestions.

For the United States Edwin Frickey has worked out a technical procedure which confirms the common-sense judgment that fluctuations more or less pervading the economy as a whole are not simply the spurious results of arbitrary trend-elimination methods.[19] It is quite true, of course, that various properties of the cycles discovered by our research methods depend on the decisions we have reached for extracting the trend, and that there exists no set rule for "correct" trend elimination. In extracting the trend, we can be guided merely by very general considerations about the probable nature of long-run tendencies. But for his period of investigation, 1866-1914, Frickey found *without* the use of any trend-elimination method in the conventional sense that thirteen important time series in finance, trade, and commodity production tended to expand and to contract together, in what appears to be a common rhythm. The amplitudes of the fluctuations were, of course, by no means the same in the various series, but this is a different question.

Frickey did not limit himself to the use of a single method. But the distinctive part of his analysis is based on the representation of time series by their link relatives,[20] after the removal of seasonal variations. This, of course, is different from using a fixed base (such as, for example, 1866 = 100) in constructing one's index numbers. Frickey's analysis leads to the conclusion that, with comparatively little further manipulation,

---

[19] Edwin Frickey, *Economic Fluctuations in the United States* (Cambridge, 1942) .

[20] Using link relatives means expressing the value of a time series for a period by a number which indicates what percent that value is of the value found for the preceding period.

these link relatives show marked similarity in their patterns of fluctuation. To obtain a common rhythm in the link-relative series, it is necessary to make allowances merely for "typical" leads or lags of some series in relation to the others. Aside from necessary allowances for leads and lags that stay constant over a long period, the various series tend to expand and to contract at about the same time. Thus there may be said to exist a common pattern or rhythm which enables us to speak of a representative turning-point chronology.

Frickey claims that his methods of processing the data and of deriving the common pattern do not include trend elimination. However, while no conventional "trend elimination" is involved in these methods, it should nevertheless be pointed out that the long-run drift of link relatives is not identical with the long-run drift of fixed-base index numbers, and that in many cases the upward drift of a fixed-base series may wholly disappear—may become wholly eliminated—when the series is represented by link relatives.[21] In the course of his work Frickey also makes further adjustments which reduce or practically eliminate secular drifts even in the link relatives. But this is not particularly important from our point of view because these further adjustments for trend do not change the common pattern which emerges without the adjustments. Only the lead-lag adjustments are essential, once we take it for granted that we are analyzing link relatives rather than fixed-base index numbers.

In our opinion, the trend-reducing implications of the link-relative method, as compared to fixed-base methods, do not destroy the claim that the "common pattern" deserves recognition. The objection that the pattern results simply from the arbitrary trend treatment implicit in constructing link relatives would be unconvincing because the link relatives possess direct, intuitive meaning. They express proportionate rates of change. Frickey's work points to the existence of a common rhythm in the *rates of change* of his various series, and if his results are thus stated, they do not depend on trend manipulations. He did not have to eliminate the trend from his link relatives to obtain a common rhythm.

Any common rhythm that could be established with the aid of the Persons method would be a rhythm of movements in relation to the trend, hence a rhythm "after" trend elimination. But a common pattern established with the Persons method would relate to the original (fixed-base)

---

[21] Take a fixed base and consider, for example, the following fluctuating but upward-drifting time series: 100, 100, 110, 121, 110, 121, 133.1, 121, 133.1, 146.4, 133.1. . . . In terms of link relatives, this reads (from the second period on): 100, 110, 110, 91, 110, 110, 91, 110, 110, 91. . . . There is no trend in the link relatives.

time series rather than to link relatives (rates of change). Furthermore, for the original (fixed-base) time series the National Bureau method *actually establishes* a common rhythm, in which only a minority of non-conforming time series fails to participate, and the method by which the National Bureau finds its turning points involves *no trend elimination whatsoever* (see Page 23). The National Bureau chronology is confirmed by the "annals," and few would dispute that in the main it is a sound chronology. In its main outline, it accords with nontechnical observation and experience, provided that we wish to take account of minor recessions as well as major depressions. Therefore, reasonable use of the Persons trend-elimination method requires identifying a trend line in such a way that its elimination should not give a significantly different turning-point chronology in the trend-corrected series from that which is initially observable in the uncorrected ones. Otherwise the turning-point chronology in the trend-corrected series would become very different from the National Bureau chronology, which is confirmed by the annals. The process of trend elimination must not change the nature of the common pattern or rhythm. For the fixed-base series, this conclusion emerges from thinking through the implications of the Persons method, in view of what we know about National Bureau results. For the link relatives of a group of significant series, the analogous proposition was advanced by Frickey.

These conclusions may appear to be somewhat paradoxical. On the one hand, we have defined cyclical movements as movements relative to secular trends. On the other hand, we now suggest that no specific decision concerning trend-extraction methods is needed to discover a common rhythm of cyclical fluctuations. Yet the contradiction here is merely apparent. The meaning of these propositions is that there exist specific problems not calling, in practice, for a distinction between absolute movements and movements relative to trend in the bulk of our time series. In particular, for the majority of time series many reasonable methods of trend fitting will give turning points relative to the trend at about the same time when turning points are observable in the absolute movements of the time series. Turning-point chronologies based on trend-elimination methods that do not satisfy this condition are very arbitrary.

This implies that turning-point chronologies become arbitrary unless, in the turning-point neighborhoods, the trend slope is found to be very moderate *relatively to the time rate of change in the series themselves.* The statement that a series "now" starts moving downward absolutely can and should, in most cases, be made to mean that a very short time ago the series started moving upward at a lesser rate than the trend, hence that a very short time ago it started moving downward in relation to the trend; and the statement that a series "now" starts moving upward absolutely can and should, in most cases, be made to mean that in very little time the series will be moving upward at a higher rate than the trend, hence that in very little time it will be moving upward not merely absolutely but also in relation to the trend. While the intuitive meaning of cyclical fluctuations is that of fluctuations relative to trend, and while thus some form of trend elimination is a necessary technique in business cycle analysis, we do not have to search our minds long to discover how uncertain the content of the cycle concept would become if, in the bulk of our time series, a technically identified peak became a very different thing from a temporary *absolute* high point, and if a technically identified trough became a very different thing from a temporary *absolute* low point. If, for example, most time series were so strongly trend-dominated that no turning points would be observable in them prior to trend elimination, and hence no trend-elimination method could leave an initially observable turning-point chronology by and large unchanged, then the concept of the business cycle would cease to be significant.

As was seen earlier, Frickey's work led to the conclusion that the common rhythm of movements in the proportionate rates of change of time series (that is, the common rhythm in link relatives) is about the same if no trend is extracted as if one of several reasonable trend-extraction techniques is used. We may now add that while the turning-point chronology in the fixed-base series is different from that in the link relatives, neither set of turning points should be appreciably modified by "reasonable" or "convenient" methods of trend-extraction. If the trend is identified in such a way that relative to that trend the turning-point chronology becomes very different from the initially observable chronology, then the chronology relative to trend ceases to have a counterpart in the "annals," that is, in common experience.

Detailed analysis of the amplitudes and of some other properties of cyclical movements, defined as deviations from trend, does, of course, depend on the choice of a unique trend representation among several "reasonable" ones. This choice will always be arbitrary in the sense that, in making it, we can be guided only by speculations of a general sort concerning the plausible character of long-run drifts. Nevertheless, it follows from what was said here that the fundamental characteristics of the phenomena called "cycles" and "trends"—the nature of these concepts—should not depend on whether we use the method exemplified by Persons' work, or the National Bureau method (as long as, subject to a one-year minimum rule, we are prepared to view the shortest type of fluctuation as "the cycle" and thus not to disregard minor recessions). Various known methods of identifying cycles and trends are more convenient or less so according as one or the other aspect of the problem of dynamic economics is investigated. But in all cases where trend elimination is undertaken in such a way that the turning points initially observable in the time series are not shifted appreciably,[22] reasonable use of the Persons method and of the National Bureau method will yield very similar chronologies. Whether we do or do not want to disregard that part of the chronology pertaining to minor recessions is a separate question.

It follows also that if we characterize the trend by listing numerically the sequence of average values of time series for successive decades or for similar periods,[23] this numerical description may just as well be interpreted as applying to the long-run sweep of Persons' trend lines as to that of the National Bureau's *intercycle* trend. The decade-to-decade movements in average values of series express drifts in such a way as to make the tracing of *intracycle* events unnecessary. In other words, the method implies replacing intracycle events by average values for the cycles, indeed, usually for periods extending over more cycles than one. Decade averages relate to *intercycle* drifts, and these intercycle drifts, of course, also dominate the long-run sweep of a Persons trend.

4. Are we faced with multiple cycles in general business activity?

A "cycle" the length of which would be six months is not considered a cycle, but is viewed as a brief interruption of the expansion or the contraction phase of a cycle. As we have seen, the National Bureau requires a length somewhat in excess of one year,[24] and for the United States the methods which were developed by the Bureau actually yield an average cycle duration of between forty and fifty months, with considerable variation in successive cycle durations.

However, if a trend is fitted to, say, a fifty-year period, it may be taken

---

[22] That is, in all cases where the turning-point chronology observable in the original series is not appreciably different from the chronology of the turning points in the *movements relative to the trend.*

[23] See Pages 4-5, *supra.*

[24] The usual practice of the Bureau is to require fifteen months.

for granted that the period as a whole can be divided into successive subperiods in such a way that some of the successive trends for these subperiods will be steeper and others flatter than is the trend for the period as a whole. The primary trend for the period as a whole "averages," in a sense, these so-called secondary or intermediate trends.

It is always *possible* to look at the secondary trends as comparatively long cycles. Assume, for example, that after elimination of a fifty-year trend from a time series we identify cycles on the basis of the one-year minimum length rule, and then smooth out the resulting "forty-month cycles" by some method of averaging the values found during such cycles. The forty-month cycle will then have disappeared from our materials, but we shall still observe longer ups and downs relative to the secular trend that is, ups and downs described by secondary trends. These may, of course, be interpreted as longer cycles. The so-called forty-month cycle is episodic in this longer cyclical pattern. The secular trend marks the drift of these longer cyclical units as well as of the "forty-month cycles." It is possible to obtain not merely one but several cycle durations lying between about forty months and the length of an entire historical period which is being analyzed.

It is always *possible* to proceed in this fashion, thus building into one's system the concept of cyclical alternations in several types of intermediate trend (hence of cycles with various durations). It is not merely possible but also *convenient* to do this if the successive durations of alternating longer periods with markedly different characteristics show sufficient regularity and if the *same* regularity is observable in a sufficiently large segment of the economy. This is the case if, for example, each successive fifty-year period can be divided roughly into two twenty-five-year subperiods—one with a steeper trend than that of the fifty-year period and one with a flatter trend—and if a great many individual series fit the pattern so described. Such findings would justify recognizing a fifty-year cycle in addition to the forty-month cycle. If, at the same time, the subperiods can be further divided in such a way that, when the twenty-five-year trend is viewed as the secular trend, the secondary trend to *that* trend should complete a steeper plus a less steep phase in roughly nine years, then this would justify recognizing an intermediate nine-year cycle in addition to the fifty-year long wave and the forty-month short cycle. It will be seen in a moment that these specific figures have been chosen for a reason. Some investigators have found it useful to proceed precisely in this fashion, a fact which was already implied in our introductory remarks in Chapter 1.

If regularities of this sort are not observable, then in most cases it is unnecessary and inconvenient to complicate the analytical apparatus by building different cycle durations into it. The statement that secondary or intermediate trends with alternating slopes are discernible is not significant *if* we have to add that the duration and other characteristics of the successive secondary-trend periods are *extremely* irregular. This statement merely means that an average value for a longer period (for example, the slope or a higher derivative of a fifty-year trend) can always be taken apart into a series of constituent values for shorter periods *in some fashion*. How could this fail to be true? Significance attaches to a statement of this kind only if certain regularities are observable for the sequence of the constituent periods and values. Such may be the case if, for example, the successive durations show some degree of regularity. Even if the durations do qualify on these grounds, the significance of the findings will stay limited to specific time series, unless a substantial number of important series participates in the same type of fluctuation.

The principle of sufficient regularity cannot, however, serve as a basis for a truly definite statement concerning the existence or nonexistence of long cycles. The reason is that even the kind of cycle which we have called the forty-month cycle, for the sake of brevity, does not show a *very high degree* of regularity. Some of the trough-to-trough durations are much longer than others, that is, the variation around the mean duration is substantial. Also, some of these cycles have mild contraction phases or expansion phases (or both), while others mark violent movements; and nonparticipating individual time series always exist. Whether longer periods with alternating characteristics show *significantly* less regularity than the short cycle will always remain a matter of subjective judgment. The attitudes of different investigators to this problem have not been the same.

5. The early emphasis on the seven-to-eleven-year cycle (one major downturn about once every decade).

The statistically less developed, common-sense procedure which underlies most early statements on business-cycle history (most statements up to perhaps the third decade of the present century) emphasized merely the *serious* disturbances in economic activity, which were also usually connected with financial panics. The earlier chronologies suggest that the

duration of a cycle is identical with the span between such disturbances. These relatively nontechnical accounts give a duration of about seven to eleven years for expansion plus contraction (*i.e.,* for upgrade plus downgrade). The following is a rather typical chronology of major downturns from the eighteen-twenties on:

> 1825
> 1836
> 1847
> 1857
> 1866
> 1873
> 1882
> 1890 (for the United States, this should probably be the year 1893)
> 1900 (for the United States, this should probably be the year 1902)
> 1907
> 1913

Continuation of this sort of chronology beyond 1913 would lead to adding:

> 1920
> 1929
> 1937

That is to say, if a chronology of this sort were extended into the nineteen-fifties, the downturns of 1920, 1929, and 1937 would have been registered for the United States and, with similar dates, also for other countries; but the minor downturns and subsequent upturns in 1923-1924, 1926-1927, 1948-1949, and 1953-1954 would have been disregarded for the United States. Similarly dated minor events in other countries would also have been disregarded. The National Bureau chronology does not, as we have seen, distinguish between major depressions and minor recessions, and thus it includes many more downturns than those listed here. (See Table 1, Page 22.) Note, however, that the National Bureau table does not go back further than 1854 and that it does not yet include the recession of 1953-54.

Down to the late 'thirties Alvin H. Hansen of Harvard University, in his presentation of the business cycle problems, rightly characterized the chronology of major downturns as (mostly) a seven-to-eleven-year chronology. Now it would have to be added that so far the 1937 downturn has been the last of its kind. The major downturns tended to be international in scope. With respect to minor interruptions the differences among the cycle chronologies of various countries are greater. The number of minor interruptions between the major downturns seem to have been greater in the United States than in most European countries, even though the secular trend has been particularly steep in the United States.

6. Long cycles.

Chronologies of the seven-to-eleven-year cycle were being widely used (and the existence of secular trends, of course, was recognized) when several investigators expressed the view that longer cycles also exist. These longer cycles are alternations in the characteristics of secondary trends, that is, of subperiod trends; they mark ups and downs in the secondary trends around the secular trend of the seven-to-eleven-year cycle. The seven-to-eleven-year cycle itself marks shorter ups and downs in subperiod trends (or shorter secondary trends) around the secular trend of the forty-month cycle. But the less readily observable forty-month cycle came to be emphasized later than the seven-to-eleven-year cycle, and more recently also than the long cycles around the trend of the latter.

Shortly after the turn of the century Arthur Spiethoff, a German scholar, used a framework for cycle analysis in which he placed considerable emphasis on the alternating characteristics of longer periods comprising several seven-to-eleven-year cycles.[25] Of the investigators of long cycles in the technical sense, the Russian economist and statistician, N. D. Kondratieff, is especially noteworthy, although he was not the first. His work falls mainly in the nineteen-twenties, the decade in which greater refinement of empirical work also resulted in the identification of the shorter movements which underlie the National Bureau chronologies of forty-month cycles.[26] But Kondratieff's research methods were not of the kind required for separating the seven-to-eleven-year cycle from shorter fluctuations. His method smoothed out all fluctuations other than his long waves.

---

[25] Arthur Spiethoff, "Krisen," in *Handwörterbuch der Staatswissenschaften*, 4th ed., (Jena, 1925), VI, pp. 8-91. An abridged English translation, by J. Kahane, was published by the International Economic Association in *International Economic Papers* (1953).

[26] N. D. Kondratieff, "The Long Waves of Economic Life," trans. by W. F. Stolper, *Review of Economic Statistics* (November 1935), pp. 105-115.

Kondratieff eliminated the secular trend from time series relating to various types of data in different countries. Some of these series could be traced back to the early periods of industrialization; others covered periods of less than a century. After removing the secular trend, he smoothed out the seven-to-eleven-year cycle by using nine-year moving averages, and in some cases he corrected for population increase by using *per capita* figures. His moving averages describe a long wave of roughly fifty years' duration for upgrade plus downgrade. He found these long waves in the price series, in the interest-rate series, and in many (but not all) physical production series. Kondratieff felt that he had established the existence of these long waves, in addition to the seven-to-eleven-year cycle, which he treated as a nine-year cycle. Alternatively expressed, he felt convinced that if we start with a model that includes merely the seven-to-eleven-year cycle and the secular trend, then we can prove that sub-periods with a steeper drift than would be expected on the basis of the secular trend slope and periods with a less steep drift alternate at reasonably regular intervals. These successive periods mark the succession of upgrades and downgrades in Kondratieff's long wave. He suggested that a great many time series participate in the common rhythm of this long cycle.

Kondratieff's long wave in general business activity has the following peaks and troughs:

Peaks:	1810-17	1870-75	1914-20
Troughs: 1780-90	1844-51	1890-96	

The original chronology ends with the downgrade that started around 1920. Kondratieff was made a victim of the Russian political system during the nineteen-twenties. It seems obvious, however, that in the Kondratieff framework a new upgrade should be said to have started in the course of the nineteen-thirties.

Most investigators now feel that the Kondratieff findings depend too much on particular trend-elimination procedures and on arbitrary decisions of dating. The thesis that long waves of approximately fifty years' duration permeate general economic activity is not conclusively established. Using different techniques in general, and different trend-elimination methods in particular, other investigators have obtained secondary trend waves of considerably shorter duration (twenty to twenty-five years) in various production series.

The Kondratieff findings are less controversial with respect to series for which they can be established without extracting a secular trend of some complexity,[27] that is to say, where the behavior of the series for the period as a whole is not very significantly influenced by a secular drift. Prices and interest rates, in contrast to physical production and consumption data, yield series of this sort. Even with respect to prices and interest rates, there arise controversial questions of dating. But it is reasonable to conclude that in these series periods with rising trends and periods with declining trends have alternated in such a way that until World War II the secular trend for very long periods was *not significantly different from horizontal.* The observable trends are "secondary" ones, around an approximately horizontal secular trend. At any rate, this statement about the approximate horizontality of the *secular trend* (that is, essentially about its nonexistence) comes nearer to the truth with respect to prices and interest rates than in the case of production or consumption series or any other series reflecting "real" economic activity. This, of course, reduces the significance of arbitrary trend-elimination techniques for prices and interest rates. In prices and interest rates we observe *alternations of long periods of uptrend with long periods of downtrend,* not merely alternations of periods of steeper uptrend with periods of less steep uptrend. Also, until World War II the periods of rising and of falling secondary trends in prices and interest rates followed each other at successive intervals, the duration of which were not so different as to deprive the findings of all significance. But even here the successive durations are far from identical.

For example, after smoothing out the shorter ups and downs in wholesale prices, Kondratieff obtained a long wave price upgrade from 1789 to 1814, a downgrade from 1814 to 1849, an upgrade from 1849 to 1873,[28] a downgrade from 1873 to 1896, an upgrade from 1896 to 1920 and a downgrade from 1920 on. The resulting schema is the following:

Peaks:		1814		1873		1920
Troughs:	1789		1849		1896	

We have here two and one-half long waves. The method would clearly indicate an upturn in the nineteen-thirties, and this would complete the third long cycle from trough to trough.[29] The successive trough-to-trough

---

[27] Some of Kondratieff's trend functions are rather complex.

[28] In the United States this upgrade ends in 1865 after the Civil War.

[29] It should be added that only the British series goes back to the late eighteenth century. Kondratieff used two more wholesale-price series: the American, which dates back to the early part of the nineteenth century, and the French, which begins at about the middle of the century.

intervals are sixty years, forty-seven years, and about forty years;[30] the successive peak-to-peak intervals are fifty-nine years and forty-seven years. The durations have been shortening. With the advent of new policies, which will be discussed in Part V, the alternation of long periods of rising price trends with long periods of falling price trends may not continue. Indeed, there is some plausibility to interpreting the Kondratieff periods of the past with reference to the institution of the metallic currency. In the late eighteen-forties gold mining started in California and in Australia; in the late 'nineties it started growing to substantial size in South Africa.

It is true, of course, also of the production and of the consumption series—of the "real" or "physical" series which are subject to a marked secular trend—that any longer period for which a "secular" trend has been selected is divisible into subperiods, with subperiod-trend slopes (secondary-trend slopes) of alternating steepness. But it depends very much on the method of "finding" the secular trend, and on methods of dating, whether any regularity is found in the alternations of secondary-trend slopes, and, if so, what sort of regularity this is. While reading long waves of some regularity into specific production or consumption series would therefore be arbitrary, it must be admitted that the *duration of business-cycle expansion periods relative to that of business-cycle contraction periods* (in the National Bureau cycle *or* in the seven-to-eleven-year cycle) seems somewhat greater in Kondratieff price upgrades than in Kondratieff price downgrades. In this particular sense, the Kondratieff price upgrades and the price downgrades do have an equivalent in the behavior of physical series. Also the most serious depressions of economic history fall in Kondratieff price downgrades. The eighteen-seventies (from 1873 on), the mid-eighties and the 'nineties (up to about 1896) had a rather generally depressed character, although not without interruptions. These depressions were long and serious. The nineteen-thirties were, of course, a very bad and fateful decade. As for earlier times, the recurrent depressions of the post-Napoleonic era were severe, up to the beginning of the eighteen-forties. All these depressions were not merely "major," in contrast to minor recessions, but they gave longer

---

[30] Something can perhaps be said for including all or part of the 1933-1938 period in the Kondratieff price downgrade which started in 1920. In the United States, for example, prices were lower at the 1937 peak than in 1929. This would raise the duration of the third long wave to somewhat more than forty years from trough to trough. If, however, the next (fourth) upgrade of the long wave is said to begin in 1933 rather than about 1938, then the third long wave must be interpreted as having had a duration of somewhat less than forty years.

periods a largely depressed character. Every one falls in price downgrades of the Kondratieff schema. Therefore, "something would seem to correspond" to the Kondratieff price upgrades and downgrades, *even in the physical series*. But it is difficult to concede more than is contained in such a vague assertion; and this vague assertion relates to a succession of "long wave" phases, the duration of which has varied a good deal even in the price series (so that the observable regularity here is very moderate). The statement that after removal of the secular trend, and after smoothing out the seven-to-eleven-year cycles, we obtain a common rhythm of about fifty years' duration in the individual physical series, is too much dependent on arbitrary techniques to be acceptable in this form.

7. Conclusions concerning multiple cycles.

Given this appraisal of the Kondratieff hypothesis, we prefer *not* to assert the existence of a long cycle of fifty years, such as would permeate economic activity in general. Hence, after elimination of the secular trend and of seasonal variations we are left merely with the business cycle in the usual sense—although we recognize, of course, that longer periods can be divided into subperiods with varying trend slopes (secondary trends). But with what sort of business cycle are we left? With the seven-to-eleven-year cycle which seems to underlie the old-fashioned crisis and depression chronologies? Or with the shorter variety of cycle which Mitchell has identified for various countries and which in the United States has an *average* duration of somewhere between forty and fifty months? Or perhaps with both types?

In view of the more refined techniques of contemporary research, we should regard the so-called forty-month cycle (the National Bureau cycle, that is, Mitchell's cycle) as *the* cycle *if* only one type of cycle is to be recognized. To maintain, for example, that downturns occurred in 1920, in 1929 and in 1937, but not also in 1923, in 1926, in 1948 and in 1953 comes so close to deliberate discarding of information as to be clearly unreasonable. At the same time, one would like to add that the 1920-1921 and the 1937-1938 contractions were very much more severe than those of 1923-1924, 1926-1927, and 1948-1949 and that the contraction of 1929-1933 is the most severe contraction on record. Consequently, we have a choice between (1) defining the short movements listed in Table 1, Page 22, as making up *the* cycle, and in this case adding that some of the contractions so listed were generally regarded as minor *recessions* while others were typically recorded as major *depressions,* and (2) distinguishing between two rhythmic movements of different and specific wave lengths (forty to fifty months and seven to eleven years). The present writer favors *the first of these two courses,* and this is the course which will be followed in the present volume. The second alternative claims too much because the hypothesis of a distinct seven-to-eleven-year cycle contains scarcely more than the proposition that among several (two or three or four) cycles of the shorter variety it is usually possible to distinguish one with a relatively severe contraction phase. Until 1937 these severe contractions usually came in intervals of between seven and eleven years.

It remains true that the significance of the major downturns listed on Page 36 was distinctly greater than that of the other contractions recorded in Table 1, Page 22. Furthermore, it is true that the significance of the *long-lasting* depressions of the post-Napoleonic era, and of the eighteen-seventies and 'eighties, and certainly that of the depression of the nineteen-thirties, was much greater not only than the significance of the minor recessions but also than the significance of the sharp but relatively short depressions that followed the *other major downturns* listed on Page 36. Therefore, longer rhythms than those accounted for in Table 1, Page 22, do seem to exist. But all these rhythms are irregular, and in such circumstances it seems preferable to state the existence of several irregular rhythms, rather than to try to identify each of these by assigning to it a spuriously precise duration.

We believe that the majority of contemporary economists would agree with this qualified rejection of the multiple-cycles hypothesis. The Kondratieff long-cycle hypothesis, and the hypothesis of the coexistence of intermediate[31] with short[32] cycles, do express significant findings, but they express them with a spurious degree of precision, which we prefer to avoid. This leaves us, after the elimination of the secular trend and of seasonal variation, with the Mitchell type of cycle[33] *and* with some informal but important observations concerning alternations in the economic characteristics of periods extending over several such cycles.

---

[31] By intermediate cycles we mean the seven-to-eleven-year cycles.

[32] By short cycles we mean forty-month cycles (more precisely, the type of fluctuation the average duration of which was found to be about forty-seven months in the United States). This is Mitchell's cycle (the National Bureau cycle).

[33] This is the National Bureau cycle, that is, the shortest of the trough-to-trough intervals that exceed a reasonable minimum length (usually one year). This concept was developed under the late W. C. Mitchell's influence.

The rhythm of alternation of these intermediate and longer periods—of the periods underlying the seven-to-eleven-year hypothesis and the fifty-year hypothesis—is none too regular. It is true, of course, that the duration of the Mitchell type of cycle also varies a good deal. But comparatively speaking, the least arbitrary procedure is to describe a method by which the shortest noteworthy movements are disclosed and then add that the interaction of several irregular rhythms produces alternations in the characteristics of longer periods too. This is less arbitrary than to distinguish a specific number of particular wave lengths.

8. Schumpeter's three-cycle hypothesis.

Some investigators would, of course, disagree with this conclusion. The late Joseph A. Schumpeter, for example, developed his analysis of economic growth, and of fluctuations in the framework of a three-cycle hypothesis.[34] The shortest of his cycles he called a Kitchin cycle;[35] the intermediate cycle he called a Juglar,[36] suggesting that three Kitchins could be found in each Juglar; and he attributed appreciable significance to a higher unit comprising six Juglars. To the last of these waves he assigned a duration of fifty-six years, and he named it the Kondratieff wave (or simply "the Kondratieff"). While Schumpeter's theory attributes fundamental significance to the existence of cycles with different wave lengths, he did not claim that there "should" be just three types of cycle in general business activity and that the wave lengths "should" be precisely fifty-six years for the longest type, about nine-and-a-half years for the intermediate, and slightly more than three years for the shortest. He merely maintained that the materials which he had examined lend themselves rather well to being interpreted in these specific terms. Schumpeter's schema is depicted in Figure 6. The schema can be interpreted as expressing fluctuations after the removal of the secular trend.

The underlying idea is that the directly observable "surface movement" of economic time series, which is illustrated by the irregular line in Figure 6, results from the superimposition upon one another of these three waves. Consequently, the turning points of Schumpeter's various

---

[34] J. A. Schumpeter, *Business Cycles* (New York and London, 1939).

[35] Joseph Kitchin found cyclical movements of approximately forty months' duration in American series. His results were published in the *Review of Economic Statistics* in 1923. So were the similar findings of W. L. Crum (see p. 108, *infra*).

[36] Clement Juglar was a French economist who in 1862 published a book on business cycles, treating these as more or less regularly recurring phenomena.

FIGURE 6—Schumpeter's Three-Cycle Schema With Approximate Dating of Schumpeter's Long Wave, and With the Dates for Kondratieff's Price Wave in Parentheses, 1786-1953

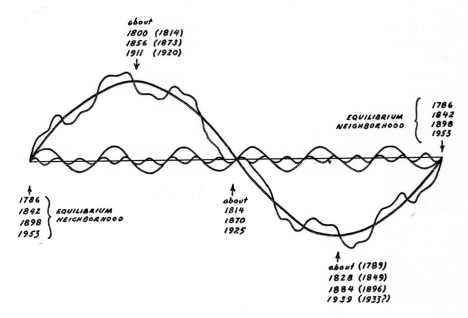

cycles need not be directly observable by simple inspection of the surface movement itself, although the surface movement usually does provide indications to the naked eye. In this regard, the Kitchin cycle of the Schumpeter system is somewhat different from *the* cycle of Mitchell's analysis.[37] Mitchell and the National Bureau staff recognize merely one cycle, and this must therefore be directly distinguishable in the surface movement of the time series. As soon as more cycles are assumed to be superimposed upon each other, dependable statements on the characteristics of these can be made only after discovering the duration of each constituent of the surface fluctuation—that is, of the duration of each pure cycle—by some statistical technique. Once this is done, the various cycles can be successively eliminated or smoothed out from the surface movement. In other words, the time series can be decomposed. The difficulty here is that the statistical decomposition of economic time series gives ambiguous results because the various rhythms lack the regularity

---

[37] That is to say, the Kitchin cycle of Schumpeter's system is somewhat different from the National Bureau cycle, although their durations are very similar.

which is a prerequisite for the proper application of decomposition techniques. We are now merely repeating in technical language what was said before—namely, that it is preferable to use the Mitchell method[38] to discover the shortest trough-to-trough intervals exceeding a reasonably selected minimum duration, and then to add that the characeristics of longer periods also seem to alternate, although with no definite regularity.

Schumpeter felt that the statistical techniques of decomposition give at least a *prima facie* indication of the existence of Kitchins, Juglars, and Kondratieffs. Combining the investigation of specific time series with a general historical analysis of the record for England, the United States, France, and Germany, he made suggestions concerning the proper turning points of the three waves. These are chronologies in the nature of "reference cycle" dates, since Schumpeter, like the National Bureau, used no composite index or time series for representing business activity in general, and yet, again like the National Bureau, he was concerned with fluctuations in general business activity as well as with the movements of specific time series. Consequently, the three Schumpeter waves (like the single cycle of the National Bureau) "lack body"—are incapable of being charted—when the cycle concept is used to express movements in general business activity. The specific time series do, of course, possess "body," and the critical points of the cycles in general business activity are clustering dates of critical points in specific time series.

The critical points of the National Bureau are troughs and peaks. These divide from each other merely two basic "phases," the expansion phase and the contraction phase. Schumpeter distinguishes four phases (in most instances). The equilibrium point corresponds to "normal" levels of activity—neither particularly prosperous nor depressed. This, in the four-phase cycle, occurs in the middle ranges of the upgrade. His waves rise from their equilibrium levels to their peaks during the phase which he calls *prosperity;* then they decline to about their normal level (that is, to the base line of Figure 6) during the phase which he calls *recession.* This part of the contraction usually does not lead to the emergence of equilibrium but is followed by the phase which he calls *depression,* and which takes business activity below the base line to a low point or trough. Finally the phase which he calls *revival* (or *recovery*) brings activity back to a level of normality, that is, to equilibrium. The cycle is usually a four-phase movement, proceeding from equilibrium to

---

[38] That is, the National Bureau method.

equilibrium through prosperity, recession, depression, and revival. Some of Schumpeter's completed cyclical movements are represented as having had merely two phases, namely, a prosperity phase raising the level of activity from normal to a peak and a recession phase bringing it back to normal. The National Bureau cycle, on the other hand, moves by definition from trough to trough in two phases through expansion and contraction. How important is this difference?

This difference, too, expresses the National Bureau's preference for building as few hypotheses as possible into the analytical apparatus itself. Schumpeter's procedure is based on the definite notion of the existence of an equilibrium neighborhood somewhere around the center of most cyclical expansions. This conception can be defended with reference to certain statistical findings. For example, Figure 5, which was reproduced from Mills' study, points to relative quiet in the middle ranges of the typical expansion. But the National Bureau method tries to avoid commitment to a hypothesis resting on the concept of "equilibrium neighborhoods." Also, the Schumpeter procedure implies a definite distinction between a recession phase and a depression phase during cyclical contractions. Since it is added that some completed cycles have had merely two phases—prosperity and recession—the hypothesis which is built into the Schumpeter apparatus formalizes a distinction between more and less severe contractions. In Schumpeter's treatment the three-cycle hypothesis itself also contributes (and perhaps more importantly than the recession-depression concept) to drawing a formal distinction between severe contractions and less severe ones because a contraction in the surface movement will obviously be more severe if all three kinds of cycle are on the downgrade than if, say, one is rising.

Distinguishing between more and less severe contractions is useful, and the terms *recession* and *depression* are suitable for expressing the distinction. Even this distinction is more suggestive than precise, but the suggestion which it carries is less hazardous than that of the existence of three waves, the movements of which are said sometimes to reinforce and sometimes to counteract each other. The National Bureau method builds neither of these distinctions into its apparatus, although it does leave the door open for recognizing the difference between more and less severe contractions and also for investigating irregular rhythms of longer duration.

As for the longer rhythms, these appeared to possess a moderate degree of regularity in Kondratieff's original presentation. But we have seen that, aside from movements in prices and interest rates, these forty-to-sixty-year cycles can be diagnosed only by methods involving a good deal of arbitrariness, and that some amount of arbitrariness enters even into the diagnosis pertaining to prices and interest rates. The precariousness of these findings is disclosed by the differences between Kondratieff's and Schumpeter's dating of the long cycles in general business activity.

Concerning the dating of the price waves, there exists no appreciable difference between Schumpeter and Kondratief (see Page 39). But Kondratieff believed he had found long waves in many specific time series, and thus in general activity, with approximately the same turning points as those established for the price wave (see Page 38). In contrast to this, Schumpeter mostly gets "equilibrium neighborhoods" (*i.e.*, middle ranges of expansion) for *his long cycles in general business activity* at about the dates where the price waves reach their troughs. Thus, Schumpeter's long wave in general business activity acquires a "lead" corresponding to about one half of the upgrade (on the average a lead of about fourteen years) over Kondratieff's long wave in general activity and in prices.

As may be noted from Figure 6, Schumpeter finds long-wave equilibrium neighborhoods[39]—mid-regions of the expansion or upgrade—in 1786, in 1842, and in 1898. The years 1786, 1842 and 1898 are close in time to *troughs* of long waves in prices and also in general activity by Kondratieff's dating (see Page 39). The duration of Schumpeter's long wave in general business activity is fifty-six years, and hence troughs occur in Schumpeter's long cycle about fourteen years earlier than equilibrium neighborhoods, while peaks occur fourteen years later than the equilibria. This results because the long-wave upgrade has an approximate duration of one-half of fifty-six years, that is, twenty-eight years. Consequently, the troughs and peaks of Schumpeter's long cycle—the troughs and peaks of *his* "Kondratieff" in business activity—come *on the average* about fourteen years earlier (from nine to twenty-one years earlier) than the troughs and peaks of the original Kondratieff waves.

This is true up to the most recent long cycle, but not of the most recent. Schumpeter anticipated the fourth equilibrium neighborhood (the beginning of his fourth long wave) for 1953.[40] Here his equilibrium neighborhood does not roughly coincide with a trough of the long wave

---

[39] In Schumpeter's schema the equilibrium neighborhoods of the long waves always coincide with Juglar and Kitchen equilibrium neighborhoods, but *vice versa* this statement is, of course, not valid.

[40] This statement in the text is based on a letter from the late Professor Schumpeter.

in prices because the duration of the long wave in prices had been shortening while the Schumpeter wave in general business activity is rigorously periodic. Consequently, the relationship between the two has been gradually shifting. In the relatively recent phase of the development a trough of the Schumpeter long wave in general activity (the trough which precedes Schumpeter's equilibrium neighborhood of 1953 by about fourteen years) roughly coincides with the trough of a Kondratieff wave in prices, and thus, presumably, with the trough of the long wave in general business activity *by Kondratieff's dating principles*. But in most cases the Schumpeter equilibrium neighborhood (middle range of the upgrade) has come close to the original Kondratieff trough, and therefore in most cases *the downgrade, or long-wave contraction, by Kondratieff's dating, corresponds roughly to the depression phase plus the revival phase of Schumpeter's long wave.*[41] In Schumpeter's schema the depression phase, is, of course, part of the downgrade or contraction, and the revival phase is part of the upgrade or expansion; but both the depression and the revival are below-equilibrium phases.

All this shows that the identification of periodic long waves in specific time series—especially in production and consumption series—is a procedure of dubious validity. In the physical series Schumpeter usually "leads" by about one-quarter of a long wave over Kondratieff. Only the price waves have roughly the same dating in the Kondratieff as in the Schumpeter chronology. In Kondratieff's account price and other long waves roughly coincide. In Schumpeter's account of the matter, which for the price wave does not differ materially from that of Kondratieff, there is a discrepancy between the long wave in general activity and the long wave in prices, and this discrepancy is explained by the distorting effect of wars, gold production, monetary disturbances, etc., on the price waves. According to Schumpeter, the price wave should "normally" have followed his own chronology of the long wave in general activity, with equilibrium neighborhoods— mid-upgrade regions—in 1786, 1842, 1898, and 1953 and with troughs about one-quarter of a long wave earlier (about fourteen years earlier).[42] Schumpeter admits that in the first three of these four cases the years here listed are more nearly dates of price-wave troughs than of mid-upgrade regions *in the price wave*, but he suggests that this is a consequence of distortions

---

[41] Similarly, the upgrade, or long-wave expansion, by Kondratieff's dating corresponds roughly to the prosperity phase plus the recession phase of Schumpeter's long wave.

[42] Precision requires adding that the chronology starts in the seventeen-eighties, and hence no statement should be made about properties of earlier long waves.

and that in the series reflecting real economic activity the years just listed do fall in mid-upgrade regions. Since Schumpeter did not base his dating exclusively on his general interpretation of economic history but relied partly, as Kondratieff did wholly, on a technical examination of time series, we see that the techniques do not yield clear-cut results for long waves in general activity. Too much depends on techniques of eliminating the secular trend and on arbitrary decisions in dating the turning points of secondary or intermediate trends.

The turning points of trend cycles (long waves) cannot be tested for their accordance with general, nontechnical experience, in the same fashion as that in which the turning points of the ups and downs in business activity are testable. Ups and downs *in the absolute level of business activity, as well as in its level relative to trend,* are the concern of investigators of cyclical fluctuations in the usual sense, regardless of whether these investigators are interested in all fluctuations which can be isolated by the National Bureau technique, or merely in the fluctuations that have resulted in the major depressions of Page 36.[43] But the so-called long cycles in general economic activity are merely alternations between intermediate trends of greater and of lesser steepness. These alternations appear to be ups and downs *only* if the secular trend is eliminated, and hence they have no very articulate or direct counterpart in nontechnical experience. Of long cycles in prices and in interest rates, this is somewhat less true because in these series there at least corresponds to the long wave an alternation of periods of uptrend with periods of downtrend, not merely an alternation of periods of steeper uptrend with periods of milder uptrend.[44]

In spite of the legitimate objections that can be raised against the concept of long cycles, we should recognize that Schumpeter's general long-wave chronology, as well as that of Kondratieff, provides valuable hints concerning sequences of longer periods with alternating characteristics. What are these hints?

On the basis of the Kondratieff chronology, we arrived earlier[45] at the conclusion that the long-wave *downgrades* in general activity (which in Kondratieff's schema are also long-wave downgrades in prices) include

---

[43] See Section 3 of the present Chapter.
[44] However, long periods of uptrend include phases with falling prices, and *vice versa*. A community does not "experience" a change from uptrend to downtrend in the same direct sense as in which it experiences a change from a phase of continuous rise to one of continuous fall.
[45] See Page 40.

the most serious, long-lasting depressions of economic history. Moving backward in time, it is possible for us to list in support of this claim the depressions of nineteen-thirties, of the eighteen-eighties, and especially of the eighteen-seventies, of the late eighteen-thirties, and of the immediate post-Napoleonic period. If we take Schumpeter's chronology, then these depressions must be said to fall in long-wave *depressions or revivals,* that is, not uniformly in downgrades.[46] Also, we noted earlier that the ratio of the duration of expansions to the duration of contractions (in the surface movement observed by the National Bureau) tends to be more favorable in periods of long-wave upgrade than in periods of long-wave downgrade by Kondratieff's dating. Here again, a difference between long-wave upgrade and long-wave downgrade in the Kondratieff model becomes in the Schumpeter schema a difference between *long-wave prosperity plus long-wave recession* on the one hand, and *long-wave depression plus long-wave revival* on the other. This latter distinction divides above-equilibrium phases from below-equilibrium phases of the Schumpeter schema.

In this respect, the Schumpeter chronology should not be regarded as inferior to the original Kondratieff chronology. It is no less plausible to attribute undesirable properties to the *low ranges*[47] of the long wave (*i.e.,* to the depression phase of the downgrade plus the revival phase of the upgrade) than to the entire downgrade and *merely* to the downgrade. Furthermore, the Schumpeter chronology is neater, in that each long wave has a duration of fifty-six years, while the data on Pages 38-39 show a successive diminution in the length of the long waves in prices (which in the Kondratieff schema roughly coincide with long waves in general activity). The greater the irregularity, the less significant are the findings, because there is nothing astonishing in the mere fact that there exist irregular alternations in the characteristics of longer periods.

In the Schumpeter schema we are supposed to have more regular alternations. But while the periodicity of Schumpeter's wave is precise, it is not *invariably* true that severe and extended depressions have become observable in the revival phases as well as in the depression phases of

---

[46] In Schumpeter's schema the period extending from the late eighteen-twenties to 1842 was a period of long-wave revival and so was the period extending from the mid-eighties to 1898. The latest long-wave revival extends from about 1939 to 1953. All these revivals are, of course, preceded by long-wave depressions and followed by long-wave prosperity, and the duration of all these phases is about fourteen years.

[47] Low ranges in the sense of below-equilibrium ranges.

his long wave. No serious depression became observable in the revival phase of 1939-1953. This, of course, could be explained away with reference to the war and to the postwar boom. Indeed, in support of the Schumpeter schema one might point out that after 1939 the large-scale American unemployment of the nineteen-thirties became absorbed rather slowly and gradually, in spite of the outbreak of war in Europe in September 1939. *But it remains a fact that while by Kondratieff's dating at least one severe and extended depression became observrable in each long-wave downgrade, the same is not literally true of each revival phase of the Schumpeter schema.* It *is* true of each depression phase of the Schumpeter schema; and it *is* true of the first two out of the three revival phases on record, but not of the last.

In this connection it should be mentioned that, according to Schumpeter, government interference and union power are gradually destroying the capitalist process, and we are likely to be engaged now in a "march into socialism." Consequently, it would be possible to take the position that according to his views the recent period *should not* fit his theory of the capitalist process too well. Yet he maintained that, perhaps surpisingly, the theory nevertheless continues to perform satisfactorily.

Considering that technical methods of decomposing production and consumption series do not yield clearcut indications concerning the existence of long waves of definite periodicity, or concerning the coexistence of intermediate waves with short ones, there is in our opinion no sufficient justification for defining these regularities into the basic analytical apparatus. But there is good reason for drawing a distinction between major depression and minor recessions, and generally between the alternating types of longer period. In some longer periods the major depressions tended to become protracted; in other longer periods they were mostly short.

It is easy to play down the Kondratieff schema and that of Schumpeter. But very much more imagination was needed to invent them than it takes to tear them down. After weighing the pros and cons of these models, one may decide against them. Indeed, on the balance of considerations we are inclined to do so. But the process of weighing the pros and cons is exceedingly instructive. Any hypothesis of which this is true has considerable merit. In our opinion, the main merit of the Kondratieff and Schumpeter long-cycle hypotheses is that they direct attention (1) to a moderate degree of regularity in the past alternation of upward and downward trends in prices and interest rates and (2) to the fact that the most severe, long-lasting depressions were concentrated in the second and the fourth quarter of the nineteenth century and in the nineteen-thirties, that is, in periods separated from one another by roughly one half of a century. We believe, however, that these findings do not stand the degree of formalization which the proponents of long-cycle hypotheses have attempted to give them.

9. The relation between Schumpeter's techniques and his theoretical position.

This Chapter is primarily concerned with methods of deriving trends and cycles from time series. We are not reviewing cycle theories and theories of the long-run drift at this juncture. But it was necessary to comment with respect to the analytical implications of the methods earlier considered, namely, those devised by Persons, the National Bureau of Economic Research, Frickey, and Kondratieff. In those cases, brief comments were sufficient because the analytical implications were not very specific. Within certain limits, the methods earlier considered are compatible with a wide range of theoretical positions. The relationship between Schumpeter's techniques and his theoretical position is closer. Schumpeter's method is the technical counterpart of a specific theory of economic development.

His long waves (or "Kondratieffs") are periods in which specific types of "innovation" were put into effect. Innovations are changes in production functions, that is to say, technological and organizational improvements. These improvements are first introduced by highly imaginative, pioneering entrepreneurs, whose activities subsequently become imitated by many followers. The innovations of each "Kondratieff" start in a specific area of the economy, or in a few specific areas, but subsequently there is a spread of these changes and the economy as a whole becomes transformed. In capitalist economies innovating activity comes in spurts and is associated with credit expansion. Aside from monetary disturbances, the basic pattern of the process can be represented by a secular upward trend with merely two-phased cycles around it. In the first of these phases, the prosperity phase, the new production functions are introduced; in the second, the recession phase, the new products reach the market and the harvest is collected. However, at this point the previous credit expansion usually leads to the necessity of monetary contraction or "liquidation": the recession is followed by depression, and subsequently by a revival toward the new equilibrium neighborhood.

The cycle becomes four-phased. In each major period, innovating activities of various spans are being carried on simultaneously, and monetary repercussions of various spans are being generated. This, according to Schumpeter, points to the usefulness of a multiple-cycle hypothesis. The three-cycle hypothesis is relatively simple, and he considers it sufficient to bring out the essential features of the development.

The first long wave in the Schumpeter sequence (his first "Kondratieff," extending from the equilibrium neighborhood of 1786 to that of 1842) is described as having been produced by a wave of innovations which centered in cotton textiles, in coal and iron, and in canals and road building. The spread of the steam engine is a characteristic feature of this wave which Schumpeter calls the long wave of the Industrial Revolution. The second wave (1842-1898) is associated mainly with railroad building and steel; and the third (1898-1953) is linked to the process of electrification, but with much of the innovating activity centering in the automobile industry and the chemical industries.

In the present volume, too, an analytical framework will be used which places much emphasis on "improvements" (the acquisition of new skills). However, our argument will be based on the idea that proper functioning of capitalist economies requires not merely a sufficient flow of improvements, but also the adjustment of the *character* of improvements to the resource requirements of the economic system, that is, to the relative resource scarcities existing in it. Furthermore, proper functioning of the economy requires that changes in the composition of output should not overtax the mobility of resources (*i.e.,* that there should exist a proper relationship between changes in the composition of output and mobility of resources) ; and it requires that the money and credit supply should keep pace with physical growth tendencies. Interruptions of the growth process will be interpreted as resulting from temporary violations of these conditions, that is, of conditions relating to the quantitative sufficiency and qualitative adequacy of improvements, to the mobility of resources and to the proper regulation of the money and credit supply. The three-cycle hypothesis will not here be used as a technical device. The shortest of the fluctuations directly observable in the time series will be regarded as the business cycle, provided that the duration exceeds a minimum of about one year. However, we shall distinguish minor recessions from major depressions, recognizing that usually more than one cycle in the foregoing sense has run its course between successive *major* depressions; and we shall attribute significance also to the succession of longer periods with alternating characteristics. This amounts to recognizing that several irregular rhythms interact in industrial economies, even though we do not believe that it is possible at present to isolate these rhythms in pure form.

10. Fluctuations in general business activity and in individual sectors of the economy.

We are implying here, of course, that concepts such as "the economy as a whole" or "business in general" possess meaning. They do, indeed, possess intuitive meaning to all of us, and this is sufficient justification. The methods used in the analysis of trends and cycles also imply that "business in general" fluctuates, that is to say, that meaning attaches to the clustering dates of critical points in the movements of individual time series. This, again, is an intuitively satisfactory judgment.

Yet all careful analysts show awareness of the existence of individual series which, from the viewpoint here sketched, appear to be highly untypical. Some of these are not typical because their fluctuations seem largely unrelated to fluctuations in "business in general." Many agricultural production series are of this character. Once a crop has been planted, its size depends largely on climatic conditions. Furthermore, it is not a generally valid proposition that a smaller crop will be planted when business conditions are expected to be weak, because the farmer may then impute to himself a lower wage rate (per unit of effort) and he may try to maintain his total earnings by producing more. Frequently, the out-of-pocket expenses are relatively small. Also, depressions may cause migration from the cities to rural areas. The business cycle is a phenomenon characteristic of industrialized economies, and its effects on the agricultural sector of advanced economies cannot be summarized by simple statements.

Where production decisions must be made for an appreciable period ahead, *and out-of-pocket expenses are comparatively small,* production does not typically show a tendency to diminish in business contractions. Not even with a lag does it show this tendency. Prices react strongly but output does not. The standard crops illustrate this, except where output restrictions are imposed on farmers from the outside.

In other agricultural pursuits production decisions must be made well ahead of time, but out-of-pocket expenses are appreciable. In these lines of agricultural activity rhythmic movements do develop, but the rhythm is strongly influenced by the length of the production lag.

The so-called "corn-hog cycle" is an example. High prices for "finished" live animals, relative to the price of fodder, result in substantially increased output of finished animals, and hence in low prices for finished animals relative to the price of fodder. This result, however, shows with a lag. When the result becomes evident, it leads to reduced demand for young animals and hence, again with a lag, to high prices for finished animals relative to the price of fodder. Producers tend to adjust their output to existing prices, but the fact that many producers adjust simultaneously tends to change the prices as soon as the adjustment is completed. There exists a tendency toward overadjustment, both upward and downward. This is because many producers adjust independently at the same time, and all must commit themselves to a higher or a lower output for a future date. After having committed themselves, they cannot change their minds without incurring high costs—usually prohibitive ones.

Specific cycles of this sort are not limited to agricultural types of activity. A tendency toward overadjustment exists also in construction, manufacturing, mining, the utilities, trade, and elsewhere. In some, production lags possess considerable significance. Would it be possible to argue that business fluctuations appear to be general merely because rhythmic movements of the corn-hog variety (so-called "cobwebs") [48] occur in all branches of the economy?

None of the research methods here surveyed suggests this way of looking at business fluctuations. The concept of reference cycles—of single National Bureau cycles, of multiple Schumpeter cycles, or of Kondratieff's long waves—clearly suggests that we are not simply faced with a great many specific cycles of overadjustment. The same is true of Frickey's standard pattern. There exist good reasons for not taking an essentially particularistic view of business fluctuations. The corn-hog variety of overadjustment can explain why certain branches of the economy periodically overexpand relatively to others, but it cannot explain why the economy as a whole periodically overexpands and overcontracts. Assume, for example, that the corn-hog type of cycle is in its overexpansion stage all over the economy, that is, not only in hog production but also in railroad construction, residential building, automobiles, textiles, etc. In this case, incomes and purchasing power should also be "overexpanded." But the meaning of this, of course, is that we have *not* explained the over-

---

[48] These cycles of overadjustment in individual time series are sometimes called *cobwebs* because the graphic representation of the movement with supply and demand curves gives the visual impression of a cobweb.

expansion of output as a whole. We have not explained in relation to what there is "overexpansion." To explain this we must be able to make clear why, in certain phases of economic development, part of the aggregate income will be used neither for the purchase of consumer goods nor for that of investment goods. We must be able to make clear also why such a condition may establish itself with a detour over an inflationary phase of development. The corn-hog analysis contains no explanation of this. It contains merely an explanation of fluctuations in specific lines relative to a given level of general business activity.

The methods which we have surveyed rightly imply that we cannot simply put together the problem of over-all trends and general fluctuations from individual overadjustment cycles. However, analysts of economic development have not overlooked that the problem of fluctuations in general activity is intimately connected with the problem of fluctuations in specific industries relative to others. On the one hand, specific maladjustments—overexpansion in one area in relation to others—may degenerate into general maladjustments because of the incomplete mobility of resources. Resources may not flow freely and promptly enough from the overexpanded lines of activity into the insufficiently expanded ones. On the other hand, general fluctuations caused by other circumstances—not by disproportionalities between specific industries—may *create* disproportionalities because of their differential impact on different branches of economic activity. Obviously, there exist important differences between the income elasticities of demand for various products. This in itself could explain why different industries react with different intensities to changes in general business conditions. But we have to take account also of the fact that for the various industries, we find different *lags* (1) in the spending of new buyers' incomes on the products of the industry in question, (2) in the reaction of the producers of the industry to changed market conditions, (3) in the completion of finished goods from resources already acquired by the industry, and (4) in the replacement of equipment earlier installed by the industry. All these lags should be taken into account in a full discussion of the differential behavior of individual time series. The research methods of economic analysts imply that significance attaches to the *differences* in behavior of individual time series, as well as to standard patterns or clustering dates for the economy as a whole.

Characteristic rhythms of overadjustment in specific time series have received a good deal of attention not merely in the area of agriculture.

For example, textile production seems to show more rapid pulsations than the economy as a whole. On the other end of the scale, in lines of activity where the durable equipment wears out slowly and where the costs created by the fixed equipment account for a high proportion of total long-run costs,[49] the observable rhythms are substantially longer than in the great majority of specific time series. Under the conditions so described, overexpanded productive capacity diminishes slowly, by gradual wear and tear. It does not pay to abandon a productive plant, even if there is too much of it for maintaining prices at a profitable level. When the plant does become contracted, through gradual wear and tear, an appreciable shortage may have to accumulate before the individual investors feel induced to build a new plant on a major scale, since this decision involves an irrevocable long-run commitment. Where many investors act independently, the result is likely to be a long rhythm of overadjustment, both upward and downward. Each investor adjusts to existing conditions, not to those which will exist when all other investors have acted as he does.

II. The building cycle and its dating.

This pattern of behavior may contribute to bringing about the fifteen-twenty-year waves which are observable in building activity, even though population movements must also be taken into account in the proper interpretation of the building cycle. Here, of course, the house is to be viewed as the "plant" which wears out slowly and the fixed cost of which accounts for a high proportion of the total cost of producing the output. The services of the house are the "output," and rents (actual or imputed) are the "prices." Simultaneous adjustment of the output of many producers to the initially given price causes the price to change and hence the "adjustment" may turn out to have been overdone. Once overadjustment has occurred, it may take a long period to change the existing quantity of "plant."

Burns and Mitchell, basing their work partly on the previous investigations of Riggleman and Frisbie, found the following building-wave turning points for the United States: [50]

---

[49] The first of these two conditions means that the Marshallian "short run" is long in terms of clock time; the second means that in the Marshallian "short run" fixed costs account for a high proportion of total costs.

[50] Burns and Mitchell, *op. cit.*, p. 422. See also C. D. Long, *Building Cycles and the Theory of Investment* (Princeton and London, 1940). For further references to work on building cycles see A. H. Hansen, *Business Cycles and National Income* (New York, 1951), Ch. 3, and R. A. Gordon, *Business Fluctuations* (New York, 1953), pp. 209-211.

Peaks (downturns): 1853   1871   1890   1909   1925
Troughs (upturns):   1862   1878   1900   1918   1933

Subsequent developments point to a further peak in 1941-1942. This peak came after a very weak upgrade in the late 'thirties, and it was followed by a short but sharp downgrade which falls in the period of World War II. An upgrade began in the immediate postwar period, and it has been exceedingly vigorous.

Building activity is a sufficiently important constituent of investment activity as a whole to make it appear likely that interactions of some importance can be found between general economic fluctuations and building waves. The mobility of resources may be insufficient—their specialization to specific activities may be too great—to enable the other sectors of the economy to expand or contract promptly when building activity contracts or expands. Indeed, the severe and extended depressions of the eighteen-seventies, of the eighteen-nineties and of the period 1929-1933, all fall in building cycle downgrades. These downgrades began two to four years earlier than the severe general business contractions in question. Yet at least two of the five building cycle downgrades of the Burns-Mitchell chronology did not produce severe *and extended* general business contractions,[51] and one decade with rather generally depressed characteristics falls in a building wave upgrade.[52] So far as the severe and long depressions of the past are concerned, the original Kondratieff schema and the Schumpeter schema provide somewhat more dependable hints than does a hypothesis linking these depressions to building-wave downgrades.

However, we are inclined to attribute some significance to the fact that the three worst depressed periods of the past one hundred years do fall in building cycle downgrades.

12. Leads and lags.

Contrasting the behavior of individual time series with the behavior of "business in general" is interesting not merely because some series show characteristic rhythms of their own which are untypical of business in

---

[51] This is true of the building cycle downgrade of 1853-1862 and of that of 1909-1918. The second of these includes the period of World War I, but the war began five years after the beginning of the building cycle downgrade.

[52] This is the decade of the eighteen-eighties.

general. Even where the rhythms are similar, turning points do not coincide in time.

The concern of the National Bureau with lead-lag relationships has already been mentioned. As was noted, studies undertaken by Mills show a slight tendency for consumer demand to turn up before other constituents of demand and output do. This is called a "lead" on the upturn. By similar methods[53] it was demonstrated that other series tend to lead by several months at both turning points, although there exist exceptions in almost all cases where the series is available for longer periods. The time series relating to orders of durable goods have been shown to "lead" both on the upturn and on the downturn. Business failures, as measured by the amount of the liabilities involved, tend to start rising before the downturn of business in general, and they tend to start falling before the upturn. Stock prices, too, tend to lead at both turning points. So do building contracts and also average hours worked in manufacturing (*i.e.*, the length of the work week). A more recent study shows that the percentage of all corporations suffering losses has typically started to rise before the reference-cycle downturns (and that this percentage has typically started to decline before the upturn), even though total profits have displayed no lead or lag relative to the reference-cycle turning points. Furthermore, the percentage of all time series participating in the expansion and in the contraction starts diminishing before the expansion or the contraction is ended, that is, before the reference-cycle turning point is reached. On the other hand, interest rates, manufacturing inventories, and some other series tend to lag behind general business activity. The length of the leads and lags vary from occasion to occasion, but the time interval elapsing between the successive turns of several leading series may give some indication of the speed with which a general turning point is approaching on any particular occasion.

It can, of course, never be taken for granted that tendencies of this sort will stay unchanged, and even if the tendency continues it cannot be taken for granted that the next occasion will not be one of the few exceptions. For example, in the nineteen-twenties and 'thirties economists engaged in business-cycle research at Harvard University were currently

---

[53] See Geoffrey H. Moore, *Statistical Indicators of Cyclical Revivals and Recessions* (Occasional Paper 31, National Bureau of Economic Research, New York, 1950); also Thor Hultgren, *Cyclical Diversities in the Fortunes of Industrial Corporations* (Occasional Paper 32, National Bureau of Economic Research, New York, 1950).

publishing a "barometer" based on the fact that time series relating to *stock-exchange* activity (labeled as group A) mostly led over "business" [54] (labeled as group B), and that "business" mostly led over series in which *interest rates* are prominent (group C). This "barometer" showed the standing of the A index, the B index, and the C index separately in a graph. Such a barometer inevitably carries the suggestion that a downturn, say, in the B series is likely to be merely apparent (merely an episodic interruption of an expansion that is going to continue presently) if the downturn in question was not preceded by a downturn in the A series. However, in some phases of economic development—notably in the significant downturn of 1929—the A-B-C sequence did not establish itself. For example, in 1929 "business," in the sense of series representative of production, turned down several months prior to the stock exchange crash. Yet the downturn was very real indeed, not an episodic interruption of an expansion which was still going strong. Later, the publication of the Harvard barometer was discontinued.

Those engaging in guesswork concerning the future (in so-called forecasting) should not disregard the "typical" lead-lag relations of the past. Nor should they, in our opinion, disregard some of the suggestions which other hypotheses of recurring sequences, *e.g.,* the long-wave hypotheses, carry. But, unfortunately, it is necessary to use informal judgment and general information as much as technical devices. By using technical devices we can arrive at conclusions concerning tendencies, sometimes merely *mild* tendencies, toward certain regularities in the past record. In what sense this is useful, and yet insufficient for prediction is a question about which it is impossible to make simple and articulate statements. The question is essentially identical with one that we encounter all the time in our everyday lives. Why is it useful to be "experienced," and why, nevertheless, does "experience" in itself not guarantee correct foresight and success? The present writer's disinclination to formalize mild tendencies in the past record into rigid models is essentially a disinclination to overstress the value of this kind of experience. Yet this is merely a qualified objection because no reasonable person will disregard available pieces of experience even if they are inconclusive.

---

[54] "Business" was represented by series among which bank clearings outside New York played an important role. These are more directly connected with the level of production than are the bank clearings in New York, since the latter are significantly influenced by purely financial transactions. In general, "business" in the sense here considered should be interpreted as standing for output-yielding activities (production).

13. Trends.

For the analysis of cyclical behavior, we need data relating to successive short periods. Take, for example, the reference-cycle chronology of Table 1, Page 22. This would be somewhat less revealing if it were based on quarterly rather than monthly dating, and its usefulness would be further reduced if the dating were based on yearly data. A peak or a trough in the yearly data may well occur one year earlier or later than the calendar year in which the monthly or quarterly peak or trough falls. This is because the peak year or the trough year, as identified in yearly data, depends on what happened before and after the trough, during the year in which the true peak or trough falls and during the years preceding and following that year. Obviously, the amplitudes (magnitudes of trough-to-peak or peak-to-trough swings) in individual time series would be spuriously reduced, and lead-lag relationships would be distorted, if we computed our results from yearly figures. Data relating to even longer intervals would be entirely useless for the analysis of the Mitchell-type cycle. National income data are not at present available sufficiently far back for sufficiently short successive intervals to be usable for establishing the turning points in Table 1.

But Simon Kuznets' estimates of the American net national product, for *overlapping decades* from 1869-1878 on, enables us to give an indication of the nature of *long-run trends* in American economic activity in general.[55] All data are expressed in 1929 prices, in addition to being listed in current values. Thus price changes are eliminated. On the balance of considerations it is desirable to do this, even though the elimination of price changes is an inevitably arbitrary procedure, especially for longer time intervals. The center points of the overlapping decades are *five years apart,* that is to say, the decade 1869-1878 has January 1, *1874,* as its center point, the decade 1874-1883 has January 1, *1879,* as its center point, etc. We have not carried Table 2 beyond the decade 1919-1928 because the last two decades covered by the Kudnets statistics (1924-1933 and 1929-1938) are strongly influenced by the severe depression of the 'thirties, and the estimates do not extend into the post-depression era. Consequently, we list in Table 2 the average of the Kuznets estimates for the years 1928 and 1929, instead of listing the estimate for the decade 1924-1933, of which January 1, 1929 is the center point. We show in the table also the rate of growth of the net national product from one overlapping decade to the next, and the per-

---

[55] Simon Kuznets, *National Income: A Summary of Findings* (New York, 1946).

centage of the net national product which in each period went into net
capital formation. The "net" figures are here derived from the "gross"
by deducting depreciation on buildings and on durable producer goods,
on the assumption of a lifetime of fifty years for buildings and a lifetime
of thirteen years for durable producer goods. One hundred minus the
percentage going into net capital formation is the percentage of the net
national product which reached households (*i.e.*, constituted "consumption"). In the Kuznets estimates, in contrast to those of the Department
of Commerce, the goods and services acquired by the government are
allocated partly to the category of consumption and partly to that of
net capital formation; they are not listed as a separate category. However,
very much the greater part of the net capital formation was private, both
in the decades covered by the table and in the postwar period.

From the decade 1879-1888 (which is centered on January 1, 1884) to
the last period shown in the table, the rate of increase of the net national
product moved between 12.4 percent and 25.2 percent *per quinquen-
nium.* For no *decade* (no sequence of two quinquennia) did the rise

Table 2—Net National Product; Percentage Rise in Net National Product; and Net Capital Formation as Percentage of Net National Product

(Decade averages. All data expressed in 1929 prices).

Overlapping Decades	Net National Product (in billions)[1]	Percentage Rise in Net National Product from Preceding Period	Net Capital Formation as Percentage of Net National Product[2]
1869-1878	9.3	—	13.7
1874-1883	13.6	46.2	14.4
1879-1888	17.9	31.6	14.6
1884-1893	21.0	17.3	16.1
1889-1898	24.2	15.2	16.2
1894-1903	29.8	23.1	14.8
1899-1908	37.3	25.2	13.6
1904-1913	45.0	20.6	13.1
1909-1918	50.6	12.4	13.0
1914-1923	57.3	13.2	11.4
1919-1928	69.0	20.4	10.2
1928-1929[3]	83.9	21.6	10.9

[1] Simon Kuznets, *National Income: A Summary of Findings,* p. 32.
[2] *Ibid.,* p. 53.
[3] Average of years. Kuznets, *National Product since 1869* (New York, 1946), p. 56.

amount to less than 27 percent, and for no decade did it exceed twice
this percentage rate. The average of the decennial rates of increase was

about 40 percent, with no tendency toward "retardation" (slowing of the proportionate rate of growth) after the mid-eighties. However, if we extend the analysis back to the beginning of the Kuznets series, then we obtain appreciable retardation in the proportionate or percentage rate of growth because the two earliest figures for the quinquennial rate of growth are by far the highest. Retardation as compared to the 'seventies or even the early part of the 'eighties may very well be a real phenomenon, but we should be aware of the fact that the estimates for the earliest periods are less reliable than those for the more recent ones.

The increase in *per capita* national product is not shown in our table.[56] The average of decennial increases in this magnitude was about 20 percent if we begin with the decade centered on 1884. There is no "retardation" from this time on, but here, too, the rates of increase are higher for the decade preceding that which is centered on 1884. Around the average of 20 percent there was considerable variation in the increases for individual decades. The rise in the *per capita* output is partly a consequence of the fact that the capital stock per unit of worker has been rising; partly it is a consequence of technological and organizational improvements, that is, of changes which are in the nature of inventions.

During the period covered in the table the percentage of the net product going into capital formation declined from a level of 14 to 16 percent to slightly more than 10 percent. More precisely, it declined to about 10 percent, after having risen in the early decades from 14 percent to 16 percent. In the past decade this percentage again seems to have been about 10 percent, if allowance is made for capital formation in the government sector (as is done in the Kuznets procedure) and if the ratio is made generally comparable to those of Table 2. During the eighty-year period as a whole the percentage of the output going into *consumption* seems therefore to have shown some rise, but not one that would be observable for each subperiod which can be put together from several quinquennia or even from several decades. The absolute amount of new investment, in contrast to the percentage of output going into new investment, has, of course, risen significantly. We shall see later that the rise in the consumed proportion of income occurred in a long period in which the share of labor in the national income increased (see Pages 260-265). It is plausible to assume that these two trends were at least loosely connected, although no close correlation emerges in any technical sense.

---

[56] See Kuznets, *National Income: A Summary of Findings*, p. 32.

Within the aggregate of net capital formation, the relative weight of construction (building activity) has become smaller than was the case in the early decades. This is likely to be connected with the decline in the rate of population growth. Within the aggregate of consumption, there has been a gradual increase in durable goods and in immaterial services. In the beginning of the period covered by Table 2 durable consumer goods accounted for about 8 to 9 percent of total consumption, toward the end for about 10 to 11 percent. In the beginning immaterial services (services not incorporated in material goods) [57] accounted for slightly less than 30 percent of total consumption, toward the end for somewhat more than one third.

The table does not carry us beyond 1929. If, by using estimates of the Department of Commerce, we compare 1929 figures with those pertaining to the late nineteen-forties, we obtain for these two decades a 30-percent *average per decade* increase in the aggregate output (GNP) of the American economy.[58] This average per decade increase lies between the highest and the lowest decade increases (joint increases for two quinquennia) in Table 2. On the whole, it is definitely on the low side.

However, the average decennial increase from the late nineteen-twenties to the late 'forties results from practically no rise between 1929 and the late 'thirties and a *more than 60-percent* increase from 1939 to the end of the 'forties.[59] The rise from the late 'thirties to the late 'forties exceeds all decade increases (joint increases for two quinquennia) in Table 2, unless the decade in question includes the first of the Kuznets quinquennia. The rise from the late 'thirties to the late 'forties is likely to be untypically high because it leads from a decade in which resources were greatly underutilized into a decade of "overfull" utilization. Yet, on the other hand, the average per decade increase from the 'twenties to the 'forties may well be untypically low because this span included the Great

---

[57] See Kuznets, *National Product since 1869,* p. 106. These services include consumer services performed by the government and also such things as education, travel, entertainment, laundering, banking services, brokerage.

[58] The difference between GNP (gross national product) and the net national product consists of the depreciation allowances on buildings, machinery, and equipment. These depreciation allowances are deducted from the gross national product to obtain the net national product (NNP).

[59] U. S. Department of Commerce, *National Income and Product of the United States, 1929-1950,* Supplement to the *Survey of Current Business* (Washington, 1951), p. 146. Considering that 1949 was a recession year, we took the arithmetic mean of the 1948 output and of the 1950 output as characteristic of the end of the 'forties. If the 1949 figure had been used, the increase from the end of the 'thirties to the end of the 'forties would have come out as 57 percent.

Depression, and because, as we shall note later, there is reason to believe that a depression of such magnitude will not return. Not all the growth potential lost in a long and severe depression is likely to be exploitable in the next decade. Some of it is likely to be lost for good. In other words, in the present circumstances it seems reasonable to expect a decennial rate of increase in aggregate output such as lies between 30 percent and 60 percent. If, as is likely, the economy is kept closer to its growth path, and thus the wastes of fluctuations are reduced, the rate of growth may turn out to lie much closer to the upper than to the lower of these two figures. Assuming such a rate of increase, the case for the "retardation" hypothesis becomes very weak, unless we compare recent rates of growth with those observable in the first two quinquennia of Table 2. It should be added that the American output-increment from 1948 to 1953 was the equivalent of a slightly higher than 60-percent decennial rate of growth (about 5 percent at an annual compound rate), but this increment was influenced by the inflationary armament boom of the Korean War.

In "maturing" *individual industries* it is, of course, not uncommon to find slackening of growth rates, frequently after periods of increasing rates of growth in output. But there have always existed new as well as maturing developments, and hence the proportionate rate of growth of aggregate output has so far shown no clear-cut signs of slackening.

Similar conclusions can be derived also from F. C. Mills' estimates, covering the six decades from 1891-1900 through 1941-1950, in terms of straight decade averages (not averages for *overlapping* decades). These estimates are given in Table 3. They provide information on decade-to-decade increases in total man-hours performed and in output per man-hour, as well as in aggregate output.

Table 3—Real Gross National Product, Population, Labor Input and Productivity, United States, by Decades, 1891-1950 [1]

Decade	Gross National Product (billions of 1929 dollars)	Gross National Product (index number based on 1891-1900)	Population [2]	Total-Man-hours of Labor Input [2]	Output per Man-hour [2]
1891-1900	294	100.0	100.0	100.0	100.0
1901-1910	455	154.8	120.6	126.1	122.8
1911-1920	603	205.1	143.4	140.5	146.0
1921-1930	838	285.0	165.4	145.1	196.4
1931-1940	843	286.7	181.9	122.8	233.5
1941-1950	1,493	507.8	201.4	180.5	281.3

[1] F. C. Mills, *Productivity and Economic Progress* (New York, 1952), p. 2.
[2] Index number based on 1891-1900.

The output concept here is that of the gross rather than the net national product (GNP rather than NNP). In other words, the depreciation charges on durable producer goods and on buildings are not deducted. These charges have shown a somewhat rising long-run trend relatively to the NNP itself.

The rise in output per man-hours performed in the economy, so-called *man-hour output,* shows no retardation in Table 3. The decennial increase moves between about 20 and 33 percent; the highest proportionate increase is observable for the transition from 1911-1920 to 1921-1930. Man-hour output—that is, output per man-hours performed in the economy—is not quite the same thing as *per capita* national product because the length of the workweek has shown a declining tendency and also because the labor force has not accounted for a constant proportion of the population.

Here again, the question of whether recent increases in *aggregate output* (GNP) are smaller or greater than the increases around the turn of the century depends on what we mean by recent increases. The percentage rise from the 'thirties to the 'forties is the highest observable in Table 3; the *average per decade increase* from the 'twenties to the 'forties is on the low side as compared to earlier experience. At present, it seems reasonable to assume a rate of growth such as is lower—at least somewhat lower—than the increase from the 'thirties to the 'forties but distinctly higher than the average per decade increase from the 'twenties to the 'forties. This gives no retardation (certainly no *appreciable* retardation) since the turn of the century.

Before turning to other countries, the attention of the reader should be called to the looseness of the connection between the *saved proportion of output* and the proportionate *rate of growth of output.* Table 2 shows that historically these two magnitudes have not moved together. The reason is that the growth rate of output depends on the output-increment obtained per unit of new capital formation as well as on the saved proportion of output. The growth rate of output is the algebraic product of these two. In recent years, for example, the saved proportion of output has been on the low side, but the growth rate of output has been significant as compared to most periods on which we have data. The high output-increment per unit of new capital formation which expresses itself in this fact is an indicator of a very substantial rate of technological and organizational progress. In principle, the high output-increment per unit of new investment could also indicate that factors of production cooperating with capital are being acquired at a much more rapid rate (relative to capital itself) than was the case further back in history. But in the present case the facts do not support this alternative interpretation. We have here an indicator of rapid technological and organizational progress.

This does not in itself *conclusively* answer the question of what would have happened recently if taxes and government expenditures had been appreciably lower. The answer depends in part on how much more investment our rapid rate of technological progress would have been capable of calling forth if we had had more savings. For, with lower taxes and lower government expenditures aggregate savings would have been higher. It is possible to speculate about the consequences of higher savings, and in one's speculations one should stress the high rate of improvement during recent periods. But it is not possible to answer the question conclusively here. We shall return to the problem in the next chapter.

Table 4 includes figures concerning growth rates in various countries. These were prepared by Raymond W. Goldsmith for a conference of the National Bureau of Economic Research.[60] Growth rates are higher for the United States than for any other country included in the table. Yet the upward trend is a common characteristic of all these economies.

Is there a tendency in the other countries toward a decline in the proportionate rate of increase, that is, toward "retardation"? It is not easy to arrive at definite conclusions in this regard.

The yearly percentage rate of growth is smaller in most countries for the period 1913-1938 than for 1860-1913, but this is inconclusive because the period 1913-1938 includes the Great Depression. The fact that the Great Depression was more severe than were the depressions of the last quarter of the nineteenth century is not, in itself, a proof of retardation. The growth rates from 1938 to 1950 were greater in some countries and smaller in others than those for earlier periods. Where the 1938-1950 growth rates were greater, indications are against retardation. But, nevertheless, retardation is not *disproved* because the twelve-year period in

---

[60] Raymond W. Goldsmith, *Financial Structure and Economic Growth in "Advanced" Countries,* Conference on Capital Formation and Economic Growth, National Bureau of Economic Research, (New York, 1953) , p. 4. At the time when this volume goes to press Mr. Goldsmith's paper is as yet unpublished, although available in mimeograph. The data for Germany were revised. The author wishes to express his thanks for Mr. Goldsmith's and the National Bureau's permission to reprint the table with the revisions.

Table 4—Growth Rates of Real National Product of "Advanced" Countries, 1860 to 1950

(percent per year)

	U.S.	Canada	Aus-tralia	New Zealand	U.K.	France	Ger-many	Nether-lands	Bel-gium	Switzer-land	Sweden	Nor-way	Den-mark
Aggregate Real National Product													
1. 1860-1913[a]	4.3	—	3.7	—	2.4	1.1	3.0	2.3	2.2	2.6	2.0	2.3	2.8
2. 1913-1938	2.0	1.7[b]	2.1	—	1.0	1.1	1.3	2.1	1.0	1.6	1.9	1.9	2.1
3. 1938-1950	5.7	5.9	2.6	3.3[c]	1.6	.2	2.3[d]	1.8	.6	2.1	2.5	3.0	2.2
4. 1860-1950	3.8	—	3.2	—	1.8	1.1	2.4	2.2	1.7	2.1	2.0	2.3	2.5
5. 1913-1950	3.0	2.8	2.3	—	1.2	.9	1.7	1.7	.9	1.8	2.1	2.3	2.1
Real National Product per Head													
6. 1860-1913[a]	2.3	—	1.7	—	1.5	.9	2.0	.8	1.4	1.4	1.3	1.6	1.8
7. 1913-1938	.9	.2	.4	—	.8	.9	0.7	.6	.6	1.2	1.4	1.2	.8
8. 1938-1950	4.2	4.0	1.1	2.4	1.2	.0	.7[d]	.6	.3	1.1	1.7	2.1	1.2
9. 1860-1950	2.2	—	1.3	—	1.2	.9	1.4	.7	1.1	1.3	1.4	1.6	1.4
10. 1913-1950	2.0	1.4	.6	—	.9	.7	0.7	.6	.5	1.2	1.5	1.5	.9

[a] First period starts with following years other than 1860; U.S. 1869/78; Australia 1886; U.K. 1870; Netherlands 1900; Belgium 1846; Switzerland 1890; Sweden 1870; Norway 1891; Denmark 1870.
[b] 1911 instead of 1913.
[c] 1938/39 to 1947/48.
[d] From 1936 to 1952.

question begins with a depressed year and ends with a year of prosperity.[61] Where the 1938-1950 growth rates were smaller than the earlier ones, we do get an indication of retardation, except that in some cases[62] the smaller growth rates of the late period may have resulted from war devastation and foreign occupation.

14. Russian growth rates.

The growth rates of the Russian economy seem to be considerably greater than those of the Western nations. There exist indications that in Russia the national income, in constant prices, has been rising for some time at an average annual rate of about 8 percent.

It is true that a growth rate of this magnitude is obtained only if the output of each year is valued in the prices of the initial year of a longer period (say, of a decade), and that smaller growth rates are obtained if the output of each year is valued in the prices of the final year of a span. This is because, in a country like Russia, the *composition* of output is shifting appreciably toward specific goods which are higher priced relatively to the other goods in the initial year of any longer period than in its final year.[63] A very high proportion of the total growth shows in the sectors producing goods which are becoming cheaper relatively to other commodities, namely, in highly processed manufactured goods (particularly investment goods). There exists in such circumstances an appreciable difference between growth rates computed on the basis of initial-year valuations and growth rates computed on the basis of final-year valuations. This phenomenon is sometimes referred to as the Gerschenkron effect because Alexander Gerschenkron of Harvard University was the first to recognize its great practical significance for the interpretation of Russian growth rates.[64] Subsequently, Gregory Grossman showed that to the 8-percent annual growth rate, on the basis of initial-year valuations, there corresponds an annual growth rate of about 5 percent on the basis of final-year valuations.[65]

It is impossible to call one of the two methods of valuation correct and the other incorrect. The ambiguity follows from the nature of the index-

---

[61] In Germany, however, 1938 was not a depressed year in terms of aggregate output.

[62] This may apply to France, Belgium, and Holland.

[63] This is another way of saying that the trends in relative prices are dominated by the *supply shift*, not the demand shift, toward these goods and services.

[64] Alexander Gerschenkron, *A Dollar Index of Soviet Machinery Output, 1927-28 to 1937* (Santa Monica, 1951), pp. 47-49.

[65] Gregory Grossman, "National Income," in *Soviet Economic Growth*, ed. by Abram Bergson (Evanston and White Plains, 1953), p. 6.

number problem with which we are faced. If the composition of the output changes, an arbitrary decision must be reached concerning the basis of valuation before a figure can be computed for the rate of increase in aggregate physical output, that is, of output in constant prices. Therefore, something can be said for averaging the two rates of Russian economic growth, as Grossman is inclined to do. Even this procedure yields disturbingly high *proportionate* rates of growth,[66] as compared to the Western world, including the United States. An 8-percent annual rate increases the output by more than 110 percent per decade, a 6.5-percent annual rate increases it by almost 90 percent decennially. The comparison has disturbing implications especially if we also take account of industrialization in the other states of the Soviet sphere of influence.

Moreover, if we are interested in the shift in power relations which would result from a continuation of past tendencies, it may be more revealing to take the higher of the two Russian economic growth rates, that is, to base valuations on the prices of the initial year of a period. This method places more emphasis on the growth of the industrial sector than does the method of final-year valuations, since the excess of the higher growth rate over the lower reflects mainly the shift in the economic structure toward the industrial sector. To be sure, the difference between the two rates is not a particularly clear-cut "measure" of the shift, but in an appraisal of changing power relations it may be more revealing to use a figure for aggregate growth which is raised by an internal shift from the agricultural to the industrial sector than to use one which is lowered.

The steepness of the Russian growth trends in aggregate output is disclosed also by a recent study which was undertaken by the staff of the Joint Committee on the Economic Report of the United States Congress.[67] This is all the more noteworthy because the data in this study are grouped in such a way that at first sight the Russian growth rates do not seem particularly high in relation to the American. But the first impression is somewhat misleading. According to the data used in the study, the Russian aggregate output grew by 43 percent from 1948 to 1953, which, of course, is far in excess of the American output-increment for

---

[66] The *absolute* yearly output-increment is as yet smaller in Russia than in the United States. But the smaller absolute yearly increment corresponds to a higher proportionate growth rate. This, of course, is no contradiction because it is probably reasonable to put the current Russian output at no more than 30 percent of the American. This is suggested by a study of the staff of the Joint Committee on the Economic Report, to which we shall refer presently.

[67] *Trends in Economic Growth, A Comparison of the Western Powers and the Soviet Bloc* (Washington, 1955).

the same five-year period (27 percent). The recent Russian quinquennial increment of 43 percent corresponds algebraically to a decennial growth rate of 104 percent; the American corresponds to a rate of 61 percent. The Joint Committee report suggests that, because of the abnormally low level of activity in the initial year, this Russian growth rate is untypically high:[68] 1948 was a relatively early postwar year in a country that suffered very great devastations during the war. The American output-increment from 1948 to 1953 may also be untypically high because in the United States the final year, 1953, was still influenced by the boom conditions of the Korean War. The Joint Committee report implies, however, that the abnormally low level of Russian economic activity in 1948 makes a bigger difference than the abnormally high level of American business activity in 1953. But *if*, for Russia, 1948 was an abnormally low initial year, then the conclusion should be that as a consequence of World War II, which Russia entered in 1941, the Russian growth process lost (skipped) more than seven years, and that therefore the period 1938-1953 calls for being interpreted as containing less than eight effective years of growth. The study tells us that during the period 1938-1953 the Russian aggregate output grew by 62 percent. If interpreted as relating to less than eight effective years, to perhaps seven effective years, this growth rate is not very much lower than that applying to 1948-1953 (it is the equivalent of a 90-percent decennial rate instead of a 104-percent decennial rate). Either way of looking at the matter suggests average annual growth rates which are considerably in excess of the typical Western rates.

The 1948-1953 experience, as well as the corrected 1938-1953 experience, points to a substantial differential between the Russian and the American percentage rates of growth. It is true that the relatively short period 1950-1953, taken in isolation, brought a Russian output-increment which algebraically corresponds to a decennial growth rate of "merely" 80 percent, or to an annual compound rate of about 6 percent. This is less than the 104-percent decennial growth rate which is the equivalent of the Russian increment for 1948-1953, and it is also a little less than what seems a reasonably corrected rate for the period 1938-1953. But the highest American decennial growth rates of the present century have so far been in the neighborhood of 60 percent, or not quite 5 percent annually,

---

[68] Also, the index-number problem discussed in connection with Grossman's study seems to have been handled by the Joint Committee staff in such a way that the "high" rather than the "low" growth rates were obtained.

at a compound rate.[69] If we wish to stay within the range indicated by past experience, it is necessary to combine consistently very high assumptions for the United States with consistently very low assumptions for Russia to obtain a differential of merely about one percentage point annually; no reversal, but merely a very moderate relaxation of extreme assumptions, is needed to obtain a differential of 2 to 3 percent annually (corresponding to a growth rate of, say, about 4 to 4.5 percent *per annum* in the United States and 6.5 to 7 percent in Russia).

The study of the Joint Committee staff sets the 1938-1953 Russian output growth of 62 percent beside the American output growth of 120 percent for the same period, and this gives the first impression that, aside from a short and possibly abnormal postwar span, the Russian growth rate is rather low. But if the reader reaches such a conclusion then he disregards two essential facts. One is that between 1938 and 1953 the Russian growth process lost (skipped) a good many years, and the other is that in the United States 1938 was a year of major depression. We should not compare a Russian span consisting of considerably fewer than fifteen effective years with an American span consisting of fully fifteen effective years, especially if the "effectiveness" of the American span, from our point of view, is further increased by moving from deep depression to very high prosperity.

While the rate of increase in Russian aggregate output has been very high, it must be pointed out that the relative insufficiency of agricultural output may give rise to difficulties, politically as well as technologically, and that the increase in the supply of consumer goods in general has been very small in the Soviet economies. In some items, including meat, *per capita* consumption seems to have declined since the nineteen-twenties. The insufficiency of the agricultural output and of the output of consumer goods seems recently to have created a serious problem in Russia and in the satellite countries, but it is not at all clear whether it will take a reduction of the investment-goods sector relative to the consumer-goods industries, and a reduction of growth rates, to render the problems of the Soviet governments politically manageable.

The continued relative inadequacy of the Russian transportation system has also been noted in the literature. But these and other disproportionalities have not so far seriously hampered the long-run growth process. This is because so much of the output-increment is used for

---

[69] This is the American growth rate for the period 1948-1953 and also the average growth rate for the decade of the 'forties.

further expansion of the investment-goods industries which feed the process of growth, and also because some of the disproportionalities among complementary sectors of the economy do, of course, gradually diminish.

The high proportionate rates of growth of the Russian output may be said to result from (1) high rates of net capital formation or investment per unit of aggregate output and (2) from high output- increments per unit of capital formation. Both these ratios seem to be considerably higher in Russia than in the West. The height of the first ratio reflects partly the low productivity of Russian agriculture, and partly the policy of expanding, in the industrial sector, the output of the heavy industries rather than that of the consumer-goods industries. The height of the second ratio—of the output-increment per unit of new capital formation —is not particularly surprising if we remember that labor resources bear a very much higher proportion to the capital stock in Russia than in the Western countries. In Russia much labor cooperates with a unit of capital or, alternately expressed, little capital cooperates with a unit of labor. This, of course, tends to make for high output-to-capital ratios and for low output-to-labor ratios. Output per unit of labor input is much smaller in Russia than in the Western economies.[70]

The question arises whether in a more advanced stage of economic development the high Russian growth rates will not automatically fall. It should not be taken for granted that this will be the case. Take, for example, the present stage of American economic development. A total-itarian government, if it could establish itself in a country such as the United States, might not find it difficult to operate the economy at a level of consumption 20 to 25 percent lower than our present consumption level, and then to let consumption rise very slowly with the rise of aggre-gate output. By such a policy, the present American net capital forma-tion could be *more than doubled,* and it is quite likely that the annual economic growth rate of the United States could be *almost* doubled. This implies, conservatively, that the "classical" tendency toward diminishing returns to capital would be somewhat less than completely offset. In view of the increased volume of investment, population growth plus improve-

---

[70] The present population of the Soviet Union is estimated at about 210 millions, and the labor force at 100 to 110 millions. The present population of the United States is 165 millions, the labor force about 67 millions. The Russian aggregate output is be-lieved to account for no more than 30 percent of the American, and the ratio of the Russian capital stock to the American must be substantially smaller even than the ratio of the outputs.

ments might become less adequate for offsetting this tendency. Also, the mobility of resources might be put under greater strain. But these limiting factors play a much smaller role in an economy where the investing agency is largely independent of market preferences than in one in which the fate of each investor depends on the verdict of the market. Furthermore, it is not even certain that diminishing returns would come into play. It is quite conceivable that by doubling net capital formation our growth rate could be fully doubled.

We would find it exceedingly difficult to double our present net capital formation and our growth rate, or even to increase these by one half, because we are paying a price for political and economic freedom of choice. A totalitarian government might not find it too difficult to produce one and one half times our growth rate, or possibly twice our rate, even in a comparable stage of economic development. This, of course, can be expressed by saying that, from the viewpoint of our value system, totalitarian governments are engaged in unfair trade practices. But the verdict of history will depend on whether the past differences between growth rates on the two sides of the Iron Curtain will or will not continue. Only if they do not continue in the long run, can we be confident about the survival of Western institutions. At present, the best appraisal of the past differentials in growth rates appears to be that with these differentials it would take the Soviet bloc roughly half a century to catch up with the West, in terms of yearly aggregate output.[71] But it might take them very much less time to catch up in terms of those constituents of aggregate output which determine relative power positions.

No one can tell, of course, how much technological advance the Russian system would be capable of producing if the free world were not ahead of it and if the totalitarian systems were in no position to transplant the more advanced industrial Western techniques. But the Communist countries could run out of further transplantable techniques only after having very nearly reached the Western level of technology.

---

[71] Comparisons of aggregate output in *Russia and the European Soviet bloc* with aggregate output in *North America and in Western Europe* have led investigators to believe that it is reasonable to put the present difference at about 4:1, or possibly at slightly more, in favor of the West. A catching-up period of fifty years then results, with the additional assumption of a three percentage-point difference between the two proportionate growth rates, in favor of the Soviet rate. A difference of two percentage points gives a catching-up period of sixty years.

Hints from Condensed Narratives
of Major Downturns

The statistical methods surveyed in the previous Chapter enable us to identify trends and cycles in economic time series. Unlike plain narratives, these methods may be expected to reveal not only the general outline of dynamic development but also some of its finer details. Yet the statistical methods would be useless—indeed, they would be outright misleading—if they pictured a development whose broad outlines cannot be confirmed by plain narratives based on the experiences of contemporaries. In the interpretation of the growth process and of cyclical disturbances, we must not disregard the hints which may be obtained from condensed historical accounts.

We shall begin with brief comments on some of the recorded early shocks in economic activity, and subsequently we shall turn to the period between 1825 and the present. What primarily characterizes these centuries is, of course, economic growth rather than crises and contractions. But crises are spectacular events to which specific dates can be attached, and it is true that many of the available accounts tend to be grouped around these dates. The story of these spectacular growth-interruptions also contains information concerning the nature of the growth process that had been temporarily interrupted.

1. Some early shocks.

1720. The French ventures of the Scotch financier John Law failed in 1720, almost simultaneously with the collapse of the South Sea Company in England. Both these undertakings were connected with colonial expansion. Initially they were aimed at the exploitation of colonial profit possibilities—the Law enterprise in the Mississippi Valley and the English company in the South Sea islands. John Law received the French note-issue privilege for his Banque Royale, which was subsequently merged with his colonial trading company. The French state could thus "pay back" its public debt with these bank notes, leaving the holders of the debt with claims against the Law companies. On the other side of the Channel, the Bank of England, which had been founded in 1694, sought a monopoly for the South Sea venture in 1711, and, had it obtained this, conditions in England might have become strictly analogous to those in France. The Bank was outbid by the South Sea Company, which could not issue bank notes. Yet the Company acquired government securities in considerable amounts, partly against its own stock and partly for cash. Thus, holdings of English government securities were converted partly into stock holdings in the South Sea Company. The speculative activity in the shares of these "bubble companies" was substantial in France as well as in England. Both projects proved unsound: the colonial profits did not materialize. After a temporary but enormous increase in the prices of their stocks, the two companies collapsed at about the same time.

These were not the only colonial "bubble" ventures of their kind. But they were the most important ones, and Law's money-issue privilege made his venture unique. It should be added that Law's bank had also engaged in financing industrial investment projects in France.

1763, 1772. In Northern Europe large business losses followed the Seven Years' War in 1763, and credit withdrawals further aggravated business conditions. The losses and the following credit stringency and bank failures of 1772 seem to have originated in Scotland, and their impact was felt mainly in Scotland and England.

1783, 1793, 1810, 1819. The English economy suffered a postwar shock in 1783, at the end of the American War of Independence, and another setback in 1793. The difficulties of 1793 were aggravated by the outbreak of war with France on February 1. However, even before the declaration of war a condition of credit stringency existed, and the number of business failures had been increasing. The first major bank failures in February seem to have been caused primarily by unsuccessful peculations in the North American market. The English crisis of 1810 has been attributed to the more severe enforcement of the Continental Blockade, and partly also to speculative overinvestment in South American markets. Some indications have also been found concerning a setback in the French economy in 1810; and after Waterloo sharp setbacks occurred both in Western Europe and in Britain (1816 and 1819).

Commodity prices in Western Europe had a rising trend from the seventeen-forties to the end of the Napoleonic Wars.

In most countries (England is the only exception[1]) the agricultural sector of the economy was still so overwhelmingly large relatively to the commercial-industrial sector that fluctuations in business activity could not have caused much instability in aggregate output. Agricultural producers benefit or suffer from short-run price increases or decreases, but agricultural output does not typically show the same fluctuations as does industrial output (see Pages 54-55).

2. Was the early causal mechanism different from the later?

Most of the recorded shocks between the "bubble" crises and the post-Napoleonic period seem to have been directly connected with wars, but they may nevertheless lie within the area to which our analytical framework can be applied. Some of these crises were probably prompted by the overexpansion in specific areas of activity and the inability of the economy to rearrange its structure of production without an intervening lag. Postwar shocks, and also the difficulties which may stem from the initial wartime economic reorganizations themselves, almost invariably possess a structural aspect of this sort. Other crises seem to have been caused or aggravated by the inability of the volume of credit to grow along with output, given the contraints imposed by a metallic currency, or given the desire to re-establish a metallic currency after periods during which inconvertible bank notes or debased coins had been used.[2] These two causes of disturbance—imperfect mobility of resources in the face of a need for sudden rearrangements in the structure of production,

---

[1] Around 1800 only about 35 percent of the English population was engaged in agriculture. By this somewhat arbitrary measure, the same degree of "industrialization" was not reached in the German empire until about 1900, at which time more than 40 percent of the French population was still agricultural. As late as 1866, more than one half of the French population was in agriculture.

[2] Monetary contraction and maladjustments in the structure of production usually supplement each other, and it is difficult, frequently impossible, to decide which should be given the primary emphasis in any given instance. However, in 1763 the elimination of debased coins seems to have played a deflationary role *sui generis* in some centers (*e.g.*, Hamburg). In the years immediately following the Napoleonic Wars the return to the metallic standard after a period of inconvertibility exerted a deflationary influence on the English economy. As for the rearrangement of the structure of business activities from previous channels to new ones, this factor is stressed in most accounts of the postwar disturbances here listed.

and disproportionalities between the growth of the money and credit supply on the one hand and of the output flow on the other—will be assigned roles in our later analysis. They seem to have played a part in the history of the early disturbances too.

Our later analysis will also emphasize the fact that in some periods the flow of improvements becomes insufficient, or qualitatively inadequate, to offset the tendency toward diminishing returns. Temporary insufficiency of improvements may be a consequence of the fact that it takes time to develop specific improvements for opening up new "leading areas" of activity when growth tapers off in the leading areas of the previous epoch. If improvements become insufficient to offset diminishing returns, investment opportunities cease to be plentiful enough to absorb savings. This may be expected to express itself in the relatively long-lasting inability of the system to recover from depressions after periods of vigorous expansion. However, the other two factors—severe maladjustments in the structure of production and long-lasting insufficiency of the rate of increase in the money supply—may also cause extended stoppages.

These three factors will be in the foreground of our analysis. They tend to interact. There remains the question of whether the early shocks here recorded lend themselves to tracing the tapering off of specific types of improvement activity in periods in which other types have not yet grown to significance. For England it might be possible to argue that the canal-construction wave reached its peak toward the end of the eighteenth century, and that the twenty-five-year period following the Battle of Waterloo included so many years of depression *because* the improvement process had run its course in one major area (canals) without yet having opened up other areas for sufficiently abundant new investment. Only the beginning of this depressed period falls in the span covered in the present section.

However, along with canal construction, the late eighteenth-century English upswings had also brought a good deal of investment in land improvements (connected with enclosures), turnpikes, textiles, iron and machinery, coal mining, etc. Several of these areas acquired considerable significance again in the upswings of the 'twenties and the 'thirties;[3] temporarily, even canal construction revived somewhat in the 'twenties. Furthermore, the construction of docks, as well as that of waterworks

---

[3] However, agriculture remained a depressed area for about twenty years after the war, except in regions where it was easy to shift from crop farming to grazing and to dairying.

and gasworks, were new fields in the early decades of the nineteenth century. Also, foreign investment (in the Americas) played a considerable role in the English expansions of the 'twenties and the 'thirties. In a sense, there was here a reasonable degree of continuity in successive leading areas for improvement activity and investment. But these various fields of development were not of equal significance. The post-Napoleonic decades, up to the 'forties, had a rather depressed character generally. The depressions of the period tended to be severe and, in some cases, also prolonged. The gap between the canal era and the railroad era— the relative slowness with which the technological-organizational pre- requisites of railroadization became satisfied—may perhaps contribute to explaining this.

3. Major downturns from the 1820's to 1930's.[4]

1825. This was mainly an English downturn. During the preceding ex- pansion large investments were undertaken in Latin American states, which had recently won independence. These were largely mining in- vestments. Domestically, textiles, coal, iron, and machinery (all of these already significant in earlier expansions) were still among the prominent sectors in which new investment seems to have been concentrated. Invest- ments in docks and in gas and waterworks also acquired significance. Canal construction was much less important at this time than in the previous decades. Early and small beginnings of investment in railroads fall in this period. The rise in commodity prices was considerable im- mediately prior to the crisis,[5] even though the price *trend* was downward from the end of the Napoleonic Wars to the late 'forties; an abrupt fall of prices is recorded for 1825. The balance of trade had turned un- favorable through the rise in imports and the fall in exports during the advanced stage of the expansion. As a consequence of this, a so-called external gold drain occurred; subsequently, the domestic liquidity crisis gave rise to an internal gold drain. The following depression lasted many years, until about 1832. Unemployment appears to have been severe.

1836. English foreign investments during the preceding expansion went mainly to the United States. Domestically, railroad construction

---

[4] In this Section we shall be concerned with the downturns listed on Page 36.
[5] The crops of the years preceding 1825 were poor. This contributes to explaining the movements of the wheat price. But the price increases of the boom and the subsequent decline were not limited to agriculture.

was still in its early stages, but was gradually growing in significance. In England the number of joint stock companies increased greatly, particularly in railroads and banking. The iron industry and coal mining were further stimulated by the railroads. There was an expansion of cities and building construction, especially in textile districts. Prices had risen temporarily, but they fell in 1836.[6] In England unfavorable balance of trade and external gold drain preceded the domestic crisis and the internal gold drain. Crisis was recorded also in continental Western Europe (France, Belgium) and in the United States. Accounts of business conditions in the United States call attention to wildcat banking, to land speculation, and also to violent cotton speculation, especially after the virtual ending of the Second Bank of the United States in 1833.

The depression lasted into the early years of the next decade, with temporary recovery tendencies in 1838-1839. Social discontent grew; in England the Chartist movement (1836-1848), with its emphasis on social equality, created a grave political problem. The sentiment for factory legislation was increasing. The Corn Laws were repealed in 1846 (after tariff revisions in 1842). The Ten-Hours Bill was enacted in 1847.

1847. The preceding expansion was largely carried by railroad investments, with many typically "speculative" traits. Railroad stocks became overvalued, some important new companies turned unprofitable (or projects were not completed). Construction of ships, still mainly sailing, was also important. Collapse of speculation occurred in 1847. During this liquidity crisis and in the midst of an internal gold drain the Peel Act of 1844 was suspended for the first time to allow the Bank of England to issue bank notes beyond the limit set by the Act.[7] The suspension restored confidence in the Bank of England's credit and hence actual excess issue of bank notes was avoided. Crisis was noticeable in England, the United States, and France. However, the early phase of the growth process was scarcely interrupted in Germany.

The approximate thirty-five-year period of falling price *trends* comes to an end at this time, that is, in the eighteen-forties. From the end of the 'forties to 1873 (in the United States to 1865), the price trend was rising and the ratio of years of prosperity to depressed years was more favorable than in the preceding decades. For the twenty-five-year period

---

6 The price of wheat rose in England until the end of the year 1836. The English wheat crop of 1836 was small, partly because the abundant crops and low prices of the preceding years had led to a reduction of the planted area.

7 See Page 178, *infra.*

from the late 'forties to 1873, the average annual increase in the monetary gold stock is estimated at 4 percent. This is roughly four times the annual average for the first half of the nineteenth century, during which the gold output seems to have been not much greater than in the late part of the eighteenth century. However, with the exception of sterling, currencies stayed mostly bimetallic up to the eighteen-seventies.[8] Silver production had been rising steadily, aside from a sharp fall during the period of political disturbances in South America in the eighteen-twenties.

1857. The previous expansion was very vigorous, stimulated in part by Californian and Australian gold discoveries (1849 and 1851, respectively). Significant English investments were made in North America and in Australia. In the United States and in Europe there was very vigorous activity in railroad building. Further noteworthy features of the expansion were shipbuilding (iron steamship), the development of telegraph networks, and the growth of cities. For example, the 'fifties were the decade of the most rapid growth in the history of the city of Paris.

In France there was substantial industrial expansion under the reign of Napoleon III. The Crédit Mobilier was founded in 1852 by Péreire brothers, who were formerly associated with the early socialist movement of the Saint-Simonists. This institution was among the first of its type ("banque d'affaires") to acquire importance. On the Continent banks of this kind founded and financed large industrial undertakings and frequently retained control of their management. In subsequent decades much of German and of Austro-Hungarian industrial development assumed this character, with large banks often in key positions.

The boom preceding the collapse of 1857 was "world-wide." It extended over Europe, North America, Australia, and South America. In Europe it included Germany and to some extent Austria too. Overvaluation of railroad and mining securities was a general feature. The Crimean War falls in this period. At that time the liquidity of the financial system was significantly reduced. The collapse affected all the countries just mentioned. In England the Peel Act was again suspended, and this time there actually occurred some excess issue.

1866. The European expansion of the 'sixties moved along lines similar to those of preceding decade. Railroads, the spread of iron steamship, and residential construction were important contributors to the expansion. In the United States this is the period of the Civil War.

---

[8] See Page 180, *infra.*

In Europe the American Civil War caused the so-called "cotton famine" (steep increase in cotton prices); America was temporarily replaced as source of supply by Egypt, India, and Brazil. The expansion was vigorous in Germany, but the following contraction was mild in spite of its coincidence with the end of the short Prusso-Austrian War (which was one of the important preludes to the later unification of Germany under Prussian leadership).

The credit crisis broke in 1866. Collapse of a prominent London banking house (bill-brokers)—Overend, Gurney and Co.—was caused by the bankruptcy of several large borrowers, including an American and an English railroad. Crédit Mobilier suffered large losses, and it liquidated. In England the Peel Act was again suspended. As in 1847 (but unlike 1857), there was, however, no actual excess issue. Henceforth, sufficient reserves were accumulated in good times to enable the bank to ease conditions in periods of stringency without requiring powers to violate the Peel Act. Also, liquidity ratios of large joint-stock banks were kept higher in subsequent decades.

1873. The preceding expansion was particularly vigorous, with strong speculative traits in Germany (which was unified in 1871 after the short Franco-Prussian War) ; it was vigorous in Austria too (the establishment of Austro-Hungarian "Dual Monarchy" had occurred in 1867 after a long period of internal struggle between Austria and Hungary). A significant building boom developed in these countries, particularly in Berlin and in Vienna.

Railroad construction in the United States and in Central Europe was resumed at a high rate. However, much of the British railroad network was largely completed prior to this expansion, and the stimulating influence of the railroad boom on the British economy now developed largely through its effect on British foreign investments and exports. In the United States the first transcontinental rail connection was completed in 1869.

The Suez Canal opened in same year.

The application of the Bessemer process which had been invented in the 'fifties, reached the stage where steel production started acquiring significance.

The collapse came first in Vienna in May 1873; the American crisis took place in September (bankruptcy of Jay Cooke and Co.). The English crisis followed, partly caused and aggravated by the weakening of foreign demand for English goods and by the withdrawal of foreign funds due to liquidity crisis abroad. The subsequent six-year period was seriously depressed in most countries. This showed *mainly* in a fall of prices and in falling profit rates. Severe unemployment seems to have been limited to shorter spans during this period. France, owing to the lost war, had not participated in the preceding boom and had a revival during part of the period of world depression, but toward the end of the decade a downturn occurred there too.

During the 'seventies and 'eighties, groups with attitudes opposed to *laissez-faire* were gaining in political weight (social democratic movement and other reformist movements in Europe; social insurance, first in Germany; gradual trend away from free trade, partly as a reaction to growing American wheat exports, etc.). The price trend was declining from 1873 until the end of the century. The average annual increase in the world's monetary gold stock from 1873 to 1895 is estimated at 1.6 percent, less than one half of the rate applying to the previous twenty-five years.[9] At the same time silver was becoming considerably more abundant. In the bimetallic countries (that is, in most countries of the European continent and in the United States) silver would now have tended to displace gold.[10] However, at this time the bimetallic countries decided to demonetize silver and changed to the gold standard. Germany went on gold immediately after unification (1871); the other European countries did so during the same decade; the United States went on gold in 1879, when specie payment was resumed after the use of inconvertible paper currency (greenbacks).

From 1873 to the end of the century, the ratio of years of prosperity to depressed years was less favorable than in the preceding twenty-five-year period.

1882. The revival after the Great Depression of the 'seventies was comparatively weak in European countries, except in France. The boom in France, now under the Third Republic, was vigorous, with strong speculative traits. In the United States, too, there was strong expansion. Mileage added to the American railroad network reached the peak of all times in the early 'eighties. Steel rose in significance in Europe and America (spread of Siemens open-hearth process which had been invented in the 'sixties; also of newly invented Thomas process, rendering impure ores usable for steel manufacturing). The steel ship starts acquiring importance for ocean transport.

---

[9] However, see in this connection Footnote 25, Page 100.
[10] See Page 180, particularly Footnote 22.

Industrialization began in northern Italy, too, soon after unification of Italy (which was completed about 1870).

The collapse of the speculative boom occurred in France in 1882. Bankruptcy of Union Générale, a French bank engaged in financing industrial ventures, fell in this crisis. The American crisis came later (1884). It was partly the consequence of a financial panic caused by reckless speculation and maneuvers in railroad shares.

1890. The preceding expansion was vigorous in the United States and in Germany. Growing steel output was a dominant characteristic of the expansion. The merchant marine was substantially expanded. The subsequent growth of electric energy production and of chemical industries (*e.g.,* fertilizers) is already foreshadowed. The beginning of streetcar construction occurred in this period. English (also German) foreign investment activity, was a significant trait of the period. Baring Brothers, London, was prominent in financing English investments in Latin America. The period still fell within the span of declining long-run trends in prices, but prices rose temporarily before the crisis.

Baring Brothers went bankrupt in 1890. In the United States the crisis developed in 1893. In the same year the silver purchase policy of the United States (a compromise with bimetallistic pressures) was abandoned, after having led to monetary disturbances. The formation of producers' "pools," the establishment of trusts, and discriminatory practices led to legislative intervention: the Sherman Anti-Trust Act was passed in 1890.

1900. In the preceding expansion the significance of electric energy production was growing. Its use for lighting and as a source of industrial power was rising. Telephone systems were spreading. Streetcar construction was developing, and the beginnings of subway construction fell in this period. The importance of chemical industries (*e.g.,* fertilizers, dye-stuffs) was growing. But steel, coal, and shipbuilding, also remained significant. Mergers (vertical and horizontal integration of enterprises) and, particularly in Germany, also cartelization brought further accentuation of the trend toward large-scale units of production and marketing.

The Spanish-American War fell in this period, and the Boer War broke out at the turn of the century.

In most European countries there was a crisis in 1900, in the United States somewhat later. However, these seem to have been relatively mild events in the history of crises.

Toward the end of the century the falling price trend gradually gave way to rising trends. Gold production rose, primarily the result of South African gold discoveries and improved methods of mining. From 1895 to 1913 the average annual increase in world's monetary gold stock is estimated at 3.7 percent. This is more than twice the rate for the period 1873-1895.

1907. The preceding expansion brought further electrification, streetcar and subway building, growth of copper production, naval construction and expansion of merchant marines, growth of chemical industries, and the beginnings of automobile production.

Credit stringency and run on banks are particularly important features of the American crisis in the fall of 1907. By the National Bank Act of 1863 the reserves of American country banks could be held in reserve cities, and those of reserve-city banks in central reserve cities. The note issue was highly inelastic, linked to government bond holdings of individual banks. In 1907 there were increasing cash needs; money was withdrawn from banks, including country banks; central reserve-city banks were unable to withstand the pressure; many banks were forced to suspend payments; a general credit crisis broke out. Need for central banking system, with elastic regulation of note issue and of bank credit, was increasingly realized, and the Federal Reserve System was established six years later.

1913. After a two-year interruption, expansion had continued from about 1909 on, along much the same lines as were characteristic of the preceding expansion. However, tight credit and scarcity of capital had not wholly subsided in the upswing. European armament expenditures were high; international relations were tense on several occasions. The Balkan wars in 1912 and 1913 between Balkan states and Turkey ended with the expulsion of the Turks from Europe, except for the area around Istanbul, and the subsequent defeat of Bulgaria by her former allies (the other Balkan states). The spectacular growth of German relative strength in the world economy (*e.g.,* in steel and the engineering industries) and the very gradual emergence of a power vacuum in the Balkans (with Russian *versus* Austro-Hungarian and German interests involved) belong among the most frequently noted antecedents of World War I. Economic downturn was registered in 1913. The Panama Canal opened in 1914, after approximately ten years of preparation and construction.

1920. This was the year of the postwar depression, following World War I (1914-1918; for the United States 1917-1918). The United States had emerged as the most powerful nation, but was shifting to an "isolationist" line in international affairs. Conditions of war boom existed in the United States even before 1917 in consequence of large credits and commodity exports to the Western powers. The status of the country changed from that of a debtor to that of a creditor.

The Soviet government came to power in Russia in 1917.

After the ending of hostilities postwar inflationary pressures were observable in all participating countries as a consequence of shortages in civilian goods and of the high liquidity which government expenditures had created during the war. In the United States and in several other countries depression came in 1920, when fiscal expenditures had been significantly reduced and when the monetary policy was tightened and price expectations turned deflationary. At the peak, American wholesale prices were more than twice as high as in 1913; after the 1920-1921 depression they were 40 percent higher than in 1913. By the time the peak was reached, English wholesale prices had risen threefold since the prewar period; after the depression they were 60 percent higher than before the war. In the defeated countries of Central Europe[11] depression came three to four years later. This happened when new and stable currencies were introduced after the runaway inflations of the postwar period. These inflations had reduced the value of the old currencies to a negligible fraction of the original. Even in France and Italy, inflation was resumed after the price fall of 1920-1921, and stabilization came at a considerably reduced level of these currencies, in the late part of the decade.

1929. The expansion after 1921 was vigorous in the United States, with a very mild downward tendency in prices after 1925. The growth of the automobile industry was perhaps the most conspicuous feature; along with it came road building and rapidly growing gasoline production. Prominent also were electric energy production and the expansion of the chemical industries. The substantial building boom tapered off after 1925, that is, the building cycle turned down several years prior to the 1929 peak of general business activity. Violent stock-exchange speculation and rapidly rising stock prices were characteristic of the last two years of the American expansion. The downturn of production occurred in the summer of 1929, the big stock exchange crash in the fall.

In England the expansion of the 'twenties was not particularly strong. The English export industries were facing difficulties, in part because

---

[11] More precisely, in Germany and in the Succession States of the dismembered Austro-Hungarian monarchy.

of competition and industrialization in the former English export markets. Also, the return in 1925 to the gold standard at the prewar parity made England a high-price economy in foreign markets. Deflationary pressures were more or less continuous from 1920 on; there was a general strike in 1926.

In France the inflation ended with the stabilization of the franc in 1927-1928 at a relatively low rate in terms of gold, with the result that France was now a "cheap" country. Thereafter, money was flowing back to France. Unlike most other countries, France was not appreciably hit by the depression until 1931.

In the defeated countries of Central Europe, there was recovery and reconstruction from about 1925 to 1929. This occurred after the runaway inflations previously mentioned and after the following depressions which accompanied the stabilization of these currencies. Exceedingly high reparation obligations had been stipulated against Germany; subsequently, compromises were made on the basis of yearly payments. After the stabilization there was a substantial flow of capital (largely American and English) into Germany and into the Succession States of former Austro-Hungarian monarchy. Much of this was short-term. This added to the instability of economic conditions in continental Europe at the outbreak of the American depression in 1929.

In 1931 a violent international financial crisis (beginning with the fall of the Austrian *Creditanstalt* in Vienna) aggravated the depressions which had been developing in most countries since 1929. The creditor countries were recalling their short-term credits from foreigners; the domestic credit stringency was getting worse everywhere. Germany and the Succession States of the Austro-Hungarian monarchy introduced moratoria on foreign payment obligations and adopted "exchange-control" systems. These are systems of foreign currency rationing. Their essential feature is that owners and current recipients of foreign exchange (including the exporters) must sell their holdings at officially set exchange rates to a domestic agency (frequently the central bank) and that those desiring to buy foreign exchange (including the importers) must apply to the agency in question, which acts as a rationing office.

England went off the gold standard in September 1931, two years after the outbreak of the depression; the pound was not tied to gold at any fixed rate thereafter. The United States went off gold in 1933; the next year the dollar was stabilized relatively to gold at a 40-percent lower level, and with no gold in domestic monetary circulation. Neither

England nor the United States rationed foreign currencies (*i.e.,* foreign exchange remained freely available to buyers in both countries).

In 1932-1933 unemployment was at an extraordinarily high level in many countries (*e.g.,* the United States, England, Germany). United States national income valued in constant prices had fallen by 40 percent since 1929. Prices, too, fell sharply. In Germany Hitler came to power in January 1933.

For the period 1913-1930 the average annual increase in the world's monetary gold stock is estimated at merely 1.8 percent. However, the average annual increase in the gold stock of treasuries and central banks was about 5 percent, that is to say, more than in previous periods of rising price trend. The difference between the 5-percent rate and the 1.8 percent is partly a consequence of the exclusion of gold from monetary circulation in countries returning to the gold standard after World War I. Under these modified gold standard arrangements of the postwar period, central banks tied their currencies to gold not by redeeming their bank notes in gold coins on demand, but merely by buying and selling gold bullion at a legally fixed price and by holding a legally required gold-bullion reserve (or a reserve in a foreign currency such as had, in turn, a gold-bullion reserve behind it). These modifications were effective gold-saving devices. It would therefore be arbitrary to attribute the collapse of the international gold standard in 1931 to insufficiency of gold production.[12] There was a maldistribution of gold reserves: from the mid-twenties on, some countries had distinctly overvalued currencies relative to their high price level and hence were losing gold, while others had undervalued currencies relative to their price level and hence were accumulating gold. For several years prior to 1931 England had been losing, France accumulating. At any rate the shock caused by the international credit withdrawals of 1931 was too great to be cushioned by gold reserves of reasonable size. Yet legal gold-backing provisions did make it more difficult in some countries, including the United States, to meet internal liquidity drains by extending central-bank credit.

1937. In the United States the recovery after 1933 was incomplete. At the 1937 peak production was at approximately its 1929 level; hence no upward trend was observable from peak to peak. Production had *not* risen in accordance with population growth or with reduced man-hour

---

[12] To a lesser extent, the same sort of arbitrariness enters also into the interpretation of earlier deflationary periods, in terms of gold insufficiency. See Footnote 25, Page 100.

requirements per unit of output. In spite of the considerable shortening of the work week during the 'thirties, almost 15 percent of the labor force was unemployed even in 1937 (in 1933 about 25 percent had been unemployed). In aggregative terms, the net investment activity of the recovery period 1933-1937 corresponded to little more than the previous undermaintenance (*i.e.,* net disinvestment) of the depression years. After this, investment activity gave out, and the 1937-1938 contraction was very sharp. By any reasonable classification this was a major depression, not simply a recession. In 1938 close to 20 percent of the American labor force was unemployed.

The problem of interpretation is highly controversial. New Deal policies are blamed by one side, but these cannot be appraised as a single unit. The compensatory fiscal policy of the Roosevelt Administration (the deficit-financed public works program) must have alleviated the deflationary conditions, but the policy was not adopted on a very large scale.[13] Wage increases are likely to have retarded the recovery, and they may well have been partly responsible for the downturn of 1937. The downturn was preceded by significant labor trouble and by upward pressure on wage rates emanating from newly organized unions, toward which the Administration was sympathetic. The results of the labor trouble must have been similar to those of a genuine labor shortage. Also, the wage increases and some other factors resulted in price increases, and these led the Federal Reserve to raise reserve requirements appreciably, thus exerting counterinflationary pressure in a period of heavy unemployment (but of a rather sharply rising price level). Finally, increased tax revenues, resulting partly from the rising level of business activity and partly from the new social security taxes, suddenly produced a balanced cash budget in 1937 after several years of deficit financing. This coincided with the impact of the anti-inflationary credit policies, and it occurred in a period in which the business outlook was adversely influenced by difficulties on the labor front and by a political climate hostile to business. Part of the responsibility may rest with these combined policies. However, the 'thirties were undoubtedly a decade with

---

[13] In the preceding years (1929-1932), the Hoover Administration in the United States as well as many European governments, including the German, had based their policies on the wrong conception that an increase in the domestically held public debt, such as is brought about by deficit-financed public expenditure, is more dangerous than mass unemployment. In the United States and in some other countries gold-backing provisions also stood in the way of expansionary fiscal policies and even of expansionary credit policies of the central bank. In the United States this specific obstacle was significantly reduced by an amendment of the Federal Reserve Act in 1932.

severely deflationary *basic tendencies,* and these raise the analytical problems which are connected with protracted depressions *in general.* We shall return to these in the present Chapter (Page 99) and also in our subsequent analysis.

The English recovery after 1932 was less incomplete than the American. There developed considerable residential building activity at low interest rates. Nevertheless, British unemployment rarely declined much below 10 percent of the labor force during the 'thirties. It is not clear how much of this should be attributed to *cyclical* factors. As a consequence of the structural reasons earlier mentioned (Page 86), British economic conditions were rather depressed even during the 'twenties.

On the Continent exchange control was spreading from 1931 on, and a highly restrictive tendency developed toward the bilateral or regional balancing of exports and imports in order to avoid balance-of-payments deficits and major capital transfers. No systematic attempt was made to bring exchange rates into equilibrium with each other. Also, American tariffs were increased. The British introduced tariffs, with preferential treatment of the Commonwealth countries. Under such conditions the recovery of world trade after 1933 was slow and incomplete. In spite of the depreciation of the pound, the dollar, and other currencies, France postponed the depreciation of the franc relative to gold until 1936. This had an unfavorable effect on her exports,[14] but when depreciation came, French prices rose rapidly, thus depriving the country of the trade advantages of cheapening her currency. Subsequently, the franc ceased to be tied to gold at an institutionally fixed price.

In Germany the armament program under Hitler had led, by about 1937, to deficit-financed full employment in a rigorously controlled economy. World War II started when Germany invaded Poland on September 1, 1939. The United States entered the war after the Japanese attack on Pearl Harbor in December 1941. Unemployment was still considerable in the United States in 1940, in spite of increasing economic aid and exports to Britain. Inflationary pressures did not begin to show in America until 1941. After Pearl Harbor comprehensive price and wage controls were adopted, scarce materials were subjected to a system of priorities, and consumer goods were rationed. About two thirds of the 90-percent increase in the American cost of living index from 1939 to the

---

14 While the stabilization of the franc at a low level had made France an inexpensive country to foreigners in the late 'twenties, this relationship became reversed in the 'thirties by the depreciation of the pound, of the dollar, and of other currencies.

present occurred after the elimination of these controls. Only one third occurred between 1939 and 1946. Prices rose sharply in the two years immediately following decontrol, that is, in 1946-1948; and they rose again in the early stages of the Korean war boom in 1950-1951.

4. No major downturn since 1937.

1948. The earlier chronology might have led to the expectation that in the second half of the 'forties there would occur a major downturn, comparable to those which in the past came about once every decade. There was a downturn in the United States in 1948, and some of the European countries showed signs of a cyclical disturbance at about the same time.[15] But the contraction of 1948-1949 was milder than those so far discussed in the present Chapter. This contraction has a legitimate place in the Burns-Mitchell chronology of Page 22, which includes both minor recessions and major depressions with no attempt to distinguish between them; but the 1948-1949 contraction has no legitimate place in the chronology of major downturns. During the recession unemployment rose to a level corresponding to 7 percent of the labor force for one quarter (three-month period). Aside from this one quarter, the unemployment rate of this recession was about 5 percent, as against a 3-percent unemployment rate at the previous peak level of business activity (when there was general agreement concerning the existence of "full employment" for all practical purposes). From the peak *month* to the trough *month,* the recession lowered industrial production (manufacturing-plus-mining production) by less than 15 percent.

There is some reason not to attribute the high performance of the American economy in the postwar period mainly to the specific war and postwar stimuli, but to regard it as a sign of the genuine passing of the

---

[15] As was seen on Page 22, the National Bureau of Economic Research records a postwar contraction also from February to October 1945. This period begins shortly before the ending of hostilities in Europe (V-E Day), and it ends shortly after the ending of hostilities in Japan (V-J Day). In other words, the very short initial phase of a surprisingly smooth postwar transition shows as "contraction" in the National Bureau materials. However, during the year 1945, eight months of which fall in this "contraction," unemployment corresponded on the average to less than 2 percent of the labor force. We shall here disregard this "contraction."

After the war there occurred, of course, a significant reduction of the size of the labor force itself because of the voluntary withdrawal of persons not ordinarily in the labor force. Most of these withdrawals came after 1945 in connection with demobilization. Reduced employment as a consequence of withdrawals from the labor force is, of course, not recorded as "unemployment." These withdrawals express a reduction of the size of the job-seeking population. Only a job-seeking person can be "unemployed."

depression tendency which plagued the country during the 'thirties. If we wish to stress these genuine or *normal* features of the expansion after 1945, we must direct our attention to the exceedingly high rate of increase of the output of the chemical industries (including the basic chemicals as well as artificial fibers, synthetic rubber, plastics, etc.); the rapid rise in the light metals (aluminum and magnesium); the substantial increase in the demand for several varieties of electric household equipment; the rapid development of natural gas; and, perhaps most of all, the exceedingly rapid further growth of the output of electric energy. We must also take account of the very significant rise in building activity. This cannot be interpreted simply as a backlog effect developing from the wartime restrictions of the four years 1942-1945. At the end, the development of atomic energy might turn out to be the most significant characteristic of the new era, but so far as direct economic impacts are concerned, this is as yet in its early stages. Around 1948-1949 the impact was strictly limited to the military field.

For the first American postwar decade a very rapid rate of technological and organizational improvement is indicated by a high output-*increment* per unit of new capital formation. As was seen in Chapter 2, Section 13, the saved proportion of output has recently been rather low as compared to earlier periods, while the proportionate rate of growth of output has been substantial. This points to a high rate of output growth per unit of new capital formation, presumably as a consequence of rapid technological and organizational improvement. Favorable recent trends may be attributed to this factor. Indeed, interpretations of recent trends along these lines carries a good deal more plausibility than do alternative interpretations.

The argument is not, of course, entirely conclusive. *Abnormal* stimuli were undoubtedly present during part of the period following World War II, and it is possible to argue that they have been with us since the end of the war. For example, the wartime shortage of physical capital relative to the output level created an abnormally high investment demand for many years after the war;[16] the depletion of the stock of consumer durables during the period of wartime restrictions gave rise to an enlarged demand for these commodities; the high liquidity generated by fiscal borrowing from banks during the war raised the level of consumer

---

[16] It was possible temporarily to "stretch" the capital stock by increasing the number of shifts and by using equipment which normally would have been scrapped. This is why the capital shortage created no unemployment.

demand in general in the postwar period, and this demand could express ·
itself freely in the market from 1946 on, when most controls had become
abolished; the military budget, after a gradual reduction in the early
postwar years, rose again to a high level when hostilities broke out in
Korea in the summer of 1950, and the postwar rise in the temporarily
diminished foreign-aid expenditures started even earlier, with the
Marshall Plan.

Some of these stimuli were of short duration. Indeed, the period over
which the economy has shown considerable resistance to downward impacts is long enough [17] to suggest that, of the "artificial" stimuli here
listed, only the high military (plus foreign-aid) expenditures could have
much relevance to the period *as a whole*. Yet the fiscal expenditures of
the postwar period were tax-financed rather than financed by cash deficits
of the federal government, when the period is taken as one unit. From
July 1, 1946, through June 30, 1954, there developed a cumulated surplus (cumulated excess of surpluses over deficits) of 16 billion dollars
in the *cash budget*. [18] At the present writing (1955) the cash budget of
the federal government is approximately balanced. It is questionable
how much net "artificial stimulus" is derived from high fiscal expenditures which are financed by high taxes, including the taxation of corporate profits at a rate of about 50 percent. [19]

---

[17] So far, this has been a period of ten-year duration, since the end of the war.

[18] V-J Day fell in the early part of the fiscal year 1945-1946, but even if we cumulate
from July 1, 1945, rather than from July 1, 1946, we obtain a cumulated cash deficit of
merely 3 billions through 1954. In the *administrative budget* of the federal government,
there was a cumulated deficit of 9.5 billions from July 1, 1946, to June 30, 1954, and
this deficit increases to 30 billions if we cumulate from July 1, 1945. The most important difference between the *cash budget* (relating to cash incomes and outgoes) and
the administrative budget is that in the latter the cash surplus on the social security
accounts is not treated as a revenue but is treated as an amount which the federal
government *borrows* from the social security reserve (*i.e.*, owes to the insured). In the
present circumstances a balanced cash budget leaves the administrative budget unbalanced by a yearly amount of $2-3 billion.

[19] If the adverse effect of taxation on the willingness to accept risk could be disregarded, then, in an economy with excess capacities, tax-financed government expenditures on goods and services would create a net addition to income and employment.
This net addition would be equal to the government expenditure. There would be no
offsetting item. This is because the government expenditure would add to the aggregate disposable income and to the demand for privately produced goods precisely the
amount which is withdrawn from that income and demand by taxation, so that over
and above the *unchanging* demand and the *unchanging* output in the private sector,
the tax-financed government output would develop as a net increment. But this assumes that the degree of confidence with which market demand is anticipated by private producers, and the willingness of private producers to satisfy this demand by production, are uninfluenced by taxation. Given the nature of the contemporary American
tax structure, such an assumption would very probably be unwarranted. Taxation has

Also, the mildness of the 1948-1949 recession in particular could scarcely be attributed to military and foreign-aid expenditures because the recession and the beginning of the recovery fall in the span which followed the gradual reduction of wartime spending and which *preceded* the resumed military expenditures of the Korean hostilities. During the span 1947-1950, in which the recession and the early recovery fall, government spending was considerably higher relative to national income than in the 'twenties, but mostly lower than in the depressed 'thirties[20] and the tax structure had become *very much* stiffer. Subsequently, the Korean war led to a renewed increase in government expenditures relative to national income, but the recovery started prior to the Korean outbreak.

On the whole, there exists a presumption that the highly unfavorable tendencies of the nineteen-thirties had been overcome, quite aside from "artificial stimuli." But an argument of this sort can never be established conclusively. In this particular instance it is possible to argue, for example, that the wartime shortage of physical capital relative to the output level had not yet been entirely overcome by 1948-1949. For the economy as a whole, the ratio of capital to output was probably smaller in the late 'forties than in the 'twenties, and it is not clear how much of this was a genuine decrease in the capital requirement per unit of output and how much of it was a backlog such as stimulates further new investment.[21] Also, the period falls in an upgrade of the "building cycle," but this in itself does not explain the mildness of the recession. We have had severe depressions in building-cycle upgrades.

It has been argued that the high income and profit taxes, the unemployment insurance, the high corporate savings (undistributed profits), and the high government expenditures of the postwar period have acted in the United States and elsewhere as *automatic cyclical stabilizers*, and

---

the effect of significantly reducing the net income from successful ventures in a risky environment in which some ventures succeed and others fail. Therefore, the willingness to accept risks is reduced. In the given circumstances, it is questionable how much net stimulus is provided by tax-financed government expenditures, or even whether any net stimulus is provided at all. This is the problem of the so-called *balanced-budget multiplier* (see Footnote 6, Page 365).

[20] However, foreign-aid expenditures were rising during the period, as a consequence of the Marshall Plan. Government expenditures on goods and services (including expenditures of the State and local governments as well as those of the Federal government) accounted for 10 percent of the national income in 1929, for 20 percent in 1933, for 18 percent in 1939, for 16 percent in 1948, for 20 percent in 1949. Later, the Korean war increased this percentage again to 27 percent.

[21] As to why this shortage did not at the same time create unemployment, see Footnote 16, Page 92.

that this should be recognized even by those who feel that the high level of activity in the favorable phases of the business cycle cannot be explained by tax-financed government expenditures. In other words, the factors here listed reduce the severity of downswings. This is because fiscal revenues from graduated individual income taxes, profit tax revenues, undistributed profits, and the net current surplus on the unemployment insurance accounts, all decline in a higher proportion than output itself when income tends to decline.[22] Government expenditures on the other hand, tend to decline in a smaller proportion than national income. Hence spendable private income ("disposable income") falls less than the value of output, and this exerts an automatic stabilizing influence. The argument is valid and significant, but it is valid and significant in both directions. A stabilizing influence may be expected from these "automatic" or "built-in" stabilizers, both upward and downward. The net tax revenues and savings here listed decline in a higher proportion than the value of output when output declines, but they also rise in a higher proportion than output when output rises. In cyclical expansion periods these same factors cause spendable private income to *rise less* than output.

Consequently, these stabilizers in themselves are incapable of explaining why the basic tendency in an economy is favorable. They merely explain why an economy is in less danger of significantly *deviating upward or downward from the path toward which it is tending*. Automatic stabilizers lower savings plus tax revenues relatively to private investment plus government expenditures as soon as there has occurred a small degree of cyclical contraction, and thus the cyclical contraction may stay small; yet automatic stabilizers raise savings plus tax revenues relatively to private investment plus government expenditures as soon as there has occurred a small degree of cyclical expansion, and thus the cyclical expansion, too, may stay small. As for the 1948-1949 recession, the automatic stabilizers help explain the mildness of the cyclical swing *if it is taken for granted* that until the late part of 1948 the economy was moving on a high path and that *from the end of 1949 on it was tending back toward that same path* (while the Korean outbreak came about six months later). But what is here taken for granted requires explanation and points to the basic strength of the economy in the period surrounding the recession. This basic strength reasserted itself very recently, when

---

[22] Indeed, in a sharp contraction the last two of the four items listed turn negative. All items here listed are included in the value of output, but we have to deduct them from the value of output to obtain the disposable (spendable) income of individuals.

the recession of 1953-1954 interrupted a vigorous growth trend only very briefly.

The proposition that cyclical stabilizers do not account for basic strength is subject to the qualification that reduced cyclical instability diminishes wastes and risk, and consequently may be expected to improve trends. This qualification is important in general, but it obviously cannot explain the difference between the character of the American economy in the nineteen-thirties and its character in the 'fifties. Cycle stabilization in the 'thirties would have meant stabilization at a low level of activity.

1953. At this writing (1955), the American economy is in a period of cyclical expansion which has followed the recession of 1953-54. The recession was very mild. In no quarter (three-month period) did unemployment exceed about 5 percent of the labor force. There also occurred, of course, a shortening of the work week (primarily as a consequence of reduced overtime), but from the cyclical peak month to the trough month this reduction did not exceed about 3 percent of the average length of the work week. Industrial production, consisting by definition of manufacturing and mining, declined by about 10 percent from the peak month of 1953 to the trough month of 1954. The gross national product and national income declined by 3 to 4 percent from the cyclical peak quarter to what seems to have been the trough quarter. The Federal Reserve counteracted the contractionary tendency by shifting toward a policy of easy credit after the tighter credit policy which was adopted during the advanced stages of the previous expansion. In the event of mild swings, central-bank policies are sufficiently effective, and they have the advantage of being much more promptly adjustable to changing business conditions than are tax policies. In the early part of 1955 central bank credit was again tightened to some extent.

Both in the United States and in Western Europe, there exists a widespread conviction that in the event of a severe depression tendency governments would not rely entirely on automatic stabilizers and on credit policy. They would presumably engage in deliberate "compensatory fiscal policy" by reducing tax *rates* and by deliberately increasing fiscal expenditures.[23] The test of this has not yet come, since the Western

---

[23] The fall in tax revenues *at given tax rates* is an *automatic* stabilizer. But the reduction of tax rates obviously is not. There is nothing automatic about such a reduction. As for an increase in government expenditures during depressions, this is "automatic" only insofar as it results from prior commitments (unemployment insurance, farm supports, etc.).

world has been faced with no serious depression tendency since the 'thirties. Later, we shall consider at some length both the merits and the limitations of compensatory fiscal policy in deflationary and in inflationary periods. But we should recognize even at this point that the limits of tolerance to unemployment have become considerably reduced in contemporary social systems. There exists reasonably general agreement in the Western World that the governments of the period 1929-1933 based their policies on a faulty diagnosis when they acted on the assumption that deficit financing (an increase in the domestically held public debt) exposes our social systems to greater danger than do severe deflation and large-scale unemployment. It is true that the American New Deal policies of the following era have stayed legitimately controversial. But this is not because in a period of heavy unemployment the New Deal engaged in some amount of deficit-financed public expenditure. The reason why the New Deal policies have stayed legitimately controversial is that in a depression a very moderate amount of deficit financing was combined with redistributive policies that are likely to have weakened the incentive to invest. To paraphrase a comment which the late Professor Schumpeter made in his posthumously published *History of Economic Analysis,* it is true, of course, that the choice between reliance on discretionary stabilizing policies and reliance on a rigid rule of thumb (balanced budget, gold standard, etc.) is to some extent a choice between two types of "vagary." Schumpeter spoke of a choice between the vagaries of gold and the vagaries of politics in connection with certain nineteenth century controversies. This phrase can be extended to a comparison of any rule-of-thumb policy with policies of discretionary action. But it is unrealistic to believe that in a twentieth-century industrial environment it is possible at all to leave the problem of the business cycle to the vagaries of a rigid rule of thumb and thus to avoid the vagaries which discretionary action might carry with it.

Neither the American nor the European economies have experienced a major downturn since 1937. At present, the currencies of the Western world are tied to gold with a very flexible string. The United States is legally committed to keeping a gold reserve, to freely buying and selling gold from foreign treasuries and central banks when these wish to sell or to buy, and to maintaining a fixed price ($35 per ounce) on its purchases and sales of gold. A close tie exists between gold and some other currencies, too, by virtue of domestic legislation. However, most currencies of the Western world are "tied" to the dollar and to each other merely by an agreement which requires the approval of the International Monetary Fund for a change in the exchange rates of any country by more than 10 percent. At the same time, most countries—not including, however, the United States—have exchange-control systems which restrict in varying degrees the right of individual citizens to buy or sell foreign exchange. Recently, there has been some liberalization of these controls.

5. What stands out in these narratives?

We were concerned here mainly with the span of 130 years lying between the second quarter of the nineteenth century and the present. This was a span of unprecedented material progress. During this period the population of Europe more than doubled; the population of the United States, which at the beginning of this period was thinly spread over about one-fifth of the present national area,[24] rose sixteenfold. Income *per head* of this rapidly increasing population rose to several times its initial height.

This development was made possible by effective offsets to the classical law of diminishing returns; by the adjustability of the internal structure of economic activity to changing demand structures; and by the flexibility of the money and credit supply, which, at the same time, was usually not so great as to produce violent inflationary instability. These factors make up the strategic elements of our analytical framework. Naturally, the development required also a policy attitude conducive to economic growth, although in no stage of the process did it require gearing the policies of governments exclusively to the beliefs or the interests of any single group in the population. In Europe the period started with compromises between the ideology of industrialism and that of feudalism. Throughout the Western world it ended with compromises between the ideology of industrialism and that of equalitarianism (more in the sense of income equality, than in that of equal opportunity to earn *differential incomes*.)

The history of growth interruptions (downturns) points to the strategic significance of the factors here listed. But the analytical framework which we are using is not nearly so rigorous as is a theory in the exact sciences, and hence at this point we can merely hope to convince the reader that the usual narratives of the process carry suggestions con-

---

[24] Practically all of the then settled (very *thinly* settled) area was east of the Mississippi.

sistent with our emphasis on a limited number of strategic growth factors. Stoppages may be attributed to temporary insufficiencies of the improvement process, that is, of the process which creates offsets to diminishing returns; and/or they can be attributed to the necessity of readjusting the structure of production; and/or to monetary disturbances.

The usual story of the major downturns which have been discussed in the present Chapter includes the development of specific fields of activity to a point where profitability is insufficient as long as other fields of activity are not further developed. The relative significance of specific fields of activity, and hence the required structure of production, usually changes from one "major" expansion period to the next, that is, from the period preceding a major downturn to the period preceding the next downturn. This amounts to saying that the structure of production must be readjusted, and the mobility of existing resources is of course always less than perfect.

If, at the same time, offsets to diminishing returns are forthcoming at an insufficient rate in the economy as a whole—that is, if technological and organizational improvement is insufficient to maintain the profitability of investment for a growing capital stock—then one would expect longer lasting and more severe interruptions of the growth process. In this case, more is involved than the overcoming of structural maladjustments. There exist some indications that the protracted depressions of the post-Napoleonic decades, the depression of the 'seventies (with relapse-tendencies well into the 'nineties), and the Great Depression of the nineteen-thirties may have had something to do with the fact that the technological and organizational revolution in already developed fields had spent itself, while in new fields the transformation process had not yet reached a stage where it could have exerted a sufficient pull on the economy. The technological and organizational prerequisites for rapid railroadization do not seem to have been met until after 1840, those of the steel age until about the 'eighties, those of electrification and automobile production until about the turn of the century. The chemical industries and the light metals were not ready for the role they have now assumed until after the Great Depression of the nineteen-thirties. A case could even be made for the proposition that prior to relatively recent innovations and discoveries electricity could perform merely the first act of its performance.

But while it is possible to find such indications in the general narratives, it must be admitted that long-lasting insufficiency of the technological and organizational improvement process is not the only possible cause of protracted depressions. The need for structural rearrangements, which indubitably played a role in most of the interruptions discussed in the present Chapter, may on occasion give rise to difficulties that last for many years. In this connection, we should recall that most protracted depressions, including that of the nineteen-thirties, fell in building-cycle downgrades, and that the specialization of resources (the limited mobility of capital as well as of labor) makes it difficult and time-consuming to shift resources from construction to other sectors of the economy. Also, in all cases where depression tendencies were very severe and protracted, it is possible to discern specific adverse factors which were peculiar to the period. All the long depressions of the nineteenth century fall in periods of relatively small gold production.[25] As for silver, in the third decade of the nineteenth century there was also a setback in silver production, and in the eighth decade an international shift toward demonetizing silver. In the nineteen-thirties the character of the depression changed for the worse at the time when the unsound financial structure of the heavily indebted Central European countries collapsed and when the arrangements by which the currencies of the Western nations were tied to each other gave way to competitive exchange-rate depreciation and exchange control. The pathology of protracted depressions must not overlook special circumstances of this sort. At the same time, it must recognize the likelihood that the flow of

---

[25] However, the argument emphasizing small gold production raises very complex questions. The ratio of bank notes and of check deposits to the available monetary metal does not remain constant. It is not at all clear whether in any of the periods characterized by slowing gold production, and by downward price trends, the rate of increase in the money supply—in the M term of the quantity equations, including bank notes and check deposits—was smaller than during the preceding period with rising price trends. Nor is it obvious whether the rise in M was smaller *relatively to the rise of output* in the periods with downward price trends than in the preceding periods with rising price trends. In other words, with the quantity equation $MV = PT$ in mind, we do not know how to distribute the responsibility for a falling P, between M, V, and T. The argument emphasizing small gold production would be stronger if we could assert the primary responsibility of M. In reality, we can merely say that more gold would have meant more M and that more M would presumably have meant a less downward-tilted or more upward-tilted price trend, whatever the trends in the other terms of the quantity equations happened to be. This implies that gold was one of the limiting factors, but it does not imply that a constant rate of increase in the gold base would have been either required, or sufficient to avoid periods with falling price trends. For a discussion of the literature, see W. W. Rostow, *British Economy of the Nineteenth Century* (Oxford, 1948), Ch. VII.

offsets to diminishing returns has occasionally been insufficient for periods extending over many years.

Monetary disturbances, to which the usual narratives frequently call attention, may well have contributed to deepening depressions of the usual kind into more severe stoppages. But monetary disturbances are capable of producing a downturn even where structural maladjustments have not previously proceeded to the danger point and where the improvement process is vigorous. Under metallic standards the elasticity of the money supply may become insufficient to finance indefinitely, and without forcing substantial price reductions, the rapid rate of expansion which characterizes a cyclical upswing. After a while, it may be necessary to tighten credit. The tightening of credit by central banks plays an important part in the usual cycle narratives. Frequently, it turns out that credit has become overexpanded, that is to say, that the banking system is in need of increasing its liquidity by reducing the volume of credits previously granted. If a country expands more rapidly than do other countries, then its imports tend to rise more than its exports and the country loses part of its monetary metals and foreign-exchange reserves. This "external drain" may force a tight credit policy. Internally, too, greater liquidity is sought and the demand for currency increases. Where gold-backing provisions or similar limitations of issue exist, this "internal drain" may, in itself, lead to credit restrictions and may accentuate the difficulties of credit institutions.

But even if the factors governing the money supply at first merely necessitate a *slowing* of the rate of expansion, *contraction* is likely to follow. Appreciable reduction of the rate of expansion is very likely to result in a temporary interruption of the growth process because a smaller rate of growth calls for structural rearrangements. The so-called acceleration principle explains how the absolute level of activity in certain industries depends on the rate of growth in other activities. Generally speaking, the absolute amount of the demand for *new* durable goods—for durable goods in addition to those required for maintaining the existing stock—depends on the *rate of increase* in the output of the goods and services produced with the aid of the durable goods in question.[26] Hence the output of the durable goods industries depends

---

[26] Given the stock of textile machinery, the absolute level of the demand for further machinery depends on the *rate of increase* in the demand for textiles; given the stock of automobiles, the demand for further automobiles depends on the *rate of increase* in the demand for passenger-miles of driving, etc.

on the rate of increase in other sectors of the economy. An appreciable reduction of the rate of expansion is likely to result in temporary contraction because, to gear an economy to a substantially reduced rate of expansion, the output of the durable goods industries must be reduced and the freed resources must be employed in other industries. These rearrangements can rarely be undertaken without intervening lags.

Hence, to understand the monetary limits of expansion, it is not necessary to assume that the institutional setting calls directly for contraction of the money and credit supply. It is sufficient to recognize that the money and credit supply cannot be allowed to go on expanding indefinitely at the rate at which it expands on the way from depression levels to cyclical peaks. Even an inconvertible paper currency must ordinarily be managed in such a way that the rate of money and credit expansion is reduced when the upswing reaches a point where further expansion at an unchanging rate would be associated with violent price inflation. If this limitation is not observed, the currency of the country depreciates. Inflation itself creates great hardships, and the subsequent stabilization, or introduction of a new and stable currency, is likely to cause a violent crisis.

It follows from this reasoning that interruptions of the growth process may result from any set of circumstances which *significantly reduces the rate of expansion.* We have stressed the possible sluggishness, in certain periods, of the improvement process by which offsets are provided to the "classical" tendency toward diminishing returns; the need for internal readjustments in the structure of economic activities; and the limits to monetary expansion. These are our strategic factors. We should now add that all these limiting factors may result in contraction even if *initially* they merely lead to an appreciable *slackening of the rate of expansion.* One of these factors—the need for sudden internal readjustments—is very likely to force temporary contractions even if this factor itself, or one of the other two strategic factors, initially forces merely a slowing of the expansion. For the internal structure required for slow growth is different from that required for rapid growth. The weight of the investment-goods industries must change relative to that of the consumer goods industries.

Once contraction is under way, it is, of course, always uncertain at what stage the expansion will be resumed. Even if the circumstances which have resulted in the contraction have been overcome, this does not guarantee that expansion will be resumed promptly. During the process of contraction the experience of the recent past is unfavorable, and it takes a psychological reorientation to eliminate the influence of the recent past on entrepreneurial decisions. However, it will be seen later that an upturn would follow at some stage—at an exceedingly low level —even if the behavior of investors were always uniquely determined by the experience of the *recent* past. Fortunately, contractions do not usually proceed to such an exceedingly low level.

The cycle narratives are consistent with this way of looking at the growth process. We believe they suggest that real significance attaches to what we have selected as our strategic factors. More cannot be claimed. We are not dealing here with rigorous models of the econometric variety. We shall consider them later—they, too, have their limitations.

Some of the narratives place emphasis, also, on the growth-interrupting effect of crop failures and the stimulating effect of abundant crops. However, the record of business-cycle history is not very consistent in this regard. At any rate, we are faced here with a special application of an argument which was considered in the previous pages in a different nexus. Crop failures may create structural maladjustments by causing specific shortages in agricultural goods and relative overproduction in the goods that farmers normally buy; they may also turn the balance of payments against the country in question, and by causing an "external drain" they may force restrictive credit policies.[27]

A final word should be said about a type of downturn which has not been listed in the present Chapter (except for the nineteen-forties and 'fifties to illustrate the difference between the characters of recent and earlier cyclical developments). These are the downturns leading merely to minor "recessions," that is, to contractions which have not usually caught the attention of the historians and analysts of major cyclical events. Burns and Mitchell do not distinguish between major and minor cyclical disturbances, and they include both in their chronologies (see Page 22). This is how they obtain an average cycle duration of between

---

[27] On the other hand, very abundant crops, too, may have harmful consequences if, as a result of low demand elasticity, they reduce agricultural prices more than unit costs. In this case, they worsen the condition of agriculture. Costs in the industrial sector are reduced, but if the elasticity of demand for agricultural products is low enough, the nature of the total impact on the industrial sector is uncertain because the buying power of agriculture from the other sectors is diminished. Yet, on the whole, rather extreme assumptions must be made to arrive at a case *against* abundant crops. It is especially unlikely that a single country should be worse off if *ceteris paribus* its own harvest is abundant than if it is poor, because the elasticity of the world demand for the output of a single country is likely to be high.

three and four years for the United States, and somewhat longer average durations for other countries. We have been using the conventional distinction between major depressions and minor recessions, even though the distinction is admittedly somewhat arbitrary. In the main Sections of the present Chapter, we limited ourselves to the major downturn which unil the nineteen-forties came about once a decade.

Recessions are minor depressions, and they can be caused by structural maladjustments or by monetary disturbances of temporary character, if these growth-interrupting factors appear merely in mild form. However, it is a rather common characteristic of minor recessions that in the course of these developments inventory fluctuations catch the eye very much more readily than fluctuations in other magnitudes. Consequently, some of these minor disturbances have occasionally been called "mere inventory recessions."

A mere inventory recession may be viewed as a typical case of mild maladjustment in the structure of production. Inventory accumulation sometimes falls behind actual needs, and the catching up process subsequently creates a greater demand for new inventories than that which can be sustained in the long run. There will follow a reduction of the demand for new inventories and therefore for goods in general. Subsequently, inventories will have become too far depleted, and inventory accumulation will start anew at a rate exceeding its sustainable long-run rate. In those cases where a recession is attributed exclusively to the temporary slackening of the demand for new inventories, it is *implied* that the trouble arises because *it is impossible to keep resources shifting between different areas of activity at short intervals.* It is impossible to shift resources back and forth all the time between, say, the production of shoe inventories and the production of industrial machinery and equipment. If the trouble had developed because investment opportunities were lacking in the economy as a whole (except in periods of temporarily excessive inventory accumulation), the correct interpretation of the temporary stoppage would not be that it was a "mere inventory recession." In this event, the causes would lie deeper. Profitable opportunities would be insufficient in the economy as a whole to keep the economy going, except when inventory accumulation was temporarily excessive. This would not be a "mere inventory recession."

Not all minor recessions were mainly (let alone exclusively) caused by structural maladjustments connected with fluctuations in inventory accumulation. But this seems to have been a rather prevalent type among the short-lived maladjustments in the structure of production.

We shall now turn to an analysis of the conditions of smooth or uninterrupted growth (dynamic equilibrium), and subsequently to a more detailed discussion of disturbances. In Part II a general analytical framework will be described. A more specific discussion of growth conditions and their corollaries will follow in Part III. In developing the analytical framework and the growth conditions we shall keep in mind the objective of adding subsequently an analysis of cyclical growth interruptions.

BIBLIOGRAPHY—PART 1

1. List of books and articles from which general supplementary readings may be selected:

Books

Bergson, Abram, ed. *Soviet Economic Growth*. Evanston and White Plains: Row, Peterson & Co., 1953.

Bouniatian, Mentor. *Geschichte der Handelskrisen in England im zusammenhang mit der Entwicklung des englischen Wirtschaftslebens, 1640-1840*. Munich: E. Reinhardt, 1908.

Burns, A. F., and W. C. Mitchell. *Measuring Business Cycles*. New York: National Bureau of Economic Research, 1946.

Cole, G. D. H. *Introduction to Economic History, 1750-1950*. London: Macmillan & Co., 1952.

Hansen, A. H. *Business Cycles and National Income*. New York: W. W. Norton & Co., 1951.

Hart, A. G. *Money, Debt, and Economic Activity*. New York: Prentice-Hall, 1953.

Kuznets, Simon. *National Income: A Summary of Findings*. New York: National Bureau of Economic Research, 1946.

———. *National Produce Since 1869*. New York: National Bureau of Economic Research, 1946.

Lescure, Jean. *Des crises générales et periodiques de surproduction*. Paris: Domat-Montchrestien, 1932.

Marshall, Alfred. *Official Papers*. London: Macmillan & Co., 1926.

Matthews, R. C. O. *A Study in Trade-Cycle History: Economic Fluctuations in Great Britain, 1833-1842*. Cambridge, Eng.: University Press, 1954.

Mills, F. C. *Price-Quantity Interactions in Business Cycles*. New York: National Bureau of Economic Research, 1946.

Moore, G. H. *Statistical Indicators of Cyclical Revivals and Recessions* (Occasional Paper No. 31). New York: National Bureau of Economic Research, 1950.

Robbins, Lionel. *The Great Depression*. London: Macmillan & Co., 1934.

Roose, K. D. *The Economics of Recession and Revival: An Interpretation of 1937-38*. New Haven: Yale University Press, 1954.

Schumpeter, J. A. *Business Cycles*. 2 vols. New York and London: McGraw-Hill Book Co., 1939.

———. *The Theory of Economic Development*. Cambridge: Harvard University Press, 1934.

Tugan-Baranowski, M. I. *Les Crises industrielles en Angleterre*, Paris: M. Giard & É. Brière, 1913.

———. *Studien zur Theorie und Geschichte der Handelskrisen in England*. Jena: G. Fischer, 1901.

U. S. Joint Committee on the Economic Report (83d Congress, 2d Session). *Trends in Economic Growth, A Comparison of the Western Powers and the Soviet Bloc.* Washington: Government Printing Office, 1955.

Articles

Garvey, George, "Kondratieff's Theory of Long Cycles." *Review of Economic Statistics,* November 1943.

Kondratieff, N. D. "The Long Waves of Economic Life." *Review of Economic Statistics,* November 1935. (This is a somewhat abridged translation by W. Stolper of a German article of 1926 which is listed below.)

Schumpeter, J. A. "The Analysis of Economic Change," *Review of Economic Statistics,* May 1935; reprinted in *Readings in Business Cycle Theory* (American Economic Association), Philadelphia: The Blakiston Co., 1944.

Spiethoff, Arthur. "Business Cycles," trans. by J. Kahane. *International Economic Papers,* International Economic Association, 1953. (An abridged English translation of Spiethoff's article listed below.)

2. Further readings relating to topics discussed in Part 1:

Books

Clapham, J. H. *A Concise Economic History of Britain, from the Earliest Times to 1750.* Cambridge, Eng.: University Press, 1949.

————. *The Economic Development of France and Germany, 1815-1914.* Cambridge, Eng.: University Press, 1936.

Court, W. H. B. *A Concise Economic History of Britain from 1750 to Recent Times.* Cambridge, Eng.: University Press, 1954.

Dupriez, L. H. *Des Mouvements économiques Généraux.* Louvain: Institut de Recherches Économiques et Sociales, 1947.

Frickey, Edwin. *Economic Fluctuations in the United States.* Cambridge: Harvard University Press, 1942.

Gayer, A. D., Anna J. Schwartz, and W .W. Rostow. *The Growth and Fluctuation of the British Economy, 1790-1850.* 2 vols. Oxford: Clarendon Press, 1953.

Gerschenkron, Alexander. *A Dollar Index of Soviet Machinery Output, 1927-28 to 1937.* Santa Monica: The RAND Corporation, 1951.

Hultgren, Thor. *Cyclical Diversities in the Fortunes of Industrial Corporations* (Occasional Paper No. 32). New York: National Bureau of Economic Research, 1950.

Juglar, Clément. *Des Crises Commerciales, et de leur retour périodique en France, en Angleterre et aux États-Unis.* Paris: Guillaumin & Cie, 1889.

Kuznets, S. S. *Secular Movements in Production and Prices.* Boston and New York: Houghton Mifflin Co., 1930.

Mills, F. C. *Productivity and Economic Progress.* New York: National Bureau of Economic Research, 1952.

Robertson, D. H. *A Study of Industrial Fluctuation.* London: London School of Economics and Political Science, 1948.

Rousseaux, Paul. *Les Mouvements de Fond de l'Economie Anglaise, 1800-1913.* Paris: Desclée, DeBrouwer & Cie, 1938.

Sartorius von Waltershausen, August. *Deutsche Wirtschaftsgeschichte, 1815-1914.* Jena, 1920.

Stolper, Gustav. *German Economy, 1870-1940.* New York: Reynal & Hitchcock, 1940.

Thorp, W. L. *Business Annals.* New York: National Bureau of Economic Research, 1926.

Wiston-Glynn, A. W. *John Law of Lauriston.* London: E. Saunders & Co., 1907.

Articles

Ames, Edward. "A Theoretical and Statistical Dilemma—The Contribution of Burns, Mitchell, and Frickey to Business-Cycle Theory." *Econometrica,* October 1948.

Crum, W. L. "Cycles of Rates on Commercial Paper." *Review of Economic Statistics,* January 1923.

Hawtrey, R. G. "Modern Banking: United Kingdom," in *Encyclopaedia of the Social Sciences.* New York: The Macmillan Co., 1930.

Hicks, J. R. "Mr. Hawtrey on Bank Rate and the Long-term Rate of Interest." *The Manchester School,* No. 1, 1939.

Kitchin, Joseph. "Cycles and Trends in Economic Factors." *Review of Economic Statistics,* January 1923.

————. "Gold," in *Encyclopaedia of the Social Sciences.* New York: The Macmillan Co., 1931.

Kondratieff, N. D. "Die langen Wellen der Konjunktur." *Archiv für Sozialwissenschaft und Sozialpolitik,* December 1926.

Persons, W. M. "An Index of General Business Conditions." *Review of Economic Statistics,* April 1919.

Spiethoff, Arthur. "Krisen," in *Handwörterbuch der Staatswissenschaften,* 4th ed. Jena: G. Fischer, 1925.

PART 2 /

Analytical Systems for the Study of Economic Growth

4

Time Sequences in Growing Economies

1. The point of departure.

The economics of growth and of fluctuations is concerned with the requirements of proper balance in the acquisition of new resources and of new skills. We shall set out by constructing a framework for the analysis of these problems of balance. Later, it will be seen that behind the framework there lies an area of largely sociological and political questions that will have to be faced separately. These are the problems of the initial conditions which must become satisfied before the technical framework of growth economics can acquire practical relevance. Section 2 of the present chapter will compare the classical analytical system with the technical framework to be used in this volume.

Our analytical framework directs attention to two propositions which have been expressed in many writings of the past fifteen years. The formulations which will be used here were taken over from a book published by the present writer about ten years ago, but the literature abounds with roughly simultaneous alternative versions of these same propositions.

The first proposition, relating to the required time-sequence of invest-ment flows. The first of our two propositions is a flexible variant of what is best known as the Harrod-Domar theory. The savings-investment framework is linked here to long-run growth tendencies, and thus a piece of equipment is constructed which is useful for the analysis of economic progress. The resulting analytical apparatus makes it clear that dynamic equilibrium positions which are derived from short-period savings-investment relations cannot help possessing implications concerning the proper time sequence of investment flows. The conclusions will be summarized briefly on page 118 before we turn to the "second proposition."

Figure 7 shows that if, in period one, the real[1] aggregate planned new investment is C_1P_1, then OY_1 is the aggregate real income which satisfies a significant short-period equilibrium condition. The condition is that the real savings of the public should equal the planned or desired new investment.

FIGURE 7—Relationship Between Output and Its Constituents in a Condition of Uninterrupted Growth

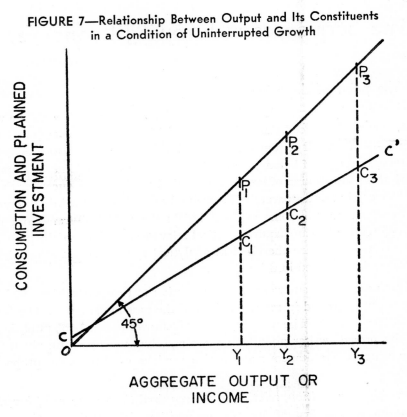

The line CC' (the "consumption function") is defined to give us the consumption at alternative levels of aggregate real income, and hence Y_1C_1 is the consumption corresponding to the income level OY_1. Con-

---

[1] By "real" we mean "physical," in the sense that a change in a "real" magnitude excludes that part of the change which reflects price changes. The difficulties connected with correcting for price changes will be considered later. However, we shall anticipate here the later conclusion that smooth growth requires a reasonably stable general price level.

sidering that $OY_1 = Y_1P_1$ (this follows from the fact that P_1 lies on a line drawn at a 45° angle from the origin), the savings of the public at the income level OY_1 are measured by C_1P_1. This is the difference between income and consumption, or, geometrically expressed, the difference between Y_1P_1 and Y_1C_1 (where Y_1P_1 is the same magnitude as OY_1). Therefore, if C_1P_1 is the planned new investment of period one, as was initially assumed, then income OY_1 is unequivocally *the* aggregate income which satisfies the condition that no more and no less than the savings of the public should find their way into planned new investment. This income or value of aggregate output can be found by moving along the horizontal axis to that point where the vertical difference between the 45° line and the CC' line equals the planned new inevestment of the period —in our case, C_1P_1 for period one. If the aggregate planned investment of period one were greater or smaller than C_1P_1, then the aggregate income at which savings equal planned investment would be greater or smaller than OY_1.

We shall not exploit in our conclusions the exaggerated rigidity of the graphic model, which assigns a unique amount of saving to each potential amount of output or income. But we shall make use of the assumption that the aggregate saving corresponding to any given amount of output is likely to be a magnitude lying within some specific range of magnitudes, and that aggregate savings are likely to grow when output grows. In a graphic presentation it is simpler to operate with specific magnitudes of saving, such as C_1P_1 and C_2P_2, than with ranges of magnitudes. Yet our conclusions will not depend on this.

Let us now examine the meaning of our first proposition, according to which short-period representations of the savings-investment equilibrium condition should be supplemented by an analysis of the time-sequence requirements which must be met for the savings-investment equilibrum to *stay* satisfied. Only if the equality of savings with planned investment stays satisfied all along (with positive savings and investment) will the system be in a state of uninterrupted growth or "dynamic equilibrium."

In Figure 7 the new investment of period one (C_1P_1) will lead to the growth of output, with the result that the income level of period two will be, say, OY_2. This means that in period two the original short-period equilibrium condition—the equality of savings with planned investment —cannot be satisfied unless new investment is now C_2P_2. Usually, it is realistic to represent C_2P_2 as being greater than C_1P_1 because the sum total of savings typically rises with aggregate income. Conditions of dynamic equilibrium—such as savings should equal planned investment—acquire significance only if they are developed for a sequence of periods. Consequently, we should not be satisfied with the conventional statement that has emerged from savings-investment analysis, namely, that in dynamic equilibrium the output of period one must be OY_1. We must add the supplementary statement that the profitability of the investments of any period hinges on further planned investment in subsequent periods, usually on the willingness of producers to undertake increased amounts of new investment in the periods that follow. Part of the new investment of each period must lead to the production of goods which will subsequently be used for a further increase in the amount of new investment. This is because in the subsequent periods the aggregate amount of savings will be greater.

If, in Figure 7, the planned new investment of period two does not reach the level C_2P_2, then at that time the market demand for the output OY_2 becomes insufficient to justify the investments of preceding periods. The reason for this is that the market demand consists of the consumer demand Y_2C_2 and of the demand coming from investors. The sum of these two demands is insufficient if it is smaller than Y_2P_2 (which is the same magnitude as OY_2). The new investment of period one, C_1P_1, gives rise to the output-increment Y_1Y_2, and hence the new investment of period one will not prove profitable unless, in period two, new investment is at least C_2P_2. Investment will not prove profitable unless aggregate demand is sufficient at the time when the output-increment created by the investment reaches the market; and whether the aggregate demand is sufficient at that time depends, in part, on the size of the further investment *then* undertaken.

This might lead one to believe that the growth requirements are particularly easily met if the output-increment per unit of new investment is low with the result that output, total saving, *and the required amount of new investment* rise little from one period to the next. But this is not so. What *is* true is merely the obvious statement that the investment requirements are more easily met with a consumption function that leaves little room for savings than with one that leaves much room for these. But if the investment needed for matching savings is forthcoming in either case, then trends in output and in the standard of living will of course be more favorable with a consumption function that leaves more room for savings than with one that leaves less room for these. The likelihood that planned investment will match savings is greater in any event if the output-increment per unit of investment is great in each industry than if it is small. This is why offsets to diminishing returns are needed for sustained growth.

We must remember that unless the aggregate income becomes redistributed in favor of the investing groups, the profitability of new investment depends on the size of the output-increment which is created by the investment. Given the investment of period one (C_1P_1), continuous growth is not promoted by making the output-increment smaller than Y_1Y_2. To be sure, this would reduce the aggregate amount of savings in period two, and thus would reduce the amount of investment required in period two for matching savings. Yet it would also reduce the probability that the required investment will be forthcoming either in period one or in period two. If the investment of period one, C_1P_1, is capable of creating a *high* output-increment, and if subsequently the output-increment which the planned investment C_2P_2 is capable of creating is also *high*, then chances are good that planned investment will be *sufficiently profitable* in both periods and therefore will be forthcoming.[2] In such circumstances investment may even have to be kept in bounds by restrictive monetary measures in order to avoid inflation.

The essential requirement here is that, when the time sequence of the aggregate flow of new savings per priod is such as C_1P_1, C_2P_2, C_3P_3, the output-increment per unit of new investment should be sufficiently *high*, at the margin of the new investment of each period, to assure sufficient profitability for a sequence of investments which matches the sequence of savings. As for the flow of new savings, this will be C_1P_1, C_2P_2 C_3P_3, . . . , if in period one output was OY_1 and if from that time on the economy stays on the path of Figure 7 (on the P_1, P_2, P_3, . . . path).

Generally speaking, if in our period two (which with the appropriate reinterpretation can represent any period in the course of dynamic development) the real planned new investment exceeds C_2P_2 or falls short of it, then output will not be equal to consumption plus planned new

---

[2] It will be seen later, that there exists a type of decrease in the output-increment per unit of new investment (for the economy as a whole) which need not diminish profitability. This develops when the relative weight of primarily labor-using sectors in the economy diminishes and that of more capital-using sectors increases, *with no change in the output-increment per unit of new investment in the individual sectors.* Such a shift increases the income share of investors in total income; and it is a generally valid proposition that a decrease of the output-increment per unit of new investment need not diminish profitability if, at the same time, the relative share of investors in total income rises. (Cf. Footnote 12, page 122.)

investment. In the graph this disequilibrium will express itself in the fact that the sum of consumption and of planned new investment, measured vertically from Y_2 as a base, will not add up to the height of the 45° line. In other words, the sum will not total the height of a line which is defined in such a way that at Y_2 its height equals the real output OY_2.

Only if planned new investment is C_2P_2 will output in period two equal the sum of consumption and of *planned* new investment. But output must always equal the sum of consumption and of actual new capital formation (new investment), *planned or unplanned.* All nonconsumed physical output is added to the capital stock either in the form of buildings, machinery, and equipment, or in the form of business inventories.[3] Output necessarily equals consumption plus actual investment, that is, consumption plus the actual additions to the capital stock. But output is not necessarily equal to consumption plus *planned* investment. It does not necessarily equal the sum of consumption and of the *desired* additions to the capital stock. When the system does not move on a path of dynamic equilibrium, the actual new capital formation (new investment) exceeds the planned or falls short of it. If, for example, in period two planned new investment is not C_2P_2, then there will be an unplanned or unwanted change in the capital stock (unplanned new investment). This is the sense in which planned new investment of the amount C_1P_1, C_2P_2, C_3P_3, . . . in the successive periods is a requirement of dynamic equilibrium, that is, of continuous growth.[4] It is a requirement of avoiding unplanned positive capital formation or an unplanned depletion of the capital stock along the time path of the economy.

Let us assume, for example, that in period two planned new investment exceeds C_2P_2. In this case, the sum of consumer demand and of the demand coming from investors will exceed the available supply of goods, and hence producers will find themselves with involuntarily reduced business inventories. As a result the statistically observable new capital formation (new investment) of the period will be smaller than

---

[3] However, as will be seen later in this Chapter, if a method of social accounting is used which includes the output produced or acquired by the government *neither* in consumption *nor* in capital formation, then a somewhat more complex analytical framework is required.

[4] It will be seen later that if the output produced or acquired by the government on the one hand and tax payments on the other are included neither in consumption nor in capital formation, then the statement here must be interpreted as implying a balanced budget.

the planned new investment.[5] Also, prices will tend to rise, and shortages will makes themselves felt. Such a process must be financed either by excessive creation of new money or by the "dishoarding" of previously idle (inactive) purchasing power. Sooner or later, the inflationary process will have to come to an end, and economic growth will be interrupted. "In principle" a tight money policy should always be able to prevent planned investment from growing beyond C_2P_2, but in practice it is not always capable of accomplishing this.

What if planned new investment falls short of C_2P_2? Then the sum of consumer demand and of the demand coming from investors will fall short of the available supply of goods at unchanging prices. Hence, producers will find themselves with involuntarily increased business inventories. Consequently the statistically observable or "actual" new capital formation (new investment) of the period will be greater than the planned new investment. Also, prices will tend to fall. The stock of machinery and of buildings will now prove oversized. The attempts of producers to get rid of their excessive inventories and of their excessive fixed capital will reduce, or turn into negative, the planned new capital formation. The growth process will become interrupted. Since total effective demand is insufficient for maintaining the growth process, either the total supply of money (currency plus check deposits) must have risen insufficiently, or the amount of "hoarded" money must have risen at the expense of the active money.

We now see why dynamic equilibrium requires that in period two new planned capital formation should be of size C_2P_2—if the antecedents of the situation include investment in the amount of C_1P_1 in period one and if they include the output-increment Y_1Y_2 from period one to period two. The profitability of the investments of period one can be sufficient only if the physical productivity of the investments is sufficient in each period *and* if a sufficient flow of further investment is generated in the subsequent periods. Where the latter condition is not satisfied, the total demand for goods does not balance with the total supply at the initial prices. Easy credit, in itself, is not always sufficient to call forth the required amount of planned new investment. As for price reductions, these diminish incomes as well, and hence their consequences are not precisely predictable.[6]

---

[5] This is an unplanned depletion of the stock (unplanned negative capital formation).
[6] The analysis of the impact of general price and wage reductions leads into a problem which will presently be considered in connection with the so-called Pigou effect.

Here again our conclusions should make allowance for the exaggerated rigidity of the graphic model. In the real world planned new capital formation or planned investment is not a specific magnitude but a range of magnitudes. If, for example, inventory accumulation is somewhat greater or smaller than would correspond to the initial best guess of the producer, this will create no cumulative disturbance. But if actual capital formation turns out to fall outside some desired *range,* then these consequences will show.

Our first proposition, then, leads to the conclusion that the investment of a period will not pay unless the investment of the next period is sufficient (which usually means that the total investment of the next period must be greater than that of the previous period). An economy in which there is new investment is a growing economy, and in a growing economy aggregate planned investment must keep pace with aggregate savings, the absolute amount of which usually rises. The conditions of sustained growth may be viewed as conditions of the appropriate time sequence or time path of aggregate new investment, and the required path is usually a rising one. The physical productivity of new investment and its profitability to the investors must stay sufficiently high to accomplish the proper time sequence. Once certain initial conditions of economic growth have become satisfied, a rising time path of aggregate new investment depends on the following: (1) the continued ability of the system to bring forth a sufficient flow of technological and organizational improvements, by which all or much of the tendency toward diminishing returns from investment can be offset; (2) sufficient mobility of resources; (3) the proper flexibility of the money-and-credit mechanism and its adjustability to the requirements of a reasonably stable general price level. It will be seen in Part 3 that it is necessary to introduce this requirement of general price stability, and also that the requirement enables us to circumvent the cumbersome distinction between expected and unexpected savings.

The second proposition, expressing an empirical generalization about time sequences in the saved proportion of output. We now turn to our second proposition, which supplements the first. The available statistical material proves that, in advanced economies, the saved *proportion* of output does not usually tend to increase with the passage of time. There exists a significant difference between the behavior of a family when it moves from a lower to a higher income class, at a given level of the national income, and the behavior of a family when its income rises roughly in the same proportion as the income of the other families in the economy. A family whose income increases relatively to that of other families saves a higher proportion of its income. This can be seen from household-budget statistics, which show that in any given period the upper-income groups save a substantially greater proportion of their incomes than the lower. Numerical data proving this proposition will be found in Appendix I to the present Chapter. Yet, when everybody's income rises along the time path of a growing economy, the saved proportion of aggregate income does not rise consistently.

In the relatively early stages of Western economic development the saved proportion of income does seem to have risen, but in no advanced economy has this proportion continued to rise appreciably. In some cases it has fallen. This is disclosed by intertemporal comparisons of national income, and of aggregate consumption, over periods during which the absolute amount of national income and of consumption rose to a multiple of their initial size.

The CC' function in Figure 7 illustrates a process during which aggregate income is rising, *with roughly unchanging income distribution.* The function is drawn in such a way that along it the saved proportion of income rises noticeably in the low ranges of aggregate income, and rises negligibly in the region of high aggregate income. This is because the function is represented as a straight line which intersects with the vertical axis somewhat above the point of origin of the axes. The linear shape of the function is merely a simplifying device, but it seems realistic to assume that with an unchanging distribution of income the main characteristics of the trend in the saved proportion of income would be about what they are along our CC' line. The saved proportion of income would presumably rise significantly in the early stages of growth (as was the case in early Western development), and the rise would cease or become small in the later stages of the process.[7] In some of the advanced Western economies we have observed not only slowness of rise in the saved proportion of income, but a moderate decline. However, this may

---

[7] Only if the CC' function were really linear, would this trend in the saved proportion of output necessarily imply that CC' intersects with the vertical axis above the origin. (But such a "positive intercept" is meaningful, in a sense, at any event. The positive intercept indicates positive consumption for zero output. Indeed, apes consume without "producing.")

be connected with a tendency toward more equal distribution of income.[8] Such a tendency should be conceived of as shifting up the CC' line, rather than as affecting its shape. Along our CC' line the saved proportion of output stays practically unchanged in advanced stages of economic growth, after having risen appreciably in the very early stages.

In our previous volume we suggested an explanation for the difference between the "cross-section" behavior of the saved proportion of income (that is, its behavior in household-budget statistics for a comparison of various income classes during one period) and its behavior along time paths. We suggested that, so far as saving habits are concerned, a family in an advanced economy behaves as if it were better off mainly (or only) if it gets to be better off *relatively to other families,* and not if, along with others, it gets to be better off *absolutely.*[9] This seems to be the reason for the failure of the typical family, in advanced economies, to save a higher proportion of its income when the national income rises, even though in any given period a high-income family saves a very much higher proportion of its income than a low-income family. Subsequently, the same interpretation has become an ingredient of James Duesenberry's thesis—now usually referred to as the relative income hypothesis—where it was technically blended with cyclical analysis.[10] Other interpretations of the difference

---

8 This assumption possesses plausibility, although the writer doubts that a precise statistical relationship could be established between trends in distribution and trends in the saved proportion of aggregate income.

9 See the present writer's *Monetary Policies and Full Employment* (Berkeley, 1946), pp. 55-73. The argument assumes that habits in the community have already become geared to a gradual rise in incomes, as is the case in advanced economies. In other words, notions about a "normal standard of living" are being continually adjusted upward as national income rises. But a family whose income rises relatively to that of others is becoming better off relatively to the then prevailing notions about "high," "normal," or "low" standards of living.

10 J. S. Duesenberry, *Income, Saving, and the Theory of Consumer Behavior* (Cambridge, 1949). In his treatment the "relative income hypothesis," in the foregoing sense, becomes technically integrated with a cyclical hypothesis which has generally been made by investigators of dynamic processes, but which had not previously become linked with other aspects (*e.g.*, the trend aspects or the "cross-section" aspects) of the problem of saving habits. Earlier, too, it was recognized that in cyclical downswings the saved proportion of income falls and that in upswings this proportion rises—in other words, that the cyclical behavior of the saved proportion of income is at variance with its behavior along the long-run trend of growing economies. *Cyclically,* the saved proportion of aggregate output or of aggregate income does rise with rising output. Duesenberry accounts for this by relating consumption to an income peak which lies in the past whenever the simultaneous income is not the highest income on record. This expresses the resistance of income recipients to reducing a standard of living which has already been reached. In Duesenberry's theory, the saved proportion of simultaneous income will change if the relative position of the income recipient in the income structure changes, *or* if his present income is not the highest income on record and the

between the household-budget behavior (or "cross-section" behavior) and the time-series behavior of the saved proportion of income have also been advanced. Recently, James Tobin has made a case for the hypothesis that the growth of assets, that is, of already accumulated wealth, along the time path of an expanding economy may contribute importantly to the understanding of the difference in question.[11] Other things equal, an increased stock of wealth may tend to reduce the saved proportion of further income.

What remains significant from our point of view is that in advanced economies aggregate savings do not tend to rise to an ever-increasing proportion of the national income. The world would be very different indeed if distances such as C_2P_2 in Figure 7 were not only greater absolutely than the corresponding distances C_1P_1, but if there occurred a consistent, steep increase in the *proportion* of the total output that must go into new capital formation to maintain the profitability of previous investments. The improvement process—the innovational mechanism— which is required for offsetting a consistent tendency toward diminishing returns would then presumably be put under an intolerable strain, and the mobility of resources, too, would be overtaxed. On the other hand, a significant decrease of savings would also create serious difficulties be- cause Western institutions are ill-suited to the needs of a stationary economy. Experience shows that the *absolute size* of the gap which needs to be filled by planned new investment (the absolute size of the *CP* gap, so to speak) usually does tend to rise with the growth of the national income, but that this gap does not typically show an appreciable and sustained increase *in relation* to the simultaneous national income. The time-series behavior of the saved proportion of income is very different from its household-budget behavior. The *CC'* line expresses a different sort of relationship from that which can be derived directly from house- hold-budget statistics. This is our second proposition.

We have now described the two propositions with which we wish to be equipped at our departure. The profitability of the new investment of any period depends on the size of the investment flows which will be generated in subsequent periods, that is, on the time path of the

relationship between his present income and the past peak-income changes. A pre- liminary statement of Duesenberry's position is contained in his contribution to *In- come, Employment and Public Policy: Economic Essays in Honor of Alvin H. Hansen* (1948).

[11] James Tobin, "Relative Income, Absolute Income, and Saving," in *Money, Trade, and Economic Growth* (New York, 1951) , pp. 135-156.

investment flow itself; and, on realistic assumptions, the matching of the time path of savings probably requires a rising time path of new investment, but not a rise (at least not a consistent or sweeping rise) of new investment relative to the simultaneous output. The profitability of new investment is obviously connected with its physical productivity (that is, with the ratio of output-increments, such as Y_1Y_2, to the size of investment flows, such as C_1P_1 in Figure 7), although a ratio of this sort is not *identical* with the profit rate.[12] Yet if, in one period, the physical productivity of investment *is* sufficient, but subsequently either the physical productivity or other relevant factors are too unfavorable to call forth a sufficient flow of *further* investment, then not even the investments of the "first period" will pay. Total effective demand, which in a growing economy must always come partly from consumers and partly from further investors, will be inadequate to justify the original investments. The analysis of the growth process, therefore, must be concerned with the factors that call forth the proper time sequence or time path of new investment. At the same time, the analysis must also be concerned with the *sufficiency of savings* to enable us to maintain, without inflation, growth rates in output which exceed the rate of population growth. We are interested in a rising trend in *per capita* income. Hence a *sufficient* time sequence of savings must be matched by a sufficient time

---

[12] The relevant proposition here is that a fall in the output per unit of capital used must be associated with a fall in interest-plus-profit rates, unless the relative share of interest-plus-profit income in total income rises. Therefore, unless the relative share of interest-plus-profit income rises, a fall in the interest-plus-profit rate can only be avoided if output per unit of capital is prevented from falling. It follows that a sustained and appreciable fall of the output-increment per unit of new capital formation must also be avoided.

Denote total output (or income) by O; interest-plus-profit income by P; and the total capital stock by V. Then to say that P/V should not fall with the passage of time is identical with' saying that $O/V \cdot P/O$ should not fall. Hence, if P/O is not rising, then the condition is that O/V should not be falling. It will be seen presently that this may be interpreted as implying that ratios such as $Y_1Y_2 \div C_1P_1$ in Figure 7 also must not fall appreciably in the long run. Only if P/O rises, is a fall in O/V, and therefore a fall in ratios such as $Y_1Y_2 \div C_1P_1$, compatible with an unchanging P/V. A shift in the *composition* of output, from primarily labor-using sectors to primarily capital-using ones, frequently raises the over-all P/O ratio, while it lowers the O/V ratio. Hence, P/V need not be lowered here. But, generally, there exists no reason to assume that when O/V falls in the individual sectors of the economy, then P/O will rise and P/V will be kept from falling.

Ratios such as $Y_1Y_2 \div C_1P_1$ are closely related to O/V ratios. Strictly speaking, the $Y_1Y_2 \div C_1P_1$ ratios are $\Delta O/\Delta V$ ratios. But, if O/V stays constant $\Delta O/\Delta V$ must also stay constant. It is true that if O/V rises at a decreasing rate, then $\Delta O/\Delta V$ may fall appreciably in a limited range. But a sustained and appreciable fall in $\Delta O/\Delta V$ would have to be associated with a fall in O/V, hence it would pull down P/V (unless P/O rises correspondingly).

sequence in planned investment. This is the point of departure for the discussion in the following chapters.

2. An old story with some new features.

Technically, the analysis which takes its start from these propositions differs from the growth analysis of the classical economists in several respects. On the whole, these technical differences should not be over-stressed. They reflect the gradual improvement of analytical tools in the course of a period extending over more than a century. However, some differences of a more fundamental character do exist.

The classical economists were very much concerned with the characteristics of the growth process. Indeed, in our appraisal this was their main theme. Yet, if they had been confronted with the model represented by our Figure 7, they would presumably have objected to the use of the consumption function (CC'), or at least to the way in which we have used it. Malthus might not have objected, but this merely illustrates that not everyone of the classical school belonged to it without important reservations. Adam Smith, David Ricardo, and the later classical economists would have argued that, if we focus our attention on long-run tendencies, then the CC' line should be interpreted as *automatically adjusting* to the equilibrium requirements of the system. This implies that the CC' line does not possess the significance we have attributed to it.

The CC' line, it will be remembered, was used for arguing that if at some potential level of output (e.g., at OY_2), planned new investment would not absorb the *difference* between that output and the consumption indicated by the CC' line (would not absorb C_2P_2), then insufficiency of effective demand will keep the system below that output level. This stays nonclassical even if we recognize, as we do, that credit policy and similar factors can change the position of the CC' line within limits and that in the real world "planned investment" is a *range* of magnitudes rather than a single magnitude.

For example, if in period two planned new investment falls short of C_2P_2, in the classical doctrine this is associated with a tendency of the CC' line to shift up in such a way that at the full-employment level of output the vertical gap between the CC' line and the 45° line becomes no greater than the planned new investment. More precisely, there takes place a mutual adjustment by an upward shift of the CC' line *and* by an increase of planned investment to somewhat beyond its initial level, since the initial discrepancy results in a fall of interest rates. From some future date on—when, according to classical doctrine, further planned net investment will be zero and the stationary state will have been reached—the upward shift of the CC' line will bear the full brunt of the adjustment. In the stationary state, with zero net investment, by definition no upward adjustment in investment can occur. But quite aside from the stationary state, the gap between the CC' function and the 45° line cannot exceed planned new investment in the long run, that is, when short-run disturbances are disregarded. Therefore, in the long run there can be no insufficiency of effective demand, nor can there be unemployment of labor. If, on the other hand, the planned new investment in period two is greater than C_2P_2, and the investors are supplied with the money required to put their projects into effect, then in the long run all prices will rise in the same proportion. The inflationary process cannot stop before the appropriate tightening of the money supply reduces planned new investment to a magnitude such as C_2P_2. Under metallic currencies this tightening was supposed to be automatic because of a loss of monetary metals by the country in which prices were rising. "In the long run" the monetary and interest-rate mechanism will again have restored dynamic equilibrium, this time by reducing planned investment and by shifting *down* the CC' line (thus by increasing savings as well as by diminishing new investment). In the long run savings always equal planned investment for the economy as a whole at any technologically feasible output level.

The classical doctrine postulating that in the long run savings cannot become excessive (investment cannot become insufficient *relatively to savings*) is known as Say's Law. One of its most effective formulations stems from Jean Baptiste Say, a French economist of the classical school.[13] The usual way of expressing Say's Law is to say that, in the aggregate, a supply of goods necessarily creates a demand of the same magnitude because the sellers of goods either buy consumer goods or use the proceeds of their sales for planned physical investment. They do not, in the long run "hoard" their money—that is, they do not in the long run hoard currency or keep idle bank deposits. If initially there were a tendency toward "oversaving" relative to planned investment, falling interest rates would direct all savings into planned investment, either by reducing savings or by increasing

---

[13] See, *e.g.*, J. B. Say, *Letters to Thomas Robert Malthus on Political Economy and Stagnation of Commerce* (London, 1821), Letter I. The same theory had been expressed also in Say's earlier works. Indeed, it was an integral part of Adam Smith's analytical system in 1776!

investment or by accomplishing both. Recently, A. C. Pigou has argued that in the interpretation of Say's Law we must remember that, with completely flexible money wage rates and prices, the interest-rate mechanism might not have to bear the full burden of the classical savings-investment adjustment.[14] An excess of savings over planned investment would, at any rate, tend to become eliminated by the decline of money wage rates and prices. This decline would be brought about by the insufficiency of effective demand when planned new investment fell short of savings. The unemployment and the unsold goods would cause wages and prices to decline, and the decline would continue until the *real* value of already existing liquid assets (their value in goods and services) had risen high enough to discourage further savings on the part of the public.[15]

These differences between the classical assumptions and the assumptions underlying our analysis are significant. They may be expressed by drawing a sharp contrast. They may, however, also be expressed by drawing a parallel.

The classical doctrine describes a growth process at full employment which gradually leads into the stationary state with full employment, by using an apparatus that does not even permit of deviations from full employment. In its more careful statements the doctrine makes it clear that its failure to allow for underemployment rests (a) on its primary concern with the long run and (b) on an assumed equilibrating mechanism which eliminates certain disturbances that are observable in the short run. This equilibrating mechanism possesses many facets, among which interest-rate adjustments at the given general price level and wage-and-price changes are prominent. In contrast to this, our apparatus incorporates a general characteristic of contemporary employment-theory models. It permits the explicit description of situations in which the conditions of continued growth are not satisfied, and, at first blush, it leaves the question open whether a long-run equilibrating mechanism will or will not eliminate these deviations from equilibrium. In our analytical framework the possibility is not excluded that the growth process may become interrupted for long periods, or that it may even come to an end, because of a tendency to save more than would

---

[14] See, *e.g.*, A. C. Pigou, *Employment and Equilibrium*, 2d ed., (London, 1949), pp. 131-134.

[15] For somewhat more detailed discussion and for the appraisal of a qualification, see Page 283.

be invested along the growth path of the economy. We do not postulate that interest-rate adjustments or wage-price flexibility would necessarily eliminate such a discrepancy. We even allow for the possibility that in continuous growth, with "full use" of equipment, there may exist appreciable unemployment of labor and that this may not become eliminated by a reduction of real wage rates. It is, of course, a very essential property of the real world that so far difficulties of this sort have not become chronic, although in some cases they have been long lasting. But we do not wish to postulate that interest-rate adjustments and wage-price flexibility would have been sufficient to preclude such tendencies.

The analysis to be developed in this framework will lead to the conclusion that the long-run tendency toward satisfying the growth conditions in Western economies has rested only partly on the equilibrating processess implied in the classical theory. The long-run growth tendency has very largely been a consequence of the fact that technological and organizational improvements have been forthcoming with much greater regularity than had been anticipated in the Ricardian doctrine. These improvements resulting from "inventions" (new skills) have tended to keep planned investment at the level needed for matching savings in growing economies. We shall attribute substantial significance to the fact that *the character of these improvements—their relative impact on capital-productivity schedules and on labor-productivity schedules, respectively—has by and large adjusted to the growth requirements of the system.* Later, we shall explain in what sense this adjustment has so far been somewhat less than complete, but nevertheless, adequate.[16] Here we shall limit ourselves to the statement that the laborsaving and natural-resources-saving effect of improvements has been sufficient to prevent a consistent and appreciable fall in the profitability of new capital formation; and yet the laborsaving effect of improvements has not been so great as to prevent favorable trends in real wage rates (or as to create a chronic excess of labor) . This is why the system has worked.

To be sure, a reasonable degree of flexibility in interest rates and in the price-wage structure has played an important role. But neither the statistical material nor common observation makes it safe to assume that the interest-rate mechanism or price-wage adjustments *in themselves* would have kept planned new investment at the required level in relation to our *CC'* line, had the improvement process not tended to accom-

---

[16] See particularly Chapter 8 and the Appendix to Part 3.

plish this result. In the secular long run—in the very, very long run—the classical equilibrating mechanism might conceivably have worked, even without technological and organizational improvements. But so far this hypothesis has remained untested; and if future history should test this hypothesis, the hardships of an extended period would probably lead to a political collapse of the private enterprise system.

The Ricardian school was unduly optimistic about the ability of the interest-rate mechanism and the price-wage mechanism to eliminate severe disturbances within reasonable periods of time. Yet this school was unduly pessimistic concerning the ability of the system to bring forth the improvements required to offset diminishing returns and hence to *avoid* severe testing of the interest-rate and price-wage-adjustment mechanisms. Consequently, the economists of the Ricardian school were optimistic as to the avoidance of excess capacity and unemployment, but they were unduly pessimistic with respect to the ultimate duration of the growth process. They expected that as a consequence of the scarcity of natural resources, diminishing returns would win out over improvements, with the result that new investment would cease to call forth output-increments such as Y_1Y_2 in our graph. The system, they thought, was moving toward the stationary state, toward a state with zero net investment. But in the classical view interest-rate and wage-price adjustments would have assured that a zero-investment economy (stationary economy) would also have been a zero-saving economy, hence that it would have been an economy with sufficient effective demand to maintain full use of capacity and full use of the labor force (but presumably with a very low standard of living). They did, it is true, feel that in England the movement toward the stationary state would become slowed if the Corn Laws were repealed, and the raw-material base of the English economy were thus enlarged. Yet the existence of very significant and distinctly profitable investment opportunities in the second half of the twentieth century, with no end in sight, is hardly in accordance with the Ricardian diagnosis.

The classics expected a low standard of living in the stationary state because they believed, on Malthusian grounds, that population growth would catch up with the increased quantity of goods consumable by workers (that is, with the classical wages fund) as soon as the capital stock should cease to *grow* at a sufficient rate. This was the classical pessimism, which was coupled with optimism concerning the ability of the economy to produce equality of planned new investment with savings[17] and to assure full use of equipment and full employment of labor.[18]

The qualifying comment should be added that the classical pessimism with respect to the duration of the growth process is more characteristic of David Ricardo (1772-1823), and of his school in the narrower sense, than of the classics in general. Adam Smith (1723-1790) considered the stationary state to be presumably in the very distant and hazy future. So did Jean Baptiste Say (1767-1832) and Nassau William Senior (1790-1864). The first of these was Ricardo's contemporary, the second was much younger. In the appraisal of John Stuart Mill, a late classic (1806-1873), the problem of the gradual transition into the stationary state did deserve attention, but there was hope that "prudential" checks on population would tame the Malthusian Devil by the time the stationary state should be reached.[19] However, they all believed that at the end of the dynamic process which they were describing was the stationary state; and, with the exception of Malthus and some other "untypical" economists of the period, they all took the validity of Say's Law for granted.[20] We shall not imply the validity of Say's Law because, like most contemporary economists, we feel convinced that equilibrating processes based on the interest-rate mechanism and on price-wage adjustments *alone* would not perform satisfactorily. If investment activity gave out, saving might continue, and this would reduce effective demand below the level required for full employment. On the other hand, we shall attempt to substantiate the view that improvements have tended to be forthcoming with sufficient regularity to produce "long-run" sufficiency of planned investment, and we shall pay particular attention to the requirement that the character of the improvements must adjust to the relative resource position of growing economies.

Continued growth, then, depends on continued performance of a

---

[17] In the stationary state, but only there, this equality was expected to establish itself with *zero saving* and *zero investment* at full employment.

[18] David Ricardo, *On the Principles of Political Economy and Taxation* (London, 1817), Ch. 6; see also J. R. McCulloch, *The Principles of Political Economy* (London, 1825), pp. 198-202 in 1870 edition. N. W. Senior, in *An Outline of the Science of Political Economy* (London, 1836), maintains that manufacturing in itself is subject to increasing returns, but the economy as a whole to diminishing returns (due to the scarcity in "raw produce").

[19] J. S. Mill, *Principles of Political Economy* (London, 1909), Book IV, Ch. 6. First Edition 1848. With the Malthusian overpopulation tendency checked, the standard of living would not have to fall in the stationary state.

[20] Most economists of the classical school accepted Malthus' position on the population problem, but they considered his views concerning Say's Law erroneous.

mechanism of induced improvements, *in addition to* depending on reasonable mobility of resources (which implies adjustability of price relations to the changing demand structure) and *in addition to* depending on a money-and-credit mechanism flexible enough to preclude chronic inflationary or deflationary pressures. Needless to say, an adequate flow of savings is also indispensable for growth. But the discussion in Chapter 2, Section 13, showed that periods in which the saved proportion of output is merely moderate can be periods of appreciable output-growth, provided that technology advances swiftly, and hence the output-increment obtainable per unit of new investment is high. Such have been the circumstances recently in the United States. This of course does not contradict the statement that, *other things equal,* a higher rate of saving, and investment brings higher growth rates of output.

The contrast which was here drawn between the classical framework and our own can now be replaced with a parallel. The ease with which this can be done and the relatively intricate character of the argument expressing the contrast make one wonder whether, after all, the parallel does not contain the essence of the matter. It follows directly from the classical doctrine that continued growth—the avoidance of the ultimate "stationary state"—requires an improvement mechanism which offsets the tendency toward diminishing returns. In addition, the classics have of course, also placed a good deal of emphasis on the mobility of resources and on a well-developed credit system as prerequisites of the growth process; and they have greatly stressed the need for an adequate supply of savings to exploit the investment opportunities while society was in its advancing stage.

The classical writers did not believe that the stationary state could be avoided. But we have just seen that their answer to the question of what *would be* necessary to assure continued growth, with no approach to the stationary state, was much more similar to our views concerning these requirements than was their answer to the question of what is likely to happen if these requirements are not satisfied. The Ricardian answer to this second question was that we would be (and, indeed, gradually are) moving toward a situation with no net investment and with no saving, with low real wage rates *but with full employment.* Our answer to this second question is that with the slackening and ultimate cessation of net investment and of growth we might well get an excess of savings over planned investment until income and employment had contracted to a level where saving ceased and hence effective demand became sufficient to maintain a reduced level of output. After a long period, perhaps many decades, we might arrive at a condition where saving would cease to be forthcoming even at the full-employment level of business activity, and at that time the stationary state with full employment might establish itself. But a very long-lasting disturbance of this sort would presumably be fatal to the institutional framework of Western nations. In our opinion, the approach to the stationary state (zero-investment state) would be very much less smooth than the Ricardian school believed. Furthermore, even if the transition could be smoothed by means of compensatory government expenditures, the essential features of a private enterprise system could scarcely be transplanted into a routinized, stationary environment. However, we see no good reason for expecting a tendency toward the stationary state in the predictable future.

3. The Marxian variant.

Karl Marx (1818-1883) and the Marxian school of economists and sociologists have shared the Ricardian conviction that the growth conditions will not stay indefinitely satisfied. However, in the Marxian analysis, it is necessary to add that while these conditions will not be satisfied *in the capitalist framework,* growth will continue under socialism. In the Marxian view, the factors interfering with continued growth in the capitalist framework are different from those which the classics had stressed.

Marx expected that the adjustment of the structure of specialized resources to the structure of demand would meet with increasingly severe difficulties and also that the insufficiency of consumer demand, a consequence of the exploitation of labor, would in the future make investment unprofitable. This second argument rests, of course, on the denial of Say's Law: capitalists will save more than what corresponds to profitable investment opportunities, *i.e.,* to planned investment. The ownership of the means of production will become increasingly concentrated in fewer hands, the lot of the workers will progressively deteriorate, crises with mass unemployment will grow increasingly frequent, and, finally, the proletariat will expropriate the remaining expropriators, whose number will have significantly diminished in relation to the proletariat itself.[21] The following "dictatorship of the pro-

---

21 The technical argument in Marx's main work *(Das Kapital)* is strongly influenced by the fact that he had a "labor-value theory." According to this, the value of goods is determined by their labor content, that is, in Marx's terminology, by the socially neces-

letariat" will ultimately be succeeded by the extinction of the state. For the function of the state is to enforce the dominance of exploiting classes over the exploited, and under the "dictatorship of the proletariat" society will gradually become classless. The underlying theory of history is usually referred to as the materialist conception (or the economic interpretation) of history.[22]

---

sary labor which must be used for the production of the goods. The capitalists are represented as exploiting the workers by withholding from them part of the value of the product (*i.e.*, by realizing nonlabor income, or, in Marxian terminology, "surplus value"), and the degree of exploitation is said to be progressively increased by the introduction of new machinery. This process is interpreted as leading to an increasing degree of exploitation, in the sense that the productivity of the worker grows, yet in the long run his wages tend to stay at the bare subsistence level. Hence, surplus value is increasing relatively to the wages of labor. Also, the degree of industrial concentration is promoted by this rise in capital intensity. Unemployment would develop even if the profit rate stayed high because of the very highly laborsaving character of technological change. However, the profit rate (in contrast to the degree of exploitation) is said to be decreasing, in other words, the amount of surplus value is expected to fall *relatively to the total capital employed.*

It is not at all clear why the capitalists should be aiming at a higher degree of "exploitation" (a higher rate of surplus value relative to the labor employed and to its wages) at the expense of the profit rate. The reasoning here moves in terms of the "labor-value theory," which makes labor alone the determinant of value, and this is an empirically wrong theory. In the third volume of *Das Kapital*, a volume published by Engels many years after the death of Marx, the labor-value theory becomes modified by recognition of the fact that producers are guided by the profit rate, not by the rate of surplus value (that is, not by surplus value relative to the wages of labor). In the text *supra* we tried to give a summary that bypasses the difficulties caused by Marx's use of the labor-value theory, except that the idea of an increasing demand-insufficiency (increasing inability of capitalists to "realize" the surplus value) possesses vague "labor-value" implications. In the Marxian theory this difficulty is expected to become increasingly grave, and it is said to be caused by the exploitation of labor. It becomes increasingly difficult to cash in on that part of the total value which is not going to labor.

The earlier classical economists, too, developed labor-value theories, but they qualified these from the outset by recognizing the influence of other factors of production on the value of goods, and they did not, of course, interpret the share of the other factors as resulting from "exploitation."

[22] In this conception of history, some elements of which are clearly expressed already in Karl Marx's and Friedrich Engels' early work, the *Communist Manifesto* (1848), the modes of production are the basic moving forces of the historical process. They determine the class relations in society, that is, the character of the relationship between dominant and exploited classes. The "outlook" prevalent in a society—including the prevalent philosophical, legal, ethical, etc. ideology—is in turn determined by the nature of the class struggle in a given stage of development. These ideologies form the superstructure; they are built on the basic structure which is determined by the modes of production (technology) and the class struggle. As the modes of production change, there develops a discrepancy between these, on the one hand, and the existing class relations and ideologies on the other. Sooner or later, such discrepancies must become eliminated by revolutionary adjustments in the nature of class relations. This is how, according to the materialist conception of history, the capitalist system succeeded the feudal, and this is how socialism will succeed capitalism. The Marxian reasoning which was sketched in the text, above, and in Footnote 21, Page 130, is developed in the general sociological framework of the "materialist conception of history."

Marx and the Marxians may have been partly right in their predictions as to what *would* happen *if* a chronic condition developed where planned investment on the scale required for matching savings, at high levels of employment, became unprofitable. A chronic condition of this sort would indeed have revolutionary consequences. Dictatorship in the name of the "proletariat" is one of the forms of government that might establish itself in such circumstances. The dictatorial state would surely not become extinguished—it would not "wither away"—and this is not the only point on which the Marxian predictions would prove wrong, even if depression tendencies were to become chronic. But, on the whole, chronic depression tendencies would prove Marx a successful prophet.

Depression tendencies have not, however, so far become chronic in the Western world, in spite of the fact that the circumstances which according to Marx should have resulted in these tendencies have by now had another hundred years to prove their allegedly destructive properties. We live in very complex systems, in which the structure of specialized resources must be adjusting constantly to changing demand structures. Also, we live in economies in which a very significant proportion of the resources is privately owned, with the result that owners of capital and of natural resources earn a sizable proportion of the national income (in the United States, probably about 25 percent of the privately produced aggregate income before taxes, a proportion that does not seem to have changed appreciably as a consequence of unionism or other more recent features of the institutional setting). But the growth tendencies have continued. Marx must have misjudged the conditions on which growth tendencies have depended, even though he may have had a better eye than most of his contemporaries for what might be in store in the event that capitalistic economies should cease to show growth tendencies. The classics, on the other hand, by focusing attention on the race between improvements and diminishing returns, as well as on the required mobility of resources and on the significance of a well-developed credit system, showed succeeding generations the way to an analysis of the growth conditions under capitalism; but, for reasons of their own, they had limited faith in the continuation of the growth process and unqualified faith in the long-run equilibrating faculty of the interest-rate and wage-price mechanisms in the event of the cessation of growth.

It could, of course, be argued that in the times of the classics the greater flexibility of the wage-price mechanism justified greater faith in the validity of Say's Law in the stationary state. Yet it is questionable whether conditions under capitalism ever were such as to warrant the assumption that the hardships of the classical adjustment process would have been accepted. They certainly would not be accepted in our epoch, which has brought a significant increase in the political power of the relatively low-income classes and their representatives. Chronic insufficiency of profitable investment opportunities would lead to radical institutional change. At the end that change might or might not turn out to be the kind of change for which the Marxians are waiting. But at any rate it would be the kind of change most of us have reason to contemplate with little pleasure.

4. Returning to the main stream.

With value judgments and conclusions peculiar to it, Marxism has so far remained a side stream of the main current of *Western* economic thought. In the last three decades of the nineteenth century the main stream continues with the neoclassical school. Much of the work of this school was concerned with the processes by which resources become allocated to specific uses when the equality of savings with planned new investment can be taken for granted (at a positive level or at the zero level of savings). Marginal-utility theory and marginal-productivity theory emerged in this period, and so did the first formalization of the general equilibrium concept. To the outstanding economists of the neoclassical school, cessation of growth, as a consequence of insufficient offsets to diminishing returns, seemed an exceedingly remote problem (although not necessarily an unreal problem in some ultimate sense). But even for the event of diminishing returns "Say's Law" was upheld as a reasonable long-run proposition. The Austrians, the neoclassics of the Lausanne school, Alfred Marshall, John Bates Clark, Knut Wicksell, would all have agreed with the classical view that for long-run analysis there existed no legitimate problem of discrepancies between full-employment savings and investment. In the event of an uncompensated tendency toward sharply diminishing returns, a competitive economy would become stationary at full employment. But it was generally recognized that Ricardo had underestimated the potency of offsets to diminishing returns. The pessimistic dissenters of the period, who expected insufficiency of investment opportunities and rejected Say's Law, as a long-run proposition, were not typical. With the exception of the Marxians, the dissenters from neoclassical economics were at that time unable to develop a systematic theoretical framework.

At about the same time the historical school of economists, which had originated in Germany in the first half of the century, was beginning to direct attention also to the problem of *early* industrialism or *primitive* capitalism. The problem of the initial social and ideological obstacles standing in the way of incipient growth, and the problem of the removal of these obstacles, received much attention from the early and the later historical school. So did the problem of continuous environmental changes.

Even though, in the so-called *Methodenstreit*, there developed clashes between advocates of the neoclassical approach (especially Carl Menger in Austria) and "historical" economists (especially Gustav Schmoller in Germany), the interest in historical antecedents and environmental change has not stayed limited to the members of the historical school. For example, Alfred Marshall in Cambridge recognized the importance of work along historical lines. Somewhat later, Vilfredo Pareto, another significant economist of the neoclassical school, developed an historically oriented theory of sociology. Nor was the interest of economists in precapitalistic history, and in the initial requirements of industrialization, new. Adam Smith and Malthus were more interested in these problems than the later classics of the Ricardian school (or some of the neoclassics). Marx's theory, too, was historically oriented, resting as it did on a specific hypothesis in the "theory of history," namely, on the socalled materialist conception of history. However, in its more mature stages the historical school made the important contribution of bringing to bear the methods of technically adequate historical research on the problem of gradual economic development. On the other hand, if the historical school had gained predominance over the neoclassical theorists and their successors, the logical framework in which contemporary economic analysis proceeds would never have emerged.

5. Three immediate antecedents.

The analytical apparatus which will be used in the present volume was sketched diagrammatically in Section 1, *supra* (see Figure 7). As has already been said, this sort of apparatus has now existed for some time in many versions. These contemporary models share a number of immediate antecedents, of which three deserve special emphasis:

(*a*) In the first place, from the turn of the century on it has become increasingly usual to analyze short-run movements of output and employment in terms of the relationship between savings and planned investment. The apparatus of our Section 1 (*i.e.,* of Figure 7) focuses attention on this relationship, that is to say, the apparatus does not *postulate* the equality of saving with planned investment.

Say's Law which takes the equality of these two magnitudes for granted, was, of course, never intended as a short-run proposition. Around the turn of the century, the Swedish economist, Knut Wicksell, much of whose work moved along the neoclassical lines of the period, first developed the idea that *short-run* economic disturbances can be discussed systematically with the aid of a conceptual framework which discloses discrepancies between savings and planned investment along the cyclical path of the economy.[23] The classical school proper had shown much less interest in the problem of short-run disturbances.

In his explanation of differences between planned investment and saving, Wicksell placed a somewhat one-sided emphasis on the role of the interest rate—or rather on the significance of discrepancies between the market rate and the equilibrium rate or "natural" rate[24] of interest—and he used savings-investment analysis primarily for a discussion of cumulative movements in the price level rather than in output and employment. However, his ideas have proved very fruitful because it did not take much to realize that the ups and downs in the general price level are caused by forces which may also produce ups and downs in output and employment.

In the work of D. H. Robertson (now Sir Dennis Robertson) during the second and the third decade of the present century, a blend of the savings-investment analysis with quantity-theory analysis was used to trace the mutual interaction between monetary expansion or contraction and movements in real output.[25] At approximately the same time, several outstanding Swedish economists—mainly, Erik Lindahl, Bertil Ohlin, Erik Lundberg, Gunnar Myrdal—undertook to analyze the general consequences of discrepancies between planned investment and saving. These economists, along with R. G. Hawtrey in England, have greatly contrib-

---

[23] Knut Wicksell, *Lectures on Political Economy* (London, 1935), pp. 193-228. Wicksell presented the problem as if the equality of planned investment with savings necessarily implied a stable general price level. The discussion that developed around his book soon made it clear that the problem of the price level must be faced separately. If we wish to define dynamic equilibrium as a condition in which planned investment equals savings at a stable general price level, then we must express both postulates.

[24] The natural rate of interest was defined as the interest rate which would keep planned investment equal to savings and which would keep the general price level stable.

[25] D. H. Robertson, *Banking Policy and the Price Level* (London, 1932).

uted to the understanding of the difference between planned and realized investment, where realized investment differs from the planned in that it includes the unintentional changes of business inventories in times of unexpectedly low or high demand for goods. Such unintentional accumulation or unplanned investment (positive or negative) exerts a significant influence on the subsequent planned investment. The Swedish economists drew a sharp distinction also between expected and unexpected savings, a distinction which we shall prefer to circumvent.

The savings-investment framework was a rather well-developed instrument by the time the Great Depression of the nineteen-thirties made its fateful appearance. During the 'thirties John Maynard Keynes, the later Lord Keynes, brought the apparatus into a shape similar to that of our Figure 7, Page 112, except that, under the influence of the depression, he was primarily interested in a different aspect of the problem.[26] He directed his attention mainly to the question of how public investment can be used to fill the gap between the CC' function and the 45° line at the full-employment level of output (if, say, in "period one," planned investment is too small), rather than to explaining the response mechanism by which planned investment has been kept from becoming chronically insufficient. He was not primarily interested in developing a theory of the proper time sequences in growing economies. Instead, he developed a theory of the approach to the stationary state, on the assumption that the equilibrating process implied in Say's Law was incapable of maintaining full use of resources during such a development, but that deficit-financed public expenditure was capable of accomplishing this objective. Keynes regarded the postulate of automatic savings-investment equality at full employment as unrealistic in the long-run as well as "cyclically." Instead he postulated for mature economies a tendency toward *chronic* unemployment by assuming that, at the full-employment level of activity, saving would chronically exceed investment and that, therefore, the full-employment level of activity could not materialize.

While the kind of analysis to be presented in this volume is concerned with the mechanism which maintains growth tendencies, the analysis does contain a Keynesian ingredient. We shall assume that *chronic* insufficiency of planned investment to match savings at full employment is

---

[26] J. M. Keynes, *The General Theory of Employment, Interest, and Money*, (New York, 1936), particularly Ch. 18, "The General Theory of Employment Re-stated" and Ch. 24, "Concluding Notes on the Social Philosophy towards which the General Theory might lead."

conceivable (i.e., that this possibility should not be eliminated by an *a priori* postulate). This is not to deny that in the secular long run the interest-rate mechanism, aided by price-wage adjustments, might eliminate a chronic discrepancy between savings and planned investment, or that the discrepancy might become eliminated simply by an adjustment of general attitudes, and thus of saving habits, to a climate created by the absence of investment opportunities. In some "secular long run," Say's Law may well possess theoretical validity. But in cases where these adjustments would have to lead the economy through a long period of great hardship, the social system would prove insufficiently resistant. The deficiency of planned investment relative to savings would, at first, result in a reduction of output and employment to a level where saving would be sharply reduced, and such a condition could persist long enough to cause irreparable damage. This is the sense in which we shall accept the "Keynesian" proposition that long-run insufficiency of planned investment is conceivable. We shall not accept the Keynesian proposition that such a tendency should be anticipated in "mature" capitalistic economies in general. Nor do we share the view developed by Keynes and A. H. Hansen that the disturbances caused by a substantial chronic insufficiency of planned investment could be eliminated in the private-enterprise framework by deficit financing.[27] We do not share this view because the institutions of a profit economy lose their essential functions if the growth process is sustained mainly by government investment, *or* if routinized stationary conditions become established in a zero-investment economy (regardless of whether in the latter case government-subsidized consumer expenditures or the automatic cessation of saving do or do not raise effective demand to the level required for full employment). It is essential to realize that significant long-run insufficiency of private investment is a possibility. But the proper functioning of a private enterprise economy depends on its ability to produce a flow of savings which is sufficient to maintain appreciable growth rates, and on its ability to match these savings by a flow of net capital formation.

In summary, the emergence of the savings-investment analysis—a type of analysis which leaves room for savings-investment discrepancies—is one of the immediate antecedents of the contemporary growth models which are exemplified by the apparatus of the present volume.

(*b*) Another antecedent is the increasing emphasis on the long-run significance of improvements as effective offsets to diminishing returns. A

---

[27] See A. H. Hansen, *Full Recovery or Stagnation?* (New York, 1938), Ch. 19.

long time has elapsed since the "classical" period in the history of economic thought, but theories of the approach to the stationary state have remained untested. The improvement process—the flow of "innovations"—has proved a reasonably dependable part of economic development.

The significance of this was clearly realized by some of the authors who were mentioned in the earlier sections (*e.g.,* Marshall, Wicksell, and Robertson). It was clearly realized and stressed also by John Maurice Clark, whose work is connected more intimately with problems to be considered later in this Section. However, Joseph Schumpeter did more than any other economist to arouse interest in the characteristics of the "innovating" process.[28] In the analysis of the present volume a response mechanism of induced improvements will be considered one of the requirements of sustained economic growth. The growth process could not continue for long if the output-increment created by a unit of new investment were falling consistently and appreciably. Considering that the absolute amount of new investment which is required for matching savings in a growing economy tends to rise from period to period, the improvement mechanism must offset diminishing returns for a gradually *rising* amount of new investment. Improvements, in the sense in which the term will be used in the present volume, result from "inventions," that is, from the acquisition of new skills.

The present volume will place a good deal of emphasis also on the fact that the growth process requires the adjustment of the *character of improvements* to the relative resource scarcities existing in the economy. In Western economies the capital stock has been rising at a much higher rate than the labor supply. Improvements must therefore shift up the capital-productivity schedules, not simply the productivity schedules of some factor of production, to prevent the yield of capital from falling below critical levels. But if improvements had a favorable impact *merely* on the capital-productivity schedules, and an unfavorable impact on the labor-productivity schedules, this could result in chronic unemployment of labor or in a consistent fall of the relative share of workers in the national income. It is not enough that improvements should be sufficiently "cost-saving." An additional requirement is that their character—

---

[28] J. A. Schumpeter, *The Theory of Economic Development* (Cambridge, 1934). The German original was published in 1911. Also, *idem,* "The Analysis of Economic Change," *Review of Economic Statistics* (May 1935), pp. 2-10, reprinted in American Economic Association, *Readings in Business Cycle Theory* (Philadelphia, 1944), pp. 1-19.

their impact on the marginal productivity schedules of the various factors of production—should by and large accord with the relative resource scarcities in the economy. This requirement we shall have to keep in mind in the later course of our argument.

(c) Development of the acceleration principle is the third of the immediate antecedents of the growth models exemplified by our apparatus. The acceleration principle, in its broadest form, maintains that the size of the output-increment to which a given amount of new investment gives rise is significant *not merely* because it reflects the physical productivity of the new investment, but also because—when interpreted in reverse—it explains the amount of new investment which is called forth by the decision to produce a given output-increment. Interpreting the output-increment per unit of new investment "in reverse" means attributing significance to the *new capital requirement (net investment requirement) per unit of the output-increment*. This latter ratio—the incremental capital-output requirement—is frequently called the "accelerator."

The acceleration principle expresses the fact that an original demand-increment (that is, demand for an initial output-increment) becomes magnified by an *additional* demand-increment, via the accelerator. The original or primary demand-increment gives rise to further "derived" demand for the new physical capital which is required for producing the output-increment. An early statement of the principle is found in the work of the French economist Albert Aftalion, particularly in Book XI of his *Crises Périodiques de Surproduction*. Essential elements of the principle were developed by John Maurice Clark during the nineteen-twenties.[29] Until recently, the interest of economists focused mainly on important cyclical aspects of the principle. With the aid of the acceleration principle, it can be shown why, during the cycle, the derived demand for instruments fluctuates with a greater amplitude than the direct demand for final services.[30] This is the cyclical aspect of the acceleration

---

[29] J. M. Clark, *Strategic Factors in Business Cycles* (New York, 1934), pp. 33-44 and Part VI. Also, *idem*, "Business Acceleration and the Law of Demand: A Technical Factor in Economic Cycles," *Journal of Political Economy* (March 1917), pp. 217-235, reprinted in American Economic Association, *Readings in Business Cycle Theory*, pp. 235-260.

[30] Assume, for example, that the demand for housing accommodations is 2000 rooms' worth of rentals per year, that the stock of buildings which is capable of providing these accommodations is 100, and that, as long as the demand for housing accommodations stays stable, two new houses must be built in the average year to replace old houses. In other words, the average lifetime of a house is assumed to be 50 years. Assume also that there are no vacancies. If the final demand for housing accommodations now rises to 2400 rooms, this demand cannot be satisfied unless the stock of buildings is

principle, the aspect that first met the eye of Aftalion. However, Clark observed also the significance of the principle for the interpretation of long-run growth tendencies. This is the aspect with which growth models, such as that expressed by our Figure 7, are directly concerned. When fitted into a long-run theory, the acceleration principle tells us that new investment is called forth by the upward trend in output, or, more generally, by processes expressing themselves in successive output-increments. In the long run the demand for new investment depends on the rate of increase of output and on the size of the "accelerator" (*i.e.,* of the new capital requirement per unit of output-increment).

In Figure 7, Page 112, the profitability of the new investment C_1P_1 depends on the sufficiency of the output-increment Y_1Y_2 which is created by the investment.[31] But we have seen in Section 1 that at the same time the profitability of the new investment C_1P_1 depends on whether, in period two, total effective demand will reach the size OY_2 (or Y_2P_2), that is to say, whether the new investment of period two will reach the size C_2P_2. From this it follows that the justified amount of new investment in period one depends on the output-increment which will find a profitable market in period two. Assuming that Y_1Y_2 is this output-increment, we may multiply Y_1Y_2 by the new capital requirement per unit of the output-increment and thus obtain C_1P_1 as the justified amount of new investment in period one. The algebraic product of the output-increment with the incremental capital-output requirement (the "accelerator") is the new investment of the period. The incremental capital-output requirement (or accelerator) may be defined as the net capital formation per unit of output-increment. If so defined, the accelerator is, of course,

---

also increased by 20 percent. But this means that the demand for new houses rises from two per year to twenty-two per year, that is, it rises more than tenfold instead of rising by 20 percent. If, subsequently, the demand for housing accommodations keeps *rising* at a yearly rate of 400 per year, then the demand for new houses will *stay unchanged,* at its increased level of twenty-two (except for a slow, gradual increase in the replacement demand). But if, after the first rise, the demand for housing accommodations is reduced from 2400 units to the original 2000 units per year, then the demand for new houses shrinks from twenty-two per year to about two per year, and even these two new houses per year will be needed only after the temporary excess of houses has disappeared through depreciation. The amplitude of the fluctuations in residential construction far exceeds the amplitude of the fluctuations in the demand for final services.

For the same reason, the demand for automobiles fluctuates with much greater amplitude than the demand for the *services* of automobiles (*i.e.,* the demand for miles of driving) ; the demand for sugar manufacturing equipment fluctuates with much greater amplitude than the demand for sugar, etc.

31 See Pages 112-122, and particularly Footnote 12 on Page 122.

the reciprocal of the output-increment per unit of new capital formation.[32]

Growth models of the kind used in the present volume imply the acceleration principle because they recognize that the amount of investment which can be profitably undertaken in any period depends on the size of the output-increment for which there will be a market, and on the new capital requirement (investment requirement) per unit of this output-increment. The output-increment for which there will be a market depends, in turn, on the consumer demand, as well as on the *further* investment demand which will subsequently be forthcoming (when part of the income-increment will be consumed and another part saved). Smooth growth would require that the new investment so determined should match current new savings in each period, that is to say, that the output-increment which will find a market multiplied by the new capital requirement per unit of output-increment should match the current savings that are forthcoming at a continuously rising income level. In the real economy growth is not continuous, and hence this condition is not continuously satisfied. But the real economy very markedly shows long-run growth tendencies, and hence the growth requirements do tend to become satisfied in the long run. The business cycle may be viewed as resulting from deviations from a hypothetical condition in which the requirements of smooth growth would be continuously satisfied.

Growth, then, depends on the sufficiency of the planned investment of successive periods to match a growing total amount of saving, where the sufficiency of planned investment may be expressed as the sufficiency of the algebraic product of the successive output-increments with the new capital requirement per unit of output-increment. One must not, however, be misled into the belief that planned investment will be the greater, the greater the new capital requirement per unit of output-increment. It is true that a higher capital requirement per unit of output-increment —that is, a higher "incremental capital-output requirement" or higher

---

[32] We shall use this definition of the accelerator, except when presenting the theories of authors who use a somewhat different definition. These theories will be considered in Chapter 11. The theories in question distinguish investment that is induced by output-increments of specific past periods from investment that is induced by other events, and they define the accelerator as the increment to the capital stock which is induced by a unit of past output-increment. This is somewhat different from our definition of the accelerator because the concept of these authors uses time lags in a formal fashion in which we will not introduce them before reaching Part IV of this volume, and also because these alternative concepts distinguish between "induced" investment which is explained by output-increments and the accelerator, and other investments to which the concept of the accelerator is not applied.

"accelerator"—makes for higher aggregate planned investment, *if the size of the output-increment is given*. But we have seen earlier that a rise in the new capital requirement per unit of output-increment (that is, a fall in the output-increment per unit of new investment) is associated with a fall in the interest-plus-profit rate, unless the share of interest-plus-profit income in total income is rising.[33] Therefore, unless there *is* such a redistribution of income, investment is increasingly less likely to be undertaken, and output-increments are increasingly less likely to materialize, if the capital requirement *per unit of output-increment* (*i.e.*, the "accelerator") is getting bigger. In general, a rising accelerator is not conducive to investment. Circumstances conducive to growth are characterized by the ability of the system to bring forth a large total output-increment with an accelerator that is not so large as to make for small profitability. This means that for a sufficiently large *total* investment the capital-requirement *per unit of output-increment* must not rise beyond the levels compatible with sufficient profitability. The total output-increment must be sufficiently large to be associated with sufficient *total* investment, even though the accelerator is not so high as to make for small profitability.

In summary, contemporary growth models such as that of our Figure 7 may be said to have had three immediate antecedents. These can be described as (a) the development of the basic principles of the savings-investment analysis, (b) recognition of the significance of improvements for the utilization of existing resources as well as for sustained growth, and (c) development of the acceleration principle. It is easy to explain why putting these ingredients together was a post-Keynesian development. Keynes' work added a great deal to the usefulness of the savings-investment framework. It added especially to the applicability of this framework to problems where it is essential *not to postulate a priori* that the interest-rate mechanism and price-wage adjustment will in the long run eliminate discrepancies between savings and planned investment. Contemporary growth models presuppose the Keynesian stage of development of the savings-investment machinery. Yet Keynes, who made this contribution in the nineteen-thirties, came very close to postulating that in advanced industrial economies *neither* the interest-rate and price-

---

[33] See Page 122 and particularly Footnote 12. We wish to repeat that a shift in the composition of output from primarily labor-using to primarily capital-using sectors of the economy is usually associated with an increase in the relative share of property income. It follows that the rise in the accelerator brought about by such a shift need not reduce the profitability of investment.

wage mechanism *nor* any other process will prevent a long-run insufficiency of planned investment relative to savings, and that the difference must therefore be made up by deficit financing. Analysis of the problems to which contemporary growth theories are directed is, of course, aided considerably by the Keynesian elaboration on the savings-investment framework. But growth analysis, instead of postulating or coming near to postulating chronic insufficiency of planned investment, must concern itself with the factors which have so far prevented such chronic insufficiency from developing. It is not surprising that growth theories of this sort are post-Keynesian products and that they build heavily on the long-run flow of improvements and on the relationship between new capital formation and the successive output-increments.

6. A family of models.

A piece of machinery which R. F. Harrod constructed in 1939 was probably the first to be based on ideas very similar to those incorporated in our Figure 7.[34] A few years later, a similar apparatus was presented by E. D. Domar.[35] The same sort of approach has now existed for years in a good many variants and, on the whole, the similarities stand out more than the differences.[36]

However, a word should be added concerning a difference in degree existing between the Harrod-Domar variant and the version we have been using. Both Harrod and Domar have formulated their models in such a way that a constant incremental capital-output requirement (constant "accelerator") is postulated, and the saved proportion of output is also treated as a constant.[37] This statement applies to the *conditions of uninter-*

---

[34] R. F. Harrod, *Towards a Dynamic Economics* (London, 1948) ; "An Essay in Dynamic Theory," *Economic Journal* (March 1939) , pp. 14-33.

[35] E. D. Domar, "Capital Expansion, Rate of Growth, and Employment," *Econometrica* (April 1946) , pp. 137-147; "Expansion and Employment," *American Economic Review* (March 1947) , pp. 34-55; "The Problem of Capital Accumulation," *American Economic Review* (December 1948) , pp. 777-794.

[36] See, for example, pp. 23-32 and 45 in the present writer's earlier quoted volume.

[37] With reference to Footnote 12, Page 122, we may say that models of this type are based on the equation $\Delta O/\Delta t \cdot \Delta V/\Delta O = sO$, where O means output, t means time, V means the capital stock, and s means the saved proportion of output (or of income) . In other words, s means S/O where S is the total saving of a period. These models postulate a constant $\Delta V/\Delta O$ and a constant s. Of these two latter magnitudes, $\Delta V/\Delta O$ is the accelerator, while s, as we have seen, is the saved proportion of output (*i.e.*, of income) . Considering that the *average multiplier* is defined as the coefficient by which we must multiply the *new investment* of a period ($\Delta V/\Delta t$) to obtain the output of the period (O) , and considering that actual new investment must always equal total savings, and therefore the average multiplier must equal $1/s$, constancy of s implies constancy of the average multiplier. Hence, the Harrod-Domar equation implies a constant accelerator and a constant average multiplier. (Footnote continued on page 144.)

rupted growth which are incorporated in Harrod's and Domar's equations. Along the growth path the realized values of all economic variables must equal their planned or warranted values; the Harrod-Domar equations suggest constancy over time of the warranted values for the accelerator and for the saved proportion of output. The assumption concerning the constancy of the incremental capital-output requirement may be interpreted as implying that the relative shares of capital and of labor in the national income are fixed and that the interest-plus-profit rate is not adjustable (must also stay fixed if new investment is to continue). With fixed relative shares in income, the interest-plus-profit-rate can stay constant only if the incremental capital requirement per unit of additional output also remains constant.[38] Hence the implied constancy of relative shares, and the implied constancy of the interest-plus-profit rate needed for growth, leads to constructing a model in which *growth can continue only with a constant (not rising) capital requirement per unit of output-increment.* Only that amount of new investment can materialize which is compatible with a constant (not rising) incremental capital-output requirement. The entire burden of the growth requirements is thrust upon offsets to diminishing returns. In the Harrod-Domar model the offsets to diminishing returns must hold the output-increment per unit of new investment *constant* when the total amount of new investment is of the size needed to match savings. This is their condition of smooth growth. In the model of these authors the needed amount of new investment rises at a constant proportionate rate. For if savings and investment correspond to a constant proportion of output, and if a unit of investment gives rise to a constant output-increment, then both investment and output must be rising at a constant proportionate rate per period of time.

We have not required a constant output-increment per unit of new investment because we wish to treat neither the relative income shares, nor

---

The *marginal multiplier* is defined as the coefficient by which we must multiply *an addition to new investment,* as compared to the new investment of the preceding period, to obtain the *addition to output* during the period. Its value equals the reciprocal not of the saved proportion of income but of the saved proportion of an *addition* to income. The saved proportion of an addition to income we may call s', in which case the marginal multiplier becomes $1/s'$. If s remains constant over time, s' also must. Hence, the Harrod-Domar equations imply also a constant marginal multiplier.

The multiplier concepts were first introduced into the literature by R. F. Kahn in 1931.

[38] This follows from Page 122. But, even aside from the technical proof there contained, it stands to reason on general grounds that if the output-increment per unit of new investment declines, then the rate of return from investment also must, unless the relative share of investors in the national income rises.

the interest rates, nor the profit margins as wholly unadjustable to the requirements of the system. Price-wage adjustments will also not be excluded, and the saved proportion of output will not be regarded as rigorously fixed. Indeed, one constituent of the total savings, the corporate savings or undistributed corporate profits, seems to show a very definite tendency to rise and to fall when investment opportunities do. The burden of the growth requirements will, in this volume, be divided among the flow of improvements; the mobility of resources in response to changes in the demand structure; and the flexibility of the credit system, that is, its adjustability to the requirements of reasonable price stability.

We are opposed to treating the incremental capital-output requirement as a constant because the available statistical materials do not point to the constancy of this ratio. However, we, too, shall assume that in a growing economy an appreciable or consistent tendency toward diminishing returns must be offset by improvements because the adjustability of the relative income shares and of the interest-plus-profit rate is limited.[39] The difference between the Harrod-Domar framework and ours is a difference in degree. Possibly it is merely a difference in method of presentation. For Harrod and Domar have presented a first approximation in the form of algebraic formulae which were explained in concise articles. Developing ideas in that form has great merit. But algebraic presentation frequently requires sweeping simplifying assumptions which introduce more rigidity into a system than is truly intended. Even our less rigid graphic model had to be further relaxed in the verbal discussion, where we recognized that in the real world *ranges* of permissible magnitudes correspond to the specific magnitudes of the graph.

7. Types of unemployment and excess capacity.

(*a*) Let us assume for a moment that *the sequence of investment decisions is insufficient* to match the sequence of savings on the continuous growth path of Figure 7, Page 112, but that it is sufficient to keep the economy on a lower time path of continuous growth with a lower output and lower saving for any specific period (say, any given calendar year). A process moving on a lower path of continuous growth may be visualized as one putting the economy into point P_1 for the specific period in which the process initially contemplated would already have placed the economy in P_3. Even if the path of Figure 7 was a full-employment path,

---

[39] See the Appendix to Part 3.

the lower path will not be that. We have here one type of general unemployment which *may* persist even along a growth path, provided that the population, too, is growing. This type of unemployment can be explained by the fact that in the given circumstances *a higher level of output and of employment than that which materializes in each period would create a volume of new savings for the matching of which the rate of planned investment is insufficient.* Therefore, a higher level of output and of employment does not materialize in any specific period. Effective demand is insufficient for a higher level of output. This type of unemployment may be temporary ("cyclical"), or chronic, according to whether the weakness of the incentive to invest is temporary or chronic. When the unemployment has the characteristics described in this paragraph, additional investment activity would clearly be desirable even if consumption is not reduced. More investment would produce no inflation.

We shall see later that, given the saving habits of the public, the difficulty here is caused by the *marginal productivity*[40] *of the existing capital stock not being high enough.* Greater additions to the capital stock do not materialize because, in view of the *relative overabundance of capital* (that is, of the relative scarcity of factors of production cooperating with capital), greater additions to the capital stock would be insufficiently productive. The laborsaving effect, and (or) the natural resources-saving effect, of the technological-organizational improvements is insufficient. To be sure, *by producing insufficiency of effective demand,* the insufficiency of investment pulls down the marginal productivity of labor, too, but this is here merely a secondary effect.[41]

b) However, unemployment may exist even though, *at a higher level of employment, aggregate savings would not outrun aggregate planned investment and thus total effective demand would be sufficient for a*

---

[40] By marginal productivity, we here mean the increment in *output-value* brought about by adding the last small unit of the factor supply actually used (or by adding a further small unit). Mathematically, this is the partial derivative of output-value with respect to the input of the factor in question. Profit maximization along functions which in the long run are here interpreted as continuous requires that the price of the factor (more generally, the marginal cost in the factor) should equal its marginal product. That is to say, under profit maximization that quantity of the factor will be employed the marginal productivity of which equals its price (more generally, equals the marginal cost in that factor). If less were employed, profits could be increased by employing more, while if more were employed profits could be increased by employing less. We shall justify the use of marginal *value* productivity at the end of Chapter 8, Section 7.

[41] The secondary effect develops because the insufficiency of effective demand reduces the increment in output-value which is obtainable by employing further labor (at the margin of the actually existing amount of employment). See the preceding footnote.

higher level of output. Unless unemployment of this sort is narrowly limited to specific regions or occupation,[42] it can be explained by the fact that the "now" available quantity of equipment is insufficient for employing the entire labor force and that savings are insufficient to bring the equipment to the required size, at a stable general price level. Were it possible to raise the level of output and of employment, there would be enough further investment opportunities to match savings at those higher levels, but the present capital stock is too small for the use of the entire labor force and savings are insufficient to raise the capital stock to the required size.

In the circumstances now considered, the monetary authority, unless it is willing to feed an inflationary process, finds itself compelled to prevent the rate of investment from growing to the size where the capital stock would be big enough to tool the entire labor force. Persistence of such unemployment—its failure gradually to disappear—would imply that real wage rates are too high to provide inducement for a gradual reconstruction of the available physical equipment in the direction of greater labor intensity (smaller degree of mechanization). Unemployment of this sort is usually recognizable by the fact that easy credit policies would call forth an amount of investment which would cause inflationary pressures at less than full employment. This is because a shortage of physical capital exists. Cyclical unemployment—depression-caused unemployment—is not this type. Shortages in physical capital do not develop in depressions. We shall note later that if we take real wage rates and the saving habits of the public as given, we are faced with a difficulty which must be attributed to the *marginal productivity of the existing labor supply being insufficiently high,* even when effective demand is as high as it can be without causing inflation. Considering that more capital and more natural resources would increase the productivity of labor, we may attribute the difficulty to the scarcity of the factors of production cooperating with labor. *Labor is relatively too abundant.* Either the labor supply must have risen in a greater proportion then the supply of the factors cooperating with labor, or the laborsaving character of the improvements must have been so great that the results are equivalent to an excessive rate of increase of the labor supply.

Both types of unemployment—that caused by insufficiently high marginal capital-productivity, and that caused by insufficiently high mar-

---

[42] That is, unless this unemployment is attributable to the *wrong location* or *wrong specialization* of the labor force.

ginal labor-productivity—may exist, or even chronically persist, in conditions where output is growing.[43] If labor and capital were the only two factors, the two types could not coexist with each other, but if both these factors become "overabundant" relative to a third factor (natural resources) the two types of unemployment may in principle be present at the same time. In this case, the willingness of producers to increase their investments (and thus to match more savings) could eliminate part of the unemployment at stable prices; another part of the unemployment could be eliminated only by more investment than is compatible, at stable prices, with existing consumption-saving propensities. Yet while both types of unemployment might, in principle, persist even in economies whose output is growing, thus far there has been no tendency toward chronic unemployment of appreciable size in the industrialized economies. Unemployment has *mainly* been a cyclical phenomenon, even though some of the cyclical contractions of output, which were accompanied by significant unemployment, were long lasting. The unemployment of cyclical contractions belongs in the first of our two types ("a" rather than "b"), while the unemployment compatible with full use of equipment and with economic growth could belong in either type.

By unemployment we mean a condition where the entire job-seeking population cannot obtain employment at prevailing wage rates. Some allowance should be made for the time which it takes to find employment. While we have seen that unemployment in this sense is compatible, in principle, with uninterrupted growth of output, *i.e.*, with what we shall call "dynamic equilibrium," excess capacity in physical capital is not compatible with uninterrupted growth. This proposition implies, of course, a specific concept of excess capacity. Output may very well grow continuously in circumstances where it would be possible to use the equipment more fully than it is actually being used. But, the economy cannot grow if the owners of the physical stock, in general, *consider* the stock excessive. Where excess capacity exists in this latter sense, disinvestment instead of new capital formation will occur, and growth will become interrupted.

The problems which were briefly considered in the present Section will be discussed in greater detail in Chapter 8, where we shall be concerned with the ability of improvements to prevent the "overabundance" of resources in relation to one another.

---

[43] In addition, the first type, but not the second, can be cyclical. That is to say, the first, but not the second, may result from a cyclical contraction of output.

8. Tax payments and government expenditures.

In our introductory discussion we maintained that growth depends on the relationship between savings and planned new investment, and we implied that the planned investment in question is *private* investment such as depends on profit considerations. The equality of savings with planned private investment was represented as a requirement of dynamic equilibrium. Appendix 2 to the present Chapter will explain why a fuller statement, in terms of the concepts used by the U. S. Department of Commerce, requires equality of savings *plus tax payments*[44] with planned private investment *plus government expenditures on goods and services*. In other words, our simplified statement of dynamic equilibrium is strictly correct only if a balanced budget is assumed.

It may be intuitively obvious, or at least immediately very plausible, that a fuller statement can be obtained by including tax payments on the one hand and government expenditures on the other. The meaning of our simplified condition in Figure 7 was that the nonconsumed part of output must be taken up by demand other than that coming from consumers. In the first approximation, it is satisfactory to present the problem as if all nonconsumed income were "saved," and as if all demand that does not come from consumers originated in "planned investments." But the statement implies a balanced budget, considering that we make no attempt here to allocate tax payments and government expenditures between the categories of consumption and saving. Generally speaking, nonconsumed income appears in the form of *tax payments as well as of savings* in the usual sense, and demand other than consumer demand may come *from governments as well as from investors* in the usual sense.

It is necessary to be aware of this throughout the analysis. But we shall find it convenient to develop the concept of uninterrupted growth (our concept of "dynamic equilibrium") at first on the assumption of balanced budgets and to take account separately of the role of budgetary deficits and surpluses.

---

[44] More precisely, we should say "tax payments *minus government transfer payments*" instead of simply "tax payments" because while the government transfer payments are essentially negative tax payments, they are not labeled as such in the national accounts. The government transfer payments consist of unemployment benefits, veterans' payments, interest on the public debt, etc., that is, of payments which the recipients treat as incomes but which they do not earn for currently produced services.

9. Behind the scenes.

The framework here considered directs attention to problems such as (a) the tendency of planned capital formation to outrun savings in some phases of economic development and to fall behind savings in others; (b) the possibility of chronic unemployment—chronic excess of labor— even where planned capital formation would not tend to fall behind savings at high levels of employment; (c) the possibility of a gradual diminution of new investment activity in advanced industrial economies, with or without corresponding downward adjustment of the rate of saving at the full-employment level of activity (that is, without or with a chronic tendency toward the underutilization of resources). The avoidance of these difficulties was said to depend on the quantitative sufficiency and the qualitative adequacy of offsets to diminishing returns, on the mobility of resources, and on the elasticity of the money and credit supply. These are the explicit growth requirements which we shall later define as "corollaries" of the condition of smooth growth. But on what do these explicit requirements, in turn, depend? Surely, much must have stayed behind the scenes.

Economic historians, and economists concerned with contemporary primitive areas, must be prepared to face directly some of the themes which so far have not been made explicit in our presentation. In primitive conditions there may be no discrepancy between full-employment savings and investment, and yet there may be great poverty. The equilibrium in Figure 7 on Page 112, may be located in the zero net-investment region, where the 45° line intersects with CC'. To be sure, if offsets to diminishing returns now began to be forthcoming at a sufficient rate, if the mobility of resources were to become sufficient, and if an adequate money and credit system were established, net investment might start developing, part of the income-increment would presumably be saved and the economy could begin to move to the right on the horizontal axis. If the movement were rapid enough to outrun population growth, *per capita* income too would be rising. But it seems obvious that what we are really talking about in such circumstances lies behind our explicit growth conditions, very largely in the realm of political and economic institutions and partly in the area of specific policies ("infant-industry" subsidization, etc.). Under certain forms of organization, with certain legal arrangements and habits, our explicit growth conditions are much more likely to become satisfied than in institutional circumstances of a different sort. In our introductory treatment this problem—the problem of what may be called the initial conditions—has so far stayed implicit.

Nor is it legitimate to lose sight in advanced economies of the initial institutional conditions, that is, of the obstacles which must be removed *and kept away* if our explicit growth conditions are to be satisfied. After a period of rapid growth, there may be a spread of organizational forms, legal arrangements, ideologies and habits which exert a damaging influence on the growth process. It is not easy to subject these so-called institutional factors to formal analysis. They tend to stay semiarticulate. But we should not lose sight of them.

APPENDIX 1—PART 2

Relationship Between Consumption and Income in Household Budget Statistics Contrasted with Same Relationship in Time Series

This Appendix is concerned with propositions developed on Pages 118-121 of Chapter 4.

Comparisons of the relationship between the income and the consumption for various income groups *during a given period* prove that "cross-sectionwise" the saved proportion of income, the so-called average propensity to save, rises very significantly with rising income. The proportion of income-*increments* going into *increments* in total saving, the so-called marginal propensity to save, rises less significantly, and the rise in this proportion does not start at the lowest income levels. But even in the range in which the marginal propensity to save is approximately constant, it is sufficiently higher than the average propensity to save to raise the latter very significantly as income rises.

Table 5 is based on satistics of the "household budget" variety, published by the Federal Reserve Board's *Survey of Consumer Finances*. This is a sampling survey. The method is that of drawing a representative sample from the entire population of the United States residing in private households. Those included in the sample are interviewed concerning their incomes, consumption, savings, liquid asset holdings, etc. The number of interviews underlying the table is 3,500. The survey is undertaken each year by the Survey Research Center in Ann Arbor, Michigan. The following comments should be added.

A spending unit consists of all people living together, and belonging to the same family, who also meet the condition that they are pooling their incomes. Money income, as the term is used by the Survey, consists of all income before taxes which individuals, including the owners of unincorporated businesses, earn in the form of money receipts (not "in kind"). Transfer income, which is not received for goods and services currently produced, is included (*Cf.* Footnote 44, Page 149, *supra*). For certain analytical purposes the top quintile obviously lumps together too many income groups, but for our present purpose the classification serves adequately.

As can be seen from the footnotes to the table, not all figures were published by the Survey in the form in which we are using them. Some figures which are essential to our computations were derived indirectly from various numerical indications contained in the Survey's published accounts. However, the indications seem conclusive in each case, aside from the possibility of some cumulation of rounding errors.

The character of the relationship between income and saving is fundamentally different if saved proportions of income are compared not for different income classes in a given period but intertemporally, for rising national outputs. This can be seen, for example, from Table 2 on Page 62, which is based on Kuznets' data and gives the saved proportion of income in the sense of "net capital formation as a percentage of the net national product" for successive decades in the United States. During those decades income per head rose more than threefold.

While the intertemporal comparisons are based on a concept of "income" or "output," and on a concept of "saving" or "net capital formation," which are different from the "income" and the "saving" concept used in the cross-section studies,[1] it is inconceivable that the sharp difference between the two behavior patterns of the propensity to save should be the result of these conceptual differences.[2]

The data of the present Appendix and those of Table 2, Page 62, illustrate the proposition developed on Pages 118-121. We see that cross-sectionwise, when various income classes are compared during a given period of time, the saved proportion of incomes rises significantly with rising income; yet in the American economy the save proportion of national income has not shown a rising trend with rising national income.

---

[1] For the Kuznets concepts used in the long-run intertemporal comparisons (time-series comparisons), see Page 62 and Page 161.

[2] In principle, the conceptual differences could explain the differences between the two behavior patterns only on the assumption that intertemporarily there has occurred a sharp fall in the propensity to save of institutions (of the government and of corporations). This is unlikely to have happened over the period as a whole. But even if there should have been a tendency in that direction, the order of magnitude of the difference between the behavior patterns of the propensity to save is such that it is quite inconceivable that any appreciable part of the difference could be explained in this fashion.

Table 5—Relationship Between Income and Saving in Household Budget Data

Money Income Class[1]	II Number of Spending Units in Each Class[2] (millions)	III Percentage of Total Money Income in Each Class[3]	IV Amount of Total Money Income of Each Class[4] (billions)	V Mean Money Income of Each Class[5]	VI Federal Income Tax Liability as Percentage of Money Income[6]	VII Amount of Federal Income Tax Liability Per Spending Unit[7]	VIII Mean Money Income After Federal Income Tax[8]	IX Consumption as Percentage of Money Income Before Federal Income Tax[6]
Highest Quintile ($4,500 and up)	10.08	47	80.6	7,996	13	1,040	6,956	73
Second Quintile ($3,200—$4,449)	10.08	22	37.7	3,740	6	224	3,516	88
Third Quintile ($2,400—$3,199)	10.08	16	27.4	2,718	5	136	2,582	92
Fourth Quintile ($1,500—$2,399)	10.08	11	18.9	1,875	4	75	1,800	98
Lowest Quintile (up to $1,499)	10.08	4	6.9	685	1	7	678	129
Totals	50.4	100	171.4					

	X	XI	XII	XIII
	Saving as Percentage of Money Income (figures in parentheses include federal income tax payments in addition to savings)[6]	Total Amount of Saving (figures in parentheses include federal income tax payments in addition to savings)[9]	Marginal Propensity to Save (figures in parentheses include federal income tax payments with savings)[10]	Marginal Propensity to Save out of Income After Federal Income Tax[11]
Highest Quintile ($4,500 and up)	14 (27)	1,119 (2,159)	21 (40)	26
Second Quintile ($3,200—$4,449)	6 (12)	224 (449)	14 (23)	15
Third Quintile ($2,400—$3,199)	3 (8)	82 (217)	14 (21)	15
Fourth Quintile ($1,500—$2,399)	-2 (2)	-38 (38)	15 (20)	15
Lowest Quintile (up to $1,499)	-31 (-30)	-212 (-205)		

1. *Federal Reserve Bulletin* (July 1949), p. 786.
2. *Federal Reserve Bulletin* (January 1950), p. 16.
3. *Ibid.*, p. 29.
4. Derived as follows: *Ibid.*, p. 14, in combination with p. 27, leads to the conclusion that 12 billions of total saving correspond to 7 percent of total gross income. Therefore, total gross income is listed here as 171.4 billions.
5. Each line in Column IV divided by figure in same line of Column II of our table.
6. *Ibid.*, p. 27.
7. Computed from Column V and Column VI of our table.
8. Column V minus Column VII of our table.
9. Computed from Columns V and X of our table.
10. Increment of aggregate saving (or aggregate saving plus tax payments) as percentage of income-increment, before federal income taxes, as we move from the mean income of the next lower class to that of the class in question. Computed from Columns V and XI of our table.
11. Same concept as that of Column XII, except that income-increments are taken after federal income tax. Hence computed from Columns VIII and XI.

APPENDIX 2—PART 2

Translation of the Analysis into the Language of National Accounting

Figure 7 on Page 112 implies a definition of net output by which this magnitude is made to consist of two constituents—namely, the goods and services going to consumers and net capital formation. It is implied also that the value of the net output equals that of the aggregate income. This, in turn, consists of income consumed and of income which is saved by individuals or corporations.[1]

Aggregate income was measured on the horizontal axis of the figure; consumption and planned net capital formation (planned net investment) were measured on the vertical axis. Dynamic equilibrium was defined as a condition where net investment consists, all the time, exclusively of planned or desired capital formation and where this capital formation is a positive magnitude. Thus, in dynamic equilibrium the aggregate income of each successive period equals the sum of consumption and of *planned* net capital formation. Alternatively expressed in the dynamic equilibrium expressed by Figure 7 savings (nonconsumed incomes) equal planned net capital formation.

Net capital formation (net investment) includes the net additions to buildings, to machinery and equipment, to business inventories, and to claims against foreign countries. Actual net capital formation may exceed the planned or it may fall short of the planned because low market demand may leave firms with a greater physical capital stock (*e.g.*, with greater business inventories) than was desired, while high market demand may leave them with a smaller-than-desired stock. In the hypothetical condition of dynamic equilibrium, actual and planned or desired net capital formation are equal all the time and they are positive magnitudes. Thus we get continuous growth. Later, we shall pay more attention to the further requirement that in dynamic equilibrium the equality of actual with planned net capital formation must be satisfied at a reasonably stable general price level. Interruptions of the growth process in the real world stem from violations of the conditions of dynamic equilibrium.

---

[1] Corporate savings are undistributed corporate profits. The individual or personal savings, too, include some *business* savings, namely, those of noncorporate business

156

It now seems appropriate to make clear the relationship between the output and income concepts of Figure 7 and those used by the national income analysts of the U. S. Department of Commerce.

In the framework which the Department of Commerce uses, net output (in their terminology, the net national product) is divided not merely into goods and services going to consumers and into net capital formation, but into three categories. It is divided into goods and services going to consumers, net *private* capital formation, *and goods and services purchased by the government.* The government purchase is not allocated to "consumption" and "capital formation," respectively.

As for the corresponding income magnitude, the Department of Commerce does not interpret this as going exclusively into consumption and savings (personal and corporate). Instead, it interprets the corresponding income magnitude as going into consumption, savings (personal and corporate), *and tax payments.*

Therefore, while the framework of Figure 7 represents net output as composed of two constituents (output for consumption, and output for net investment or net capital formation), the Commerce framework views net output as consisting of *three basic constituents* (output for consumption, output for net private investment or net private capital formation, and the government purchase of goods and services); and, while the framework of Figure 7 represents income as going into two channels (consumption and saving), the more detailed Commerce framework adds a *third channel* (tax payments). Figure 7, if taken literally, and not viewed as a mere shorthand device for the more complex Commerce apparatus, implies that the government purchase of goods and services were allocated to consumption and capital formation, respectively.

Also, in the Commerce framework the income magnitude consisting of the sum of consumption, of savings, and of tax payments does not precisely equal the value of the net output (net national product); government transfer payments must be deducted from the sum of the three to arrive at equality with the net output (net national product). This is because such consumption and such "saving" as are undertaken out of so-called transfer payments are treated as consumption and saving *out of income* by the Commerce analysts. That is to say, so-called transfer incomes which, by definition, are *not earned for a contribution to current output,* are nevertheless included in the "income" out of which consumption is said to take place.[2] For example, veterans' benefits and also unemployment compensation are "transfer income"; the interest on the public debt is also treated as transfer income (although it is distinguished from the other transfer items). Commerce calls the sum of consumption and of personal savings, including the consumption and the personal savings undertaken out of "transfer income," the *disposable income* of individuals. This is the income which individuals are viewed

FIGURE 8—Analogous to Figure 7

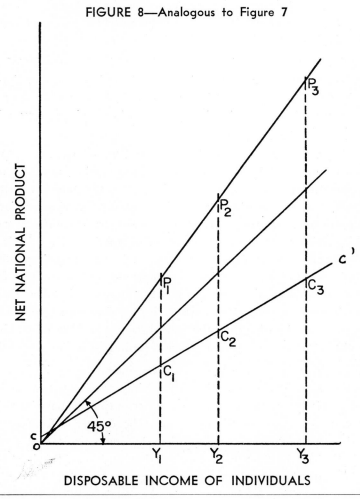

---

[2] Where "transfer income" is not treated as income, the consumption "out of it" appears as dissaving, and the nonconsumed part of the transfer income appears neither as saving nor as dissaving.

as allocating between consumption and savings. It follows that the net national product is not precisely the equivalent of an aggregate income magnitude consisting of *disposable income of individuals plus corporate savings plus all tax payments,* but that it is the equivalent of this aggregate income *minus government transfer payments.* The framework of Figure 7 does not treat "transfer income" as income, and hence it implies that output and aggregate income are definitionally equal. Indeed, something can be said for the conception that transfer income is not *true* income, although for some purposes it is advisable to include it in the income concept. But if government transfer payments are included in aggregate income, then current income will exceed the value of current output by these payments.

When translated into the Commerce terminology, the propositions expressed in Figure 7 assume the form reflected by Figure 8.

We now define the highest line in the graph so that the vertical distance from this line to the horizontal axis should measure the net national product; and the vertical distance from the CC' line to the horizontal axis is defined as the consumption expenditure. From this it follows that the vertical distance between the highest line in the graph and the 45° line measures, by definition, corporate savings plus all tax payments minus government transfer payments. The vertical distance between the 45° line and the CC' line, on the other hand, measures personal savings, that is, the difference between the disposable income of individuals and their consumption expenditure. This is because the vertical distance from any point on the horizontal axis to the 45° line is identical with the horizontal distance from the same point of the horizontal axis to the point of origin. Consequently, magnitudes such as C_1P_1, C_2P_2, C_3P_3, . . . measure personal savings, plus corporate savings (*i.e.,* undistributed corporate profits), plus all tax payments, minus government transfer payments.

Dynamic equilibrium now requires that, in the successive periods, planned net private capital formation plus the government expenditure on goods and services should be just sufficient to "absorb" the magnitudes C_1P_1, C_2P_2, C_3P_3, ... In other words, in terms of the Commerce concepts, dynamic equilibrium requires that planned net private capital formation plus government expenditures on goods and services should equal personal-plus-corporate savings plus tax payments minus government transfer payments; or, differently expressed, that planned net private capital formation plus government expenditures on goods and services plus government expenditures on transfer payments should equal all savings plus tax payments. If this condition is satisfied, net output consists exclusively of three categories of goods and services, namely, of goods and services going to consumers, of the government-acquired goods and services, and of *planned* net private capital formation. This means that there exists no difference between the actual and the planned net private capital formation. The dynamic equilibrium condition formulated in the present paragraph becomes identical with that of Figure 7, "savings equal planned net capital formation," on the simplifying assumption that government expenditures on goods and services plus government transfer payments equals tax payments (and that by "capital formation" we mean private capital formation). In this case, the "third items" on the output side and on the income side of the Commerce framework cancel each other (Page 157). In our analysis Figure 7 will be interpreted as a shorthand device implying this simplifying assumption. The assumption is essentially that of budgetary balance.

We have seen that, alternatively, Figure 7 could be interpreted not as implying budgetary balance in the Commerce framework just described, but as implying instead a procedure by which the "third items" on the output side and on the income side of the Commerce framework (Page 157) are divided between the first two. This means placing some tax payments in the category of consumption (because the public "consumed" government services of the equivalent value) and placing other tax payments in the category of savings (because the government acquired tangible assets of the equivalent value), while a third category of tax payments may be interpreted as having purchased merely instrumental services, the value of which is not included in current net output.[3] Correspondingly, the government-acquired tangible assets must then be included in net capital formation, along with the *private* net capital formation, while the remainder of the government expenditure must be viewed either as producing consumer goods (government services "consumed" by the public) or as producing merely instrumental services which do not enter at all into the value of the current net output. Also, if Figure 7 is to be literally valid as an illustration of dynamic equilibrium and is not to be interpreted simply as a shorthand device implying budgetary balance, transfer incomes must not be included in income,

---

[3] Once the finished product is included, the output of instrumental services which are incorporated in the finished product must be excluded. Inclusion of both would create "duplications."

and hence the consumption out of them must be regarded as dissaving. The procedure sketched in the present paragraph is, by and large, that employed by Simon Kuznets. Consequently, Figure 7 is directly or literally applicable if procedures such as those of Kuznets are used, while it is merely a shorthand device (implying the simplifying assumption of budgetary balance) if the underlying concepts are those of the Department of Commerce. *In general, we shall use Figure 7 as a shorthand device in the Commerce framework.*

Throughout the analysis we have meant by output the *net* output of an economy during an accounting period. In the Commerce terminology this is the net national product,[4] sometimes abbreviated as NNP. The gross national product (GNP) differs from the net output in that depreciation allowances for the use of durable capital (buildings, machinery, and equipment) are *not* deducted. In other words, interpreted as output, the GNP includes the *gross* capital formation, with no allowances for current depreciation, instead of the net capital formation which enters into NNP. The corresponding income concept includes the amounts spent on consumption, the tax payments and the *gross* savings of the period (where, in the Commerce framework, government transfer payments must again be deducted to create equality of aggregate income with output). The gross savings differ from the net in that they include the depreciation charges. But not even the *gross* national product includes in any stage of the structure of production the output which, in the same period, was used up for further production in the same industry or in other industries; consequently, not even *gross* savings includes that part of the receipts which is the equivalent of raw materials and services used up in the productive process. Even the gross national product is "net of duplications" in this sense. It is the sum of the "values added" in the various stages of production, except that, in contrast to the net concepts, no allowance is made for the use of the existing durable capital goods.

The output-increment per unit of *net* capital formation, from period one to two, may be obtained from Figure 8 by dividing the total net capital formation (which is part of C_1P_1) into the difference between Y_2P_2 and Y_1P_1. In this graph Y_1Y_2 is not the output-increment; it does not equal Y_2P_2-Y_1P_1.

---

[4] "National income," in the technical sense, is defined as the net national product minus indirect business taxes (such as excises) but not excluding the corporate profit taxes.

BIBLIOGRAPHY—PART 2

1. List of books and articles from which general supplementary readings may be selected:

Books

Baumol, W. J. *Economic Dynamics.* New York: The Macmillan Co., 1951.

Clark, J. M. *Strategic Factors in Business Cycles.* New York: National Bureau of Economic Research, 1934.

Duesenberry, J. S. *Income, Saving, and the Theory of Consumer Behavior.* Cambridge: Harvard University Press, 1949.

Harrod, R. F. *Towards a Dynamic Economics.* London: Macmillan and Co., 1948 (particularly Lecture 3).

Keynes, J. M. *The General Theory of Employment, Interest, and Money.* New York: Harcourt, Brace & Co., 1936.

Kuznets, Simon. *National Product since 1869.* New York: National Bureau of Economic Research, 1946.

Lundberg, Erik. *Studies in the Theory of Economic Expansion.* London: P. S. King & Son, 1937.

Morgan, Theodore. *Income and Employment.* New York: Prentice-Hall, 1947.

Pigou, A. C. *Employment and Equilibrium.* London: Macmillan & Co., 1949.

Robertson, D. H. *Banking Policy and the Price Level.* London: P. S. King & Son, 1932.

Robinson, Joan. *The Rate of Interest and other Essays.* London: Macmillan & Co., 1930.

Ruggles, Richard. *An Introduction to National Income and Income Analysis.* New York and London: McGraw-Hill Book Co., 1949.

Schelling, T. C. *National Income Behavior.* New York: McGraw-Hill Book Co., 1951.

Schumpeter, J. A. *The Theory of Economic Development.* Cambridge: Harvard University Press, 1934.

U. S. Department of Commerce. *National Income and Product of the United States, 1929-1950,* Supplement to the *Survey of Current Business.* Washington: Government Printing Office, 1951.

Articles

Clark, J. M. "Business Acceleration and the Law of Demand: A Technical Factor in Economic Cycles." *Journal of Political Economy,* March 1917; reprinted in *Readings in Business Cycle Theory,* (American Economic Association), Philadelphia: The Blakiston Co., 1944.

Domar, E. D. "Expansion and Employment." *American Economic Review,* March 1947.

———. "The Problem of Capital Accumulation." *American Economic Review,* December 1948.

———. "Economic Growth: An Econometric Approach." *American Economic Review, Papers and Proceedings,* May 1952.

Fellner, W. J. "The Capital Output Ratio in Dynamic Economics," in *Money, Trade, and Economic Growth* (in honor of J. H. Williams). New York: The Macmillan Co., 1951.

Hamberg, D. "Full Capacity vs. Full Employment Growth." *Quarterly Journal of Economics,* August 1952.

Harrod, R. F. "An Essay in Dynamic Theory." *Economic Journal,* March 1939.

Tobin, James. "Relative Income, Absolute Income, and Saving," in *Money, Trade, and Economic Growth* (in honor of J. H. Williams). New York: The Macmillan Co., 1951.

2. Further readings relating to topics discussed in Part 2:

Books

Aftalion, Albert. *Les Crises périodiques de surproduction.* 2 vols. Paris: M. Rivière & Cie, 1913 (particularly Bk. XI, Vol. II).

Marshall, Alfred. *Principles of Economics.* London: Macmillan & Co., 1920.

Mill, J. S. *Principles of Political Economy,* ed. by W. J. Ashley. London: Longmans, Green & Co., 1909 (particularly Bk. III, Ch. 12 and Bk. IV, Ch. 6).

Ricardo, David. *On the Principles of Political Economy and Taxation.* London: J. Murray, 1817.

Robertson, D. H. *A Study of Industrial Fluctuation.* London: London School of Economics and Political Science, 1948.

Say, J. B. *Letters to Thomas Robert Malthus on Political Economy and Stagnation of Commerce.* London: Sherwood, Neely & Jones, 1821.

Smith, Adam. *The Wealth of Nations,* ed. by Edwin Cannan. New York: Modern Library, 1937, (particularly Bk. II).

Wicksell, Knut. *Lectures on Political Economy.* 2 vols. London: G. Routledge & Co., 1935.

Articles

Alexander, S. S. "The Accelerator as a Generator of Steady Growth." *Quarterly Journal of Economics,* May 1949.

———. "Issues of Business Cycle Theory Raised by Mr. Hicks." *American Economic Review,* December 1951.

Baumol, W. J. "Notes on Some Dynamic Models." *Economic Journal,* December 1948.

Burns, A. F. "Hicks and the Real Cycle." *Journal of Political Economy,* February 1952.

Domar, E. D. "Capital Expansion, Rate of Growth, and Employment." *Econometrica,* April 1946.

Robinson, Joan. "Mr. Harrod's Dynamics." *Economic Journal,* March 1949.

Schelling, T. C. "Capital Growth and Equilibrium." *American Economic Review,* December 1947.

Tobin, James. "Asset Holdings and Spending Decisions." *American Economic Review, Papers and Proceedings,* May 1952.

Wright, D. M. "Mr. Harrod and Growth Economics." *Review of Economics and Statistics,* November 1949.

PART 3

Requirements of Uninterrupted Growth (Dynamic Equilibrium)

5

The General Price Level in Dynamic Equilibrium

The analysis of Part II led to the conclusion that in the event of budgetary balance, continuous or uninterrupted growth depends on the ability of an economic system to conduct its savings into planned investment at a reasonably stable general price level. This ability, in turn, depends (1) on the quantitative sufficiency and the qualitative adequacy of offsets to diminishing returns, (2) on the proper relationship between changes in the demand structure and the mobility of resources, and (3) on the proper functioning of the money and credit system. Here we define these three technological-institutional factors as the corollaries of the condition of continuous growth (or of dynamic equilibrium). But we shall begin with the condition itself rather than with its corollaries. The condition of dynamic equilibrium is composed of the requirement of reasonable general price stability (Chapter 5) and of the requirement that planned investment should equal savings (Chapter 6).

I. Dependence of the price-stability requirement on specific institutional arrangements.

In dynamic equilibrium, that is, on paths of uninterrupted growth, the behavior of the general price level would have to meet certain conditions. The nature of these conditions depends on law and customs because what matters here is not the price tendencies *per se*, but the reactions which they call forth. These reactions must not have the consequence of interrupting the growth process. It is impossible to state whether some specific behavior of the price level is compatible with continuous growth if we know nothing about the nature of payment contracts and of payment habits in an economy. However, enough is known about typical Western arrangements to justify the statement that in such an environment dynamic equilibrium requires a reasonably stable general price level. An appreciable degree of inflation[1] or of deflation[2] is incompatible with uninterrupted growth.

2. Appreciable inflation must be excluded: the money rate and the real interest rate.

The usefulness of money as a store of value for reasonable periods, and therefore its usefulness as a means of deferred payment (later payment on the basis of present agreements), would be destroyed if the price level kept rising at a substantial rate.[3] A complex economy cannot function in the long run without a monetary standard which performs reasonably well as a store of value and as a means of deferred payment. Unfitness to perform these two functions sooner or later destroys the usefulness of a currency as a medium of exchange, too.

To understand the nature of the inflation problem, it is necessary to realize that institutional arrangements can be *described* which would neutralize the consequences of violent inflation and would smoothly gear an economy to a rapidly rising price level. The character of these arrangements would have to be such that money itself would cease to be used as a store of value and the *claims* to money which would be used for this purpose would appreciate always in the right proportions. A description of such a model shows clearly enough that no economy would be capable of adopting its essential characteristics.

Let us assume that the general price level is known to be rising at a rate of 100 percent per year. Let us assume also that *with a stable price level* the "pure" rate of interest (the rate on safe securities with no risk of default) *would be 3 percent* in our economy. For the sake of simplicity, we shall disregard compounding during the year and also the problem of rate differentials between loans of different maturities: we shall interpret our assumption as meaning that the lender of $100 would, in

---

[1] By inflation, we shall mean in this volume an increase in the general price level.

[2] By deflation, we shall mean a fall in the general price level.

[3] If a medium cannot perform properly as a store of value, its usefulness as a means of deferred payment is also impaired. A person receiving deferred payment is "storing" a claim to the medium in question, and these claims can become suitable "stores" only if they appreciate or depreciate all the time just in the proportion required to offset the deficiencies of the medium itself as a store. This problem will be taken up presently in the text.

the event of stable prices, be repaid $103 after a year. Neutralizing the assumed degree of price inflation of 100 percent per year requires in such circumstances a rate of interest of 106 percent. The lender of $100 would have to be repaid $206 after a year to receive back the same number of commodity equivalents as he lent, plus 3 percent. In Irving Fisher's terminology, a money rate of interest (market rate) of 106 percent would here correspond to a *real interest rate* of 3 percent.[4] The real rate of interest, which in the event of price stability is identical with the money rate, expresses the goods, or rather equivalents of goods, which are repaid in addition to the repayment of the principal in such commodity equivalents. On our assumption, price inflation raises to 106 percent the money rate of interest which corresponds to a real rate of interest of 3 percent. If the money rate rose, say, to merely 50 percent per year, then the real rate would be a high negative percentage. In terms of goods, the lender would receive back considerably less than the principal. It is obvious that this would create serious distortion.

However, the "proper" interest rate (in this sense) is not in itself sufficient to neutralize the economic effects of the inflaion and thus to gear an economy smoothly to the inflationary process. This is because in the real world not all assets and claims earn interest for their owners. It would be necessary to provide for an entirely prompt and continuous revaluation of all numerically fixed money claims; and it would be necessary to exclude the use of banknotes and coins and to substitute for these check deposits, which would also have to earn interest[5] at a rate which compensates the owner for the depreciation of the currency. If these further requirements were not met, then a significant penalty would be imposed upon all persons whose money incomes and other money receipts were fixed prior to the date of payment, and even persons who avoided *this* penalty would suffer another penalty for not being able to spend their incomes or money receipts without a time lag. In other words, large groups of the population and essential economic activi-

---

[4] Irving Fisher, *The Theory of Interest* (New York, 1930) , Chs. 2 and 19.

[5] Under such arrangements, it would be desirable to treat check deposits as "claims" to money rather than as part of the money stock itself. These arrangements would accomplish the result that, instead of money itself, claims to money would be used as a store of value, and these claims would always appreciate in the right proportion. Hence, money as a standard of deferred payment would depreciate always in the right proportion, per time unit of deferment of the payment.

Under the actual institutional arrangements of Western economies, check deposits do not usually earn interest, and they are regarded as money rather than as claims to money.

ties would become penalized. Perhaps the simplest way of expressing the result is to say that a severe penalty would be imposed upon all persons whose net economic position is influenced mainly by the fact that they are claimants and holders of money, rather than debtors.

Needless to say, it is inconceivable that an economy should succeed in providing for prompt and continuous revaluation of money claims, and for the exclusion of hand-to-hand currency from common usage, as well as for the "correct" interest payments on check deposits. Money would still have to be used as a store of value and as a means of deferred payment, but it would perform these functions exceedingly badly. It is likely that at first the rate of price inflation would increase because various groups would obtain upward revisions (although incomplete ones) of their money claims and also because the attempt to get rid of money would increase the velocity of circulation of the monetary unit. Past experience with inflation shows that the process does tend to become cumulative for these reasons. Sooner or later, the process would have to collapse because of the inefficiency which it caused. If the monetary authority does not in time adopt measures to stop an inflation, the public will increasingly turn away from money and try to use instead of it some unit of measurement which, while very inefficient, is in the circumstances less deficient than the currency of the economy. Specific goods and foreign currencies have been used for this purpose in violently inflationary economies. At the end the inflation must be stopped either by monetary measures which prevent further price increases in terms of the old currency or by the introduction of an entirely new currency. Such a complicated sequence of events is not precisely predictable, and therefore even money loans in the usual sense do not command the "correct" interest rate in an inflationary period.

When a violent inflationary process comes to an end, economic contraction is practically inevitable. The penalty which inflation places upon liquid assets is equivalent to the relative subsidization of investment in physical assets. Removal of this subsidy is certain to result in abrupt reduction of investment activity, and it causes significant losses to previous investors. Only after a period of contraction and readjustment can economic growth start again.

Violent inflation is incompatible with dynamic equilibrium. This does not necessarily imply that a very mild increase in the general price level must lead to the interruption of the growth process. Nothing works perfectly, and it would be unreasonable to expect that money as a store of value and as a means of deferred payment should. It is impossible to describe numerically the limits of tolerance of the system to inflationary tendencies. The limits depend on the reactions of the public. They depend mainly on how small the rate of price inflation must stay in order not to induce the public to accelerate the initial rate considerably, by raising the velocity of circulation. To sufficiently small distortions practically no reaction will be forthcoming, especially if the direction of these distortions is unpredictable from one period to the next. It is even conceivable that creditors may accept a small penalty without reacting to it,— that is, without "fleeing" from money into real goods and thus accelerating the inflationary process—while debtors and investors become stimulated by a small subsidy. However, partly under the influence of groups with debtor interests, the limits of tolerance of the system to inflation are sometimes overestimated. This is true especially if we have a consistent (unbroken) inflationary movement in mind.

3. The sensitivity of the system to deflation.

The limits of tolerance to price deflation are narrow indeed. Let us assume again that with a stable general price level we have a 3-percent money rate of interest on perfectly safe loans (on loans with no risk of default) and therefore also a 3-percent real rate of interest. Price reduction at a yearly rate of 3 percent or more makes it impossible to prevent the real rate—the rate in terms of commodity equivalents—from rising beyond 3 percent, and from thus exerting an adverse influence on investment activity. For with price deflation proceeding at a yearly rate of 3 percent, a zero money rate would correspond to a real rate of 3 percent, and any positive money rate would raise the real rate beyond this level. It is impossible to establish a negative money rate of interest, or even a zero rate, unless holding of currency and of check deposits is taxed at a definite rate per period of time. No one will lend money at an appreciable cost to himself (at a negative money rate), if cash or deposits can be held free of cost, or at a negligible cost of storage. Considering that the inconvenience and the institutional costs of loan transactions, small as they may be, exceed those of keeping bank deposits or of holding cash, the lowest level of the money rate at which loans are forthcoming must be at least slightly higher than zero. This would not be true—the money rate could become negative—if cash holdings as well as deposits could be subjected to a tax per period, that is, if cash gradually lost its value. But taxation of this sort seems impracticable. Disregarding the theoretical possibility of a tax on cash, we may conclude that general price deflation at a yearly rate of 3 percent *necessarily raises the real rate of interest beyond 3 percent.* If, with a stable price level, smooth growth of the economy required a money (and real) rate of 3 percent, the deflationary process here assumed could not help but distort economic relations by raising the real rate of interest and thereby discouraging investment. Generally speaking, if the real rate of interest must not rise beyond x percent, then the rate of decline of the general price level must be *less* than x percent.

On the same assumption concerning the real rate required for smooth growth (3 percent), the system could, in principle, stand a continuous price decline of, say, only 2 percent per year; and it could, in principle, stand price deflation at the rate of 3 percent or more if the real interest rate compatible with smooth growth were correspondingly higher than 3 percent. The nominal rate would, of course, have to be lower than the required real rate, but it could stay positive. However, while this *is* possible in principle and conceivably also in practice, the political and social institutions of most advanced Western nations are not particularly well suited to maintaining growth trends at falling prices, even if the rate of price decline were somewhat smaller than the required real rate of interest.

For example, we *can* describe an economy in which money rates on safe loans of various maturities are, say, between 0 percent and 1 percent; in which price deflation proceeds at a yearly rate of 2 percent; and in which the real rate of almost 3 percent, which corresponds to these assumptions, is theoretically "just right" (in the sense of creating equilibrium between planned investment and savings). However, in most advanced economies the difficulty would arise here that even in such a very mildly deflationary economy the long-run distribution of the fruits of progress would be different from what corresponds to the internal distribution of influence and power.

Under mild deflation owners of cash and of check deposits would automatically receive a share in the rising output, since the real value of their money assets would be continuously rising. These potential beneficiaries are usually politically weak groups. In the contemporary Western scene they are weaker than the entrepreneurial groups with mainly physical assets (rather than money claims), and weaker also than labor unions. Under the mild deflation now considered, owners of physical assets would have to share in the productivity gains with owners of money claims. Wage earners, it is true, would receive real-wage increases, but they would receive these through the continuous rise in productivity in the form of falling prices and not in that of rising money wages. In these circumstances, it could not easily be claimed that the leadership of unions had accomplished the rise in real-wage rates. When prices stay stable, wage earners obtain their share in rising productivity in the form of a gradual rise in money wages, such as corresponds more or less to the gradual increase in output per man-hour. This leaves room for a type of bargaining activity from which established institutions would not readily withdraw.

We may now summarize. Even a rate of price deflation which is not very radical (say, 5 percent *per annum*) must bring an interruption of the growth process, if the deflationary process is continuous and predictable. The *real* rate of interest on "safe" loans inevitably exceeds the yearly rate of price deflation, and a real rate of more than 5 percent is very rarely compatible with smooth growth. If, for a short period, such a high real rate should accidentally prove to be in accordance with the rise in real productivity, and hence should not interrupt the growth process, we may safely infer that an interruption would soon take place. Indeed, it is reasonable to assume that a 3-percent yearly rate of price deflation is too high because in Western economies the growth process rarely permits of a real rate structure which exceeds this level for the safest loans of short-term variety. Furthermore, even the attempt to gear the economy to a milder deflationary trend (say 2 percent per year) would raise difficulties, if only difficulties of an institutional sort which would spring from the effect of such a trend on the distribution of the fruits of progress. The limits of tolerance of the growth process to deflation are exceedingly narrow. The limits of tolerance to inflation are also likely to be narrow. But it might be less convincing to argue with a claim to near generality that an increase in the price level at a yearly average rate of, say, 2 percent *must* in the long run prove incompatible with dynamic equilibrium (or that such a rate would *necessarily* have to become accelerated by secondary reactions of a velocity-rising kind).

4. Direct controls.

Rationing and price control will receive no systematic treatment in our analysis of the growth process in private enterprise economies. However, we may add a suggestion here. It is preferable to conclude that the prevention of an inflationary process with the aid of such controls does not genuinely satisfy the condition of reasonable stability of the general price level. In a private enterprise economy controls of this sort are never fully effective: they inevitably result in processes which are the equivalents of inflation. Quality deterioration and the disappearance from the market of specific commodities are examples, quite aside from black markets. Furthermore, in the type of economy which we are considering, controls of this sort are always temporary, and a delayed inflationary movement is predictable for the period in which the controls are abolished. Suppressed inflation—that is, inflation the consequences of which are suppressed by price control and rationing—is sometimes preferable to open inflation, but it should not be regarded as compatible with the concept of dynamic equilibrium.

5. Alternative quantity equations.

The price-stability requirement can be formulated in terms of the money supply needed for uninterrupted growth. Let us designate by M the existing quantity of "money," defined as hand-to-hand currency plus check deposits, excluding currency in bank vaults and excluding the deposits of banks in other banks;[6] let us designate by V the transactions velocity of money, that is, the average number of times money changes hands during a period, against goods and services whose prices are included in the "general price level"; by P the general price level itself; and by T the physical volume of goods and services for which payment is made during the period; then it follows that $MV = PT$. In dynamic equilibrium, the rate of increase of MV must not be very different from that of T. If the velocity of circulation of money always remained unchanged, the quantity of money would have to increase in about the same proportion as the goods and services which change hands. However, the velocity of circulation of money is not a constant, and hence it is not M but the product of M and V (the magnitude MV) which must keep pace with T. Alternatively expressed, M must keep pace with T/V; that is, with T when correction is made for changes in the transactions velocity of money. A footnote below contains some numerical information concerning the terms here defined and also concerning the income velocity of the dollar.[7]

---

[6] By excluding interbank deposits, we exclude also the reserve balances of commercial banks in the central bank.

[7] At present, the supply of money (M), in the sense here defined, is about $130

Quantity equations can be formulated in several ways.[8] They are valid in many alternative forms. We shall not review this subject here, but shall merely add that it is always possible to substitute for a velocity-of-money concept its reciprocal, namely, the concept of a *liquidity ratio,*

---

billion in the United States. Of this amount, $100 billion consists of check deposits (demand deposits) in the commercial banks. In addition to the currency and check deposits included in the $130 billion, we have about $70 billion of time deposits which, not being *directly* used as means of payment, are usually considered promises to pay money (claims to money) rather than money. We have no precise numerical information concerning V, but we know that the average annual rate of turnover of check deposits is at present in the neighborhood of 35 in the city of New York, and somewhere between 20 and 25 in American banks outside New York. This turnover comprises, however, a larger volume of money payments than that which buys the "goods and services" whose price is included in the P term of the quantity equations. It includes, for example, wage payments, tax payments, dividend payments, security purchases, intrafirm transfers. On the basis of recent money-flow estimates it would seem a good guess that V is less than ten per year in the United States.

The *income velocity* of money (Vy) is much smaller than its *transaction velocity* (V), that is, much smaller than the V term in $MV = PT$. The income velocity is defined as the number of times money gives rise to net income per period. In other words, it is defined as the factor by which M must be multiplied to yield the aggregate net income of an economy. This factor (Vy) is much smaller than V. At present in the United States, it is approximately 2.5 per year. MV includes many duplicating transactions (such as wheat purchases plus flour purchases plus purchases of bakery products, etc.), while the net aggregate output or income $(M \cdot Vy)$ is the equivalent merely of the *values added* in each stage.

[8] Clark Warburton, in "Elementary Algebra and the Equation of Exchange," *American Economic Review* (June 1953), pp. 358-361, has pointed out that on the righthand side of the quantity equation $MV = PT$ we have to watch an index-number problem. We want to measure P and T in such a way that a changed P mulitplied by a changed T should give us a correct expression for the change in PT (which must equal the change in MV when the latter is converted into index numbers). Say we are concerned with the comparison of year one with year zero. From the change in P and the change in T we want to obtain $\frac{\Sigma\, p_1 t_1}{\Sigma\, p_0 t_0}$, where the p and the t terms relate to individual prices and volumes of transactions, and the subscripts to periods. Our objective *cannot* be accomplished by weighing the individual prices according to the transactions of year zero, and the individual transactions according to the prices of period zero. For

$$\frac{\Sigma\, p_1 t_0}{\Sigma\, p_0 t_0} \cdot \frac{\Sigma\, t_1 p_0}{\Sigma\, t_0 p_0}$$

is *not* the same as

$$\frac{\Sigma\, p_1 t_1}{\Sigma\, p_0 t_0}$$

Nor would it help to weigh both prices and transactions by weights of period one. However, it is well known that Irving Fisher's ideal index number solves this problem. A simpler way of getting around the difficulty is to weigh the p terms by weights of year one and the t terms by weights of year zero, or *vice versa*. For

$$\frac{\Sigma\, p_1 t_1}{\Sigma\, p_0 t_1} \cdot \frac{\Sigma\, t_1 p_0}{\Sigma\, t_0 p_0} = \frac{\Sigma\, p_1 t_1}{\Sigma\, p_0 t_0};$$

also

$$\frac{\Sigma\, p_1 t_0}{\Sigma\, p_0 t_0} \cdot \frac{\Sigma\, t_1 p_1}{\Sigma\, t_0 p_1} = \frac{\Sigma\, p_1 t_1}{\Sigma\, p_0 t_0}.$$

defined as the amount of money held per unit of transactions. For example, if in the foregoing equation $V = 10$ per year, then the quantity of money held, on the average, per unit of yearly money expenditures (or money receipts) is $1/10$. On the average, one tenth the magnitude designated as PT is held as money during the period. If the money stock per unit of expenditures (or of receipts) is designated as k, then we may write $M = kPT$. This must be true, since $k = 1/V$. In terms of this equation, we may conclude that in dynamic equilibrium M should rise in about the same proportion as kT; that is, in about the same proportion as T, when correction is made for changes in liquidity ratios. This, of course, is no different from saying that M must keep pace with T/V.

6. The ability of the monetary authority to change the supply of money.

The central bank, in the United States the Federal Reserve, can increase the supply of money by purchasing assets from the public. These assets may consist of securities[9] or of monetary metals. To a practically negligible extent the central bank also acquires goods and services, for example, the services of its employees. All these transactions place "money" (check deposits or currency) in the hands of the public. At the same time, these transactions have a tendency to increase the lending potential of the commercial banks because, for each dollar which the central bank pays into a commercial bank for the account of a person or institution, the commercial bank increases its reserve balance in the central bank by fully one dollar. Commercial banks acquire a 100-percent reserve on such payments, and neither law nor custom requires that they should maintain such a high reserve ratio. If the commercial banks make use of the additional lending potential, there is a further increase in the supply of money. Increased lending by banks expresses itself in more deposits in the banks, and check deposits are definitionally included in the supply of money. The commercial banks create money by making loans and by buying securities. It is a misconception to believe that they simply "lend out" money that was initially deposited with them.

The central bank can also increase the supply of money by purchasing government securities directly or indirectly from the treasury. Thereby it places new money in the hands of the public via the treasury, unless the

---

[9] In the United States this means in practice government securities, at present exclusively short-term ones.

treasury fails to engage in new expenditures to the extent of its borrowings.

The central bank can, of course, also increase the lending potential (check-deposit-creating potential) of the commercial banks by acquiring assets directly from them.[10] Thereby it can increase the reserve balances of the commercial banks in the central bank. In the United States the lending potential of the commercial banks can frequently be increased also by a reduction of the legal reserve requirement, that is, by reducing the size of the reserve balances which the commercial banks must maintain, in the central bank, per dollars of deposits held by the public in the commercial banks. However, the size of the reserve balances which the commercial banks actually hold in the central bank, per unit of deposits, depends only in part on legal requirements. Indeed, in some countries, including Britain, the actual reserve ratio is entirely determined by custom and by the judgment of commercial banks. But at any rate the reserve position or lending potential of the commercial banks depends on the amount with which they have been credited in the central bank, and this amount depends primarily on the asset acquisitions of the central bank.

To each of these activities of the central bank, there corresponds a reverse activity by which the supply of money is contracted. For example, by selling securities to the public or to the commercial banks, the central bank can lower the supply of money and/or reduce the lending potential of the commercial banks. The second of these two objectives can also be accomplished by raising reserve requirements (except, of course, in countries where no legal requirements exist).

7. Limits of the control over M.

In a highly developed economy, most of the "money" consists of check deposits in the commercial banks. In the United States at present, about $100 billion out of a total money supply of $130 billion consist of such deposits in the commercial banks.[11] These deposits come into existence when the commercial bank credits one of its customers with the corresponding amount. But, as we have seen, this does not mean that the influ-

---

[10] In the United States (and probably practically everywhere) this means one of three things. The central bank may buy government securities which were previously held by the commercial banks; it may make advances to the commercial banks, *i.e.*, give them direct short-term credit, usually with government securities serving as collaterals; or it may rediscount commercial paper which is in the portfolio of a commercial bank.

[11] The remainder consists of hand-to-hand currency.

ence of the *central bank* on the money supply is almost wholly indirect. The influence of the central bank is not exerted exclusively by raising or lowering the lending potential of the commercial banks. The central bank can directly increase or diminish the volume of the deposits of the public in the commercial banks by buying securities and monetary metals from customers of the commercial banks or by selling to these customers (and the customers include the treasury).[12] Nevertheless, a large part of the influence of the central bank, in the United States of the Federal Reserve Banks, is exerted indirectly through changing the lending potential of the commercial banks.

Central banks would be in full control of the supply of money were it not for certain legal or conventional limitations. At present, these limitations are very mild.[13]

The limitations of the control over the supply of money were much more severe in the heyday of the international gold standard. Indeed, for a while in England the economic philosophy of *laisser faire* was interpreted as implying that the supply of means of payment in general should be made to rise and to fall mechanically with the monetary gold stock. At the time when the Peel Act was passed (1844), a qualified and not very articulate variant of this "principle" became adopted. According to the Peel Act, the *issue department* of the Bank of England was obligated to maintain 100-percent gold backing for each pound note issued,[14] but the *banking department* of the Bank of England (which could obtain pound notes only from the issue department against gold) could buy and sell securities and could make advances in the market without maintaining a 100-percent bank note reserve against its obligations. In other words, the reserve ratio of the banking department was

---

[12] For the Treasury maintains balances in the commercial banks as well as in the Federal Reserve.

[13] In the United States, for example, there exists a fractional gold-backing requirement, but the American gold stock is exceedingly large. Also, the Federal Reserve Board can change the reserve requirements for the commercial banks only within stated limits (but the Federal Reserve is subject to no significant limitation in influencing through the purchase and sale of assets, the total size of the reserve balances held by the commercial banks). However, *de facto* the Federal Reserve must try to avoid disorganizing the market for government securities, and this does set limits to anti-inflationary (money-contracting) action such as would require that the central bank should sell government securities on a major scale within a short period (or should not support the market when others are selling on a major scale). In such cases, compromises are likely to be made. For these reasons, it is more appropriate to say that at present the limitations of Federal Reserve control over the supply of money are relatively mild than that the Federal Reserve is in full control of the money supply.

[14] Except for an amount which was *fixed by the law* and which was backed by government securities.

allowed to vary. Thus the banking department of the Bank of England was free to let the other banking companies of England have a greater or a smaller amount of reserve balance[15] for credit creation and for the creation of check deposits *by them.* This meant that in good times the banking department of the Bank of England could accumulate cash reserves and that it could use these for alleviating panics by granting credits in times of crisis.[16] Fortunately, therefore, the Peel Act did not fully put into effect the "principle" that the supply of means of payment should be made to rise and to fall mechanically with the monetary gold stock.

It is true not only of England but of the nineteenth-century gold standard world in general that deliberate anti-inflationary and anti-deflationary regulation of the supply of money (*M*) could be practiced in a moderate degree. But the limitations were severe. As a consequence of gold-backing requirements,[17] sustained and appreciable changes in the supply of money could not usually take place unless there was an appreciable change in the quantity of gold available, and the price levels of individual countries could not be allowed to get too much out of gear with one another. This was the cost of maintaining institutionally stabilized exchange rates among the various currencies, and of thus creating an environment conducive to international capital movements. Also, the system had the advantage of never leading to severe price inflation; there was not enough gold for that.[18] On the other hand, the system occasionally made is difficult to counteract deflationary pressures. But on the whole the long-run upward trend in Western economic activity was very vigorous during the period in question. Prior to the eighteen-seventies, in most countries (but not in England)[19] the restraining influence

---

[15] A greater or a smaller amount of deposits in the Bank of England.

[16] The banking department, too, needed, of course, reasonable reserves against its obligations, even though there existed no legal reserve requirement. After the eighteen-sixties, it did have enough extra reserves to alleviate stringencies in times of crisis. But in 1847, 1857 and 1866 the Peel Act had to be suspended to make sure that the banking department could borrow from the issue department. See the discussion of these crises in Chapter 3.

[17] In general, these were requirements prescribing fractional gold reserves against the note issue (not a 100-percent reserve). Ususally, the central bank was obligated to redeem its bank notes in gold coin on demand.

[18] Severe inflation, such as that in England during the Napoleonic Wars and in the United States during the Civil War, always required that the country in question should temporarily abandon its metallic currency and should use inconvertible paper money.

[19] When, a few years after the Napoleonic Wars, sterling again became convertible, England adopted the gold standard instead of returning to bimetallism. By the 'seventies most of the Western world was on gold.

of the metallic currency system was tempered by bimetallism, which led to the substitution of silver for gold as a monetary metal whenever gold became sufficiently scarce relatively to silver.[20]

The period of the international gold standard came to an end with World War I, although there occurred a brief and rather unsatisfactory revival of modified gold standard arrangements during the nineteen-twenties (see Page 88). At present, the central banks of individual nations are much freer to regulate the supply of money as they see fit. The M term in the quantity equations is much more under control. The constraints created by flexible international agreements and, in some countries, by domestic legislation, are mild (see Page 97, also Footnote 13, Page 178). The fear of deflation and of unemployment is sufficiently great to suggest that in the changed circumstances the management of the money supply and of fiscal affairs will be such as to tilt price trends upward, although reasonable governments should find it possible to prevent a chronic and significant upward pressure on the price level.

8. V (or k) is not under control.

Control of the central bank over M does not necessarily assure ability to regulate the money supply in such a way that M should precisely keep pace with T/V or with kT, thus leaving the general price level unchanged.

V (or k) depends on two sets of circumstances.[21] Part of the money stock consists of *active balances (or working balances)*. These are being

---

[20] Under a bimetallic currency the mint is obligated to supply a gold coin of given nominal value (a dollar, or a franc) for a specified quantity of gold, and it is obligated, also, to supply a silver coin of the identical nominal value (a dollar, or a franc) for a different, but also specified quantity of silver. Implicit in this is a fixed mint ratio, that is a specific value-ratio of gold to silver. But in the market the ratio does not usually stay fixed for long. If, in the market, one of the two metals becomes scarce enough, relatively to the other, and if its market price rises sufficiently, relatively to that of the other, then the other metal will replace the scarce one as a monetary metal because it becomes profitable to melt down the coins made out of the scarce metal and to buy *in the free market* that quantity of the abundant metal for which the mint supplies a coin of the same nominal value. This tendency of "good money" to be displaced by "bad money" is known as Gresham's Law because it was commented upon by Sir Thomas Gresham, financial agent of Queen Elizabeth I.

[21] See J. W. Angell, "The Components of the Circular Velocity of Money," *Quarterly Journal of Economics* (February 1937), pp. 224-273. H. S. Ellis, "Some Fundamentals in the Theory of Velocity," *Quarterly Journal of Economics* (May 1938), pp. 431-472, reprinted in American Economic Association, *Readings in Monetary Theory* (Philadelphia, 1951), pp. 89-128.

held because, for each spending unit in the economy, there exist differences between the time shape of the receipts and the time shape of the expenditures of a period, and because it is not profitable to invest money for very short periods. Hence "inventories" of active money are maintained. In the quantity equations, the k factor, by which the transactions of a period (PT) must be multiplied to obtain the money balances held, reflects *in part* a demand for active money or working balances. Consequently, other things being equal, k will be greater or smaller depending on whether a greater or a smaller time interval elapses between the receipts of individual spending units and the regular expenditures for which the active money is held. The length of these intervals —the extent of this nonsynchronization, so to speak—depends on technological lags and on payment habits (payment lags or "terms of payment").

However, the public holds money also as a general liquidity reserve without definite ideas about when and how this money will be spent. These are *idle balances or hoards;* if their size increases relatively to the transaction of a period, then, too, the k factor in the quantity equations rises (the V factor falls). For k in the quantity equations measures the sum of the active money and the idle money which is being held per unit of the value of transactions; and V in the quantity equations is the reciprocal of this k.

The demand for idle balances depends in part on the total size of assets (old and current accumulations) in the economy, since, other things equal, a wealthier public presumably desires to hold more money as well as more physical asset and claims to physical assets. But the demand for idle balances also depends importantly on how attractive the alternative forms of holding assets are, or, more specifically, on how attractive it is to invest at any time.

In certain circumstances, the central bank may find it impossible to regulate M in such a way as to avoid an offsetting change in V or in k. This means that the central bank may find it impossible to change MV or M/k, or, differently expressed, to keep M in line with kT or with T/V. Assume, for example, that past investments now lead to an increase in output (and hence in T) and that the monetary authority would like to raise M correspondingly, with an allowance for possible changes in V. In other words, M should be raised in the same proportion as kT or as T/V, so that P should stay unchanged. But assume that all the additional money which the central bank might provide, or all of it beyond a fixed amount, goes immediately into idle balances.[22] Then it is impossible to raise MV in the same proportion as T (or M in the same proportion as kT or as T/V) because k *is getting increased and* V *is getting lowered pari passu with the increase in* M. For analogous reasons, limiting the quantity of money does not accomplish its anti-inflationary objectives if the public starts spending the remaining money stock at a correspondingly more rapid rate.

The important conclusion emerges that we cannot describe the conditions of dynamic equilibrium simply by requiring that the "correct" quantity of money should be supplied in each period. Dynamic equilibrium depends on whether the available money is spent for goods and services at a rate consistent with continuous growth, that is to say, whether an ever-increasing quantity of goods and services is acquired at a reasonably stable general price level. In the next Chapter we shall therefore turn to an examination of the factors determining the willingness of the public to acquire goods and services for consumption and investment. Continuous growth requires that this demand should be rising at the proper rate, provided that the supply of money is being increased at a rate which keeps the general price level reasonably stable. This is essentially a *joint condition* or a double requirement. It implies that the spending propensities of the public must be such that methods of regulating the money supply should *exist* by which MV is kept in line with T. The requirement implies also that, given the possibility of so regulating the money supply, this supply must actually be so regulated. For, if it is not so regulated, then growth will either not materialize at all, or it will materialize in violently inflationary circumstances which preclude continuity of the process. In our terminology the proper spending propensities of the public as well as the proper regulation of M are incorporated in the *condition* of dynamic equilibrium. The technological and institutional requisites of satisfying the condition of dynamic equilibrium will later be called the "corollaries" of the condition.

From the price-stability condition we now turn to the other half of the joint condition of dynamic equilibrium, namely to the condition of proper spending propensities. There are propensities to invest as well as to consume. They express themselves in the relationship between savings and planned investment.

---

[22] This cannot happen if the government borrows the money with the purpose of spending it.

6

Savings and Investment in Dynamic Equilibrium

1. Introductory statement of the condition.

Uninterrupted growth or dynamic equilibrium requires that individuals and private institutions should in each period *desire* to hold (own) those additions to the physical capital stock which actually come into existence. In a continuously growing economy the size of the capital stock is, of course, always smaller than the size toward which investors are working with future requirements in mind. This is merely a way of saying that net investment takes place continuously in such an economy. But uninterrupted growth requires that the ever-existing gap between the actual size of the stock and that size toward which private investors are working should stay "normal," in the sense that no efforts should be made to bring about an abrupt change in the size of this continuously existing gap. This is what we mean by the statement that in dynamic equilibrium the actual net private capital formation would all the time have to equal the desired net private capital formation. If actual and desired new capital formation are always equal, than the gap between the actual size of the privately owned stock and the size toward which investors are working with future requirements in mind always stays a "normal" gap to which investors have become used and which they do not attempt to change.

We distinguish between the private sector of the economy and the government sector because the private sector is motivated by individual utility and by profitability in the accounting sense, while the motivation underlying the activities of governments is different.

If, in a period, the private sector acquires *more* additional physical capital than what it desires to add to the existing capital stock during that period, the consequences of overstocking will show. These are incompatible with uninterrupted growth.[1]

Assume now that in some period the private sector acquires *less* than the desired addition to the capital stock, in the sense that for the subsequent period an appreciably greater further addition will be desired than would otherwise be the case. Investors start the next period with an undesirable "backlog" rather than with what they consider the normal current need for additions during that period. Therefore, new investment will rise to a level from which sooner or later it will have to shrink abruptly. Actual accumulations may or may not catch up with desired accumulations within a reasonable span, that is to say, investors may or may not succeed in eliminating the abnormal and undesirable "backlog." If they do eliminate it, part of the former investment demand ceases, and this is very likely to bring a sudden shrinkage of new investment; if they do not, then the continued attempt to make up will sooner or later create bottlenecks and an inflationary situation.

Here again, there exist margins of tolerance, but we need not speak of them explicitly because the concept of "desiring" to add a given quantity to the stock already includes a margin of tolerance: individuals and corporations do not "desire" to add some precise magnitude to their stock of physical capital. In each period they "desire" to add capital falling within some range. We need not therefore modify the statement that dynamic equilibrium requires equality of the actual net private capital formation (net private investment) with the desired rate of addition to the stock. By this we mean that, on the one hand, there must develop no tendency to reduce the capital stock because of *overstocking* and that on the other hand, there must not develop a *shortage* of such size as would create an abnormal or nonsustainable relation between the desired and the existing physical capital.

Our condition is expressed in terms of aggregative magnitudes for the economy as a whole, without regard to the relationship between different

---

[1] It is conceivable that *at first* there will be no desire to reduce the stock but merely a reduced desire to add further increments to the stock. Even this effect is usually incompatible with uninterrupted growth, unless the effect is small. Significant, abrupt changes in the rate of further new investment could become compatible with continuous growth only if they happen to coincide with abrupt changes in savings, and if the mobility of all resources were very great (so that the resources could be shifted rapidly from the investment goods industries to the consumer goods industries).

sectors of the economy. But we shall see later that the aggregative condition cannot stay satisfied unless the shifts in the sector-to-sector relations in the economy are reasonably gradual. This, in turn, implies that changes in the rate of growth must also be gradual.

2. Linking the condition to an accounting identity.

We have concluded that in dynamic equilibrium the actual net private capital formation, that is, the actual additions to the privately owned capital stock, must equal the desired additions to that stock. We shall now refer to an accounting identity which, by definition, must always be satisfied when the budget of the government is balanced. The possibility that the government may deliberately unbalance the budget even in a condition of continuous growth will be considered in Part V of this volume. Until then, we shall not complicate the discussion of dynamic equilibrium with the problem of budgetary imbalance. In the past record of Western economies the long-run growth tendency has not typically resulted from fiscal-policy techniques which would have created appreciable imbalance on normal growth paths. On the assumption of budgetary balance our accounting identity must always be satisfied, regardless of whether the system is or is not in dynamic equilibrium.

The accounting identity, to which we now turn, says that actual net private capital formation must always equal net savings when the government budget is balanced.[2] The reason for this is that, in the event of

---

[2] By budgetary balance, we must mean here one of two things. We must mean either that tax revenues equal government expenditures on goods and services, or that tax revenues equal government expenditures on goods and services *plus government transfer payments*. We must mean the first if we include in our concept of "income" merely the value of the current output and *not* also the government transfer payments (such as veterans' benefits, unemployment benefits, interest on public debt, etc.), so that the nonconsumed portion of these transfers does not show as "savings" and the consumed portion does show as "dissavings"; we must mean the second if, in addition to the value of the current output, the government transfer payments *are* included in our "income concept," and hence the nonconsumed portion of these transfers shows as "savings" and the consumed portion does not show as "dissavings."

The proof is as follows. Let us first adopt the first of the two courses (*i.e.,* income = output). Then, since

net income = consumption + net savings + tax payments......................(1)

and at the same time

net output = consumption + net additions to the private capital stock + government expenditures on currently produced goods and services..................(2)

we may conclude that net savings will always equal net additions to the private capital stock, provided that tax revenues equal government expenditures on currently produced goods and services. If the government also buys old physical assets, these must be deducted from private capital formation. *(Continued on page 186)*

budgetary balance, the aggregate savings of any accounting period (*i.e.,* the non-consumed part of the aggregate income after taxes) must have a precise equivalent in such output as has remained on stock; and that part of the net output which has remained on stock is defined as net capital formation. In view of this accounting identity, we may rewrite the dynamic-equilibrium requirement of the preceding Section of this Chapter, and we may obtain a more useful formulation of the requirement. According to the preceding Section, dynamic equilibrium requires the equality of desired additions to the privately owned capital stock with actual additions to that stock. We now know that actual additions always equal net savings; hence, in dynamic equilibrium, desired or planned additions to the privately owned stock must equal net savings. This is true aside from the possibility of unbalanced budgets in dynamic equilibrium, a possibility to which we shall return in Part 5.

3. The scope of private capital formation.

The following are always considered constituent parts of the net private capital formation of a period: additions to the stock of privately owned residential buildings (new residential construction); additions to the stock of business building (new business construction); additions to the stock of privately owned machinery and equipment (new durable producer goods); additions to the stock of privately owned business inventories and to stocks of unfinished goods in the "pipelines"; additions to private claims against foreign countries (the net export surplus on private account). The last of these items must be included because it, too, represents an increment of the privately owned wealth. Alternatively expressed, the

---

If we now switch to the alternative (and more frequently used) income concept, which includes transfer payments, then each of our two equations remains valid, but the sum in Equation 1 will exceed the sum in Equation 2 by the government transfer payments. Consequently, the accounting identity of net savings with net additions to the privately owned capital stock will now presuppose "budgetary balance" in the sense of equality of tax revenues with government expenditures on goods and services *plus government transfer payments.*

These explanations, and our analysis of dynamic equilibrium in general, imply the conceptual framework used by the U. S. Department of Commerce. The Kuznets framework, on the other hand, not merely postulates identity of aggregate income with aggregate output, but it also involves allocating taxes, as well as government expenditures, partly to consumption and partly to capital formation. If this framework were used, aggregate net savings would always be identical in magnitude with aggregate net capital formation (private plus public), regardless of budgetary balance or imbalance. But here we are using concepts such as those of the Department of Commerce. These result in an accounting identity between aggregate net savings and aggregate net *private* capital formation, on the assumption of budgetary balance.

For a more detailed treatment, see Appendix to Part 2.

net export surplus represents part of the current output whenever the exports do not result in an offsetting negative item (deduction) under the heading of inventory reduction. Consequently, the net export surplus must be included in capital formation, which, in conjunction with consumption and the government purchase, must account for the entire current output.

The items so far considered are always interpreted as constituents of net capital formation or investment. The logic of the matter would call for including also the additions to stocks in the possession of households. However, it is not usual to include the additions to these stocks. If the additions to consumer stocks were included, we would have to interpret as investment the acquisition of a new automobile by a consumer. We would have to look upon the consumer in question as saving and investing the amount for which he bought the automobile. It would be difficult to indicate where one should stop applying this principle, because similar considerations would favor treating new furniture or even shoes as investment. Consumption would then consist of the *using up* of these stocks, and the rate of depreciation per period would measure the rate of consumption. On the other hand, if we exclude from investment the additions to consumer stocks, we are implying that a commodity becomes "consumed" as soon as it *reaches* the consumer. This is what we usually do imply.

There are two reasons why we exclude from private capital formation the additions to consumer stocks. One reason is that the motivation which underlies the acquisition of durable or semidurable consumer goods is different from the motivation underlying the acquisition of producer goods. A firm acquires producer goods with a view to selling a product in a market. This is not true of consumer goods, and consequently the determinants of one type of acquisition are different from those of the other type. Secondly, it is difficult to obtain even approximate data on household inventories in general, and on their rate of depreciation. For producer stocks, there at least exist accounting data, but even these are unavailable for consumer stocks. The two reasons which lead us usually to exclude consumer stocks are obviously interrelated; they stem from the absence of a truly businesslike attitude with respect to these stocks. These reasons apply to residential buildings in a smaller degree than to other goods in the possession of consumers. Consequently, new residential construction is included in capital formation, even though other additions to "consumer stocks" are not.

The capital to which additions are made when investment is undertaken is a stock. By this we mean that capital exists at a *moment* of time. It can be measured without reference to a period of time. On the other hand, magnitudes such as output, consumption, new capital formation, are flows. They are measured per *period* of time, and their size depends on whether we choose to define them per day, month, year, or decade.

4. The meaning of discrepancies between planned investment and savings.

In the event of a balanced budget actual net capital formation always equals net savings. This is true regardless of whether the economy is or is not in dynamic equilibrium. But desired or planned net capital formation may be different from net savings. This is because some of the capital formation may be unplanned or undesired, as is the case when the conditions of dynamic equilibrium are not satisfied.

In dynamic equilibrium only those additions to the privately owned stock would materialize which investors had planned at the time of their investment decisions. If the additions that acutally materialize exceed those which have been planned *at the time of the investment decisions,* then this must be because business inventories turn out to be greater (the demand for goods smaller) than has been expected. In this event it will usually be true *also at the time of the completion of the investments,* that the actual additions to the stock exceed the desired. Attempts will now be made to reduce the capital stock, or at least the desired capital formation of the next period will become smaller.[3] If, on the other hand, the additions that actually materialize fall short of those which were planned *when the investment decisions were made,* then this must be because business inventories turn out to be smaller (the demand for goods greater) than has been expected, and/or because resource shortages cause delays in the delivery of new equipment. In this event, it will usually be true *also at the time of the completion of the investments,* that the actual additions to the stock fall short of the desired, in the sense that investors move into the next period with what they consider an abnormal backlog. They will try to eliminate the backlog.

This is subject to the qualification that, between the planning and the completion of additions, there might occur an abrupt change in desired additions. Such changes do occur in the neighborhood of cyclical turn-

---

3 See Footnote 1, Page 184.

ing points. In these neighborhoods the desired capital formation changes so abruptly that an excess of the formerly planned capital formation over the "now" realized turns into an excess of the "now" realized capital formation over the *"now" desired,*[4] or that an excess of the "now" realized capital formation over the formerly planned turns into an excess of the *"now" desired* capital formation over the "now" realized. Business-cycle theory points to good reasons for believing than an inequality between actual and desired additions will at those critical junctures not be changed into equality. It will be changed into inequality in the opposite direction. The reason for this can only be briefly suggested here.

If, in advanced stages of expansion, shortages or the anti-inflationary action of the monetary authority make it impossible to bring actual capital formation to the desired level, then sooner or later the growth process will be interrupted by contraction; once this has happened, the desired stock will become smaller even than the existing stock. This is how the discrepancy between desired and actual capital formation changes its direction (its algebraic sign) at the upper turning point or downturn. The change at the lower turning point or upturn is analogous. If, as a consequence of demand insufficiencies, the actual stock exceeds the desired, then disinvestment (shrinkage of the stock) and the fall in output will sooner or later create a situation where more stock is desired than the available. We shall see in Part IV how business-cycle theory explains these processes of overshooting.

Here it is sufficient to say that a discrepancy between actual additions to the stock and *initially planned* additions produces a discrepancy also between actual additions and the additions which are *desired at the time of completing the new investments.* For some time the two discrepancies move in the same direction and reinforce each other; in turning-point neighborhoods the two discrepancies are typically in the opposite direction because in turning-point neighborhoods a sharp change in desired additions occurs, and this reverses the direction of the discrepancy between actual additions and desired ones. What matters here is that a discrepancy between actual additions to capital and initially planned additions is incompatible with dynamic equilibrium. Such discrepancies result because the aggregate demand for output may fall short of the available output, or may exceed it, and thus more addition or less addition to the stock materializes than has been planned.

---

[4] "Now" in this paragraph means "at the time when additions to the stock become completed."

7

The Joint Condition of Dynamic Equilibrium

I. General statement of the joint condition.

We shall now merge our two requirements of dynamic equilibrium. The first requirement is that of approximate stability of the general price level. Secondly, on the assumption of balanced government budgets, we require equality of desired net capital formation with net savings at positive levels of both these magnitudes. The discussion of unbalanced budgets in dynamic equilibrium will be postponed until we arrive at the policy sections of our analysis, in the final Chapter of this volume. By merging our two requirements we obtain the joint condition that desired net capital formation should equal net savings when the general price level stays reasonably stable. This formulation of the condition enables us to circumvent the cumbersome distinction between "expected" and "realized" *savings,* and to limit ourselves to the relation of planned to realized *investment.*[1]

The condition implies that the required equality of desired capital formation with net savings should not be a consequence of the stimulating effect of inflation. An otherwise too small rate of desired capital formation may become increased by an inflationary encouragement, and the equality of desired capital formation with net savings may be established in this fashion; we do not wish to say that in this case the condi-

---

[1] If planned and realized investment are equal, a difference between expected and realized savings would have to express itself in changes in the general price level. On the other hand, appreciable changes in the general price level are practically certain to create differences among all planned and realized magnitudes in the system. This follows from the discussion in Chapter 5.

tion of dynamic equilibrium is satisfied. The reason for this is that in such circumstances a subsequent interruption of the growth process is predictable.

As we saw in Chapter 5, the joint condition of dynamic equilibrium requires a gradual increase in the supply of money at the rate of the gradual increase in T/V (which can also be expressed as a gradual increase in $k \cdot T$). The joint condition, which from now on we may call *the* condition of dynamic equilibrium, implies that it is possible to regulate the supply of money with this result. Otherwise, the condition cannot be satisfied.

Should "reasonably full employment of labor" be made a further condition of dynamic equilibrium? It was pointed out briefly in Chapter 4, Section 7, and it will be explained more fully in Chapter 8, that chronic unemployment may exist in a condition of uninterrupted growth, provided that real-wage rates are not instantaneously adjustable to the requirements of full employment. Such unemployment may either be the consequence of the fact that, at a higher level of employment, *savings would exceed planned investment,* or it may be a consequence of the insufficiency of the capital stock for "tooling" the entire labor force (and of the *insufficiency of savings* to raise the stock to the required size). The avoidance of appreciable chronic unemployment is essential to the workability of our social systems. This will be taken into account in the subsequent analysis. However, we prefer not to *define* full employment into the concept of dynamic equilibrium. By the concept of dynamic equilibrium, we want to express the idea of continuous growth, and this does not logically imply full employment of *labor.* As was pointed out earlier, dynamic equilibrium does imply the absence of excess capacity in *equipment,* in the sense that investors must be willing to accumulate further capital rather than consider their given equipment excessive.

2. The psychological character of the joint condition and the problem of objective corollaries.

The formulation of the condition in the preceding pages places a psychological relationship in the foreground. The condition has been presented as requiring that *desired* capital formation should meet certain requirements. Placing a psychological relationship in the foreground seems justified, because smooth growth depends on desires which become translated into action. However, we must attempt to penetrate the psychological surface of economic decisions. We shall have to examine the circumstances in which desired capital formation is likely to meet the condition here developed. One way of expressing this is to say that we have to turn to the *corollaries* of the condition of dynamic equilibrium. If the condition which we have formulated in the present Chapter is to be satisfied, then certain other conditions must also be. It is desirable to express the corollaries in question with reference to technological and institutional circumstances which link the concept of desired capital formation to more readily observable magnitudes.

The analysis of these more tangible corollaries to the condition of dynamic equilibrium focuses attention on the question of the realism or the lack of realism of the condition. A discussion of the corollaries follows in the subsequent Chapters. Before turning to these, we shall go through the preliminary exercise of formulating the joint condition of dynamic equilibrium in an alternative fashion. The alternative formulation helps clear the way toward a discussion of the technological-institutional corollaries.

3. An alternative formulation of the joint condition, in terms of the incremental capital-output requirement and the rate of growth.

The joint condition of dynamic equilibrium can be expressed with the aid of a concept that relates desired capital formation to the rate of increase in output. In Chapter 4 we introduced the concept of the incremental capital-output requirement, that is, of the desired addition to the capital stock per unit of output-increment.[2] If, for example, an increase in output by one unit per period is associated with a two-unit desired increase of the capital stock,[3] then we say that the increment capital-output requirement is two (or that the "accelerator" is two). It follows that the desired capital formation of a period equals the algebraic product of the rate of increase in output with the incremental capital-output requirement. Consequently, the joint condition of dynamic equilibrium can be expressed in the following way: with an approximately stable price level, *the rate of increase of output times the incremental capital-output requirement must equal net savings.*

It should not be assumed that the incremental capital-output require-

---

[2] This is the reciprocal of the output-increment per unit of new capital formation. See Pages 114-115 and 140-141.

[3] The units in question may be conceived of as dollars of constant purchasing power (*i.e.,* corrected for price changes).

ment compatible with dynamic equilibrium is necessarily a constant. However, a rise in the incremental capital-output requirement tends to pull up also the average capital requirement per unit of total output; and in Chapter 4 we saw that a rise in the average capital requirement per unit of output must be associated with a fall in the rate of return on capital (interest-plus-profit rate) if the relative share of interest-plus-profit income in total income does not rise at the same time.[4] There may, of course, occur offsetting changes in the relative share of interest-plus-profit income, and in this case the average capital-output requirement may change without causing a change in the interest-plus-profit rate. When, for example, the composition of output changes, there usually occurs a change in the average capital requirement per unit of output, and also a change in the relative share of property income. The service industries have a lower average capital-output requirement than does the steel industry, but from this it does not follow that the service industries are more profitable. For, the share of interest-plus-profit income in total income is greater in the steel industry than in the service industries.

However, a change in the capital requirement per unit of total output may result from changing requirements in specific industries, rather than from changing weights of the individual industries in the total economy. If the capital requirement per unit of output changes (say, rises) in specific industries, there is no general presumption that the relative share of interest-plus-profit income in total income will also change (say, rise), thus leaving the interest-plus-profit rate unchanged. Hence, a change in the capital requirement per unit of output in any given industry does tend to change the interest-plus-profit rate. It is true that dynamic equilibrium does not require constancy of the interest-plus-profit rate. But dynamic equilibrium does require that the interest-plus-profit rate should not fall to a level at which the investment needed for matching savings in a growing economy would not materialize. If the interest-plus-profit rate should fall so low, then output would cease growing. Thus the capital requirement per unit of output which is compatible with dynamic equilibrium does not possess unlimited upward flexibility. The average capital-output requirement must not rise so high (the profit rate must not fall so low) that there should cease to exist a desire to engage in the required amount of new investment per period,

---

[4] This should be an almost obvious proposition, even without algebraic proof. However, for more detailed analysis see Footnote 12, Page 122.

when the price level stays reasonably stable. This is an alternative version of the condition which was formulated earlier in this Chapter, namely, of the condition that desired capital formation must equal savings at a reasonably stable general price level. The present alternative version has the advantage of calling attention to technological-institutional factors which will be in the center of our discussion of the growth corollaries in the Chapters that follow.

4. The long-run tendency toward dynamic equilibrium on a lowered path.

Our economies are not growing without interruption, and hence they do not move on paths of dynamic equilibrium. The condition of dynamic equilibrium is not, properly speaking, realistic. However, as was suggested in Part 1, it is methodologically fruitful to look at our economies as systems that have shown a long-run tendency toward lowered paths of dynamic equilibrium.

Trend lines which are fitted to the actual output series of our economies belong in the family of paths of dynamic equilibrium. Yet the actually observable trend lines are lowered paths of dynamic equilibrium, where the lowering is a consequence of the fact that failure of the economy to move continuously along a path of dynamic equilibrium causes maladjustments. Abrupt, unpredictable changes in the level of activity, and in its composition by industries, lead to excessive capital formation in some periods and to insufficient capital formation in others; they lead also to wrong specialization of resources. These maladjustments have the same effect as a loss of resources. The subsequent discussion of the corollaries of dynamic equilibrium (smooth growth) should show why dynamic equilibrium must necessarily be an unrealistic concept, and yet why, *in the form of observable trend lines, it tends to become realistic for the purpose of longe-run analysis, except that an allowance must be made for the "waste" caused by fluctuations.* This leaves open the question of how much of this "waste" is unavoidable in a type of economy which is capable of producing steep upward trends with reasonably free markets. But there exists good reason for assuming that, as compared with the performance of Western economies up to World War II, the waste of fluctuations can be considerably reduced, without sacrificing the essentials of the market mechanism and of the private enterprise system.

8

The First Corollary of the Condition of Dynamic Equilibrium: The Improvement Process

Sections 2, 4, and 6 of this Chapter are more technical than the other Sections. It is possible to follow the general line of argument without reading these Sections, even though full appraisal of the problems raised requires reading them.

1. Offsets to diminishing returns.

If the input of one factor of production rises at a higher rate than that of the cooperating factors, then, on a given level of technological and organizational knowledge, the rapidly rising factor should become subject to diminishing returns.

In Western industrial economies population has, on the whole, been rising at a considerably lower rate than the capital stock. In all countries there have probably existed subperiods of which this statement is not true, but the numerical data in the Appendix to Part 3 will support the claim that an excess of capital growth over population growth is a normal feature of economic development. The numerical results are, of course, not identical for the various countries. But they generally show a long-run excess of capital growth over population growth, and this is confirmed by "common observation," which makes us say that in industrial societies the quantity of equipment increases *per capita*. Consequently, *on a given level of technological and organizational knowledge,* there should develop an increasing abundance of capital relative to labor

195

(increasing labor scarcity), and the investment of capital should be running into diminishing returns.

This conclusion is reinforced if we consider natural resources. On a given level of organizational and technological knowledge, the available stock of natural resources is literally fixed. The acquisition of hitherto unknown (unavailable or inaccessible) natural resources should always be interpreted as reflecting progress or improvement, based on some technological invention or discovery or on some new organizational move. This reinforces the conclusion that organizational and technological improvements are needed to avoid sharply diminishing returns to capital.

Were it not for technological and organizational improvements, diminishing returns would have to express themselves in rising capital requirements per unit of output in the various sectors of the economy. Both the average and the incremental capital requirements would have to rise. Moreover, at the margin of new investment, rates of return (interest-plus-profit rates) would have to be falling. The essence of the process can best be understood by visualizing an economy in which increasing quantities of capital are added to unchanging quantities of cooperating factors, at an unchanging level of technological-organizational knowledge. In such circumstances the gradual fall in the output-increment per unit of new capital formation would surely have to translate itself into falling net rates of return to investors, at the margin of new investment, because the investors could not compensate themselves at the expense of the cooperating factors. The prices of the scarce cooperating factors would be rising, not falling.

2. An appraisal of two analytical difficulties.

The statements of the previous Section, according to which the capital stock of Western economies has been growing in a higher proportion than the supply of the other factors of production, assume the measurement of capital. These quantitative propositions, to which we shall return in the Appendix to Part 3, are based on estimating the size of the capital stock by adding the net investment of successive periods to an initial stock.[1] The net investment or net capital formation of each period is valued at the *buyer's (investor's) cost of acquisition of the new*

---

[1] The valuation of the initial stock is a thorny problem. However, in long-run analysis the quantitative significance of the problem is reduced, provided that we can go back far enough to make the initial stock small as compared to the present. The Kuznets estimates, which start in 1869, enable us to do this for the United States. The

capital goods produced, with a correction for price changes (that is, the capital goods are valued at the prices of some given base year).

Such numerical appraisals of the "size of the stock" possesses inevitable weaknesses. These are perhaps even more pronounced than the weaknesses of the corresponding procedure for valuing real or physical *output*. The physical character of the capital goods cannot help changing in the course of the investment process. Aside from technological improvements—that is, on a given level of technological knowledge—the physical character of capital would have to change, because, if the stock increases per unit of labor and per unit of natural resources then equipment of a different kind must be used. Needless to say, technological progress, too, changes the physical character of capital. With the changing character of the goods produced in successive periods, valuation in constant prices (correcting for price changes) becomes a logically objectionable procedure. Yet when, in the present analysis, we state that the capital stock is rising at a rate different from that at which the supply of cooperating factors increases, then, of course, we mean physical capital. We *must* try to eliminate price changes from our series.

The objection cannot be answered to the satisfaction of the logical purist. If we move from decade to decade—*i.e.,* are concerned with decade comparisons—the physical characteristics of many goods certainly do change. Changes in the composition of physical aggregates (such as inter-sector shifts in the composition of aggregate output or of aggregate investment) cause difficulties which cannot be resolved to full satisfaction. In all such cases we must require that the general results of the statistical computations should accord with intelligent judgment or common observation. If they do accord with general judgment, we may perhaps rely more confidently on technical procedures for discovering details in a movement which would not be disclosed by common observation alone. This is how we are forced to proceed in such matters. In the present case we may derive quite a bit of consolation from the fact that the general conclusions to which capital stock estimates lead are in harmony with intelligent informal judgment. To take one example, it is obviously reasonable to conclude that the quantity of physical capital per man has shown a substantial rise in the long run.

---

difficulty would obviously disappear completely if we could start with zero stock. It should be added that the net investment which is being cumulated here to obtain the size of the present capital is net in the sense of having been made subject to allowances for depreciation and obsolescence.

However, only on very special assumptions would other methods of measuring physical capital yield the identical numerical results as the cost-of-acquisition method described on Page 196. Let us consider, for example, the alternative method of discounting, at the pure rate of interest, the stream of future net earnings to which the use of capital goods gives rise. Only in perfect competition, that is, in the complete absence of monopoly or monopsony power, and with no uncertainty ("risk"), would the present market value of the future net earnings, arrived at by using the pure rate of interest as a discount factor, equal the buyer's (investor's) cost of acquisition of new capital goods.

If the producer acquiring the capital goods possesses monopoly power, then monopoly rents will express themselves in an excess of the discounted present values over the investor's cost of acquisition[2]—except at the margin of investment (where the monopolist stops investing precisely because no further rent increments are obtainable by investing more). This is another way of saying that on the cost of acquisition of his assets the monopolist usually enjoys a higher yield than the yield corresponding to the market rate of interest (except that at the margin or his investment he enjoys precisely this yield). It should be added that the market rate of interest, which is properly used for obtaining the present market value of assets by way of discounting the future earnings, would be the pure rate of interest (the rate on perfectly safe securities) only if the future earnings of all assets were foreseen with complete certainty. Under uncertainty the relevant market rate is usually higher. The market will usually charge an uncertainty premium, with the *intention* of obtaining a higher yield than that of perfectly safe securities (say, of government securities). But whether at the margin of investment the yield on cost of acquisition will actually be more or less than the pure market rate of interest depends on how good the judgment of the market was.

We are concerned here with intertemporal comparisons. Our interest is in changes of the capital stock. In this regard, capital values arrived at by discounting at pure rates of interest would give numerically identical results with valuation by the investor's cost of acquisition only if the influence of the monopoly and monopsony element, the attitude to uncertainty and the quality of foresight, remained unchanged. Dis-

---

[2] Such an excess develops also under monopsony. It develops even under otherwise pure competition, if entry into the market becomes institutionally limited. However, the excess does not develop under monopolistic competition in the special case where a so-called tangential equilibrium is reached. It does not, of course, develop in perfect competition with free entry.

counting at "risky" rates of interest would still result in including capitalized monopoly and monopsony rents into capital values. In this regard the method would be like that of discounting at pure rates and unlike that of valuation at cost. The difficulties connected with correcting for price changes would have to be faced at any event. Which of the two methods—investor's cost of acquisition or discounting—is preferable depends, of course, on the analytical purpose. At present, we are interested in comparing the rate of growth of physical capital with that of cooperating factor supplies. We see no reason for believing that the approximation provided by the investor's cost-of-acquisition method, on which the statements of the preceding Section are based, should be considered inferior to the approximations which other methods are capable of providing. The inclusion of capitalized rents would be a disadvantage from our point of view. The Appendix to Part 3 contains a supplementary discussion of the problem.

We now turn to the second difficulty which was bypassed in the analysis of the preceding Section. The statement that, on a given level of technological and organizational knowledge, a relatively rapidly growing factor should be running into diminishing returns disregards a complex of problems connected with economies of scale and complementarity. Aside from improvements, the average product per unit of the relatively rapidly growing factor, as well as the rate of return from that factor, should be falling. But this obviously does not mean that in a primitive economy the returns from the first small unit of investment should yield more than the second, third, etc.

Assume that in a primitive economy, too, capital is the relatively rapidly growing factor, and assume for a moment that there develop no technological and organizational improvements. Then, as soon as the cooperating factors are capable of receiving a positive price, diminishing returns should set in for capital,[3] but this is likely to mean that the average yield of the first, say, thousand units of investment is greater than that of the second thousand, etc. It is not likely to mean that the yield of the first small unit is greater than the second. There will exist a range in which economies of scale, and complementarities among different sorts of specialized equipment, have the effect of increasing the yields. A great many small units of physical equipment may be needed

---

[3] The marginal productivity, and hence the price, of the cooperating factors (that is, of the relatively fixed factors) could not become positive before there was enough of the rapidly growing factor to produce diminishing average returns for itself.

to exploit the economies of scale; and the complementarity existing among various types of equipment and among various industries may require investments in more lines than one. In the meantime, yields will be rising in the range in which economies of scale and complementarities become more fully exploited. We are here faced with the consequences of indivisibilities.

We shall see later that this may be of great significance for the understanding of conditions in primitive economies. To use our simplified terminology, these economies may have less than 1000 units of physical capital. On the way toward the first 1000 units, returns from new investment may be rising, quite aside from improvements. Subsequently, too, there will occur similar ranges of rising yield. While, on the assumption of a constant level of technological and organizational knowledge and with a fixed quantity of labor and of natural resources, returns would be diminishing from the 1000-unit capital input to the 2000-unit input, there may be an intermediate rise in the range lying between, say, 1500 units and 2000 units. Even in an advanced economy, we must be aware of a qualification stemming from these indivisibilities. A new "offset" to diminishing returns—a further dose of progress—prepares the way not for one unit of new investment but for what we have here called "thousands of units." However, the danger that the economy may get stranded in a region of low returns between, say, 10,000 and 11,000 units is much smaller than the danger that it may get stranded prior to acquiring the first 1000 because the intensity of the use of already existing physical equipment can temporarily be increased and the complementarities thus exploited.

3. Persistently and appreciably diminishing returns incompatible with sustained growth and probably also with full utilization in the capitalist framework.

In an economy with imperfect foresight of business results, those engaging in net capital formation (*i.e.*, "investors") expect that, after the deduction of all costs other than interest, a yield will materialize which, at the margin of their investment, includes three constituents. These are (1) an uncertainty premium ("risk premium") for undertaking the physical investment itself, (2) a similar premium for lending money to business investors rather than to an absolutely safe borrower,[4] (3) the

---

[4] In some circumstances the absolutely safe borrower is a mere abstraction. It is, however, reasonable to say that under contemporary conditions, the federal government of

pure rate of interest on perfectly safe loans, *i.e.,* the money rate of interest of Chapter 5.[5] The sum of the second and third constituents is the *rate of interest on business loans.* The first constituent is the profit which, in the presence of uncertainty, even a purely competitive firm expects to make after deducting interest on borrowed money. A firm investing its own money expects to earn the sum of the three constituents, although it may be satisfied with a smaller first-plus-second constituent than two independent persons would be.

We are describing here the yield that is expected to be earned on the *marginal* unit of investment of each investor because we are interested in how yield requirements determine the point to which new investment activity will be carried. For clarification, we may add, however, that a firm with monopoly or monopsony power will usually make an additional gain (monopoly or monopsony rent) on the cost of inframarginal units of investment because monopoly and monopsony power usually result in the ability of a firm to acquire physical assets at a lesser cost than corresponds to their value, if the value is obtained by discounting their earnings at the market rate of interest (including risk premia). Even under monopoly or monopsony the *discounted value or market value of all assets*—inframarginal as well as marginal—is computed so as to yield on this value neither more nor less than the three "constituents" described in the preceding paragraph; but under monopoly or monopsony all assets other than the marginal yield more than our three constituents *on the cost which the investing firm incurs when acquiring the*

---

the United States (like the governments of many other countries) is a practically safe borrower in the sense that it will never default. The federal government can always be enabled to issue new money instead of defaulting. However, the money which the federal government pays back may have lost part of its purchasing power. There is, of course, always the possibility that the federal government will turn out to have borrowed at a negative *real* rate of interest (see Chapter 5). In this sense, the government is not an absolutely safe borrower. But in the text we are now concerned with the constituents of *money* yields. The fact that even the owner of "perfectly safe" securities accepts certain risks will be taken into account later. The "perfectly safe" security is perfectly free merely from the *risk of default.*

[5] The pure rate of interest (*i.e.,* the rate of interest on absolutely safe loans) is different for different maturities. The short-term rates may be expected to rise (or to fall) in the course of a longer period, and this in itself would raise (or lower) the long-term rates relatively to the short-term rates. But it seems probable that a vague expectation of unchanging interest rates would produce higher long rates than short rates. Subjectively, the risk that interest rates will rise (bond prices will fall) is usually *weighed* more heavily than the possibility that interest rates will fall (bond prices will rise). This hypothesis, and generally the hypothesis of risk aversion or of the conservative bias, is perhaps indistinguishable from the hypothesis of the declining marginal utility of money earnings. It hurts more to lose than it is pleasant to gain.

assets. The difference is monopoly rent, and it expresses itself in capitalized form in an excess of the market value of the inframarginal assets over their cost of acquisition.[6] The firm stops at the margin precisely because at the margin the three constituents of the yield just barely materialize on cost of acquisition. That is to say, for the marginal asset there exists no difference between discounted value and cost of acquisition. On either of these values a yield is expected to be earned which includes the three constituents described on Page 200.

In a risky world the sum of the three constituents of the yield cannot fall below a minimum rate at the margin of new investment. Investment that yields less income than a minimum requirement will not be forthcoming (unless price inflation is expected, and physical assets are therefore expected to bring capital gains in terms of money). This is why persistently and appreciably diminishing returns would sooner or later cause a permanent stoppage of the growth process. A temporary sharp diminution of returns stops the growth process temporarily.

Yet, within limits, the sum of the three constituents does possess adjustability to the requirements of the economy. Alternating longer periods of mildly diminishing and rising returns would be compatible even with uninterrupted growth. A very mild downward trend which flattened out asymptotically might also be. The sum of the three constituents has leeway, even though for investments actually undertaken this sum cannot fall below a minimum.

The first and second constituents cannot fall below a minimum level, and they may even show no tendency to adjust to the strength or weakness of investment opportunities. The third constituent—the pure rate—does have considerable adjustability, within wide limits. Keynes maintained that even the pure rate is subject to a floor because even in periods of weak investment opportunities there exists the possibility of a rise in pure interest rates (of a fall in bond prices), and this would prevent the public from lending money at exceedingly low rates, quite aside from the question of business risks.[7] The argument is controversial, but it is not very important to decide how much validity attaches to it. The sum of the three constituents obviously *is* subject to a floor, or minimum requirement, and this is sufficient to establish the proposition that,

---

[6] See Footnote 2, p. 198.

[7] J. M. Keynes, *The General Theory of Employment, Interest, and Money* (New York, 1936), Ch. 15.

in an inevitably risky market economy, persistently and appreciably diminishing returns would be incompatible with continued growth.

If diminishing returns should stop the growth process, then, at the output level already reached new savings would have to diminish and ultimately to cease, to keep the economy at that level. Otherwise, output and employment would have to fall to a level where savings would diminish and ultimately cease. For, as was seen in Chapters 4 and 6, an excess of saving over planned investment causes output to fall.

Some components of savings would presumably decline more or less automatically, even without a fall in output and employment. Corporate savings (undistributed corporate profits), and also the savings of unincorporated business,[8] seem to be largely, though not wholly, geared to investment opportunities. In the United States these seem to account for about one half of total savings at high levels of employment. With a significant lag, all new saving might disappear in the absence of investment opportunities. If wages and prices had unlimited downward flexibility, then the so-called Pigou effect might lead to this result.[9] Even aside from the Pigou effect, the general attitudes of the public may adjust to the absence of growth tendencies, and new saving could thus cease at high levels of output (at capacity production). But these adjustments might be very long and painful. Meanwhile persistently and appreciably diminishing returns would not merely stop the growth process but would make it exceedingly difficult to maintain output near the capacity level of private enterprise economies. The merits and limitations of compensatory fiscal policies for overcoming such an impasse will be considered later.

4. A diagrammatic excursion.

We shall first express the difference between the marginal productivity of capital and the marginal efficiency of new investment in a simplified model. This distinction was first drawn explicitly by A. P. Lerner. Conceptually, the marginal productivity schedule (or marginal productivity function) of capital indicates, for alternative stocks of capital, the addition to the value of the output-flow, obtainable by adding to the *already existing capital* stock a very small further unit of capital, given the

---

[8] These are usually included in the savings of individuals.

[9] In other words, the increase in the real value of already existing liquid assets—the increase in their value in terms of goods and services—might reduce or eliminate the desire to accumulate new savings out of current income, even at the full capacity level of output (See Page 124).

quantities of the factors cooperating with capital; while the marginal efficiency schedule (or function) of new investment indicates, for alternative amounts of new investment, the addition to the value of the output-flow obtainable by adding to the already forthcoming new investment *per period* a very small further unit of new investment per period, given the quantities of the factors cooperating with capital.[10] Both these magnitudes are expressed as percentage yields on the cost of production of the added (marginal) physical capital.

Assume that we start from scratch, so that the first unit of new investment in the next period will also be the first unit of capital in the economy. The supply of cooperating factors is fixed, that is to say, the assumption that capital is the relatively fast-growing factor is here incorporated in an extreme fashion. In Figure 9 the highest line, going

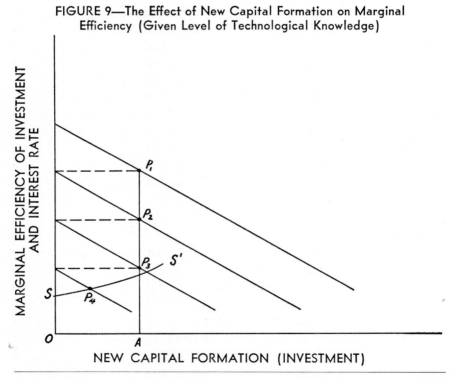

FIGURE 9—The Effect of New Capital Formation on Marginal
Efficiency (Given Level of Technological Knowledge)

MARGINAL EFFICIENCY OF INVESTMENT
AND INTEREST RATE

NEW CAPITAL FORMATION (INVESTMENT)

[10] The concept of adding a very small further unit should in both cases be interpreted in terms of the differential calculus. We are concerned with limits which are being approached as the additions are made to approach zero. The added output-flows should be conceived of as perpetual net flows, after deduction from the gross output of what is required for the perpetual maintenance of the capital.

through P_1, will then be the marginal productivity schedule of capital, as well as the first period's marginal efficiency schedule of new investment.[11] Assume now that the new investment of the first period is OA. Assume also that the marginal productivity schedule of capital remains unchanged (continues to be the line going through P_1 because the level of technological and organizational knowledge stays unchanged). Then the marginal efficiency schedule of new investment for the second period will be the line going through P_2. With new investment amounting to OA in the second period, too, the marginal efficiency schedule of new investment for the third period will be the line going through P_3. Whenever new investment takes place, a constant marginal productivity schedule of capital corresponds to a downward-shifting (leftward-shifting) marginal efficiency schedule of new investment. The reason for this is that when n units of capital exist in the economy the marginal efficiency of the *first* unit of new investment is equal to the marginal productivity of n units of capital; while, when $n + m$ units of capital exist in the economy, the marginal efficiency of the *first* unit of new investment is equal to the (lower) marginal productivity of $n + m$ units of capital.[12]

To keep the yield of a continuing and constant amount of new investment unchanged from period to period, the marginal efficiency schedule of new investment would have to stay unchanged, and this implies upward shifts of the marginal productivity schedule of capital. To keep the yield of an increasing absolute amount of new investment unchanged from period to period, the marginal efficiency schedule would have to shift upward, and this implies an even more pronounced upward shift of the marginal productivity schedule of capital. Assuming a fixed input of the factors cooperating with capital, technological-organizational improvements are required to shift up the marginal productivity schedule of capital. The same is true if the cooperating factors are not fixed but

---

[11] The schedule is drawn as sloping downward from the beginning and without interruptions, because we disregard the indivisibilities which were discussed in Section 2 of this Chapter.

[12] In the figure the successive marginal efficiency functions are drawn parallel to the marginal productivity function of capital. This is because we assume that the addition to the capital stock along the marginal efficiency functions takes place in precisely the same circumstances as those in which capital is added along the marginal productivity function. In other words, optimum adjustment of the *physical character* of all factor inputs is here assumed for all functions. If merely the marginal productivity function were so defined, while the marginal efficiency functions were interpreted as assuming *short-run* conditions (with incomplete adjustments due to immobility), then the marginal efficiency functions would have to be steeper than the marginal productivity functions.

if their input is growing in a smaller proportion than that of capital, as is the case in the real world.

The demand curves for funds to be used for planned new investment are closely related to the marginal efficiency schedule of new investment. If, in an economy with a constant general price level, there were no uncertainty, the demand curves for funds to be used for planned new investment would be identical with marginal efficiency schedules, except that for the purpose of drawing these schedules *as demand curves* we would have to measure the interest rate on business loans (rather than marginal productivity or marginal efficiency) along the vertical axis. A marginal productivity or marginal efficiency of x percent on the vertical axis of Figure 9 would have to be interpreted as an interest rate of x percent. Investors would demand 100 units of funds for new investment at some rate of interest if, and only if, the yield on the one-hundredth unit of new investment were the same as the rate of interest charged for the funds. This simply means that each firm invests on a scale such that it should be barely worth while to undertake the marginal unit of investment. The yield on the cost of the marginal physical investment unit is the marginal efficiency of new investment. Hence, in the absence of uncertainty, the demand curves for funds to be used for planned new investment would be marginal efficiency functions (with interest rates on business loans measured on the ordinate).

Uncertainty, so-called business risk, probably places the demand curves somewhat below the expected marginal efficiency schedules. The first constituent of the yield of investment (see Page 200) expresses itself in this difference. Those engaging in risky investment intend to do so on a scale which leaves them an uncertainty premium or safety margin, over and above their best guess concerning the obtainable rate of return at the margin. While the demand curves for funds to be used for planned new investment are thus presumably somewhat lower than the corresponding marginal efficiency schedules of new investment, for the present purpose it is not misleading to read the marginal efficiency schedules as demand curves, with interest rates on business loans measured along the vertical axis.

Given these demand curves, the height of the interest rates on business loans depends on the supply of funds to investors. The amount of funds supplied and used for planned new investment need not be equal to the net savings of the period (except, of course, in dynamic equilibrium).[13] The probable shape of the supply curve is illustrated in Figure 9 by SS'. This is the supply function prevailing in the period in which the marginal efficiency function is that going through point P_4. Hence, in that period the demand function for funds used for planned net investment intersects with the supply function of funds for net investment in P_4. We must assume that the SS' function was shifting downward as new capital became accumulated and as output was growing. Earlier, the SS' curve went through point P_1, then through P_2, then through P_3. In the course of the growth process, savings and the supply of funds to investors tend to rise for any given interest rate. But the position of the SS' curve which is shown in the graph may be regarded as the lowest attainable position. The risks involved in lending funds for investment will preclude the use of funds for this purpose at rates lower than OS even in advanced stages of the growth process. At the interest rate corresponding to the distance OS, returns are insufficient to induce any lending whatsoever for investment; at higher rates of interest, returns become sufficient to induce the lending of funds for gradually increasing amounts of investment.

The supply of funds to investors depends on how much the public and the commercial banks are willing to place at the disposal of investors for net investment (where the supplier may or may not be the same person or institution as the investor). That part of the existing funds which is used neither for consumption purchases, nor for the replacement of wear and tear, nor for accumulating additional idle balances,[14] becomes a supply of funds for net investment. Within rather wide limits, the central bank (in the United States, the Federal Reserve) can influence this supply by increasing or decreasing its own credits. It can do this with the aid of the techniques described in Chapter 5, Section 6. *The supply curve of funds for net investment can thus be made steeper or flatter,*

---

[13] The market equates the supply of funds for investment projects (planned investment) with the demand for funds destined for planned investment. But savings (unconsumed income) need not be equal to the SS' supply. Savings must equal the total investment, planned plus unplanned. If there develops unplanned investment, that is, if unwanted stocks accumulate then this expresses insufficiency of the aggregate demand for goods. Either the supply of money was not increased in accordance with the needs of a growing economy or money is being hoarded.

[14] Net additions to idle balances constitute a deduction from the supply to investors, and a net diminution of idle balances constitutes an addition to this supply. The sum of the deductions from the supply which were listed in the text is likely to decrease with rising interest rates. Therefore, the supply is likely to increase when interest rates rise.

and the point of origin of the curve on the ordinate may also be influenced to some extent. But there exist limits to what the central bank can achieve. Even if it can increase the supply of money, it may in certain circumstances not be capable of preventing the entire addition from going into idle balances. This is because the central bank cannot cause a supply of business loans to be forthcoming at interest rates *falling short* of some irreducible minimum requirement set by lenders' risk, that is, by the second constituent of the yield, as defined on Pages 200-201.[15] The *SS'* curve cannot be shifted below the position shown in Figure 9. If the marginal efficiency schedule became sufficiently downward-shifted, then the interest rate would decline to a level where little or no supply is forthcoming to investors, regardless of how much money the central bank supplies. In other words, the interest rate on business loans may decline to the point where the lowest attainable *SS'* function originates. In Figure 9 the rate has not declined quite to that level; yet it has already become impossible to prevent new investment from falling below the amount *OA*. This is quite sufficient to bring out the difficulties with which we are concerned here. Further downward shifts of the marginal efficiency schedule would make that schedule go through point *S* of the vertical axis.

A growing economy needs technological and organizational improvements by which continuous and significant downward shifts of the marginal efficiency schedule of new investment are prevented. If the marginal efficiency schedule shifts to the left to such an extent that it intersects with the *SS'* curve on the vertical axis itself (in point *S*), then the funds used for further net investment shrink to zero and growth ends. Furthermore, it is likely that at the full-employment level of income savings would be forthcoming even if the marginal efficiency schedule did intersect with the *SS'* curve in point *S* on the vertical axis, and it is likely that savings at the full-employment level of income would not become *reduced* correspondingly when the funds used for new investment were reduced below *OA* (as is the case in the graph). In this case net saving would exceed the supply of funds for planned net investment, and the difference would go into additional idle deposits (money hoards).[16]

---

[15] The central bank could eliminate these risk premiums only if it supplied risky loans directly to business enterprise on a major scale. This would amount to an arbitrary policy of subsidizing specific firms.

[16] Savings would then exceed the *planned* investment to which our investment demand functions (marginal efficiency functions) relate. The difference would accumulate in the form of undesired stocks, that is, of unplanned investment. Aggregate demand

This would render the total effective demand insufficient for maintaining the full-employment level of output. Income and output would have to decline to a level where net saving ceases.

Offsets to diminishing returns are needed to prevent consistent downward shifts of the marginal efficiency schedule. These offsets must have the effect of *shifting up* the marginal productivity schedule of capital and of thus keeping the marginal efficiency schedule of new investment at a satisfactory level in each successive period.

5. Properties of the required offsets.

The required offsets to diminishing returns can be characterized as technological and organizational improvements. These result from the acquisition of new knowledge or new skills. But not just any improvement or cost-saving innovation will do. It is not enough to state that improvements must be sufficiently plentiful. Within reasonable limits, the character of improvements must adjust to the resource scarcities in the system. The meaning of this requirement is that not only the total impact of the improvements must be sufficient, but their differential impact on the demand for the various factors of production must not be badly out of line with differential rates of increase in the supply of the various factors. In advanced economies capital tends to be the most rapidly rising factor, and this may have been true even of earlier stages of development.

We shall discuss this problem in terms of the marginal productivity theory of factor demand. This implies that profits tend to become maximized along functions that, in the long run, may be interpreted as continuous, and that therefore the demand for each factor tends to be such that the marginal productivity of the factor quantity demanded should be equal to its price (or more generally, should be equal to the marginal cost of acquiring the factor).[17] From this it follows that in our presentation *the demand for factors will be governed by their "marginal productivities,"* which are to be interpreted here as marginal value productivi-

---

would be insufficient to prevent the accumulation of these unwanted stocks, and this would have to be the consequence of the hoarding of money.

[17] A firm buying more or less of a factor than is required for satisfying this condition does not maximize its profits, because such a firm could increase its total profits by reducing or by increasing its factor purchase. By the marginal productivity of a factor quantity, we mean here the increase in the *output-value* which is occasioned by the last very small unit of factor input within that total quantity. More precisely, we mean the limit of the increment in output-value per unit of additional factor input, when the addition to the factor input approaches the limit zero, and the input of all other factors stays constant.

ties. But the essential part of our conclusions should be acceptable even to readers who believe in some other theory of factor demand. These readers should *substitute "change in the demand for a factor" whenever we say "change in the marginal productivity of a factor,"* and they should apply their own theory of the demand for factors. The essential part of our conclusions will stay valid.

We now turn to a discussion of the requirement that not only the total impact of improvements but also their differential impact on the individual factor demands must be in line with the resource position of the economy.

For illustration, take two extremes.

Imagine an improvement that raises the marginal productivity of the existing supply of labor and also the marginal productivity of the existing quantity of natural resources, but fails to raise the marginal productivity of the existing quantity of capital. Such an improvement would illustrate in rather extreme form a change which is capital-saving relatively to the other two factors of production. Considering that the market tends to equate the prices of factors of production with their marginal productivities, our improvement will increase the demand for labor and the demand for natural resources. Wage rates and rents will rise. But unless more labor and natural resources are available, the demand for capital will not increase. If, nevertheless, more capital is accumulated, while the supply of the cooperating factors does not rise *correspondingly,* the rate of return on capital will have to fall. An improvement that fails to raise the marginal productivity of capital for the amount of capital already invested will not offset the tendency toward diminishing returns on the investment of new capital. Insufficiency of the marginal productivity of capital, in the range in which the economy actually operates, will sooner or later stop the growth process. Insufficiency of the marginal productivity of capital is likely also to create the kind of unemployment which is attributable to the fact that a higher level of output than that which exists would bring about more savings without leading to more capital formation. *In other words, at the full-employment level of output there would develop a deflationary pressure (oversaving), and hence the full-employment level of output does not materialize.*

Now take a rather extreme illustration of technological progress such as is laborsaving relatively to the factors cooperating with labor. Imagine improvements which raise the marginal productivity of the existing stock of capital a great deal—by more than is required for calling forth at fixed interest rates the amount of new investment which will match savings—but which keep the marginal productivity of the existing supply of labor unchanged.[18] In the long run a flow of such improvements would create unmanageable social friction. For a fixed supply of labor, these improvements would keep real-wage rates constant. For a rising supply of labor, these improvements would be lowering real-wage rates all the time. In reality, a significant secular upward trend in real-wage rates is an essential part of the record of industrial societies, and in reality the labor supply has been rising, albeit in a smaller proportion than the stock of capital. Consequently, improvements would be creating social friction not merely if they prevented the marginal productivity of labor from rising for a constant population but even if they failed to shift up the marginal productivity of the existing supply of labor sufficiently to bring about an appreciably rising trend in real-wage rates for a growing population.

Also, if improvements merely caused the marginal productivity of capital to rise, without eliciting an appreciable rise of the marginal productivity of labor, then continuously rising chronic unemployment might well be one of the observable results. We have just seen that with an increase in the supply of labor, wage reductions might be called for; the failure of wage rates to fall, or the slowness and incompleteness of their downward adjustment, would create unemployment. In other words, the laborsaving character of improvements (their relatively unfavorable impact on the productivity of labor and hence on the demand for labor) could change the existing labor scarcity, in relation to capital, into overabundance of labor. *This sort of unemployment is not attributable to the fact that at given real-wage rates a higher level of employment would bring about an excess of savings over planned investment.* It is attributable to the fact that, given the laborsaving character of the improvements, too little labor is needed with the given capital stock; and that not enough saving is available for raising the capital stock to the size at which the entire labor force would be needed. With sufficiently easy credit it would be possible to call forth more new investment. But unless consumption were reduced, this would lead to inflation.

---

[18] This somewhat extreme illustration implies that the improvement lowers the marginal labor productivity below the level at which it *would be*, without improvements, when the quantity of capital had risen by the amount of the new investments. To a higher input of capital there should correspond higher labor productivity. But an extremely laborsaving improvement could keep the marginal labor productivity unchanged even though the capital stock were rising.

6. Technical elaboration.

In general, improvements can have the following three effects:

(*1*) They may raise the marginal productivity of the existing quantity of capital, given the existing amounts of cooperating labor and of natural resources. If this is their main effect, their impact on the demand for labor and on the demand for natural resources will be smaller than their impact on the demand for capital. Such improvements will be labor-saving and natural-resources-saving, *relatively* to their effect on the demand for capital.

(*2*) They may raise the marginal productivity of the existing labor force, given the existing amount of cooperating capital and natural resources. If this is their main effect, the improvementss will be capital-saving and natural-resources-saving, *relatively* to their effect on the demand for labor.

(*3*) They may raise the marginal productivity of the existing stock of natural resources, given the existing supply of cooperating capital and of labor. If this is their main effect, the improvements will be capital-saving and laborsaving, *relatively* to their effect on the demand for natural resources.

Improvements too little slanted toward the first of these three effects—improvements that are insufficiently laborsaving and natural-resources-saving and thus are too capital saving[19]—will not prevent the yield

---

[19] An improvement that, for given inputs, raises the marginal product of capital in a smaller proportion than that of the other factors, shifts up the average productivity function of capital in such a way that this function becomes less elastic at the point expressing the given inputs of all factors. *Any improvement must raise the value of the average product of all factors of production in the identical proportion for the initially given inputs, namely, in the proportion in which the output is increased for unchanging inputs.* If now, with unchanging inputs, an improvement raises the marginal product of capital in a smaller proportion than the marginal product of the other factors, then the marginal productivity of capital must rise less than its average productivity. The percentage gap between the average and the marginal product of capital must increase. This is another way of saying that the elasticity of the average productivity function must decrease in the point under consideration. *Improvements of this sort diminish the relative share of capital in total income* because the relative share is determined by the relationship between average and marginal productivity. This is why the average productivity function cannot become less elastic, or more elastic, for all factors. If the relative share of one factor in total income decreases, then that of others must increase.

The analogous statements hold for improvements that are primarily laborsaving (*i.e.*, raise the marginal productivity of the existing labor supply less than that of the other factors); and for improvements that in the same sense are primarily natural-resources-saving.

J. R. Hicks, who in his *Theory of Wages* (London, 1932), Ch. 6, first suggested a general classification of inventions along similar lines, used the concept of the elasticity

of capital from falling if the input of capital increases more rapidly than the input of the other factors (as is actually the case). Therefore, improvements too little slanted toward the first effect may prove unsuitable for sustaining the growth process. Also, such improvements may lead to one of our two kinds of general unemployment. This unemployment can be explained by the statement that the amount of new investment needed to match savings at full employment would not be sufficiently profitable.

Improvements too little slanted toward the second of our three effects— improvements that are insufficiently capitalsaving and natural-resources-saving and thus are too laborsaving—will create unfavorable trends in real-wage rates. In addition, they may also create the kind of unemployment which is usually explained by the statement that, given the character of the technology used, there does not exist enough capital to make for full employment.

We have here an explanation of the two types of general unemployment which were distinguished in Chapter 4, Section 7. These, along with the more limited unemployment attributable to the "wrong specialization" or "wrong location" of part of the labor force, exhaust the analytically significant types of unemployment for the purpose of the present volume.

The first of our two types of general unemployment could be eliminated by more investment, to match more savings, at a stable general price level. The second type could be removed only by reducing real-wage rates, and/or increasing the saved proportion of income (so as to stimulate the replacement of the existing equipment with equipment that is more labor-using, and/or to stimulate the construction of more equipment without inflation). Accumulating a budgetary surplus may have the same effect as increasing the saved proportion of income.

Our two types of unemployment may occasionally coexist. This is the case where part of the existing unemployment could be eliminated by more investment, without inflation, but where the capital stock that would be available if this additional investment were forthcoming would still be insufficient to equip the entire labor force. There are two reasons why our two types of unemployment could coexist. One reason is that

---

of substitution for tracing distributional effects. But the concepts here employed seem simpler. See also Joan Robinson, "Notes on the Economics of Technical Progress," in *The Rate of Interest and Other Essays* (London, 1952), pp. 33-65, and *idem*, "The Classification of Inventions," *Review of Economic Studies* (February 1938), pp. 139-142, reprinted in American Economic Association, *Readings in the Theory of Income Distribution* (Philadelphia, 1946), pp. 175-180.

the improvements may be slanted too much toward raising the marginal productivity of natural resources (our third effect of Page 212). In this case, they are too capital-saving, as well as too laborsaving, relatively to the demand for natural resources. The other reason is that we may become faced with over-all weakness or fewness of improvements so that even if they are wholly slanted toward raising the marginal productivity of capital and of labor they will not prevent both marginal productivities from falling when the supply of capital and that of labor rise relative to the supply of natural resources.

By over-all weakness or fewness of improvements, we mean a condition where the improvements, regardless of how they are slanted toward saving individual factors, would be incapable of preventing a fall in either the marginal productivity of labor or in that of capital. In other words, when improvements are too few or too weak the objective of maintaining both the marginal productivity of capital and that of labor cannot be achieved, and this is a consequence of insufficient over-all cost-saving, not simply of excessive slanting of the improvements toward the capital-saving and the laborsaving effect. However, over-all weakness or fewness of improvement, in this sense, cannot exist if the *average* product per unit of factor input fails to decline *even for the most rapidly growing factor*. In this case the total output has not become insufficient relatively to any of the factor inputs, and therefore we are not faced with fewness or weakness of improvements. With the proper slanting of the labor-saving, capital-saving, and natural-resources-saving character of the improvements, it would in this case be possible to ensure that the marginal productivity *of no factor* should decline. For example, if the average product of the most rapidly rising factor stayed unchanged (which implies a rise in the average product of the other factors), and if the elasticities of all average product functions stayed unchanged in the successive equilibrium points, so that the gap between average and marginal product, too, stayed constant for all factors,[20] then the marginal productivity of the most rapidly rising factor would stay unchanged and the marginal productivities of the less rapidly rising factors would in-

---

[20] The average product per unit of any factor input is attributable to all factor inputs, not to a specific factor. The marginal productivity, on the other hand, is a value-increment attributable specifically to one factor, given the quantities of the co-operation factors. The demand for the individual factors is governed by their marginal productivity. The marginal product equals $AP - \dfrac{AP}{\eta}$, where AP is the average product and η the elasticity of the average productivity function. (See Footnote 19, Page 212.)

crease. The statement that for the actual inputs the average product per unit of the most rapidly rising factor has not declined over time implies either that the marginal product of no factor has declined or that, with a different "slanting" of the same total cost-saving effect toward the individual factors, none of the marginal products *would have* declined. It is reasonable to conclude that in this event the over-all strength—over-all cost-saving effect—of the improvements has been sufficient. Later we shall see that, in the United States at least, the over-all strength of the improvements does seem to have been sufficient in the foregoing sense.

Even if improvements are sufficiently plentiful and sufficiently strong in this over-all sense, they may, of course, still be of excessively capital-saving or excessively laborsaving character, or both.[21] This would express itself in unfavorable tendencies in the *marginal* product of one or both of these two factors, that is to say, in a corresponding decline of the elasticity of the average product function of capital or of labor, or of both. With such a wrong "slant" of improvement activity, either the yield of capital would be falling while the real-wage rate was rising, or the real-wage rate would be falling while the yield of capital was rising, or rents would be rising at the expense of both. But if the average product does not fall even per unit of the most rapidly rising factor, we may be sure that (owing to the improvements) there is "enough" total output in the sense that, if the marginal productivity and the price of one factor nevertheless declines, then this happens because another factor gains at the expense of that which is becoming cheaper. This is wrong slanting and not over-all weakness or fewness of improvements. Only if, with the growth of factor inputs, the average product per unit of one factor input shows a decline, may we be faced with over-all weakness of the improvement mechanism in the sense that it may be impossible to describe a "slant" (laborsaving, capital-saving, natural-resources-saving slant) which would prevent the marginal product of at least one of the factors from declining.[22]

---

[21] To say that improvements are too much slanted toward both the laborsaving and capital-saving effects means that they are too much slanted toward the third effect listed on Page 212.

[22] Assume, for example, that with growing factor inputs the average product per unit of capital declines. If at the points expressing the successive capital inputs the elasticity of the average product function of capital stays the same, then this implies a decline not merely of the average but also of the marginal product of capital. Taking it for granted that the average product of capital is declining, this fall of the marginal productivity could be prevented only if the elasticity of the average productivity function of capital were increasing. Yet if the elasticity of the average product function of capital increases, with the result that the marginal product of capital (in contrast to

7. Returning to the general argument.

Smooth functioning of an industrial economy requires that technological and organizational improvements should raise the marginal productivity of the existing capital stock sufficiently to prevent consistently and significantly diminishing returns to investors, in spite of the relative scarcity of the factors cooperating with capital. Once this is accomplished, the more the remaining effect of improvements serves to raise the marginal productivity of labor, the more does it probably contribute to the social workability of the system. The impact of improvements on the various factor markets—their effect on relative factor demands—must by and large adjust to the existing relative factor scarcities. *Improvements, by raising the marginal productivity of capital for given capital inputs, that is, by not letting the marginal productivity of capital fall too low for rising capital inputs, must achieve the result that new investment should stay sufficiently profitable, in spite of the relative land-labor scarcity. But while a substantial laborsaving effect is implied in this, the laborsaving character of improvements must not overshoot the mark to such an extent as to turn the relative labor scarcity into a chronic over-abundance of labor.*

In industrial societies the improvement mechanism has by and large functioned in this fashion. This, of course, can be maintained only with respect to the long run. The story of many shorter periods and even of some decades is far from harmonious. But the analysis of long-run trends leads to the conclusion that, in spite of successively growing amounts of new investment, *very much* of the tendency toward diminishing yields from investment has been offset by improvements. As we shall see later, statements claiming high numerical precision must be avoided. It may be stated, however, that a persistent and significant trend toward diminishing yields from investment has not been observable. While thus technological and organizational improvements have, by and large (perhaps somewhat incompletely), offset the scarcities in factors cooperating with capital, the laborsaving character of the improvements has not typically

---

its average product) does not decline, then the average product function of one of the other factors must become less elastic, and hence the marginal product of this other factor may decline even though its average product does not. Indeed, if with growing factor inputs the average product of the most rapidly rising factor declines, and that of no other factor increases, then *we may be sure* that no "slanting" of the improvements can ensure that the marginal product of each factor will be maintained. In this case, we may be certain that we are faced with over-all insufficiency of improvements. All these considerations are based on the propositions described in Footnote 19, Page 212.

overshot the mark. There has been no tendency toward a chronic excess of labor.

Real-wage rates have shown a significantly rising trend. In many countries, including the United States, the long-run rise in real-wage rates has tended to proceed at a rate similar to that of the rise in output per man-hour input, or even at a somewhat higher rate. In the United States this is in the neighborhood of 2 percent per year. In no event do the data suggest a long-run decline in labor's relative share. They suggest a *rise* in some periods of longer duration, with no equal decline in others.

The laborsaving character of improvements does not seem to have overshot the mark. On the contrary, the improvement mechanism seems to have "erred" more in the direction of permitting some consequences of the relative labor scarcity, and perhaps also of the relative scarcity in natural resources, to "come through." There does seem to have occurred a mild decline in yields from investment. This is presumably a consequence not of the over-all weakness or fewness of improvements but of their insufficient "slanting" toward the laborsaving effect (if precise maintenance of the yield of investment were considered the goal).

As will be seen in the Appendix to Part 3, long-run trends in *average output (or average product) per unit of physical capital* have so far shown no traces of decline. This is true even though the stock of capital has been rising in a considerably higher proportion than the supply of the other factors. Consequently, it would be wrong to conclude that the *over-all effect* of technological and organizational improvements has been too weak, or that improvements have been too few, or that they have been gradually weakening or becoming too few. Indeed, since improvements in the very special sense of the expansion of capitalism into vacant or primitive areas has been losing in significance, improvements in the more usual sense have presumably become increasingly sufficient to offset the tendency toward a decline of average output per unit of capital. On the other hand, distributive shares do show traces of uncompensated labor scarcity: the relative share of labor in income before taxes has risen somewhat in the long run, with the result that rates of return to investors seem to have been somewhat lowered. This lowering of rates of return to investors has occurred in spite of the fact that output per unit of physical capital has not declined. There is no contradiction here because rates of return to investors depend both on average output per unit of capital and on distributive shares. From the materials to be examined later, it does seem reasonable to infer that with the increase in the relative share of labor there has been associated a mild long-run decline in rates of return to investors, even though the evidence here is inconclusive.[23] The indications therefore point to a somewhat too small "slanting" of the character of the improvements toward the first of the three effects listed on Page 212. In other words, the indications point to a *somewhat insufficiently laborsaving character* (somewhat too capital-saving character) of the improvements, in the sense that with a very significant rise in real wage rates there has probably been associated a mild fall in the yield of capital. The improvements do not seem to have increased the demand for capital, relative to the demand for labor, sufficiently to prevent a moderate decline in the yield of capital. But the decline in yields has not been consistent or significant in the long run. Moreover, as long as a decline in yields to investors, such as is coupled with a significantly rising trend in real-wage rates, is not so pronounced nor so sustained as to render the inducement to invest too weak, the social workability of the system is thereby probably increased. By and large, the improvement mechanism has tended to adjust to requirements in the long run.

In the Appendix to Part 3 we shall examine the statistical data that justify these propositions. But, as was already said, it must be remembered that the statistical methods which we are forced to use in long-run analysis have limitations, and it is therefore advisable for us to ask the question whether the main propositions arrived at by statistical analysis do or do not accord with the results of broad, non-technical observation. The details cannot be traced without statistical techniques, but the main results can frequently be tested for their accordance with nontechnical "experience." We may suggest here that the conclusions formulated in the present Section are very likely to be found plausible by experienced nontechnical observers. Expressed in nontechnical terms, we were concluding that the *proportion in which yields from investment have declined in the long run is exceedingly unlikely to have been greater than the proportion in which the share of property income in total income has declined.* If this is accepted as a plausible proposition, it follows by necessity that the improvements were sufficiently plentiful to keep output per unit of capital from declining, and that any decline in

---

[23] This implies an increased gap between the average product of capital and its marginal product. Hence, it implies decreased elasticity of the average product function (see Footnote 20, Page 214).

yields that may have occurred *is fully explained by the diminished share of investors in the available product.* This is what we mean by saying that a decline in yields may have occurred because of insufficiency of the laborsaving slant of the improvements but not because of fewness or over-all weakening of improvements.

In the United States, at least, it is very unlikely that the increase in the labor share before taxes should have resulted from the activities of labor unions. From 1929 to the end of the nineteen-forties, the increase in labor's share in privately produced income was very small, and this increase reflects, almost *in toto,* changes in the composition of output. In the early decades of the century the rise in the labor share was greater while the strength of unions was much smaller. Unions are capable of raising money wage rates, but the effect of this on labor's share tends to be counteracted with a lag that may be rather short. It will be seen later that an attempt was also made to minimize the effect on our observed "yields" of another political force, that of changing tax burdens.

A final word should be included about the possibility that our results concerning the effect of resource scarcities and of improvements on factor prices may be spurious because we have not eliminated the effect of changing degrees of producers' monopoly on factor prices. Technically this expresses itself in our use of marginal *value* productivity functions rather than physical productivity functions, but the criticism could be expressed without reference to marginal productivity. In our analysis we could have spoken simply of the demand for factors, instead of placing the marginal productivity theory behind this concept, and the objection could be expressed in the same manner. This would not change the nature of the possible objection. Have we not spuriously traced the consequences of changes in the monopoly power of producers, instead of tracing the character of technological and organizational improvements?

When stating that output per unit of capital has been maintained in the economy as a whole, we certainly are making a statement about technology and not about monopoly. But we have asserted also that the rate of return from investment seems to have been somewhat less than fully maintained while the average product of capital has surely not fallen (may have risen) and real wage rates have risen sharply. Here, to be sure, we are expressing a fact that could be influenced by changing degrees of producers' monopoly. This is because the relationship between the demand for labor on the one hand, and rates of return from investment on the other, is influenced not merely by factor supplies and technology, but also by monopoly power. Yet the essential content of the findings here relates to the fact that trends in the average product of capital have been *somewhat more favorable* than trends in rates of return to investors, and that trends in real wage rates have been *very much more favorable* than trends in rates of return to investors. It is inconceivable that these specific findings would result from changes in the monopoly element. This could be the case at best if, with the passage of time, an extremely monopolistic economy had changed into an extremely competitive one. The essential characteristics of the data we were discussing result from the interaction of differences between factor supplies with technological progress. They do not result from changes in the element of monopoly.

8. Induced improvements.

Approximate adjustment of the character of improvements to existing resource scarcities suggests the existence of a mechanism which tends to *induce* the required type of improvement. A theory of induced improvements can be based on one of two assumptions.

One assumption is that of pure competition, or near-pure competition, in the purchase or hiring of factors of production. In this case only a specific (but plausible) way of interpreting past successes and past failures can lead a business firm to prefer an improvement which accords with the resource position of the economy as a whole to an improvement which does not.

Imagine, for the sake of simplicity, that in the economy as a whole the labor supply stays completely fixed, but that new savings make it possible to increase the aggregate capital stock. Assume also that the individual producer is capable of making or buying improvements (inventions), and that he may concentrate his efforts either on finding improvements that shift up mainly the marginal productivity of capital or on finding improvements that shift up mainly the marginal productivity of labor. The resource position of the economy would call for making the first rather than the second kind of effort, so that primarily the demand for capital, rather than that for labor, should be increased. However, there exists no good reason for believing that a purely competitive buyer will notice *direct indications* of the labor scarcity, which in the interest of the growth process should induce him to seek improvements that shift up primarily the marginal productivity of the existing *capital stock*. The purely competitive firm can hire any amount of additional labor at the going wage rate. An atomistic unit is faced with infinitely elastic supply curves in all the factor markets, regardless of relative scarcities in the economy as a whole. The fact that in our economy the wage rate is "high" relatively to the interest rate does not, in itself, ensure that our firm will prefer an improvement which calls for using more capital with the same amount of labor to an equivalent improvement which calls for using more labor with the same quantity of capital. For if these two impovements are equivalent, in the sense of reducing the total cost of production for the initial output by the same percentage, and if the increase in output which is elicited by these two improvements does not make the firm run into steeper marginal costs in one case than in the other,[24] the firm will initially believe that its profits will increase in the same proportion with the "wrong" as with the "right" kind of improvement. Yet even in this case it will, of course, turn out that the wrong kind of improvement is much less profitable, *provided that attempts are being made all over the economy to put such improvements into effect.* It then becomes apparent that more labor is not available. Merely the wage rate is being bid up. Now one specific way of interpreting such an experience leads to the conclusion that a large part of the expected profits did not materialize for the individual firm because it had acquired the wrong kind of invention. High profits would have materialized for the individual firm if it had been in possession of "the other type of improvement." On the whole, this is a plausible way of interpreting individual experience, even under conditions of purely competitive buying. Groups of atomistic buyers are thus likely to become *conditioned* to seeking the right kind of improvement.

Where factors are hired and purchased with some degree of monopsony, the indications become more direct. Monopsony power is defined as the dependence of price on the quantity purchased by the individual firm (analogously to monopoly power, which is defined as dependence of the price on the quantity sold by the individual firm). Where monopsony power is present, that is, where the individual buyer is big enough to affect the price of the factors which he acquires, there exists a strong presumption that for an increase in output the marginal cost curve will be steeper if the firm is hiring more of the scarcer factor than if it is using more of the factor that is less scarce. Therefore, even if the two

---

[24] There is no reason to believe that the marginal cost curve of a purely competitive buyer will have a greater slope for the improvement that requires using more labor than for the improvement that requires using more capital.

improvements are equivalent (in the sense of equal cost reduction for the initial output), they are very unlikely to be equivalent for the enlarged profit-maximizing output with the improved method. Firms possessing monopsony power are likely to have direct indications of the superiority of improvements which economize the scarcer factors relative to the more abundant.

In the real world competitive elements are mixed with monopsonistic and monopolistic elements. It is impossible to describe the existing combinations in quantitative terms. But there does seem to exist a somewhat imperfect mechanism which tends to direct improvement activity in the right channels. Improvements that are forthcoming—are being "produced"—regularly on a large scale are likely to be consciously directed to reasonable objectives of a period. They are likely to bring onto the market products which satisfy a demand that has been increasingly felt in an economy, and they are likely to make use of additional quantities of those factors which are relatively freely available in additional quantities. This is what improvements have tended to accomplish, and they have tended to accomplish it without turning chronic relative resource scarcities into a chronic relative overabundance of the same resources.

9. The potential consequences of a sharp diminution of savings.

In the United States and in several other advanced economies the saved proportion of aggregate output seems to be somewhat lower at present than was the case several decades ago. Data such as those discussed in Chapter 2, Section 13, do not enable us to diagnose a clear-cut trend in the saved proportion of output, but there seem to have existed periods in the past during which a higher proportion of output went into saving and new capital formation than is the case now in advanced economies. We do not know what the future may bring in this regard, even aside from the contemporary tendency to redistribute income by means of taxation. There exists no reason to anticipate a cessation of the desire to save, but a reasonably general analysis must not take past relationships between the growth of the capital stock and the growth of the labor supply for granted.

Significant diminution of new saving might conceivably reverse the discrepancy between growth of capital and growth of the labor force. There exists no reason for expecting such a reversal, but it is conceivable that in some future epoch the labor supply might grow faster than the capital stock. In such circumstances "adjustment" of the character of improvements to relative resource scarcities would imply that the improvements should bring about a relatively smaller upward shift in the marginal productivity of capital and a relatively greater upward shift in the marginal productivity of labor than has been the case in the past. It was already pointed out that in economies with a significant *labor scarcity relative to capital,* there has occurred no rise in capital requirements per unit of output; but a mild tendency toward a rise in the relative share of labor, and therefore also a mild (and not very consistent) tendency toward a decline in rates of return to investors, do seem to have "come through." In this sense, the unfavorable effect on profitability of a significant relative labor scarcity has not been quite fully offset. If the nature of the relative factor scarcities should change in the future, the favorable effect on capital productivity of a significant *labor surplus,* and its adverse effects on wage trends, would perhaps also not be wholly offset by adjustments in the character of improvements. But it is likely that the consequences would be at least partly offset, in other words, that improvements would become distinctly more capital-saving and less laborsaving.

Sharp diminution both of new savings and of population increase might still be compatible with growth of output, provided that improvements continued. In principle, some amount of improvement activity is compatible with zero net saving (in the usual accounting sense), and with no population growth.[25] But this possibility has been of no empirical significance in the past, and it is unlikely to acquire empirical significance in the future. Gradual cessation of the desire to save would presumably be accompanied by the emergence of static or near-static conditions. Such conditions would place our social and political institutions under a heavy strain. It is an essential characteristic of a workable capitalist societies that as a consequence of significant capital formation and improvement activity, real-wage rates are rising gradually but appreciably, and that profits are connected with the ability of private business enterprise to initiate and to sustain the growth process. Our systems need growth.

Somewhat lowered capital formation, relative to output, need not be historically associated with reduced rates of output-growth. This is well illustrated by recent American experience. The output-growth obtained *per unit* of new capital formation has recently been very high. It is

---

[25] Improvements would then express themselves *exclusively* in the fact that the depreciation allowances on the capital stock are used for replacing less efficient units with more efficient ones, and that the existing labor force is becoming more productive.

quite possible that in the future the increasingly systematic research efforts of industrial nations will keep the rate of improvement, and thus the output-increment obtainable per unit of new investment, at a higher level than that to which we have been accustomed. This would keep at a reduced level the amount of thrift needed for each percentage point of output-growth. At the same time, the higher the rate of improvement, the more likely is it that increased saving could bring more planned investment and therefore more growth.

While thus saving-requirements in a workable private enterprise system are flexible within limits, it must be emphasized that the social advantages of savings (such as are matched by investment) are much greater than the rewards going to savers. This is because a higher capital-labor ratio and technological advance express themselves in rising real-wage rates. If for example, our economies can obtain a yearly output-increment of between 0.20 and 0.50 units for each unit of additional capital formation,[26] then the economy as a whole obviously "recovers" the cost of saving and investing in much less time than does the saver or the investor.

---

[26] See Pages 244-245, *infra.*

9

The Second and the Third Corollary

I. The second corollary: gradualness of structural changes and sufficient mobility of resources.

Smooth growth requires that so-called bottlenecks stemming from wrong specialization of resources be avoided. The improvement mechanism described in the preceding Chapter can take care at best of discrepancies among factor supplies in the general or unspecialized sense of the terms land, labor, and capital. But in reality factors of production, or resources, are used in specialized forms, and the mobility of factors can never be sufficient for prompt adjustment of the pattern of specialization to abruptly changing needs. A textile worker in New England does not easily become part of the work force of an oil company in California; and only very gradually can the capital invested in textile machinery be freed or recovered and reinvested in oil-drilling equipment. Localized surpluses, coupled with localized scarcities in specialized resources, may interrupt the growth process. In the short run availability of the required factors of production (in the general, unspecialized sense of the term) means little if the factors are wrongly specialized. Initially, an excess of desired over actual capital formation in one sector may on paper "offset" a deficiency of desired capital formation in another sector; yet if the expansion of the first of these two sectors is impeded by bottlenecks, then desired capital formation will be reduced in that sector, too, and the aggregative balance will not persist. We cannot say that a violation of the first corollary is responsible for the resulting imbalance. A second corollary must be added by which shortages in specialized resources become excluded.

The chances of avoiding these obstacles are best where the structural shifts are predictable, where they are gradual, and where the specialized resources change their regional and occupational specialization rather rapidly in response to changes in demand. By mobility of resources we usually mean the last of these three factors, that is, the quickness of response to changes in demand.

Abrupt structural changes are necessarily unpredictable. Moreover, only to a limited extent could the pattern of specialization be fitted to abrupt changes in demand, even if these were predictable. Predictability and gradualness are important because of the incomplete mobility of resources.

Gradualness of changes in the composition of total demand and of output requires gradualness of the adjustment of consumption patterns to a rising total income. It must be taken for granted that the structure of demands—that is, the weight of specific demands in the total effective demand—changes with the growth of output. There exist substantial differences among the income elasticities of demand for the various goods produced in any economy. This tendency toward shifts in composition with the growth of output possesses an important bearing on the improvement mechanism because the shifts point to specific areas of potential growth where "new things" will be needed. The improvement mechanism must adjust to these demand tendencies as well as to the resources position of the economy (that is, to relative factor supplies). But while gradual shifts of this sort are inseparable from the growth process, abrupt major shifts in the composition of output must lead to interruptions. We must assume that in a continuously growing economy there exists no general excess capacity because this would stop the growth process by eliminating further new capital formation; and in the absence of general excess capacity major abrupt shifts in the composition of output must create specific shortages in particular sectors of the economy. The pattern of specialization must become wrong if the economy experiences abrupt shifts. It must be taken for granted that the mobility of resources is less than complete.

An important instance of such wrong specialization is that of sudden changes in the rate of new capital formation. If, with a balanced budget, individual-plus-corporate savings do not equal planned new investment, then, a condition of dynamic equilibrium becomes violated at any event. For example, an abrupt diminution of planned capital formation, with no accompanying reduction of saving out of the initially given income, would cause output to fall. But in the event of an abrupt diminution of planned capital formation, wrong specialization would create difficulties even if the over-all balance were maintained by a simultaneous diminution of savings. One might be tempted to conclude, on the purely aggregate level of analysis, that in this case an expansion of consumer demand would neutralize the consequences of a contraction in new private capital formation. But a major readjustment of this kind requires a different pattern of resource-specialization from that which existed before. The specialized labor and equipment required in one group of industries is different from the specialized labor and equipment required in the other group. Specific shortages will emerge. The important proposition follows that in continuous or uninterrupted growth (dynamic equilibrium) all changes in the rate of growth would have to be slow and gradual. This proposition can be deduced from the second corollary of dynamic equilibrium, which excludes wrong specialization, that is, requires that no specific shortages should develop.

In the real world, abrupt changes in the structure of demands and in the composition of output do take place. But here, as with the first corollary, we may say that the difficulty tends to become eliminated in the long run. The pattern of specialization tends to adjust to requirements. Observable trends shows that so far there has been enough long-run flexibility in Western economies to assure the gradual removal of prohibitive bottlenecks. To be sure, there is a lag, and by the time the adjustment is completed there are further shifts, calling for further adjustments. Consequently, what results is not dynamic equilibrium but a long-run tendency toward lowered paths of dynamic equilibrium.

Some recent institutional changes are not particularly conducive to satisfying the second corollary. Organized groups of farmers, of non-agricultural producers and of industrial workers have become more capable of slowing, or conceivably even blocking, the outflow of resources from areas of relative overproduction. This is done partly by maintaining prices and wages in these areas above competitive levels and partly by securing government subsidies for the areas of activity in question. However, it would take a good deal of pessimism to expect that these difficulties will grow to a point where disturbances rooted in the second corollary would decisively interfere with the growth process.

2. Balance-of-payments disturbances are rooted in the second corollary.

The second corollary may become violated because of structural changes calling for a sudden expansion of one industry and a sudden contraction of another, even though both are located in the same narrower area.

Or, as was implied in one of our illustrations, the corollary may become violated because needed readjustments involve an industry in one region, such as New England, and a different industry in another region, such as California. The need for sudden readjustments which overtax the mobility of resources expresses itself in a discrepancy between desired and actual net capital formation *in specific industries*—although initially, for the economy as a whole, there may exist no discrepancy *in aggregative terms*. Insufficient mobility of resources makes it impossible to cancel one specific discrepancy with the other, and hence in these circumstances the aggregative magnitudes will not stay in balance. Now if one of these two industries is located in one country, and the other industry is located in another, the difficulty assumes additional characteristics which call for further observations. If international economic disturbances possessed no special characteristics *under the second corollary,* they would automatically be subsumed under the preceding analysis.

However, the international mobility of resources is much smaller than is their interregional mobility within the area of one nation. Consequently, a shift which would be gradual enough not to overtax interregional mobility within the territory of one nation might well overtax international mobility. Bottlenecks may develop. Furthermore, in the event of a permanent structural shift, some of the specific maladjustments tend to persist: the mechanism by which the discrepancy between the needed and the actual structure should become eliminated may be inoperative rather than merely slow.

Assume, for example, that after a period of smooth growth in two countries—in "our" country and in the "foreign" country—there occurs a permanent shift in the international demand structure, as a consequence of which, other things being equal, "they" would be buying more from "us" without selling more. Assume also that we do not wish to acquire more claims against them, and that they own no claims against us which they could now liquidate. From this it does not follow that the corresponding international migration of resources will tend to come about within a reasonable period of time, or that it will tend to come about at all. No part of our labor supply or of our capital stock may become relocated abroad to satisfy their needs; and our specialized natural resources, which are wholly immobile, may in part be unique. If the disturbance had developed between two regions of the same country, the tendency toward relocation would be more pronounced. Even those hardships which might persist would hit, in the long run, merely an untypical segment of the population, namely, an immobile section in the specific area which was adversely affected. In the event of an international disturbance the hardships may persist *in toto,* and they may hit nations as a whole or typical segments of an economy.

In the case just considered, the foreign country is compelled to reduce its imports and/or to increase its exports. It will have to adopt one or more of the following measures:

a. A lowering of its prices and of its income level by restrictive monetary policies (as would automatically happen under the gold standard);

b. Depreciation of its currency in terms of ours;

c. The granting of subsidies to its exporters, who would thereby be enabled to sell us more;

d. The introduction of tariffs or of quantitative import quotas;

e. The introduction of an exchange-control system by which "our" currency is rationed to buyers in the foreign country, and the exporters of the foreign country are legally compelled to place their holdings of "our" currency at the disposal of the rationing agency.

A "once-and-for-all" lowering of standards of living is involved in any of these measures, although the distribution of the burden is different under each. One reason why the first three of the five measures are apt to eliminate the disturbance is that they tend to lower foreign prices relatively to ours, thus normally worsening the terms of trade of the foreign country. Also, the first of the five measures tends to lower the level of output and employment in the foreign economy, and thus to reduce its demand for imports. The last two measures become effective mainly by placing administrative obstacles in the way of the foreign country's imports from us. Obviously, only the first two changes are adjustments of prices to prevailing market conditions. The others are interferences with the workings of the market.

What matters here is that all these measures force structural rearrangements in both economies. They also put into effect a once-and-for-all lowering of the standard of living in the foreign country, unless a further dose of the initial disturbance develops in each phase of further growth. In the event of repetitive disturbances, the fruits of progress may even in the long run be partly or wholly absorbed by the need for continuing adjustments. Furthermore, the last two of the adjustment measures may hamper growth tendencies in the long run because they put essential parts of the market mechanism out of commission.

The initial disturbance (the initial strengthening of the foreign country's demand for our products relatively to our demand for foreign products) need not have had the consequences here considered if, at the same time, we had increased our desired investment in the foreign country, or the foreign country had possessed claims against us which it could have liquidated. In the preceding discussion of permanent structural shifts, we explicitly assumed that the structural shift is not accompanied by such desired capital movements. However, in the event of shifts which are assumed to be temporary and reversible, the equilibrating capital movements, which in this case are short-term capital movements, may be promptly forthcoming. These may eliminate the disturbance which would otherwise develop.

The equilibrating capital movements of the free market may become supplemented by the use of reserves of the central bank, such as are held in currencies of other countries or in gold. This requires that central banks should own a sufficient stock of internationally acceptable reserves, and that these reserves should be used in a flexible manner (as buffer stocks, so to speak). The danger with such a policy is merely that, even where the disturbance is permanent rather than temporary, the reserves may become used up as if the country were facing a temporary disturbance. In the meantime, the initial maladjustment may become deeply imbedded, and it may become all the more difficult to adopt the necessary measures of readjustment with a lag. But this provides no argument against adequate liquid reserves in the currencies of other countries (or in gold). All we mean to say is that in the event of imbalance among the demands of various countries for each other's products it is necessary to have a diagnosis concerning the permanent or merely cyclical or seasonal character of the imbalance. Using up existing reserves does not cure a permanent imbalance.

In conclusion, we may repeat that sharp disturbances in the international balance are incompatible with dynamic equilibrium. They violate the second corollary under circumstances which are aggravated by the fact that the international mobility of resources is typically smaller than the interregional.

3. The third corollary: legal and institutional factors must be compatible with proper regulation of money supply.

If the first or the second corollary is not satisfied, the monetary authority may not, even in principle, find it possible to keep the general price level approximately stable. Interruptions of the growth process as a consequence of the erratic short-run functioning of the improvement mechanism may, in themselves, make it impossible to keep M in line with T/V or with $k \cdot T$ (see Chapters 5 and 8). Shortages in specialized resources may also make it impossible to regulate M accordingly. This is because, when diminishing returns or the unavailability of specialized resources lead to a fall in V (a rise in k), and hence to a fall in prices, then the additional M which the monetary authority can create may remain wholly unspent; or it may be spent in a small sector where goods are short, while the prices of most other goods continue to fall.

But from this it does not follow that our discussion of the first and of the second corollary takes account of all circumstances esential to dynamic equilibrium. It is necessary to add as a further requirement that if violations of the first two corollaries do not prevent the monetary authority from keeping the general price level approximately stable, then the monetary authority should have powers and the desire to do so. In other words, the central bank must not be bound by legal limitations or conventions which would preclude keeping the rate of increase of M in proportion with that of T/V or of $k \cdot T$, and the central bank must be willing to promote a gradual rise in M at a rate that neither greatly exceeds nor greatly falls short of the gradual growth of T/V or of $k \cdot T$. This is the third corollary of the joint condition of dynamic equilibrium. It requires that no legal or institutional obstacles, and no competing policy objectives, should prevent the monetary authority from regulating the supply of money in accordance with movements in T/V or $k \cdot T$. If this condition is satisfied, and if, *while it is satisfied,* the first and second corollaries also are, then the economy will move in dynamic equilibrium.

Not all fluctuations of the general price level are attributable to legal or institutional limitations or to competing objectives of the monetary authority which prevent the proper regulation of the money supply. Fluctuations of the general price level are frequently by-products of disturbances which are rooted in the first or the second corollary. General price fluctuations frequently take place because the first or the second corollary would not be satisfied under any conceivable method of regulating the supply of money. But if this were the only reason for fluctuations in the general price level, some of the past inflationary processes would not have occurred. Also, in some periods there would have been less deflation. Legal and institutional factors and competing policy objectives have produced deviations from dynamic equilibrium such as were rooted in the money supply.

Legal and conventional limitations which in the past were imposed upon national governments by the gold standard, and which in a milder form must exist under any variety of reasonable international monetary cooperation, may force monetary expansion or contraction even where these changes cause fluctuations in price levels. Furthermore, the needs of national treasuries, especially the wartime needs and also the needs of refinancing already existing public debts, frequently force central banks to engage in inflationary monetary operations. In periods of such operations interest rates are kept too low, and there is a too far-reaching liberalization of credit conditions, in the sense that the desired rate of capital formation substantially exceeds the rate of net saving. In the history of many economies there have occurred periods of devastating inflation. The social consequences of such developments have in some cases been disastrous. These processes have been particularly ruinous for the middle classes of some countries where a large portion of the middle-class wealth had been kept in the form of money claims, notably in government securities. Disturbances of this sort were rooted more in our third corollary than in the first or the second.

However, all three corollaries are interrelated to some extent. We saw in Chapter 5 that one difficulty with a significant inflationary movement is that it cannot come to an end smoothly because its ending causes a sharp decline in capital formation. A sudden expansion of the consumer-goods industries, and thus a sudden rearrangement of the structure of production, would be required to prevent general contraction in such circumstances; thus the second corollary becomes violated. The first corollary is equally unlikely to be satisfied in such a period because the improvement mechanism cannot function properly during a phase of significant discrepancies between needs and available supplies in specialized resources. The three corollaries may therefore be stated in the fashion here suggested, but it should be added that they stand and fall together.

It is true of the third corollary, as of the first two, that actual economic development does not satisfy it. But at the same time it is true of the deviations from the third corollary, as it is of the deviations from the first two, that they have not so far blocked the long-run growth process. No specific disturbance has persisted long enough to cause permanent stoppage. In this sense there has existed a long-run tendency to satisfying all three corollaries. The characteristics of the disturbances—their directions—have alternated. The disturbances have become smoothed out in the trend lines. But presumably they have lowered these trend lines as compared to what would have been the genuine equilibrium paths of economies.

Figures 10 and 11 illustrate the meaning of these statements with respect to trends in wholesale prices in the United States and in England. No *precise* statement can be made as to the horizontally or mild slope of secular trends in wholesale prices. Statements of this sort would depend too much on the period in which we start and on that in which we end our investigation. In the American and the British series the alternation of longer subperiods with rising and falling trends (secondary trends) stands out much more clearly than any truly secular drift. The dollar and the pound, of course, have stayed the American and the English currency since the beginning of the period with which we are concerned.

We have had inflationary and deflationary violations of the third corollary. Some of the short-run violations were mild, others very marked. Also, in both the English and the United States series, longer periods (twenty- to thirty-year periods) are observable during which the *average* yearly price increase or decrease was in the order of 2 percent. But not even for countries that were compelled to adopt new currencies after violently inflationary developments would it be convincing to argue that the secular price tendency was *dominated* by interludes of runaway inflation or of violent deflation. These interludes were limited to specific historical periods. For the United States and England, as well as some other countries, we may even say that the secular trend in wholesale prices has not been far removed from horizontal. Crude estimates of long-run trends in cost-of-living type consumer indexes suggest that these trends are more likely to have had an upward slope.

The future may prove different from the past in this regard. Automatic stabilizers and deliberate anticyclical policies are likely to produce smaller deviations from output trends (see Pages 94-96). Monetary and fiscal policy is perhaps more likely to err somewhat in the inflationary direction than to let significant cyclical contractions develop. Furthermore, unionism is likely to reduce downward price movements, *even in periods of cyclical output-contraction*. On the whole, the long-run price trend is likely to become tilted upward, perhaps from about 1940 on. However, if the slope of the price trend is very mild, this will not

FIGURE 10—Wholesale Price Index—All Commodities, 1801-1951—United States, 1926 = 100

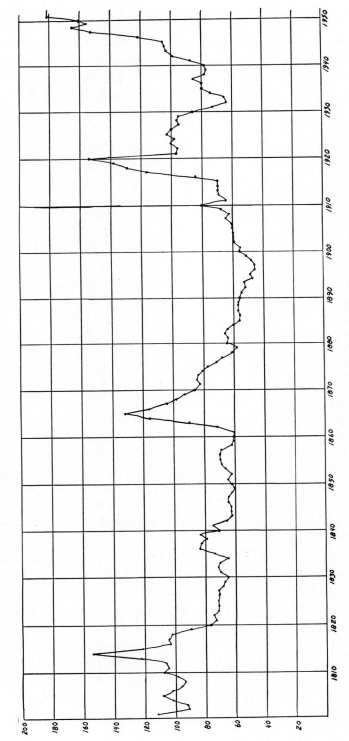

BUREAU OF LABOR STATISTICS (HISTORICAL STATISTICS OF THE UNITED STATES)

FIGURE 11—British Wholesale Price Index 1779-1953

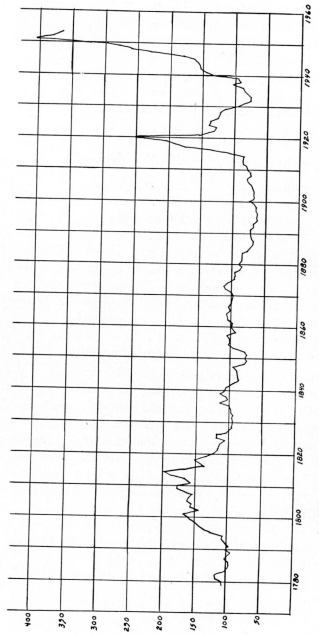

BASED ON SILBERLING, 1779-1845; ON SAUERBECK - STATIST, 1846-1953

impair the efficiency of our economies. A sharp inflationary tendency would call for direct controls—price controls supplemented by rationing and the allocation of scarce materials—and this would, of course, significantly lower the allocative efficiency of economic systems. But unless our anti-deflationary monetary and fiscal policies become too ambitious or dogmatic, it should be possible to avoid these dangers. For example, from 1951 to the present the price level of the United States has been fairly stable.

4. No separate corollary for effective demand?

All three corollaries described in Part 3 are concerned with avoiding the consequences of relative scarcities. The first corollary is required for preventing scarcities in labor and in natural resources, relative to capital, from stopping the growth process. Land, labor, and capital are viewed here as general categories, in the unspecialized sense. The second corollary is concerned with overcoming scarcities in specialized resources. The third relates to the avoidance of an imbalance between money supply and output, by stipulating that neither of these should become scarce or overabundant relatively to the other. All our technological-institutional corollaries bear on the avoidance of relative scarcities, that is, on creating balance among various requirements of growth.

While none of these corollaries is explicitly oriented to the sufficiency of effective demand, they do possess implications with respect to demand. For what does it mean to say that the corollaries are satisfied, and that the consequences of relative scarcities have thus been overcome in the required degree? This must mean that the relative resource scarcities have been *overcome sufficiently to call forth the amount of net investment which, at an approximately stable general price level, matches savings in a growing economy;* and that the required amount of new investment will be forthcoming, *given the prevalent appraisal of uncertainty ("business risk").* If this is so, aggregate effective demand is just right. What is withdrawn from the effective demand in the form of savings re-enters the stream in the form of planned investment. A further explicit condition concerning effective demand would make the list of corollaries redundant.

APPENDIX—PART 3

The Character of Improvements, in the Light of Factor Supplies, Yields And Distributive Shares

I. The propositions.

Had it not been for the compensating effect of technological and organizational improvements, growing industrial economies should have been subject to increasing raw-material and labor scarcities, relative to the physical capital stock.

If the expansion of the industrialized world into "primitive" areas is correctly viewed as organizational improvement, we must conclude that aside from improvements the available stock of natural resources would be literally fixed. The Western world would have become exposed to the consequences of raw-material scarcities. In addition, it would have become confronted with a significant labor scarcity. For we observe that with the passage of time the average worker has become much more fully tooled or equipped—in other words, in the advanced economies the labor supply has been rising much less rapidly than the physical capital stock. In the leading economies of the Western world, substantial industrialization and a substantial rise in *per capita* incomes have been taking place under these circumstances for between one and two centuries. Without the compensating effect of technological and organizational improvements, this process would have resulted in a significant rise in capital requirements per unit of output and in a significant decline of the rate of return to investors.

The available data are not very precise, but they suggest that these consequences have not shown in a sweeping way. There have occurred short-run and longer-run oscillations of considerable size in capital requirements per unit of output and in the yield of investment. Such oscillations have also taken place in the ratio of raw-material prices to the prices of manufactured goods,[1] and in the relative share of labor

---

[1] See Norman J. Silberling, *The Dynamics of Business* (New York and London, 1943), Ch. 7. Costs of producing raw-materials and raw-material prices rose relatively to the prices of finished goods in the nineteenth century. Subsequently there occurred a reversal, and it is impossible to tell in what phase of these long waves we are at present. But, at any rate, raw-material needs per unit of final output have declined sufficiently to have caused extended periods of agricultural "overproduction."

in national income. In some of the data it is even possible to discern a secular tendency in the direction in which a sweeping trend would be expected. However, while the expected secular drift shows to some extent in a rise in labor's relative share and in a decline in rates of return to investors, *it does not show in rising capital requirements per unit of output* (nor, therefore, in falling average output per unit of capital). Considering that capital has been the most rapidly rising factor, this means that improvements have been sufficiently plentiful by any reasonable criterion, although the character of the improvements may not have been quite sufficiently laborsaving to prevent the relative labor scarcity from expressing itself in falling relative income shares for the owners of capital, and in somewhat reduced rates of return to investors.

This is all the more noteworthy because the differential between the rate of increase of the capital stock and the rate of increase of the labor supply has not so far tended to diminish (except that during the nineteen-thirties and part of the 'forties capital formation was abnormally low and hence at that time there was no such differential). Moreover, the significance of a very special sort of improvement—that of the acquisition of previously unused resources through capitalistic expansion into vacant or primitive areas—has greatly diminished, so that the observable trends must have resulted increasingly from technological and organizational improvements in the more usual sense. These improvements have prevented a diminution of output per unit of capital, even though capital has been the most rapidly growing factor. As for the laborsaving and natural-resources-saving character of the improvements, this has enabled us to avoid disturbing labor and raw-material scarcities, albeit the laborsaving effect has not been so great as to suppress a mildly rising tendency in the relative share of labor and thus probably not so great as to keep yields to investors constant. But there has so far developed no *significant* long-run discrepancy between the character of improvements and the requirements set by the relative factor scarcities. In the economically advanced countries the laborsaving effect of improvements has certainly not "overshot" in the sense of turning the scarcity of labor, relative to capital, into a chronic labor surplus.

In the earlier phases of growth, for example, in England during the first half of the nineteenth century, trends in income distribution seem to have been distinctly less favorable for labor. In these earlier phases the laborsaving effect of improvements may conceivably have "overshot" for some time, especially in countries where the reconstruction of the agricultural sector was carried out by improvements of very highly labor-saving character. However, in some cases the unfavorable trend in the labor share during early phases may simply have been the consequence of the initial existence of unemployment and also of "disguised unemployment" (where the latter expresses itself in substandard jobs or occupations whose discontinuation does not reduce the total product). Even where from the outset the laborsaving effect of improvements has *not* "overshot," the initial unemployment, actual and disguised, may for some time have kept the relative share of labor down, since absorption of the initial excess of labor must have been a gradual process. Consequently, so far as the Western world is concerned, there exists no very strong indication of sustained "overshooting" of the laborsaving effect even for the early phases. Nevertheless, a mild presumption of early "overshooting" does exist in some cases. If, for example, distributive trends were more favorable for English labor during most of the eighteenth century than during the first half of the nineteenth, as might be inferred from some of the available information, then this points more to "overshooting" of the laborsaving effect in the first half of the nineteenth century than to the gradual absorption of an initial labor surplus. Moreover, there are good reasons to believe that in England there was a tendency toward increasing unemployment in the immediate post-Napoleonic decades; the frequency of cyclical depressions in that period and lags in structural adjustments do not seem to contain the *full* explanation of this tendency. This adds up to mild suggestions of temporary "overshooting" in some early phases.

However, for a more recent period—a period that in some of the advanced Western countries now extends over the past eighty years—we have strong indications of a steeply rising long-run trend in real wage rates, of a mildly rising trend in the relative share of labor, and of less than full maintenance of rate of return to investors. This is the contrary of "overshooting."

2. Capital and population.

It is reasonable to infer that the average worker of industrialized economies has become more fully "tooled" or "equipped." At the same time, the length of the work week has shown a falling trend so that the amount of capital per unit of labor input must have risen even more. For the past eight years it is possible to lend this statement some amount of statistical support, but statistics of this sort are, of course, never fully dependable.

Even in the early phases of Western European industrialization the capital stock may have risen more rapidly than the labor supply for economies as a whole.

Walther Hoffmann estimates the annual rate of increase of industrial production in the United Kingdom from 1700 to 1780 at somewhat less than 1 percent (about 0.9 percent).[2] The growth rate of the capital stock in the industrial sector is very unlikely to have been smaller (rather, is likely to have been greater) than the growth rate of industrial output. It is true that in the early part of the eighteenth century the English economy was still predominantly agricultural, and thus no direct conclusion can be established concerning the growth rate of physical capital for the economy as a whole. However, the relative significance of the nonagricultural sectors was growing very rapidly. By the end of the century, the weight of the nonagricultural sector seems to have been greater than that of the agricultural. The rate of population growth was very low: the usual estimates put it at less than one half of one percent for the eighteenth century as a whole, and at considerably less up to 1750. The growth rate of the capital stock may well have been higher, more in the order of one percent than in that of one half of one percent.

By the early part of the nineteenth century the British rate of population growth had greatly increased. The death rate had fallen substantially. From the turn of the century to 1880, the typical decennial growth of the British population moved, in all decades but two, between a lower limit of about *12 percent* and an upper limit of about *15 percent*. Around 1880 the fall in the birth rate—presumably a consequence of birth control—started outweighing the fall in the death rate, and the rate of population growth declined first into the range between *10 percent* and *12 percent* and, after 1910, below this range.[3] The labor force, consisting of that part of the population which is at work or is job seeking, grew at a decennial rate of 14 percent about 1880, and this rate of increase, too, declined to somewhat below 10 percent in the course of the first half of the present century (with a decennial rate of merely

---

[2] Walther Hoffmann, *Wachstum und Wachstumsformen der Englischen Industriewirtschaft von 1700 bis zur Gegenwart* (Jena, 1940), p. 28.

[3] Great Britain, Central Statistical Office, *Annual Abstract of Statistics* (London, 1953), No. 90, Table 6; Hoffmann, *op. cit.*, p. 273; R. R. Kuczynski, "Population," in *Encyclopaedia of the Social Sciences* (New York, 1934), XII, p. 243. These figures for the nineteenth century are influenced by immigration into Britain (*e.g.*, from Ireland) and by emigration to overseas areas.

6 percent for the third decade of the century and a recent increase in the rate of growth).[4]

While the nineteenth-century British population growth was thus very much higher than that of the eighteenth century, the growth rate of industrial production seems to have risen in an even higher proportion, that is, considerably more than the rate of population growth. Hence, for this period, too, the increase of the capital stock would have to be *very much smaller* than the growth rate of industrial production (less than one half of it) to be smaller than the rate of population growth.[5] It must be admitted, of course, that this is a very indirect way of arriving at a guess concerning the relationship between the growth of capital and that of the labor supply. To the late part of the nineteenth century and the first half of the twentieth, somewhat more adequate methods have been applied. The methods in question are similar to those which will be described in the discussion of American capital stock estimates from the eighteen-seventies on (Page 243). For Britain, Messrs. E. H. Phelps Brown and B. Weber obtained a doubling of the capital-labor ratio from 1870 to 1940.[6]

In the United States the early rate of population growth was, of course, substantially higher than that of any Western European nation. The American decennial rates of increase, including immigration, exceeded 30 percent from 1790 to 1860. After 1860 there was a decline from 30 percent toward the 1910-1920 decennial increase of about 15 percent. From the decade 1910-1920 to the decade 1920-1930 there was an insignificant rise in the rate of population growth to somewhat above the level of 15 percent, but for the decade 1930-1940 the rate fell to about 7 percent.[7] Subsequently, there has occurred a rise which has refuted the population forecasts of many experts. During the decade 1940-1950 population grew by 14 percent. At present the *yearly* net increase is somewhat in excess of 1.5 percent. There exists no consensus as yet as to how much of the recent rise merely expresses a fluctuation around

---

[4] Great Britain, Central Statistical Office, *Annual Abstract of Statistics* (London, 1936), No. 79, p. 112.

[5] Hoffmann obtains an average *annual* rate of growth of between 2 percent and 3 percent for industrial production in the United Kingdom (Great Britain and Ireland) during the period 1793-1817; an annual growth rate of between 3 percent and 4 percent for 1818-1855; of between 2 percent and 3 percent for 1856-1876; of 1.7 percent for 1875-1913; and of 1.9 percent for 1923-1935. Hoffmann, *op. cit.*, pp. 28, 30, 44.

[6] E. H. Phelps Brown and B. Weber, "Accumulation, Productivity and Distribution in the British Economy, 1870-1938," *Economic Journal* (June 1953), pp. 263-288.

[7] U. S. Bureau of the Census, *Historical Statistics of the United States, 1789-1945* (Washington, 1949), B-13.

"normal" (caused by preceding postponement of marriages and of first babies) and how much of it expresses a reversal of the previous trend toward smaller families.

In the early decades, with a decennial population growth of between 30 percent and 40 percent, the capital stock in the American economy rose at an even higher rate. This conclusion seems justified on the basis of Raymond W. Goldsmith's estimates, which will be referred to later in this Appendix. Here we shall use mainly Kuznets' estimates which go back to 1869, but no further. During the period to which the Kuznets data relate population growth was much smaller than capital growth.

The following are *decennial growth rates of the physical capital stock* in the United States for ten-year periods, beginning with 1869:[8] about 50 percent from 1869 to 1879; 65 percent from 1879 to 1889; 60 percent from 1889 to 1899; 50 percent from 1899 to 1909; 40 percent from 1909 to 1919; about 30 percent from 1919 to 1929; a negligible quantity from 1929 to the end of the 'thirties; and about 25 percent from 1939 to 1949 (or 1950).

Comparison of these data with the American population figures earlier listed shows a considerable excess of the long-run growth of the capital stock over that of the population. If we are interested in the ratio of the capital stock to labor input in the sense proper (man-hours performed), the conclusion becomes reinforced by the shortening of the work week. Allowances should also be made for changes in that percentage of the population which is included in the labor force. As is obvious from the data listed in the footnote below, these allowances do not alter the character of the conclusions.[9] The long-run rate of capital

---

[8] These estimates are based on Simon Kuznets' data up to 1929, and on a cruder method of moving from 1929 to the end of the 'forties. The latter method is described in the second of the two publications quoted in Footnote 12 below.

[9] The percentage of the population included in the "labor force" (consisting of those at work and the jobseeking) increased until the beginning of the present century, and it subsequently declined slightly. The following are the decennial percentages of increase in the United States labor force from 1870 on, with the approximate increase in the capital stock listed in parentheses:

1870-1880	35	(50)
1880-1890	34	(65)
1890-1900	25	(60)
1900-1910	28	(50)
1910-1920	13	(40)
1920-1930	15	(30)
1930-1940	8	(negligible)
1940-1950	15	(25)

growth has been much greater than the long-run rate of population increase.

However, there was very little difference between the growth rate of capital and that of the labor supply in the specific period extending from 1929 to 1950. During the nineteen-thirties there was practically no net growth in the American capital stock; and little of the capital formation of the war period 1941-1945 should be included in the permanent (peacetime) stock of the economy. At present, again, the capital stock is rising in the United States at about twice the rate of the population growth, even though the rates of increase in the population and in the labor force are substantial. A permanent reversal of this discrepancy would require continued rapid population growth, coupled with a very significant decrease of the saved proportion of output.

Our figures for the growth rates of the American physical capital stock were computed by adding to an initial stock estimate the net capital formation of successive decades. Net capital formation means, of course, gross capital formation minus depreciation allowances (which include allowances for obsolescence caused by technological and organizational progress). In the Kuznets series, on which we have mainly relied, the value of unimproved land and the value of stocks in the possession of households are excluded from the capital stock, but residential buildings are included. The significance of the initial capital-stock estimate decreases as we move on in time because the stock of, say, 1869, was very small as compared with the stock of any year in the present century.[10]

While it may be taken for granted that the physical capital stock has been rising more rapidly than the labor supply as a whole in *advanced* economies, and while the discrepancy may well have been in the same direction even during relatively early phases of Western European and North American industrialization, it is conceivable that the opposite discrepancy will establish itself in some of the contemporary "underdeveloped countries." This is because it has by now become possible to

---

It should be added that the data up to 1940 are based on the Census Bureau's concept of "gainfully occupied," while from 1940 on they are based on a somewhat revised concept. However, the 1940 estimate was adjusted (made comparable) for purposes of the 1930-1940 comparison. U.S. Bureau of the Census, *op. cit.*, D-2.

[10] In Chapter 8, Section 2, it was explained that only on specific simplifying assumptions would our estimates of capital growth be identical with estimates of the growth of *"capital" in the sense of discounted value of expected earnings.* Only if neither the appraisal of uncertainty (business risk), nor the relative significance of monopoly, changes is the parallelism between the two concepts complete. The current market value of assets is the discounted value of expected earnings.

reduce the death rate in these countries to a lower level than that which prevailed in Western Europe a century or more ago. Hence, during the interval in which the death rate is already falling but the birth rate is still very high, the rate of population growth may be higher than was the case, say, in England from the mid-eighteenth century to the second half of the nineteenth. Indeed, it has been estimated that in some of the now underdeveloped countries the annual rate of population growth could reach a level as high as 3.5 percent. But this seems an improbably high estimate. The present rates for some South American countries are said to be in the neighborhood of 2 percent per year.[11] In the contemporary environment, early phases of industrialization will bring an excess of proportionate capital growth over proportionate growth of the labor force only where investment and output-growth get under way rapidly enough to offset the relatively great rapidity with which the death rates can be made to decline.

3. The ratio of output to capital.

Since, with respect to Britain, we engaged in speculations which implied that the ratio of output to capital is unlikely to change at a very rapid rate, we shall add here a few numerical estimates concerning American capital-output relations. We shall make use of these estimates in the subsequent Sections, too.

The American output flow grew at a lesser percentage rate than the capital stock from the eighteen-seventies to the end of the century; output grew at roughly the same rate as the capital stock during the next thirty-year period, taken as a whole, that is, during the thirty years ending in 1929; and it grew at a higher rate than capital in the subsequent twenty-year period. But, aside from temporary distortions owing to excess capacity and wartime shortages, there was no violent instability in the over-all ratio of output per year to capital stock. The following figures are obtained for this ratio: 0.35 in 1879; 0.34 in 1889; 0.30 in 1899; 0.30 in 1909; 0.27 in 1919; 0.31 in 1929; spuriously low figures for the nineteen-thirties as a consequence of excess capacity; and between 0.35 and 0.40 for 1950.[12] The output *increment* per unit of capital *increment* moved

---

[11] United Nations, Department of Economic Affairs, *Measures for the Economic Development of Underdeveloped Countries* (New York, 1951), p. 45.

[12] William Fellner, "The Capital Output Ratio in Dynamic Economics," in *Money, Trade, and Economic Growth* (New York, 1951), pp. 126-134; "Long Term Tendencies in Private Capital Formation," in *Long-Range Economic Projection*, Conference on Research in Income and Wealth, National Bureau of Economic Research (Princeton,

between about 0.20 and almost 0.50 for the successive decades up to 1929, with no clear-cut trend. However, a higher incremental output-capital ratio (about 0.65) is obtained for the transition from 1929 to 1950. This may be partly a consequence of the fact that not all wartime shortages of equipment were fully eliminated by 1950. There may still have been some temporary overutilization of capacities at the end of the 'forties. But most wartime shortages had disappeared by that time, and hence not merely the "apparent value" but also the "true value" of the incremental output-capital ratio must have been high in recent periods (including the early 'fifties). This was seen also in Chapter 2, Section 13.

4. The yield of capital: introductory.

Aside from improvements, it would be reasonable to expect that, due to the law of variable proportions, diminishing returns should show in the long run in the diminution of net rates of return to owners of physical capital, when capital goods are valued at original cost of acquisition in constant prices (in the prices of some selected base year), and net earnings are valued in the prices of the same period as the capital goods.[13] In the long run it would be reasonable to expect also that diminishing returns should show, secondly, in the ratio of net earnings to the current market value of physical assets; thirdly, in rates of return on loans to business, including risk premiums; and fourthly in rates of return on loans which are free from risk of default.[14] But the link between each of the last three series on the one hand, and returns on investment in physical capital on the other, is somewhat indirect because of errors in business expectations and changing attitudes to uncertainty and because of changing rates of taxation. In this connection, we refer to Chapter 8, Section 2, where it was explained also that the changing significance of "monopoly power" influences the rates of return on cost of acquisition (our first concept above). This factor does not influence the rates of return on market values because market values contain the rents in capitalized form.

1954), XVI, pp. 275-331. In our summary in the text we spoke of approximate constancy of the output-to-capital ratio from 1899 to 1929, when the period is taken as a whole. Instead, we could have distinguished a low point in 1919. This would be a more precise way of describing the movements, except that 1919 was a year with very special (untypical) general characteristics.

[13] The problem of price correction is extremely complex, and it cannot be solved really satisfactorily. But this difficulty is inherent in any empirical application of the law of variable proportions.

[14] All this follows from the analysis in Chapter 8.

Whether, to test diminishing returns due to the law of variable proportions, trends in the rates of return on market values should be computed before or after taxes is a difficult theoretical problem. The answer depends on whether the taxes, too, become capitalized. The business taxes, at least, probably do become largely capitalized. If so, it seems preferable to examine series which express earnings from investment after deduction of profit taxes, provided that we are concerned with yields on the *current market value of assets* (e.g., interest rates, stock yields, etc.). But even if taxes are capitalized, we should examine series expressing earnings from investment before taxes where we are concerned with yields *per unit cost of physical investment* (as in our P/V ratios, which are defined on Page 255, below).[15]

A further complication develops because expected changes in the general price level influence the rates of interest on money claims: diminishing returns may not become translated into falling nominal interest rates if prices are expected to rise. Anticipated inflationary gains from investment will tend to maintain or to raise interest rates.

However, it seems reasonable to expect that a *consistent and significant secular trend toward diminishing returns would show more or less across the board, in all series here described.*

5. The yield of capital: interest rates and P/V ratios.

No real precision can be claimed for statements about secular trends in interest rates in Western economies. Some of the available time series do show indications of diminishing yields, but on the whole the indica-

---

15 We are here concerned with the effect of technological forces and of market forces on trends in yields *for the actually forthcoming amount of investment*. We must try to define these yields in such a way that the introduction or the removal of the tax should not change them (*except* indirectly in that the amount of investment is influenced by the tax, and the yield may depend on the actual amount of investment which we take for granted). Consequently, we should ask ourselves the question what the yield would be to investors, on the actually forthcoming amount of investment, if we removed the present tax. Assuming that the tax is capitalized, the yield on current market values would then be what it now is *net of the tax*. Therefore, if we observe the yield, net of tax, on current market values, then this will be uninfluenced by the removal of the tax, for the now given amount of investment. But after removal of the tax, the yield on cost of production of investment goods would be what it now is "before the tax" (without deducting the tax). Therefore, when concerned with yields on cost of production, we should observe yields before taxes. The fact that the yield on cost of production would become greater than the yield on market values explains the additional inducement to invest which would be created by removal of the tax. This additional investment would equalize the two yields. But we want to observe the yield on the now actually forthcoming amount of investment, and we want to observe that yield magnitude which is uninfluenced by the tax.

FIGURE 12—British Consol Yields, 1849-1954

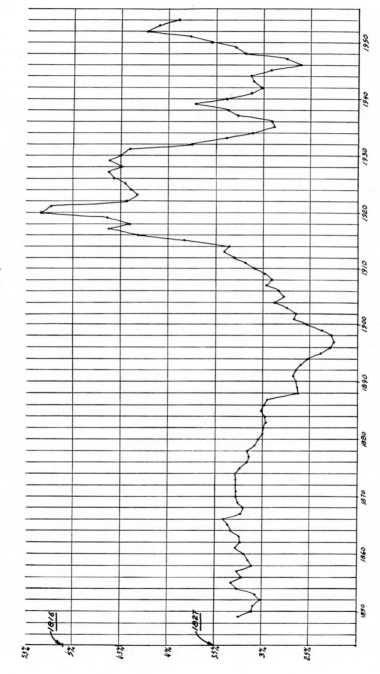

1849-1936 FROM J. STAFFORD (MANCHESTER SCHOOL, 1937); 1937-1952 FROM BRITISH ANNUAL ABSTRACT OF
STATISTICS (VOLS. 85 AND 90); 1953-1954 FROM LLOYD'S BANK REVIEW, JULY 1954

tions are neither strong nor entirely clear-cut. Some series do not show them at all.

The yield of British consols is charted in Figure 12.

We know that the rate at which the British Treasury could borrow during the eighteenth century was at times, though not always, lower than the present long-term rate. Adam Smith, for example, tells his readers that at the time of the publication of *The Wealth of Nations* (1776) the government could borrow at 3 percent,[16] while the ceiling set by the usury laws was 5 percent. At present, the rate is close to 4 percent.[17] The series shows no secular downtrend since the late part of the eighteenth century (although the diagnosis becomes less certain in this regard if we assume that the present rate is appreciably influenced by the expectation of rising commodity prices, and that it thus corresponds to lower "real rate of interest").

In charts expressing yields of capital, alternating longer periods of rise and of decline are clearly observable. Kondratieff obtained his long periods after eliminating a secular trend the character of which was strongly influenced by the limits of the total time span used for his analysis. But even if we assume no secular drift (*i.e.*, if we assume a horizontal trend), we observe for the British consols a sharply falling tendency after the Napoleonic Wars. This fall from a level exceeding 5 percent to one barely in excess of 3 percent occurred in the decade following the Battle of Waterloo, and it is not charted in our Figure. The subsequent period can be viewed as one of an approximately horizontal tendency up to the end of the 'sixties (with an exceedingly mild rising tendency in the late part of this period); then a falling tendency until nearly the end of the century; then a markedly rising tendency until about 1920; then a markedly falling tendency, which ends in the nineteen-forties (but with practically no further fall from the mid-thirties on); and finally a rising tendency after World War II. In some periods in which the consol yield was rather high, the *real* rate of interest was low or even negative, as a consequence of a rise in the price level,[18] and in some periods in which the consol yield was rather low, a fall in the price level made the low money rate correspond to a high real rate. But a marked secular trend is observable neither in the British consol yields, nor in the wholesale price series.

---

[16] Adam Smith, *The Wealth of Nations* (New York, 1937), Cannan edition, p. 89.
[17] *Lloyds Bank Review* (July 1954), p. 49.
[18] The period following World War II is a recent and strong example. In many cases the price changes were obviously not correctly anticipated.

FIGURE 13—American Railroad Bond Yields, 1857-1952

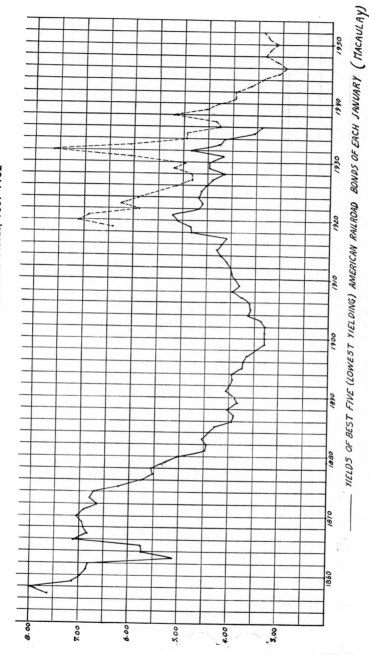

——— YIELDS OF BEST FIVE (LOWEST YIELDING) AMERICAN RAILROAD BONDS OF EACH JANUARY (MACAULAY)

--•--•-- YIELDS OF 40 BONDS FROM MOODY'S

FIGURE 14—Yields of 20 Year, Highest Grade, American Corporate Bonds, 1900-1945

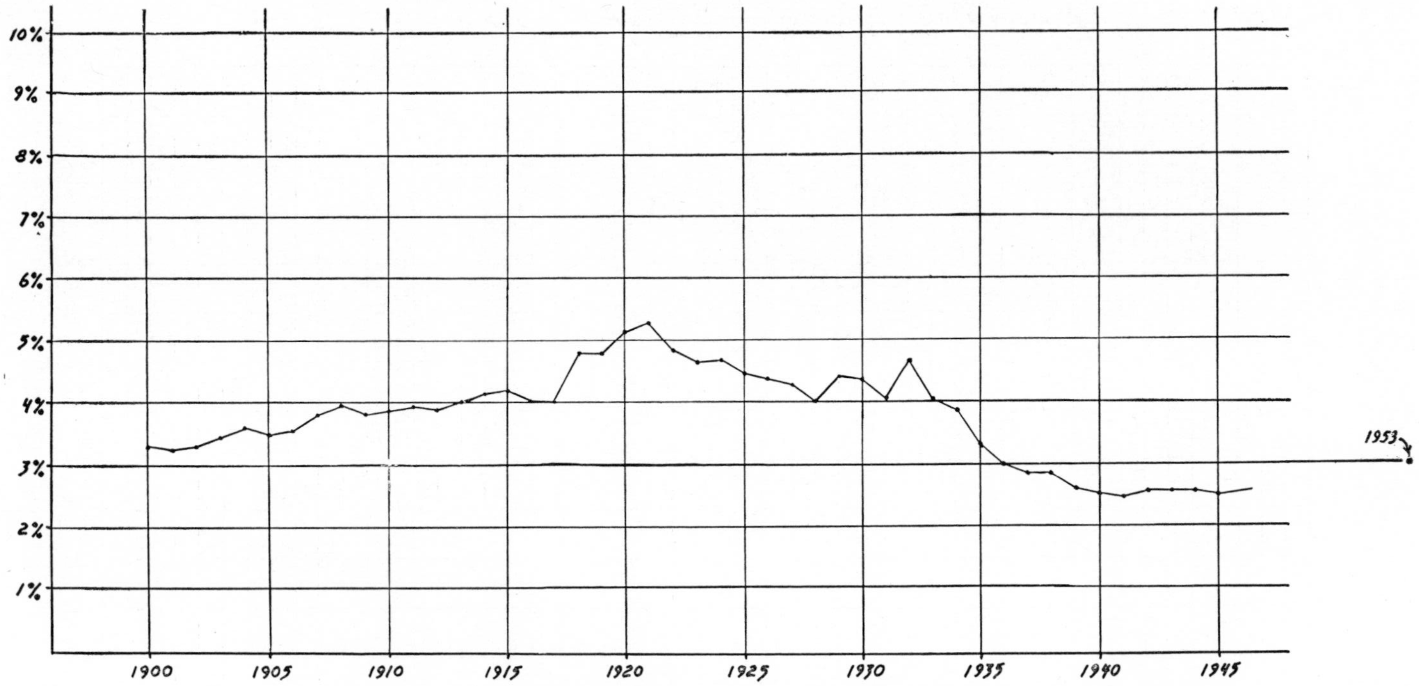

FEDERAL RESERVE BOARD (HISTORICAL STATISTICS OF THE UNITED STATES)
Approximate 1953 values added from current statistics.

The American materials lend themselves to distinguishing similar periods of rising and falling tendencies. There was a falling tendency during most of the second half of the nineteenth century, a rising tendency from the last years of the century to 1920, a falling tendency until after World War II, and a slightly rising tendency in the postwar period. Continuous series are available for the yields of railroad bonds from about the middle of the nineteenth century on (see Figure 13), and for the yields of high-grade corporate bonds in general from the beginning of the present century (see Figure 14). The railroad bond series shows distinctly lower rates for the present century, including the contemporary period, than for the middle nineteenth century and the following decades. In this sense, the series shows not merely alternating periods with rising and falling tendencies but a strong downward secular drift. However, the downward secular drift seems to have spent itself almost wholly by the end of the nineteenth century. The secular tendency seems to be tilted downward very little from then on, both in the railroad series and in the series pertaining to high-grade corporate bonds in general. It is true that World War I and the Great Depression brought much higher yields than those later observable. But it seems to us that this should be disregarded in the interpretation of the secular drift.

World War I and the immediate postwar period brought very high yields because the Treasury policy was one of borrowing at high rates, and commodity prices were rising rapidly in a short period. The Great Depression brought high yields because the risk premiums were very high and in some stages of the process there existed acute credit stringency. The Treasury policy of World War II was one of keeping the market liquid and of permitting a limited amount of private borrowing at low rates of interest. During the late war the government relied heavily on commodity rationing and allocation, rather than on restrictive credit policies, to combat inflation. After the war, and after decontrol, commodity prices rose significantly, but even at that time the bond-support policy of the Federal Reserve kept interest rates low. The natural tendency would have been toward a rise at least in some stages of the process. Only from 1951 on were interest rates on long-term government securities allowed to rise again, and the high-grade corporate bond yields differ from the government bond yields merely in that the former include a risk premium. Very recently, high-grade corporate bond yields have been moving in a narrow range surrounding the 3-percent mark. In the first decade of the present century they moved in a range lying between

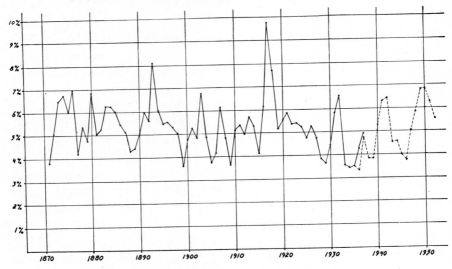

FIGURE 15—American Stock Yields, 1871-1952, All Stocks

————1871-1937 COWLES (HISTORICAL STATISTICS OF THE UNITED STATES)
------1935-1952 MOODY (SURVEY OF CURRENT BUSINESS)

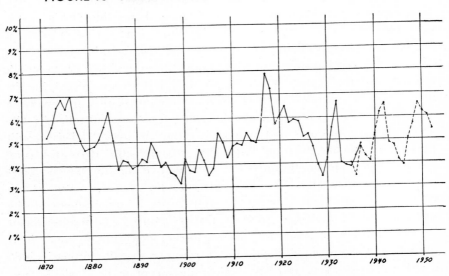

FIGURE 16—American Stock Yields, 1871-1952, Industrial Stocks

————1871-1937 COWLES (HISTORICAL STATISTICS OF THE UNITED STATES)
------1935-1952 MOODY (SURVEY OF CURRENT BUSINESS)

3.25 percent and 4 percent, and the bonds of fifty years ago were on the whole less high-grade. There may exist a downward tendency in the American bond series, even for the most recent fifty-year period, but the tendency is not very powerful.

The steep downward drift of the second half of the nineteenth century (and perhaps also the more doubtful, small downward tendency of the past fifty years) may well be a reflection of the diminution of a specific sort of risk. It is noteworthy that American "stock yields" (in the sense of dividends divided by the market value of common stock) show no downward drift for the period for which continuous series are available, that is, from 1870 on. This is apparent from Figures 15 and 16. One possible explanation of this may be that the risk premium attaching to bonds did decline very significantly in the late part of the nineteenth century, while until very recently the riskiness of stocks may not have declined similarly. In other words, it is conceivable that the surviving corporations of the present century, and the newly founded ones, are deemed less likely to default on their bonds but are deemed no less likely to suffer losses. But such a statement is difficult to distinguish from the alternative proposition that institutions managing the savings of the public (insurance companies, trust funds, etc.) have followed conservative rules of thumb. Until very recently they favored bonds more than stocks. The significance of institutions of this sort has greatly increased, and these institutional circumstances may go a long way toward explaining the difference between bond and stock yields. Whatever the true explanation may be, it is a fact that the stock yields, in the sense of dividend to market-value ratios, show no secular downward drift for the period covered by our tables. If undistributed profits are added to dividends, the indications might even turn out to be toward an upward drift. In contrast, railroad bond yields show a markedly falling trend for the second half of the nineteenth century, and a somewhat declining trend is observable in corporate bonds yields, generally, for the past half-century, too. However, in the past·few years of rising stock prices, dividend-to-price ratios have fallen a good deal for common stock, and it is questionable whether this is a merely *cyclical* phenomenon. It is quite conceivable that the difference between the appraisal of the two types of risk is becoming reduced, with the result that after some time the secular trend in stock yields will become more similar to the trend in bond yields.

Series expressing yields of the bonds of the United States federal government start in the inflationary period of the First World War. For reasons discussed earlier in this Section, a steep downward drift should be expected if we compare that specific period with the present. The drift is clearly observable, but it is strongly influenced by differences between earlier and more recent government policies.

Short-term interest rates show a secular downtrend in the United States and in some other advanced countries, but by no means in all. The relationship between long and short rates gives rise to analytical problems of great complexity which will not be discussed here. One reason for the fall in American short rates is that the market for the short-term securities has become broadened and better organized: these securities have become a much closer substitute for money.

A different way of getting at the yield of dollars invested in physical capital is to compute the value of the existing physical stock at the buyer's (investor's) initial cost of acquisition, net of depreciation, and to estimate the ratio of property income to this value (with correction for price changes). We shall now turn to such computations, even though the margins of error of estimating these yields or ratios are considerable.

In Section 3 of this Appendix, we saw that in the United States the ratio of output as a whole to the capital stock seems to have risen somewhat since the beginning of the century. If, as before, we designate output by O and the capital stock by V, we may call this the O/V ratio. As was seen, the rise in this ratio since the beginning of the century is about 25 percent (of the ratio itself) for the economy as a whole. We shall assume that O/V rose in the same order in the private domestic sectors of the economy, that is, if we limit ourselves to domestically produced output and exclude the government sector.[19] The ratio of property income (nonlabor income) to aggregate national income originating in the private domestic sector of the economy seems to have declined in the United States since the beginning of the century. The proportionate fall in this ratio (in the P/O ratio, where P means property income before taxes) is likely to have been somewhat greater than the rise in O/V, namely, about 30-35 percent of the property share itself.[20] The P/O ratio seems to have fallen by this 30-35 percent, regardless of whether

---

[19] Perusal of Raymond W. Goldsmith's estimates in "The Growth of Reproducible Wealth of the United States of America since 1870," in Kuznets (ed.), *Income and Wealth of the United States* (Cambridge, England, 1952), suggests that no great error is involved in this assumption.

[20] This corresponds to a rise in the labor share from nearly 65 to 75 percent, and therefore to a fall in the property share from slightly more than 35 to 25 percent.

we consider the P/O ratio of the private domestic sector as a whole, or merely that of the nonagricultural private domestic sector. The algebraic product of the O/V ratio with the P/O ratio is the ratio of property income before taxes to the capital stock, since $O/V \cdot P/O = P/V$. Consequently, computations of this sort also point to the likelihood that the change in the ratio of property income to the capital stock has not been significant over the last fifty years as a whole, although a decline does seem to have occurred. The decline, as here computed, is about 15 percent of the P/V ratio which was observable in 1900, (that is, 15 percent of about 10-11 percent). The P/V ratio is a crude measure of the yield of privately owned physical capital, as valued at cost of acquisition, provided that the relative significance of *rent from natural resources* has not greatly changed.[21] The most we can do to reduce the effect of changes in the rent share on changes in the P/O ratio is to use for the economy as a whole the P/O ratio of the nonagricultural sectors.

So far, we have seen that the interest-rate series, and, to some extent, also the yields of physical capital (computed from O/V and P/O), indicate some decline since the turn of the century. The "stock yields," as computed from stock-exchange data, give no such indications, although if the very recent experience is not merely cyclical, trends in stock yields may now gradually become adjusted to trends in bond yields. On the whole, it is reasonable to speak here of some degree of secular decline.

However, subperiods with alternating characteristics are, of course, discernible. Several of our time series illustrate this clearly. The average yield of new physical capital, computed as the algebraic product of O/V and P/O, also shows a succession of rising and falling secondary trends. In the United States such subperiods can be distinguished within the last fifty years, which, taken as one unit, show but a small change (small decline)[22] in P/V. From the turn of the century up to about 1920, there was a marked fall;[23] during the 'twenties there was not much change;[24]

---

[21] Statistically, we cannot distinguish the rent from natural resources from other property income with any claim to precision, and hence it is included in P. Theoretically it should not be because V does not include "unimproved land."

[22] A decline corresponding to about 15 percent of the initial P/V ratio iself (which was almost 11 percent in 1900).

[23] In this subperiod, both the output-capital ratio (O/V), and the ratio of property income to output (P/O), seem to have fallen. Interest rates had a rising tendency, but prices, too, were rising, and "real" rates of interest (with correction for price changes) were falling increasingly below the apparent or nominal rates of interest.

[24] From 1920 to 1929 there was little change in O/V or in P/O. Nominal interest rates showed a falling tendency, but there was also a fall in the price level.

and from 1929 to the late 'forties, that is, during a relatively recent sub-period, there was a *rise*.[25]

As for the decades preceding the turn of the century, we saw that the steep fall in bond yields during that period is likely to have resulted partly from a reduction of risk premiums. But this need not be the whole explanation. It is noteworthy that the P/V ratios, too, point to somewhat falling yields for the decades immediately preceding the turn of the century. In the late decades of the nineteenth century the ratio of output to physical capital was falling, and there was no corresponding rise in the ratio of property income (nonlabor income) to total income. The decline of the so computed P/V ratio from the eighteen-seventies to the end of the century was about 15 percent of the initial ratios. The fall in the O/V ratio, which alone caused this decline in P/V, occurred in a period in which an internal shift occurred toward heavily capital-using sectors within the economy. Some of these sectors (*e.g.,* the public utilities, which are subject to significant economies of scale) seem to have had particularly low O/V ratios in the earliest stages of their development, when capacity was built ahead of time in anticipation of later demand. On the other hand, in recent decades O/V ratios in the American economy have had more a rising than a declining tendency, and *if this tendency does not become reversed, then a future fall in the P/V ratios will, of course, not exceed the rate at which the P/O ratios might continue to fall.* Indeed, we saw that in the period 1929-1950 there was a small *rise* in the P/V ratio because the fall in P/O was smaller than the rise in O/V. But this happened to be a period in which the capital stock grew no faster than the labor supply.

These statements are based partly on the capital-output data on Page 242 and partly on P/O data derived from Edward C. Budd's study, *Labor's Share of National Income,* originally a doctoral dissertation (University of California, Berkeley) but soon to be published as a book. This study distributes the earnings of the self-employed, including the farmers, between labor income and income from capital, by a principle which will be explained in Section 7 below.

---

[25] For the two decades following 1929, when these are viewed as one subperiod, the rise in O/V was greater than the fall in P/O, about 25 percent as against 15 percent. Hence P/V rose by 5 percent or somewhat more. Interest rates showed a declining tendency, even though prices were rising during the 'forties (and thus the decline in "real" rates of interest was that much greater). But it must be taken into account that in this period the monetary authority was a lender at artificially low interest rates, and that during part of the period rationing and allocation prevented borrowers from bidding up interest rates to levels which would have been appropriate to market conditions.

We may conclude that some (though not all) of the available materials give indications of diminishing returns to investors. While much of the tendency has become offset by the improvement mechanism, there exist signs of a residual that may have stayed uncompensated. But the uncompensated residual *does not show in increasing physical capital requirements per unit of output:* according to the data on Page 242 there has been no such increase in the United States, and estimates by Messrs. E. H. Phelps Brown and B. Weber suggest that this statement can be extended to Britain, too.[26] An uncompensated residual shows in several (though not all) of the series expressing *rates of return to investors.* For example, the P/V ratios show such an uncompensated residual for the United States, and similar techniques point in the same direction for Britain. There is no contradiction involved in maintaining that some of the rate-of-return series show signs of diminishing returns, while physical output-capital relations do not, because rates of return to investors depend on the relative share of capital and of labor in the aggregate income *as well* as on physical output-capital relations. The character of the improvements may not have been sufficiently laborsaving to prevent a mild secular rise in the relative share of labor[27] and thus to prevent a mild declining tendency in some of the rate-of-return series. But the total effect of the improvements has been sufficient to maintain, even to increase, the physical output per unit of capital, in spite of the fact that the capital stock has been rising in a higher proportion than the supply of cooperating factors.

6. A diagrammatic presentation of the properties of improvements.

These propositions may be illustrated graphically. In the long run offsets to diminishing returns have tended to be somewhat less than complete in the sense in which a rightward shift of capital's marginal productivity schedule from MP_1 to MP_2 in Figure 17 expresses less than complete offsets. The underlying assumption here is that C_1C_2 is the new capital formation of the period during which the rightward shift of the marginal productivity schedule from MP_1 to MP_2 takes place. This new capital formation will then reduce the marginal productivity of capital from the D_1B_1 level to the D_2B_2 level. The rightward shift of the schedule is

---

[26] Phelps Brown and Weber, *op. cit.*

[27] Considering that the labor supply has been rising in a much lower proportion than the capital stock, this trend in relative shares implies a *sharply* rising trend in real-wage rates.

FIGURE 17—Joint Effect of Capital Formation and of Improvements on the Average Product (AP), and Marginal Product (MP) of Capital

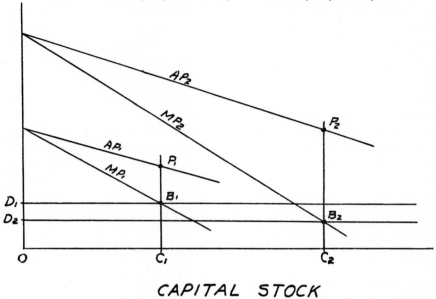

CAPITAL STOCK

insufficient to prevent a decline in the *rate of return to investors*. But in Figure 17 *output per unit of capital* does not decline. Indeed, it increases: the value of the new average productivity function of capital (AP_2) is higher in point C_2 than was the value of the old average productivity function of capital (AP_1) in point C_1. The increment in total output (or in income) which develops during the period *per unit of the period's new capital formation* is greater than the initial output per unit of capital input. This is a consequence of improvements. The yield of capital is governed, however, by the *MP* functions which relate to some given level of technological knowledge. In other words, the investment-limiting forces of any period are observable along functions which disregard the possibility of *further* improvements. More investment would not, in any given period, bring more improvement than that which takes place and expresses itself in the position of a given *MP* function. The linearity of the functions in the graph is of course an unrealistic feature, adopted for the sake of simplicity.

The decline in the rate of return from C_1B_1 to C_2B_2 in Figure 17, is brought about by a fall in the ratio of property income to total income. $OC_2 \times C_2B_2$ (which is the income going to owners of capital after the shift of the marginal productivity schedule) bears a smaller proportion to $OC_2 \times C_2P_2$ (which is the total income after the shift of the marginal productivity schedule) than does $OC_1 \times C_1B_1$ (which is the income going to owners of capital prior to the shift) to $OC_1 \times C_1P_1$ (which is the total income prior to the shift). This is because the shifted average productivity schedule (MP_2) has been drawn with a smaller elasticity than the old average productivity schedule.[28] Consequently, the average product of capital exceeds its marginal product *in a higher proportion* after the shift than before. The result here is that *output per unit of capital (the average product of capital) rises, but the share of property income in total income declines sufficiently to reduce the rate of return to investors.*

Figure 17 is used to sketch the nature of the change that occurred in the United States,[29] say, between the eighteen-seventies and the present. But it should be added that, within this period, a less favorable account seems appropriate for early subperiods and a more favorable one for a recent subperiod. From the 'seventies to the turn of the century there occurred a decline in the average product as well as in the marginal product of capital, presumably with not much change in the size of the gap between these two. On the other hand, from 1929 to 1950 a rise took place in the average product of capital, and this rise was sufficient to be associated with a rise in the marginal product, even though the gap between the average and the marginal product of capital increased somewhat (the relative share of capital in total income decreased somewhat). It is true that in the period 1929-1950 the improvement mechanism operated against little pressure, since there was no noteworthy discrepancy between the rate of increase of the capital stock and that of labor.

To each specific process ("industry") there corresponds a set of functions such as that of Figure 17. The O/V and P/V magnitudes for the economy as a whole, and thus the "representative" Figure 17 for the

---

[28] MP_2 has been drawn steeper than MP_1. But even a parallel rightward shift would somewhat reduce the elasticity of the function for given values of the ordinate. In other words, even if the shift leaves the slope unchanged on the arithmetic scale it increases the slope on the logarithmic scale (for given values of the ordinate).

[29] For England the Phelps Brown studies, to which reference was made earlier, may be interpreted as suggesting approximate long-run stability of the average product of capital, coupled with some decline in the P/V ratios, and hence in the marginal product of capital. For the United States, too, Figure 17 gives an exaggerated impression of the rise in the average product of capital from the 'seventies to the present. After ups and downs, the average product of capital now seems to be *very little* higher than in the 'seventies, but appreciably higher than around the turn of the century, and especially than in 1919.

economy as a whole, are influenced, however, by interindustry shifts as well as by intraindustry movements.

7. Distributive shares.

The previous Sections attributed significance to the relative share of labor and of property in aggregate income only because it is sometimes convenient to derive estimates of the yield of capital by means of multiplying the output-to-capital ratio by the ratio of property income to output. But there also attaches direct interest to relative shares.

In the United States the share of the "compensation of employees" in the national income rose by about six percentage points from 1929 to 1950.[30] This rise corresponds to about 10 percent of the employee share itself (which was about 65 percent in 1950). But about one third of this six percentage-point rise is attributable to the fact that in 1950 the government produced about 10 percent of the national income, while in 1929 it had produced only 6 percent. In the government sector there exists, by definition, no property share, when the accounting methods of the Department of Commerce are used. Even the interest on the government debt is treated as a "transfer," and hence it is not included in national income.[31] The remainder of the rise in the share of employees —a rise of about four percentage points—is a consequence of other shifts in the composition of the output. On balance, these shifts were from activities with a lower labor share to activities with a higher share. Aside from intersector shifts, the share of employees shows very little change from 1929 to 1950. In other words, in this period there was very little intrasector change in the relative shares for the economy as a whole.[32]

As for earlier periods in the United States, Simon Kuznets' estimates indicate that the relative shares did not change appreciably from 1920 to 1929. But there does seem to have been a rise in the share of employees during the second decade of the present century. The further back one goes, the more conjectural do the data become. By cruder

---

[30] E. F. Denison, "Distribution of National Income: Pattern of Income Shares Since 1929," *Survey of Current Business* (June 1952), pp. 16-18. National income is net of indirect business taxes, but individual and corporate income taxes are *not* deducted.

[31] "Personal income" does include these transfers. The "national income" consists of the net national product minus indirect taxes, such as excises, etc.

[32] This, of course, does not imply constancy of relative shares in each sector. It merely implies that the rise of, say, the labor share in certain sectors is offset by a fall in other sectors. It must also be remembered that such findings always depend on how many sectors are distinguished.

methods, longer periods with alternating characteristics are observable in the earlier materials, too. The American materials suggest, however, that on the whole a *secular* rise *has* taken place not merely in the share of employees, but also in the labor share, when this is corrected for the labor constituent of the earnings of the self-employed, and that this secular rise is observable even if we limit ourselves to a concern with intrasector changes in the relative shares. The rise is observable particularly if we exclude agriculture, but to some extent even if we include it. Yet *from 1920 to the present* there has been very little *intrasector* change in the relative share of employees; nor has there been any noteworthy intrasector change in the share of labor, when this is defined to include the labor income of the self-employed. The rise from 1920 to the present is a consequence merely of changes in the relative significance of various sectors in the economy.

One of several difficulties which must be faced in comparisons of this sort is created by the falling weight of the self-employed (particularly farmers). The increase, over time, in the relative share of employees produced by the individual farmer's or the individual grocer's becoming an employee is not, in itself, a genuine increase in the share of labor. In an attempt to estimate the labor share, we must correct for this apparent change either by "imputing" a labor income (as well as a property income) to the farmer and the grocer *while they are self-employed persons*,[33] or by correcting for the same shift in a roundabout way. An approximate roundabout (or implicit) correction is obtained if we trace, *not* the relative wage-plus-salary share in national income, but the relationship between the trends, say, in hourly wage-and-salary incomes on the one hand, and in total produced income per man-hour input on the other. Materials to be found in the work of E. H. Phelps Brown and Sheila V. Hopkins can be used as a point of departure for such comparisons with respect to several countries. If hourly wage-and-salary rates rise in the same proportion as total produced income per man-hour, then in the first approximation we may conclude that the share of labor income in the total income remains unchanged, with an implicit correction for the change in the weight of the self-employed. This inference implies the somewhat arbitrary working hypothesis that the self-employed, whose

---

[33] Plausible ways of correcting for the labor income of the self-employed lead to the conclusion that the *total labor* share in the privately produced American national income is at present about 75 percent, while the share of the employees is only about 65 percent.

weight has been decreasing, earn *labor income* at the average rate of compensation which the employed receive.[34]

Other methods of correction for the self-employed have also been attempted. Edward C. Budd's study, the findings of which were used in Section 5 of this Appendix, employs a method based on the explicit working hypothesis that the labor income of the self-employed is the same as the average income of the employees. Budd derives his total labor income ("service income" in his terminology) by supplementing the wage-and-salary income with the imputed labor income of the self-employed. Wherever this is possible, he imputes this labor income on the basis of the wage-salary income in the sector in which the self-employed operate. But Budd takes account also of comparisons of trends in wage rates with trends in produced income per head. His data relate to privately produced domestic output or income.

As was said before, for the United States the results generally support the assumption of a mildly rising secular tendency in the labor share, especially when agriculture is excluded. When agriculture is included, the alternations in the characteristics of successive longer periods become very marked, and it is difficult to make any clear-cut statement on the long-run drift (although, on balance, there seems to have been a small increase from 1870 to 1950). However, the oscillations attributable to the agricultural sector are likely to be caused in good part by fluctuations

---

[34] Frequently, we are faced with two further difficulties. The available data for earlier periods usually relate to wage rates in the narrower sense rather than to wage-plus-salary rates. It is likely, however, that if from wage-rate statistics in the narrower sense we obtain indications toward approximate constancy or a mild rise in the share of labor, then wage-plus-salary rate materials would indicate at least a mild secular rise in labor's share. For while salary rates have tended to decline *relatively* to wage rates in the narrower sense, they have stayed higher than wage rates, and a rising proportion of the population has come to earn "salaries" rather than "wages." Also, an increasing proportion of the population has come to earn the higher wage rates of the skilled and semiskilled workers rather than the low wage rates of the unskilled. Consequently, the comparison of trends in produced income per man-hour with trends in hourly wage rates of manual workers is likely to give less favorable results for labor's relative share than those which would result from the more relevant comparison of trends in produced income per man-hour with properly weighted hourly wages plus salaries.

However, the second difficulty which is sometimes encountered when the available statistical materials are used works in the opposite direction. We are sometimes forced to rely on a comparison, not of trends in produced income *per man-hour* with hourly wage trends, but on a comparison of produced income *per year* with hourly wage trends. Considering that hours per week or per year have had a declining trend, produced income per man-hour has risen more than the more easily traceable produced income per year. Wherever changes in the length of the work week must be neglected, this circumstance taken in itself makes the trend in the share of labor appear to be more favorable than it actually was.

in the rent share rather than in the share of income from investment in reproducible assets. The rising tendency observable in the labor share when agriculture is excluded seems to have been interrupted in some decades by approximate constancy, and occasionally by a slight fall. We have seen, for example, that from 1920 to 1929 there seems to have been approximate constancy in the labor share, and that from 1929 to 1950 the share of labor in privately produced national income rose somewhat, but that this increase disappears if we abstract from the consequences of intersector shifts in output (that is, if we compute labor's share as if the relative weight of all sectors in the economy had remained unchanged).[35] These statements concerning trends since 1920 are valid not merely for the share of employees; they remain valid if, following Budd, we make allowances for the labor constituent of the income of the self-employed, and they remain essentially valid, regardless of whether we do or do not include agriculture. Budd's study suggests that in the decade Ending in 1920 the share of labor rose about 10 percent of the share itself, regardless of whether agriculture is included or excluded. This corresponds to a fall of the property share (nonlabor share) by about 30-35 percent of itself. The period 1870-1910 seems to have contained decades with rising, approximately constant and falling tendencies in the labor share, but in the nonagricultural sectors taken as a whole there seems to have been merely a very slight rise from the beginning to the end of this forty-year period.[36] In 1950 the labor share in private domestic income was in the neighborhood of 75 percent,[37] including the imputed share of the self-employed.

Various indications point to the likelihood that over the past fifty to one hundred years there has been some rise in the relative share of labor in the Western world in general. This, of course, implies a steep secular rise in real-wage rates. Even constant relative shares would imply rising real-wage rates, since output per man-hour has been rising appreciably. The relative share of income from work in national income as a whole shows, of course, appreciable short-run variations in the course of the business cycle. In depressions the share is very high because profits are

---

[35] For computing the P/V ratios of Section 5 from O/V and P/O ratios, we had to take into account all changes in P/O (and hence in the labor share), not merely the intrasector changes.

[36] If agriculture is included, the labor share *fell* by somewhat less than 10 percent of itself from 1870 to 1910, owing to a decline that occurred in the last decade of the nineteenth century.

[37] See Footnote 33, Page 261.

low or negative. Consequently, when we engage in long-run analysis it is essential to select for comparison periods during which the cyclical factor may be assumed to have canceled out.

Economic historians admit that they have very little to go on when they try to reconstruct trends in the standard of living of workers for earlier periods. In the footnote, below, we shall engage in some speculations which perhaps point to the likelihood that in England the relative share of labor increased between the time of Gregory King and that of Adam Smith.[38] However, there seems to have been a decline not merely in labor's relative share but also in real wage rates during the Napoleonic Wars, when the cost of living of the English population rose significantly.

---

[38] Adam Smith quotes Gregory King's figure of fifteen pounds per year for the typical *family income* of common laborers in 1688. Smith's figures for England (we must exclude Scotland for the present comparison) correspond to from eighteen to twenty-three pounds *per worker* for the seventeen-seventies, on a yearly basis. From Smith's comments on Cantillon's speculations concerning the relative earning power of husband and wife in workers' families, we may conclude that Smith did not consider it unreasonable to assume that the family income of workers was about 1.5 times the common worker's income. (We should add here that he did not wish to *commit* himself to this ratio.) It seems, therefore, that Smith's estimate of the yearly family income of the common worker of his time was hardly lower than from twenty-seven to thirty-five pounds, that is, 1.5 times the income per worker. The lower limit of Smith's range may be more representative because the passage gives the impression that the low-wage districts are not included in the range. Even this implies near doubling of common workers' money incomes since 1688. After listing some commodities the prices of which fell during this ninety-year interval, and less important commodities the prices of which rose, Smith concludes that real wages must have risen *more* than money wages. It is safe to conclude that if both Gregory King's and Adam Smith's observations were approximately correct, real-wage rates must have risen at an average yearly rate of *at least 1 percent* between the sixteen-eighties and the seventeen-seventies.

Taking into account Walther Hoffmann's estimate of the growth of total *industrial* output, this output, and therefore also aggregate output including agriculture, are very likely to have risen at a yearly rate of rather less than 1 percent. While the growth rate of industrial output seems to have been slightly *less* than 1 percent per year for the United Kingdom, including Scotland, it may be reasonable to assume that for more rapidly growing England (to which the King-Smith comparison relates) the growth rate of industrial output was somewhat in excess of 1 percent. The growth rate of English *aggregate* output, including the agricultural sector, can scarcely have been more than *about 1 percent*. It probably was smaller. Output per man-hour must have increased somewhat less than total output. Therefore, these figures imply a rise in real-wage rates that exceeded the rate of increase in man-hour output. This, in turn, points to an increasing share of workers in the national income for the period between Gregory King and Adam Smith.

During the Napoleonic Wars there seems to have occurred a fall, not merely in the relative share of labor, but also in real-wage rates. The use of Norman J. Silberling's cost-of-living index on the one hand, and G. H. Wood's industrial money-wage index on the other, suggests that during the war period real-wage rates first fell steeply and then recovered, but that they reached their 1790 level only in the second decade of the century. On the other hand, a comparison of Silberling's cost-of-living index with his

But there was probably a subsequent rise in labor's relative share as well as in real-wage rates when prices fell after the war. In the course of the nineteenth century there seem to have been longer-run oscillations in relative shares, with the 'seventies and 'eighties identifiable as a period of rising labor share. For England as well as the United States, there exist indications of a rise in labor's share, when recent decades are compared with the late part of the nineteenth century.

Before concluding this Appendix, we should add a comment on the difference between income distribution by functional shares and distribution by size of income. Even without statistical investigation, it must be obvious to most observers that in several Western countries, including the United States, there has been since the nineteen-thirties a shift toward a more equal distribution of income. How is this observation compatible with indications that, aside from intersector shifts in the composition of the American output, there has been since about 1920 no *significant* change in the relative shares of labor and property, respectively? One would expect the shift toward less inequality to be discernible in the

---

own agricultural money-wage index points to a small rise of agricultural real wages beyond their prewar level, even in the course of the first decade of the century.

In the decade following the Battle of Waterloo, there was a steep fall in the British price level, accompanied by a much smaller fall in money wages, and the resulting rise in real-wage rates is likely to have exceeded the rise in output per man-hour. At that time, there seems to have been a rise in the relative share of labor. The period was also characterized by increasing unemployment, but we are here concerned with relative shares in the income produced, not with the general condition of the laboring classes.

The period from 1825 to 1873 very probably included spans during which the relative share of labor fell. Judging by a comparison of real-wage rates with man-hour output data, the period as a whole may well have brought a fall in labor's relative share. However, during the eighteen-seventies, and especially the 'eighties, there seems to have occurred a distinct rise in labor's relative share in the British economy. This problem is discussed extensively by W. W. Rostow, and the proposition is supported by a variety of indications.

It should be added that Hoffman's data permit of a comparison of the growth rate of the value of industrial production with that of wages paid in the industrial sector from 1841 to 1931. This comparison shows a *very slightly* higher growth for wages paid than for value of production when 1931 is compared with 1841, but a much greater discrepancy in the same direction for some subperiods, including the 'eighties. This, of course, is offset by the opposite discrepancy in the other subperiods.

For sources see: Gregory King, *Natural and Political Observations and Conclusions upon the State and Condition of England* (Baltimore, 1936), p. 31; Smith, *op. cit.*, Bk. I, Ch. 8; W. W. Rostow, *British Economy of the Nineteenth Century* (Oxford, 1948), p. 8; Part 1, Ch. 4, pp. 90-108; see also Part 4; Hoffmann, *op. cit.*, pp. 32 and 54; N. J. Silberling, "British Prices and Business Cycles, 1779-1850," *Review of Economics and Statistics* (October 1923), pp. 219-261; George H. Wood, "Real Wages and the Standard of Comfort since 1850," *Journal of the Royal Statistical Society* (March 1909), pp. 91-103.

DISTRIBUTION OF FAMILY PERSONAL INCOME
AMONG QUINTILES AND TOP FIVE PERCENT OF CONSUMER UNITS

Table 6

Percentage Share of Family Personal Income
(All Consumer Units)

Quintile	1935-1936	1941	1944	1946	1947	1950
Lowest	4.1	4.1	4.9	5.0	5.0	4.8
Second	9.2	9.5	10.9	11.1	11.0	11.0
Third	14.1	15.3	16.2	16.0	16.0	16.2
Fourth	20.9	22.3	22.2	21.8	22.0	22.3
Highest	51.7	48.8	45.8	46.1	46.0	45.7
Top 5%	26.5	24.0	20.7	21.3	20.9	20.4

Table 7

Lower Income Limit (All Consumer Units)
(in current dollars)

Quintile	1935-1936	1941	1944	1946	1947	1950
Second	$ 560	$ 740	$1,510	$1,660	$1,730	$1,840
Third	930	1,370	2,450	2,680	2,800	3,040
Fourth	1,380	2,040	3,410	3,650	3,830	4,200
Highest	2,120	2,940	4,800	5,130	5,470	5,960
Top 5%	3,910	5,010	8,240	9,180	9,560	10,500

SOURCE: Selma Goldsmith, G. Jaszi, H. Kaitz, and M. Liebenberg. "Size Distribution of Income since the Mid-Thirties," *Review of Economics and Statistics* (February 1954), p. 9.

individual sectors of the economy. If the shift is caused by a strengthening of the relative power of labor groups, one would expect it to be observable in the relative share of labor.

Statistics relating to distribution by the size of income show a change quite clearly. Table 6 ranks all consumer units in the United States by their size, listing them from the lowest 20 percent (lowest "quintile") to the highest, and showing separately the top 5 percent. Table 7 characterizes these population groups in terms of the income limits within which a consumer unit had to fall in order to belong in a given population group. A consumer unit is a weighted average of families and individuals, where the requirement is that the unit should live mainly by a common budget. The table relates to the distribution of personal income, before personal taxes.

From the mid-thirties to 1950, the relative share of the upper income groups declined appreciably. The shift was practically completed by 1944. We have indications pointing to the likelihood that the shift started (at least) somewhat earlier than in the mid-thirties.

Why doesn't a similar shift show in the relative share of labor in the individual sectors of the economy? To assure full statistical comparability of *distribution by functions* with *distribution by size of income* would be a difficult task indeed. But at least three circumstances come to mind which help explain the apparent discrepancy between these findings.

In the first place, the share of labor in "national income" is its share in an income magnitude from which corporate income taxes are not deducted.[39] In such statistics, the corporate income-tax payments are interpreted as entering into "property income" (nonlabor income). On the other hand, distribution by size of income relates to personal income, that is, to the income of individuals. Personal incomes do not, of course, include *corporate* income taxes, even though the personal incomes listed in our tables are "before *personal* taxes." During the period covered by the tables the corporate income tax increased significantly as a percentage of national income (from which it is not deducted).

Secondly, undistributed corporate profits also increased significantly relatively to national income. This is especially true if we compare the

---

[39] In other words, "national income" includes the corporate taxes. It is *not* net of these. Thereby indirect business taxes, such as excises, are deducted from the net national product.

chronically depressed 'thirties with 1944 or with 1950. But a relative increase would be observable even in a comparison of the 'twenties with either of the two latter years. Undistributed corporate profits are included in national income, and hence in the property share (nonlabor share), but they are not, of course, included in personal income. Here we have a second reason why the share of the upper income groups in personal income does not contain the full equivalent of the share which is assigned to them in functional distribution statistics based on national income. Both these reasons may have quite a bit to do with taxation—one of the two reasons certainly has. Much of the corporate profits tax is a deduction from upper-bracket incomes, since surely not all of the burden is shifted to buyers in the form of higher prices. At the same time the relative growth of undistributed corporate profits may be partly a consequence of high *personal* taxes. Steeply graduated personal taxation increases the attractiveness, for important stockholders, of reinvesting the corporate earnings in the corporation itself, and of thus avoiding the double taxation of dividends. In other words, while we observe a shift toward more equality even in personal incomes *before personal taxes,* this shift is nevertheless partly a consequence of increased corporate and personal taxes.

There exists also a third reason why "personal" income distribution shows an equalitarian shift, while the "functional" shares in national income do not show it (or do not show it appreciably). *Within* the aggregate of wage-salary incomes, before personal taxes, there has undoubtedly occurred a shift toward less inequality (smaller differentials). It is conceivable that some reduction of inequality has also taken place within the aggregate of property incomes. Such shifts would, of course, produce less inequality in personal distribution without showing traces in the pattern of functional distribution.

At present, it does not seem possible to appraise the relative significance of these three reasons quantitatively. An explanation based on the first two would place much of the emphasis on taxation. Such an explanation would suggest that the diminution of the relative share of the upper brackets in personal income is largely a consequence of taxation, even though the personal incomes in question are computed before personal taxes. The third reason is much less intimately connected with high taxation. It is connected with high taxation only because high marginal tax rates may reduce the interest of high-income recipients in further improving their incomes. Capital gains, which are not included in "income," have the advantage of being subjected to considerably lower taxation, and within certain limits it is sometimes a matter of choice whether given earnings accrue in the form of income or in the form of capital gains.

However, the reduced inequality within the aggregate of wage-salary incomes is likely to be partly the result of the leveling influence of unionism. While, as we shall presently see, there exist no indications that unionism has changed the share of labor income in total income before taxes, the wage-salary structure (the relationship between types of labor that are unionized and types that are not) may well have been influenced by the existence of unions. The mechanism by which the share-raising efforts of unions seem to have become largely or wholly offset [41] does not necessarily eliminate union influence on the internal wage and salary structure when we compare organized and unorganized labor belonging to two types with appreciably different specializations. Over the past twenty-five to thirty years wage trends for unionized labor seem to have been very similar to wage trends for nonunionized labor, if we compare rather easily interchangeable labor categories (similar "specifications"). But a different problem is posed by the existence of organized and unorganized labor belonging in categories differently specialized between which there is comparatively little direct competition. Take for example skilled versus unskilled or clerical versus manual labor. Here relative positions may well have become influenced. The influence is likely to have been exerted in the equalitarian direction, because within the ranks of labor the relative power of the unskilled groups has increased, and because clerical workers are largely unorganized. But it should also be recognized that the spread of schooling and other circumstances have probably reduced the scarcity value of many skills and of white-collar quality. This contributes to explaining the observable diminution of skilled-unskilled and of clerical-manual differentials, in the United States and in other countries. [42]

On the whole, it seems to us that a substantial part of the change in the distribution of personal income *is* a consequence of increased taxation. The high tax burden of the upper income groups—that is, the high level of corporate taxation and the high graduation of personal taxes—

---

[41] This seems to be a mechanism operating partly through wage-induced *price increases,* and partly through additional incentives toward laborsaving improvements.

[42] For an analysis of narrowing differentials, see Lloyd G. Reynolds and Cynthia H. Taft, *Essays in Wage Structures* (to be published by the Yale University Press in 1956).

has resulted to no small extent from the increased political power of the relatively low-income groups. For the understanding of this sociological process, it is very important to take account of the significance of the organization of labor. But it is questionable, to say the least, whether labor unions have, by means of collective bargaining, brought about a change in the before-tax distribution of national income as between labor and capital. In the United States, for example, there surely exists no indication that *prior* to the nineteen-thirties, when unionism became powerful, there was a trendlike decline in the labor share. Indeed, in the early part of the century there seems to have been a rise, and in the period 1920-1929 there was very little change. In this regard, the period 1929-1950 is not different in any obvious way from the period 1920-1929, even though the strength of unionism has increased very greatly. During the period 1929-1950 the moderate rise in the share of labor was attributable wholly to intersector shifts in the composition of output. Any appreciable consequences of unionism on functional shares should show *within* individual sectors of the economy. Shifts from industries with a relatively low labor share to industries with a higher labor share do, of course, tend to raise the over-all share of labor, but such a rise cannot be explained by the power of unions. If unions have anything to do with these shifts, their effect on them should be discouraging. Indeed, their effect may very well have been discouraging, but this effect may have been insufficient to suppress the shifts completely.

Whatever effects unionism may have on money-wage rates is likely to be partly offset by price increases. The remainder of the effect may well "tend" to show in a rise in the relative share of labor in the unionized sectors, but this "tendency" may become largely offset by induced labor-saving improvements. We have seen that the tendency toward relative labor scarcity has, in general, become largely offset by the laborsaving character of the improvement process. Wherever the unions of an industry succeed in increasing product wage rates (that is, money-wage rates relatively to the prices of the products of the industry in question), the mechanism must work through the ability of unions to increase the existing degree of relative labor scarcity. Increased labor scarcity may call forth improvements of more definitely laborsaving character. At any rate, if we compare labor-share trends during the period 1929-1950 with earlier trends, we obtain no indication of a share-raising effect of unionism in the United States.

BIBLIOGRAPHY—PART 3

1. List of books and articles from which general supplementary readings may be selected:

Books

Fisher, Irving. *The Theory of Interest.* New York: The Macmillan Co., 1930.

Hicks, J. R. *The Theory of Wages.* London: Macmillan & Co., 1932.

Robinson, Joan. *The Rate of Interest and Other Essays.* London: Macmillan & Co., 1952 (particularly her essay "Notes on the Economics of Technical Progress").

Rostow, W. W. *British Economy of the Nineteenth Century.* Oxford: Clarendon Press, 1948.

Shaw, Edward S. *Money, Income, and Monetary Policy.* Chicago: Richard D. Irwin, 1950.

Silberling, N. J. *The Dynamics of Business.* New York and London: McGraw-Hill Book Co., 1943.

Viner, Jacob. *Studies in the Theory of International Trade.* New York and London: Harper & Bros., 1937.

Wood, Elmer, *English Theories of Central Banking Control, 1819-1858,* Cambridge: Harvard University Press, 1939.

Articles

Goldsmith, Raymond. "The Growth of Reproducible Wealth of the United States of America from 1805 to 1950," in *Income and Wealth of the United States,* ed. by S. Kuznets. Income and Wealth Series II. Cambridge, Eng.: Bowles & Bowles, 1952.

Hamberg, D. "Full Capacity vs. Full Employment Growth." *Quarterly Journal of Economics,* August 1952.

Kuznets, Simon. "Long-Term Changes in the National Income of the United States of America Since 1870," in *Income and Wealth of the United States,* ed. by Kuznets. Income and Wealth Series II. Cambridge, Eng.: Bowles & Bowles, 1952.

Spengler, J. J. "Population Theory," in *Survey of Contemporary Economics,* Vol. II, ed. by B. F. Haley. Homewood, Ill.: Richard D. Irwin, 1952.

2. Further readings relating to topics discussed in Part 3:

Books

Aftalion, Albert. *Les Crises périodiques de surproduction.* Paris: M. Rivière & Cie, 1913.

Ashton, T. S. and R. S. Sayers, ed. *Papers in English Monetary History.* Oxford: Clarendon Press, 1953.

Bowley, A. L. *Wages and Income in the United Kingdom Since 1860.* Cambridge, Eng.: University Press, 1937.

Clapham, J. H. *A Concise Economic History of Britain, from the Earliest Times to 1750*. Cambridge, Eng.: University Press, 1949.

————. *The Economic Development of France and Germany, 1815-1914*. Cambridge, Eng.: University Press, 1936.

Cole, G. D. H. and Raymond Postgate. *The Common People*. London: Methuen & Co., 1949.

Court, W. H. B. *A Concise Economic History of Britain from 1750 to Recent Times*. Cambridge, Eng.: University Press, 1954.

Cowles, Alfred. *Common Stock Indexes, 1871-1937*. Bloomington: Principia Press, 1938.

Dupriez, L. H. *Des Mouvements économiques Généraux*. Louvain: Institut de Recherches Économiques et Sociales, 1947.

Ernle, R. E. P. *English Farming, Past and Present*. London and New York: Longmans, Green & Co., 1936.

Fisher, Irving. *The Nature of Capital and Income*. London: Macmillan & Co., 1906.

————. *The Purchasing Power of Money*. New York: The Macmillan Co., 1911.

Goldsmith, Raymond. *Financial Structure and Economic Growth in "Advanced" Countries,* Conference on Capital Formation and Economic Growth. New York: National Bureau of Economic Research, 1953.

Hayek, F. A. von, ed. *Capitalism and the Historians*. Chicago: University of Chicago Press, 1954.

Hoffmann, Walther, *Wachstum und Wachstumsformen der Englischen Industriewirtschaft von 1700 bis zur gegenwart*. Jena: G. Fischer, 1940.

King, Gregory. *Natural and Political Observations and Conclusions upon the State and Condition of England*, in *Two Tracts*. Baltimore: The Johns Hopkins Press, 1936.

Macaulay, F. R. *Some Theoretical Problems Suggested by the Movements of Interest Rates, Bond Yields, and Stock Prices in the United States Since 1856*. New York: National Bureau of Economic Research, 1938.

Rousseaux, Paul. *Les Mouvements de Fond de l'Economie Anglaise, 1800-1913*. Paris: Desclée, DeBrouwer & Cie, 1938.

Sauerbeck, A. *The Course of Average Prices of General Commodities in England*. London: P. S. King & Son, 1908.

Smith, Adam. *The Wealth of Nations,* ed. by Edwin Cannan. New York: Modern Library, 1937 (particularly Bk. I).

U. S., Joint Committee on Economic Report (83d Congress, 2d Session). *Trends in Economic Growth, A Comparison of the Western Powers and the Soviet Bloc*. Washington: Government Printing Office, 1955.

Usher, A. P. *An Introduction to the Industrial History of England*. New York: Houghton Mifflin Co., 1920.

Articles

Angell, J. W. "The Components of the Circular Velocity of Money." *Quarterly Journal of Economics,* February 1937.

Denison, E. F. "Distribution of National Income: Pattern of Income Shares Since 1929." *Survey of Current Business,* June 1952.

Ellis, H. S. "Some Fundamentals in the Theory of Velocity." *Quarterly Journal of Economics,* May 1938; reprinted in *Readings in Monetary Theory* (American Economic Association), Philadelphia: The Blakiston Co., 1951.

Goldsmith, Selma, G. Jaszi, H. Kaitz, and M. Liebenberg. "Size Distribution of Income Since the Mid-Thirties." *Review of Economics and Statistics,* February 1954.

Hawtrey, R. G. "Modern Banking: United Kingdom," in *Encyclopaedia of the Social Sciences.* New York: The Macmillan Co., 1930.

Hopkins, S. V. and E. H. Phelps Brown. "The Course of Wage Rates in Five Countries, 1860-1939." *Oxford Economic Papers,* June 1950.

Kahn, R. F. "Some Notes on Liquidity Preference." *The Manchester School,* September 1954.

Kondratieff, N. D. "Die Preisdynamik der industriellen und landwirtschaftlichen Waren." *Archiv für Sozialwissenschaft und Sozial politik,* August 1928.

Kuczynski, R. R. "Population: History and Statistics," in *Encyclopaedia of the Social Sciences.* New York: The Macmillan Co., 1934.

Phelps Brown, E. H. and B. Weber. "Accumulation, Productivity and Distribution in the British Economy, 1870-1938." *Economic Journal,* June 1953.

Robinson, Joan. "The Classification of Inventions." *Review of Economic Studies,* February 1938; reprinted in *Readings in the Theory of Income Distribution* (American Economic Association), Philadelphia: The Blakiston Co., 1946.

Silberling, N. J. "British Prices and Business Cycles, 1779-1850." *Review of Economic Statistics,* 1923 supplement.

Stern, E. H. "Capital Requirements in Progressive Economies." *Economica,* August 1945.

Sultan, P. E. "Unionism and Wage-Income Ratios: 1929-51." *Review of Economics and Statistics,* February 1954.

Wood, G. H. "Real Wages and the Standard of Comfort Since 1850." *Journal of the Royal Statistical Society,* March 1909.

PART 4 /

Cyclical Disturbances

10

The Paradoxes of Disequilibrium

The discussion in Part 3 gave a spuriously harmonious account of economic development because it disregarded cyclical growth interruptions. We shall now turn to an analysis of these disturbances and shall start with an attempt to show how certain well-known paradoxes of disequilibrium can be resolved.

1. Scarcities create overabundance.

The discussion of the first corollary in Chapter 8 demonstrated that the growth process tends to become interrupted when uncompensated scarcities of labor and of natural resources develop, that is, when the relative scarcities of the factors cooperating with capital are not offset by improvements. Factor scarcities were here interpreted in the general sense, without regard to regional or industrial specialization. The rate of overcoming the relative scarcity of labor and of natural resources must be sufficient to make it profitable for producers to engage in the amount of new capital formation which corresponds to the rising amount of new savings in an expanding economy.

The analysis relating to the second corollary pointed up another reason for interruptions of growth. Scarcities in specialized resources—a pattern for the specialization of equipment and of labor which has ceased to fit the needs of the economy—may result in interruptions. This is a matter of the insufficient mobility of resources in response to changes in the demand structure.

The third corollary makes it clear that on realistic assumptions further growth in any period requires sufficient expandability of the supply of money, that is, the avoidance of money scarcity. Insufficient expandability of the money supply may be the consequence of a scarcity of monetary metals, but it may also result from policy objectives competing with that of domestic price stability,[1] or from institutional factors (regulations or conventions) which are binding for the central bank. These may have an effect similar to that of a scarcity of monetary metals under the gold standard. Violations of any one of the corollaries frequently makes it difficult or impossible to satisfy the others.

The analysis of the corollaries leads to looking upon interruptions of the growth process as being caused by relative scarcities. Considering that the proper rate of overcoming scarcities is one that calls forth the rate of investment which matches savings, the business cycle expresses alternations of the rate of overcoming scarcities, complicated by alternations in the appraisal of risk (uncertainty). This is our central proposition here.

When the relationship between the rate of overcoming scarcities and the rate of saving is placed in the center of dynamic analysis, it is necessary to call the reader's attention to the somewhat hidden role of uncertainty in the analysis. A given degree of scarcity of the resources cooperating with capital may or may not be too great for continued growth, according as the uncertainty attaching to business expectations is greater or smaller. The reason why scarcities can stop growth is that they reduce profitable investment opportunities; whether investment opportunities are or are not sufficiently profitable depends partly on the appraisal of uncertainty.

Yet in periods when the growth process is interrupted, all factors of production appear to be overabundant. How does this appearance of pathological overabundance develop if the fundamental phenomenon here is that of scarcities?

The paradox is mainly rooted in the fact that once scarcities force an appreciable *slowing* of growth, this will lead to *contraction*. The acceleration principle tells us that an appreciable slowing of the growth process must be connected with a reduction of the rate of new investment. New capital formation derives its justification from the ability of the system to grow. If scarcities lead to a sudden and appreciable slowing of the growth process, new investment becomes insufficient to match savings, and effective demand becomes insufficient even to maintain the output level already reached.

Moreover, in the event of an appreciable slowing of the growth process,

---

[1] For example, international exchange-rate stability may be a competing policy objective.

output would have to contract even if savings were reduced concurrently. Shortages in specialized resources—in specific kinds of equipment or of labor—would stand in the way of promptly rearranging the structure of production in such a way as to accomplish the stabilization of output and to avoid contraction. For under these conditions the output of consumer goods would have to rise promptly, as the output of investment goods was falling. The essence of the matter is that scarcities in relation to what would be required for continued growth, at a sufficient rate, give rise to contraction and to all-around overabundance of resources in relation to the requirements of a contracted economy.

It cannot be taken for granted that the all-around overabundance of resources in the contracted state of the economy will always induce investors to create full employment. For if it is more or less predictable that at previously attained levels of activity the economy would immediately run into the same scarcities which had originally forced the system into contraction, then the expectations of producers may not lead them into the abortive experiment of expansion. Only when the initial scarcities become eliminated by improvements and by the mobility of resources (in some cases also by greater flexibility of the money supply) will approximately correct expectations lead to expansion.

2. The oversaving paradox.

If the interruptions of the growth process are properly attributed to scarcities, how can it be true that a reduction of the rate of saving would sometimes prevent these interruptions? It seems paradoxical that the consequences of scarcities could have been avoided or alleviated by saving less out of given incomes. For saving less means consuming more. How can the consequences of scarcities be alleviated by consuming more?

The inference that reduced saving would sometimes help to prevent contraction follows from the fact that if, at a given level of output, there were less saving, then a smaller amount of desired new capital formation would be required to keep the economy from contracting. Contraction takes place because of the insufficiency of desired capital formation to match savings. Even if initially there developed no discrepancy between desired net capital formation and savings, specific shortages—maladjustments in the structure of production—or a contraction of the supply of money could still force a fall in the rate of output, but one significant cause for such a fall would be removed.

By saving part of its income, an economy expresses its unwillingness to use the entire producible output *unless* a given proportion of the output assumes the form of goods for new investment, that is, unless a given proportion is made to serve the purpose of further growth. This further growth is what is hampered by scarcities. Saving less and consuming more would express a willingness to use a kind of output the composition of which would be such as to guarantee that the output in question could be produced without running into scarcities. Continued production of the net output already attained does not create further scarcities.[2]

This is mainly the explanation of the oversaving paradox. Occasionally, a somewhat different explanation may acquire significance, but essentially this is merely a variant of the foregoing. Uncertainty (business risk) is greater in an economy in which the investment-goods sector is very large relatively to the consumer-goods sector than in an economy with relatively more consumption and less new investment. This is because consumption is a more predictable constituent of output. The underlying habits of the public are less unstable. Consequently, for matching increased saving (relative to aggregate output) by increased net investment, business firms may have to accept a higher average degree of uncertainty. If they are reluctant to do so, we still may say that resource scarcities prevent the rate of new investment from growing to sufficient size. This stays true because greater abundance of resources would induce firms to accept the additional risks of new investment. But what has *changed* from one period to the next, when more saving is not matched by more investment, may sometimes be the appraisal of uncertainty rather than the relationship between investment needs and resource scarcities.

3. The difference in emphasis between blaming the rate of overcoming resource scarcities and blaming the rate of saving.

It is natural to blame a disturbance on variables that, under given conditions, show volatile behavior rather than on variables that change little. If, in a period, the rate of overcoming scarcities by improvements and by the mobility of resources declines significantly, but the rate of saving does not change much, it is natural to blame the scarcities (that

---

[2] This is true unless population starts contracting or unless the so-called "net" output is computed incorrectly without sufficient allowances for the goods, materials or natural resources which are being used up.

is, diminishing returns or the wrong specialization of resources). In this case net investment comes to fall short of the usual rate of saving. If, on the other hand, the rate of overcoming scarcities (and thus the desired amount of new investment) stays "normal," but savings rise substantially, it is natural to blame the savings for exceeding net investment. This is not a very precise distinction, but it is nevertheless a distinction which has common-sense foundations.

Periodic declines in the rate of overcoming general labor scarcities and natural-resource scarcities by improvements, are, of course, inevitable. So are periodic difficulties stemming from the wrong specialization of resources and from their insufficient mobility (that is, difficulties stemming from specific scarcities). Periodic increases in the rate of saving are also inevitable, especially in an economy in which durable and semidurable consumer goods play an important role. Consumer expenditures on durable and semidurable goods tend to become bunched in periods in which old goods are being replaced, while in the intervening periods there is more saving for future purchases or for the repayment of consumer credit. The acquisition, by households, of durable and semidurable consumer goods is conventionally regarded as consumer expenditure, not as investment. These goods are not included in the "capital stock." Consequently, fluctuations in the purchase of these goods are viewed as fluctuations in saving rather than in net investment.

There exists one important type of fluctuation in planned net investment which is very much like a fluctuation in net savings, and does not stem from fluctuations in offsets to "diminishing returns" (or from other scarcity phenomena). Replacement waves in housing and machinery are like changes in the rate of net saving. In periods during which comparatively little replacement activity takes place, the unused depreciation allowances of firms have the same effect as increased net savings. However, technically we do not call these unused depreciation allowances net savings because the value of the capital goods which are being amortized is currently declining, and thus the unused depreciation allowances are the equivalents of "costs," rather than net savings out of income.

In the terminology of national accounting we must say that bunched replacement of capital goods—of goods conventionally included in the capital stock—gives rise to fluctuations in planned investment,[3] while

---

[3] This is because net investment is equal to gross investment (gross capital formation) minus depreciation allowances. If the rate at which the current wear and tear is being actually *replaced* is reduced, there is less gross investment. Since current depreciation allowances stay unchanged, "net investment" declines.

bunched replacement of durable consumer goods generates fluctuations in net savings. But what fluctuates when the replacement of capital goods becomes bunched is *not* the rate of overcoming scarcities for the sake of expanding output. The fluctuating element here is that part of the current depreciation allowances which is not currently used for replacement and hence is available for expanding output. The temporarily unused depreciation allowances are available for expanding output, unless they are paid out to stockholders and consumed by them. The fact that the value of the temporarily "undermaintained" capital goods declines to some extent is of no significance for the problem we are now considering. Everything proceeds as if these capital goods were in their former shape, except that operating costs may temporarily be slightly higher. For growth to continue, the unused part of the depreciation allowances, as well as the "net savings" in the sense proper, must be matched by additions to the stock somewhere in the economy. What conclusions may we derive from this for the problem at hand?

In most cases, blaming the amount of planned net investment for falling short of a "normal" amount of saving implies suggesting that the rate of overcoming scarcities is "abnormally" low. This differs in emphasis from blaming savings for being "abnormally" high. However, if planned net investment falls short of a "normal" amount of savings *merely* because current depreciation allowances are temporarily not used for replacement, then the difficulty is not caused by an "abnormally" low rate of overcoming scarcities. Unused depreciation allowances have become "abnormally" high, and this is different merely in form, not in substance, from saying that savings have become "abnormally" high.

4. General wage reductions need not always reduce unemployment.

We now turn to another conclusion suggested by the analysis of the previous Sections. Considering that insufficient investment, relatively to the savings which would accrue at capacity output, results in low output and low employment, it should not be *taken for granted* that general wage reductions will always increase the demand for labor. Here we do not have in mind the obvious proposition that if wage reductions lead to the expectation of further wage reduction, investment decisions may be postponed rather than stimulated. This is quite true, but all that can be said about it is that such an expectational spiral will not last forever. What happens if the wage reductions are believed to have run their course? Will the increase in planned investment be greater than the increase in savings? Will investment increase relatively to savings even though redistribution of income at the expense of wage earners may lead to more saving out of aggregate income?

In principle, it is conceivable that a reduction of the money-wage level will diminish rather than increase the rate of saving. The money-wage reductions will usually be accompanied by price reductions, and these may raise the real value (the value in terms of goods and services) of the existing liquid assets so high that even at high levels of output the public will wish to engage in little or no further saving out of income. The argument is not based on the assumption of reduced *real*-wage rates or of a changed distribution of income; it is based entirely on the consumption-raising effect of the price cuts which accompany the lowering of money-wage rates. But this effect—the Pigou effect—assume sharp wage reductions and correspondingly sharp price reductions, and it is somewhat undependable, in any event, because an appreciable portion of the liquid assets is matched by the cash liabilities of individuals and corporations, whose real wealth *shrinks* with falling prices and who, for this reason, may wish to save more.[4] Whether a moderate reduction of the general price level will increase the demand for labor via the Pigou effect is uncertain. Let us, therefore, consider cases where we may completely disregard the Pigou effect, an effect which need not come into play at all. Let us disregard also the stimulus to investment which develops from price and wage reductions because of the interest-lowering consequences of these cuts. Here again the effect is not created by a reduction of *real*-wage rates. The effect is caused by reduced needs for working balances at reduced wage and price levels. The money released may go into the loan supply, and the lowering of interest rates may increase the amount of planned investment. But this effect, like the Pigou effect, is somewhat undependable (or may prove to be quantitatively insignificant) because in periods of unemployment the released money may largely go into idle balances rather than into the loan supply. We shall not now be concerned with this effect. *The interesting cases from our point of view are those in which the wage and price reductions are ex-*

---

[4] Not all liquid assets are matched by cash liabilities of the public; some are matched by liabilities of the government or the central bank. But it is not necessarily true that the Pigou effect per unit of liquid assets will be precisely as great as the offsetting effect per unit of cash liabilities. See James Tobin, "Asset Holdings and Spending Decisions," *American Economic Review, Papers and Proceedings* (May 1952), pp. 109-123.

pected to increase the demand for labor because prices fall less than money-wage rates.[5] In this case, investment is stimulated by a fall in *real-wage* rates, but there occurs also a redistribution of income in favor of groups with a high propensity to save.

If, as we now assume, prices fall less than money-wage rates, it is not quite certain that investment will then be increased relatively to savings. The question here is whether the decrease in product-wage rates and in real-wage rates[6] induces *at least as much* additional new investment as is necessitated by the increase in the saved proportion of aggregate income which will occur as a consequence of the redistribution of income. For the reduction of real-wage rates presumably changes the distribution of income in such a way that for any given level of output savings now become increased. If the decrease in real-wage rates induces *less* additional new investment than corresponds to the additional savings—either because further new investment causes returns to diminish rapidly or because the uncertainty attaching to business expectations rises rapidly when the consumed proportion of income falls—then effective demand will be insufficient, and not even the little new investment with which we started will be sustained. Only if investment rises by a required minimum amount can it rise *at all*. The traditional proposition that wage reductions increase the aggregate demand for labor possesses merely qualified validity.

The significance of this qualification depends on how much greater the saved proportion of output becomes when real-wage rates are reduced. There exists a presumption that the saved proportion of aggregate income would not rise very sharply. It is true that the saved proportion of income is substantially higher for the high-income than for the low-income groups, but when income is taken away from one of these two groups and is assigned to the other, the saved proportion changes for these two groups in the opposite directions. For example,

---

[5] It is likely that producers expect prices to fall less than money-wage rates. If this is so, prices actually tend to fall less than money-wage rates. This is because the investment outlays of investors will be such as to create a total effective demand which is sufficient to keep prices from falling in the same proportion as money-wage rates.

[6] By a change in product-wage rates, we mean a change in money-wage rates corrected for the change in the prices of the goods produced by the workers in question. By a change in real-wage rates, we mean a change in money-wage rates corrected for the change in the prices of goods consumed by workers (*i.e.,* corrected for changes in the cost of living). But we are assuming here that a general reduction in money-wage rates, which results in a reduction of real-wage rates, leads also to a lowering of product-wage rates. Hence we place no emphasis on the difference between real and product-wage rates.

a reduction of the income of the wage-earning groups decreases the saved proportion of their incomes, and a simultaneous increase of the incomes of nonwage earners increases the saved proportion of their incomes. Aside from *undistributed* corporate profits, these two effects might be of a similar order, although they would not cancel precisely.[7] However, when, by means of wage reductions, real income is redistributed in favor of nonwage-earners, undistributed corporate profits (corporate savings) are also likely to rise to some extent. All in all, the saved proportion of aggregate income should be expected to rise, but this proportion is likely to change no more than moderately, unless much of the benefit goes to the highest percentiles of the income structure and remains there as a consequence of monopolistic rigidities.

We recognize the potential validity of the qualification which emerges from this discussion: general wage reductions need not always reduce existing unemployment. They *may* raise savings as much as planned investment, or more. For the same reason, reshuffling a given tax burden in favor of business firms and against the lower income groups need not always reduce existing unemployment. The qualification possesses potential validity with respect to the type of unemployment which is caused by the insufficiency of investment to match the savings that would accrue at capacity output. This is one of the two types of unemployment discussed in Chapter 4, Section 7, and in Chapter 8, Section 5.

However, the reason why, under contemporary conditions, it is rarely possible to reduce this sort of unemployment by appreciable wage reductions is not that the qualification here considered may occasionally possess practical as well as potential validity. The reason is that such policies would give rise to too much social friction. Crudely expressed, the analytical qualification which we have been considering in the present Section acquires practical importance only if the system will not stand the increase in the saved proportion of income that accompanies the wage reductions. Yet the record of the system shows that it has stood considerable variations in the saved proportion of income, while, as was seen, the changes in the propensity to save brought about by wage

---

[7] In technical language, the difference between the wage earner's and the nonwage earners' *marginal* propensities to save is appreciably smaller than the difference between their average propensities to save. See in this context Table 5 in the first Appendix to Part 2.

The statement in the text should be qualified by pointing out that redistribution at the expense of the top 1 or 2 percent of the income recipients *would* have an appreciable marginal effect on saving, since for these groups the marginal propensity to save may well be in the order of 50 percent.

adjustments or by a redistribution of tax burdens need not be significant. The difficulties here are mainly social-political, not genuinely economic.

When unemployment is caused by the insufficiency of savings to create (without inflation) the capital stock required for the full employment of labor,[8] the analytical qualification discussed in the present Section possesses not even theoretical or potential validity. In this case the system obviously needs more saving, and it is not necessary to weigh the two effects here discussed—the invetment-increasing and saving-increasing effects—to arrive at the conclusion that a reduction of real-wage rates will increase output and employment.

Nevertheless, the apparently paradoxical proposition expressed in the title of the present Section is a valid proposition in the theory of economic disequilibrium.

5. The undersaving paradox.

From the preceding analysis, the inference may be drawn that with a positive rate of saving, the economy will always be able to grow if it is profitable to engage in at least as much new capital formation as is required for matching the new savings of successive periods. How is it then possible that a low rate of saving relative to planned investment can lead to contraction?

The explanation of this apparent contradiction is that an excess of desired new capital formation, over what would be the rate of net saving at a stable general price level, tends to lead into an inflationary process which will have to stop sooner or later, and will then be followed by deflation and contraction.

Even if the price level were not rising, an excess of desired capital formation over net savings would have to express itself in an undesired reduction of inventories and perhaps in delays in the delivery of new capital goods. In view of this, actual capital formation would become smaller than desired capital formation, and this is how the accounting identity between savings and actual capital formation would become satisfied. If the excess of desired capital formation over savings lasts long enough to generate an appreciable inflationary pressure, the accounting identity will become satisfied by two distortions, not merely by one. Actual capital formation will be smaller than the desired, and at the same time savings will usually be greater than what they would be at a

---

[8] This is the other type of unemployment discussed in Chapter 4, Section 7, and in Chapter 8, Section 5.

stable general price level. In the business-cycle literature this artificial, inflationary increase in total savings is called forced saving. That part of the public not consisting of business investors or highly organized workers is apt to suffer a diminution of its real income: prices rise between the earning and the spending of their money incomes, and the size of their money incomes does not take this subsequent rise into account. The difference accrues, in the form of real income and savings, to those who are acquiring physical assets with borrowed and depreciating new money. For the process must be associated with the creation of more new money than that corresponding to the rate of increase of T/V or of $k \cdot T$, that is, with the creation of more new money than would be required to keep the price level stable. Forced savings show in an increase in capital formation such as is attributable to the taxing of noninvestors by a price rise.

Appreciable insufficiency of saving, *at stable prices,* as compared to the desired rate of new investment creates dynamic disequilibrium by leading to inflationary "forced savings" as well as to smaller-than-desired actual investment. Moreover, after a while the desired rate of capital formation is likely to become further increased because of the penalty which price increases place on liquid asset holdings. This process tends to reinforce itself for some time, since these conditions strengthen the desire for even further capital accumulation at an accelerated rate. But the monetary authority cannot continue to feed this process indefinitely. When the process is stopped, the inducement to invest shrinks rapidly. Stabilization of output would require a thorough rearrangement of the structure of production. Some sectors of the economy, particularly the investment-goods industries, would have to become suddenly reduced, and others would have to expand simultaneously. This is certain to overtax the mobility of resources. Output will contract. Appreciable undersaving leads indirectly, with a lag, to interruptions of the growth process and to contraction of output because, once excess capacities are used up, inflation must develop, and because inflation is followed by an abrupt reduction of investment activity.

Undersaving as compared to desired new investment can alternatively be characterized also as overinvestment. This could, in principle, always be avoided by a sufficiently restrictive central-bank policy and by the accumulation of budgetary surpluses. A restrictive credit policy which goes with high interest rates reduces the desired rate of new investment. But policies relying on these methods cannot usually be adopted fully enough, nor can they be adopted promptly enough, to eliminate a tendency toward overinvestment and undersaving, if this tendency is substantial and if it makes its appearance suddenly.

6. A conventional classification of theories of the downturn.

Theories placing the emphasis on the processes described in the previous Section are usually called *overinvestment (or undersaving)* theories. The claim that they give a satisfactory general explanation of cyclical instability would have to rest on the assumption that once growth gets under way the desire to invest continues to outrun savings *until monetary policy becomes restrictive enough to stop an inflationary process.* At that time, the need for sudden rearrangement of the structure of production creates scarcities in specialized resources (special kinds of equipment and of labor) and these scarcities force contraction. The reason for this is that the proper relative size of the investment-goods industries and the consumer-goods industries, respectively, depends on the rate of expansion of economic activity. The internal structure of a rapidly expanding economy precludes immediate stabilization at an expanded level.

This account of the course of events is realistic in some cases, but by no means in all. The overinvestment theories possess no general validity. The process of expansion may become discontinued before the monetary authority intervenes to stop an inflationary movement. This is because desired investment may fall behind the rate of new saving, instead of exceeding the rate. But even if this is the situation, it remains true that the impossibility of suddenly readjusting the structure of production after a period of rapid expansion is one of the two circumstances which force the system into actual contraction (*i.e.,* which preclude immediate stabilization). The other circumstance is that if desired new investment falls behind new saving, then *aggregate* demand becomes insufficient because the demand-reducing effect of saving is incompletely compensated by investment demand.

The theories which emphasize the inability of desired new investment always to keep pace with new savings, even before the monetary authority engages in anti-inflationary credit restriction, may either be called *under-investment* theories, or *oversaving (underconsumption)* theories. It is usual to call them oversaving (underconsumption) theories if they blame the excess of savings over investment primarily on the high rate of saving, taking it more or less for granted that desired investment could not for long match the assumed high rate of saving. On the other hand, the theories which interpret the downturn as being typically caused by the failure of investment to keep pace with saving, but which attempt to analyze the causes of fluctuations in the rate of investment, are more adequately described as theories of periodic underinvestment. These theories almost invariably direct attention to the wavelike appearance of important new improvements. The distinction between oversaving (underconsumption) theories, on the one hand, and theories of periodic underinvestment is essentially identical with the distinction that was drawn between two types of theory in Section 3 of the present Chapter.

Arthur Spiethoff, Gustav Cassel, and F. A. Hayek, among others, have been called overinvestment or undersaving theorists. The observation is sometimes added that Spiethoff's analysis and that of Cassel stress the necessity of sudden readjustments in the structure of production, once investment commitments have exceeded the willingness to save, while Hayek pays much attention to the essentially *monetary* phenomenon of forced saving, by which excessive investment can be prolonged for some time, but not indefinitely.[9] J. A. Hobson and the joint authors, Foster and Catchings, belong among those usually referred to as oversaving (underconsumption) theorists.[10] Of the older economists, Simon de Sismondi and T. R. Malthus expressed underconsumptionist views, and one of the several hypotheses which can be found in Karl Marx's discussion of disequilibrium under capitalism is essentially an underconsumption or oversaving hypothesis.[11]

Attempts to characterize the opinions of economists with a single phrase are sometimes inevitable. But this usually does them less than justice. Indeed, from Gottfried Haberler's *Prosperity and Depression,* which was the first book to use such a classification in a systematic fashion, it became clear to most readers that these distinctions relate to differences in emphasis.[12] The work of significant contributors to business-cycle analysis has usually taken account of more than one of the

---

[9] See A. Spiethoff, "Krisen," in *Handwörterbuch der Staatswissenschaften,* 4th ed. (Jena, 1925) ; G. Cassel, *The Theory of Social Economy* (New York, 1932) ; F. A. von Hayek, *Prices and Production* (London, 1941).

[10] See *e.g.,* J. A. Hobson, *Economics of Unemployment* (London, 1931) ; W. T. Foster and W. Catchings, *Profits* (Boston and New York, 1925).

[11] Another Marxian line of reasoning emphasizes maladjustments in the structure of production, *i.e.,* discrepancies between the changing demand-structure and the output-structure which can be produced with given specialized resources.

[12] G. Haberler, *Prosperity and Depression* (Lake Success, 1946).

possible causes which are treated in isolation by the purified hypotheses described in the present Section.

This can well be illustrated with the analysis of authors who, in their theories of the downturn, showed particular interest in the intermittent appearance of significant technological and organizational improvements —for example, Joseph Schumpeter, Sir Dennis Robertson and John Maurice Clark. On the one hand, the hypotheses of these authors fit into the category which we labeled theories of periodic underinvestment. Theories such as that of Robertson or Clark are capable of explaining how, in periods of sluggish improvement activity, investment *may* fall behind savings, even with a liberal credit policy. On the other hand, the authors of these theories show awareness also of the fact that the downturns of some periods are rather well explained, in the first approximation, by the overinvestment theories. Indeed, any author placing great stress on the intermittent appearance of highly important innovations is apt to combine a theory of periodic underinvestment with an overinvestment theory, where the latter applies to those longer periods in which innovating activity is powerful enough to create a basic inflationary tendency. This is the reason why it would be difficult to place Schumpeter, Robertson, or J. M. Clark in any of the "categories" of the present Section. Indeed, they usually are not placed in any of these. In our opinion, the same reason precludes proper "classification," in these terms, of several authors who frequently *are* placed in a single category.[13] For example, Spiethoff, who usually is considered an overinvestment theorist, threw much light on the wavelike development of improvements.[14] While he was an overinvestment theorist for longer periods with high improvement activity, he recognized that in other longer periods investment tended to be weak as compared to what the community was capable of saving.

The categories listed in the present Section are worth distinguishing as types of hypothesis. But the significant contributors to business-cycle theory used more than one of these categories in developing their analysis.

So far we have been considering hypotheses of the downturn. Views about the upturn, after contraction, are organically connected with the

---

[13] This was explained very clearly by R. A. Gordon in *Business Fluctuations*, (New York, 1952), Ch. 11.

[14] See J. A. Schumpeter, *The Theory of Economic Development* (Cambridge, 1934); *idem, Business Cycles* (New York and London, 1939); D. H. Robertson, *Banking Policy and the Price Level* (London, 1932); J. M. Clark, *Strategic Factors in Business Cycles* (New York, 1934).

analysis of downturns. In any consistent theory the upturn is supposed to occur when the obstacles causing the interruption have disappeared. But the upturn may be delayed by the pessimism which develops in the contraction because of the influence of the recent past on the minds of the public.

In our own general presentation, the theories discussed in the present Section are not in the foreground. It seems more fruitful to us to place the emphasis on the relationship between the rate of overcoming various scarcities, on the one hand, and the rate of saving, on the other. By using such a framework it is possible to recognize the partial validity of each of the older business-cycle theories on which we have been commenting in this Section. The paradoxes of disequilibrium fall into their places. The central proposition which develops in our framework is that contraction develops when the rate of overcoming relative scarcities in general factor categories, and the rate of overcoming scarcities in specialized resources, becomes insufficient for keeping output on the time path which corresponds to the time path of new savings.

7. Instability and stabilizers.

Enough has now been said about disequilibrating forces to prove that paths of dynamic equilibrium are unstable. If planned investment exceeds savings, an involuntary reduction of inventories will occur, delays in delivery will retard the completion of plant and equipment, and, in general, the actual capital formation will fall short of the desired. Therefore, subsequent planned investment will tend to become even greater. If the process lasts long enough, prices must rise appreciably, and the inflationary tendency further increases the desire to reduce liquidity and to accumulate physical capital. On the other hand, if planned investment falls short of savings, excessive inventories accumulate and prices are likely to fall. These consequences of the initial discrepancy further reduce planned capital formation.

However, such an abridged presentation of so-called cumulative processes overstates the existing degree of instability. Earlier in this volume it was emphasized that actual capital formation must fall outside a *range* of magnitudes to cause cumulative disturbances, since planned capital formation should be conceived of as a range of magnitudes rather than a specific magnitude. But this is not the only reason why simplified models overstate the instability of the economy. We have in our economic systems "automatic stabilizers" or "built-in stabilizers" [15] (insta-bility-reducing factors), such as the tendency of individual savings, and particularly of corporate savings, to rise and fall in a higher proportion than aggregate income; the tendency of tax revenues *at given tax rates* to show this same behavior; the automatic tendency of certain govern-ment transfer payments (*e.g.,* unemployment insurance benefits and re-lief) to fall in expansion and to rise in contraction; sometimes, but not always, an automatic tendency for credit to become more stringent in expansion and less so in contraction.[16]

Aside from these automatic stabilizers, we sooner or later (sometimes promptly) get deliberate anti-cyclical measures. These include restrictive central-bank policies in inflationary periods and easy money policies in contraction; and in the present circumstances severe contraction is likely to lead to a reduction of tax rates and to an increase in government expenditures on goods and services. These are stabilizing *policies,* pro-ducing stabilizing effects of nonautomatic character. Moreover, the basic causes which initially produce a deficiency of desired investment relative to savings have so far always disappeared after some time: the growth corollaries of Chapters 8 and 9 have not become permanently violated.

The economic system has been unstable, but it has not been explosive, and recently the importance of the automatic stabilizers has grown. In-creased taxation and the increased weight of budgetary expenditures have produced greater "automatic" stabilizing effects. Higher corporate savings—more self-financing of investment—is also likely to have strength-ened the "automatic" stabilizing influences because changes in the vol-ume of investment have tended to become associated with change in the volume of business saving. This last factor earmarks a considerable proportion of the corporate profits for reinvestment in their own enter-prise, and hence it may not always conduct resources into the most economic channels. Most automatic stabilizers possess potential disad-

---

[15] A. G. Hart started emphasizing the importance of these and estimating their quan-titative significance already at a very early stage of the discussion pertaining to post-war economic conditions. Later an analysis of the problem was included in his *Money, Debt, and Economic Activity,* (New York, 1948) . See particularly Ch. 22.

[16] Yet an automatic tendency toward credit stringency in expansion and ease in con-traction cannot be taken for granted. The demand for credit does increase in expan-sion, and it decreases in contraction; but the supply also tends to do so. This is be-cause the desire to accumulate idle balances, which are items of deduction from the supply, usually increases in contraction, while in expansion the demand for idle bal-ances usually decreases or even gives way to a desire to reduce the existing idle bal-ances.

vantages as well as merits. We have seen earlier that while the increased size of the automatic stabilizers (including high budgetary expenditures and revenues) is apt to keep the economy closer to its long-run path, and thus is likely to reduce the waste of fluctuations, there exists no sound basis for a general appraisal of the net effect of these stabilizers on the height and the slope of the long-run path itself. We shall return to this problem in Chapter 14.

11

Expansion and Contraction

I. Permanent stoppage provides a convenient point of departure.

Inflationary deviations from the conditions of smooth growth deserve as much attention as do deflationary deviations. Nevertheless, in the analysis of deviations, the nature of the contraction process should be given logical priority because the growth-interrupting effect of inflation is indirect. If inflation could be continued indefinitely, it would not have to interrupt the process of growth. We shall therefore first examine the forces which may throw a smoothly growing economy directly into contraction. However, we should remember that sooner or later an inflationary process inevitably brings some of these forces into play, and that thus we are here dealing with the indirect effects of inflation as well as with the direct effects of deflation.

It is an essential characteristic of Western economies that violations of the corollaries of the growth conditions have remained temporary, in the sense of having merely interrupted, but not permanently arrested, the process of growth. But the nature of the forces causing these interruptions can best be understood by first assuming a *permanent* interruption. The analytical results so obtained must then be modified by recognizing that renewed expansionary tendencies have, so far, always lifted the economy out of the state which in the preliminary analysis is represented as permanent.

In principle, a chronic insufficiency of capital formation could develop from violations of the second or of the third corollary. The immobility of resources could be great enough to prevent the gradual elimination of scarcities in specialized resources, once such scarcities had developed. Or the supply of money could be entirely inflexible, and hence deflationary

294

pressure might strangle any incipient growth process. In the present stage of Western development these illustrations are not only far-fetched but would require starting the analysis with a rather complex list of artificial assumptions. It is to be hoped that illustrating the possibility of a permanent stoppage with the consequences of a permanent insufficiency of the improvement mechanism is also far-fetched, or at least unrealistic. Nevertheless, this illustration, for which the first corollary serves as a point of departure, possesses the advantage of simplicity; and it connects the analysis of a permanent stoppage with the most fundamental condition of growth, namely, with the proper functioning of the improvement mechanism.

2. Schematic illustration of permanent stoppage.

We shall assume that the net output and income of an economy, which so far has been smoothly growing, amounts to 100 units. Of these, 20 units are saved by individuals and corporations. The budget is balanced, and consequently we need 20 units of desired net private capital formation for smooth growth. The new capital required per unit of output-increment is 2 per period, that is, the output-increment per unit of new capital is one half. Therefore, in dynamic equilibrium, the net output of the subsequent period would be 110. With the same proportion of the income saved, the savings of the next period would be 22 units; assuming that these savings will again be matched by desired net investment, the output of the following period would be 121 units, etc. We assume that so far the technological and organizational improvements have offset the scarcity of natural resources and of labor, relative to capital, but have not turned the relative labor scarcity into overabundance. Thus labor is fully employed, and real-wage rates are rising approximately in proportion with output per man-hour. Of course, no excess capacity such as would have prevented continuous new capital formation has existed.

However, in the first period with which we are concerned, in the period in which desired net capital formation should be 20 units, the improvement mechanism gives out, and no more improvements will be forthcoming in the future. For a while, some net capital formation may still occur, if interest rates can be lowered sufficiently. But in the face of consistently diminishing returns this is a buffer of limited capacity. Let us disregard it, assuming, as it were, that the buffer effect has been fully used up in a span of time to which we need pay no attention here.

This, of course, amounts to disregarding the adjustment in question, knowing that it will not change our analytical results for more than a limited interval. The clock-time duration of this limited interval need not be negligible in all cases, but the presentation would become unduly complicated if we made explicit allowances for the interval at this point. We therefore assume that the net capital formation of the first period will be zero instead of 20 units. Prior to the first period, producers undertook all new investment that was deemed profitable with the given supply of cooperating factors and on a given level of organizational and technological knowledge. There is nothing that would justify further net capital formation, now or in the future.

In these circumstances, output will not merely fail to rise from 100 units to 110 units, but it will contract sharply.

At first, output will have to fall to a level where savings become negative. For ultimately there will have to flow a constant output stream in our economy, and therefore ultimately output and income will have to be at a level where savings are zero. Assume that this zero-saving level of output is 70 units. But the production of 70 units of output requires a much smaller stock of capital than that exising in our first period, when 100 units of output were produced. The economy cannot settle down at the 70-unit level before getting rid of a substantial proportion of its capital. The owners of this physical capital (inventories, equipment, etc.) will attempt to diminish their stock by selling more goods than they buy for production. In the case of inventories, this simply means that they will attempt to sell a larger quantity of, say, shoes than that which they currently produce. In the case of durable capital goods, the same attempt will express itself in not replacing the wear and tear caused by the production of the goods which are being sold. This too, of course, diminishes incomes and the output of the capital-goods industries. It is obvious that the owners of capital cannot succeed in diminishing their stock—in "disinvesting" or bringing about "net capital consumption"—before output has fallen to a level where the savings of the public become negative, that is, are turned into dissavings. This is because negative capital formation ("disinvestment") requires that consumption should exceed the current output and income. The difference must show in dissavings. Thus the output will at first have to fall below the *zero-saving* level—below 70 units in our example. Say it must fall to 50 units for some time. Later it can settle down at 70 units, provided that real-wage rates stay unchanged.

At the precontraction level of real-wage rates, the 70-unit output is associated with chronic unemployment of substantial magnitude. It is possible that the unemployment can be diminished appreciably—or, in principle, even eliminated—by a significant reduction of real wage rates. This change would lead employers to produce any given output with a smaller capital stock and a greater labor force, and it might also induce them to increase the level of aggregate output. We have seen earlier that the effects of such a policy are not fully predictable. The policy might lead to a reduction of unemployment, but it would presumably create considerable social friction. Further population growth, without improvements, would sooner or later result in increasing chronic unemployment (unless the problem can be met by a progressive reduction of real-wage rates). It is true that, even in the absence of improvements, population growth would alleviate the scarcity in one of the resources cooperating with capital, but it would do nothing toward alleviating the relative scarcity of natural resources. Therefore, population growth alone would not in the long run maintain the yield of further new investment.

We conclude that with no offsets to diminishing returns output will at first fall below the zero-saving level and that it will subsequently settle down at the zero-saving level—presumably with a substantial fraction of the labor force unemployed. Of course, the level of 70 units need not prove to be a literally stable one. For some time, in the beginning, it is even unlikely to stay stable. The system may well produce recurrent fluctuations between our 100-unit level and our 50-unit level. We know that with the given labor force, the given stock of natural resources and the given state of organizational and technological knowledge, the productivity schedule of capital was in the past such as to justify capital accumulation up to the level corresponding to 100 units of output. It is therefore conceivable that from the condition where output is 70 units, and the capital stock corresponds to this output, the system will expand to 100 units and then run into precisely the same difficulty which we have already described. This is a difficulty leading to a contraction down to the 50-unit level. There might occur a few swings of this sort, but the process would soon become so predictable that the economy would rarely rise much beyond the 70-unit level.

The reader is now requested to look once more at the numerical illustration contained in the first two paragraphs of the present Section. If, instead of assuming there that the improvement mechanism gives out completely, we had assumed that it tends to call forth investment at the insufficient rate of 10, 11, 12.1, . . . in the successive periods, we would have arrived at the conclusion that after a drop of output below 70 units, and after the elimination of part of the capital stock, output would rise somewhat beyond the 70-unit level, and that subsequently it would keep rising, but with part of the labor force chronically unemployed. To keep output at a path of full employment, the sequence of new investments for the successive periods would have to be 20, 22, 24.2, ... The sequence 10, 11, 12.1, . . . is compatible with a lower growth path along which the total amount of saving is lower (and probably even the saved percentage of income is). In the event of an insufficient but positive amount of investment, just like in our earlier case of *zero*-investment, chronic unemployment is a consequence of the fact that a higher output level than that which is attained would produce an excess of saving over planned investment. In either case occasional spurts may occur that raise the economy to full utilization, or near that level, but subsequently the system will tend to return to the path for which savings do not exceed the long-run rate of investment. Moreover, the excessive capital formation of these spurts calls for the disinvestment and hence the spurts call forth a temporary drop of output below the path for which the growth requirements are met in the long run.

We preferred to discuss the problem on the assumption of zero investment because this simplified the problem by bringing out the characteristics of the difficulty in extreme form. In the analysis of problems created by a chronic insufficiency of the improvement mechanism, we shall continue to use a terminology implying zero investment, but it is easy to make allowances for the difference between this and insufficient investment (that is, for the difference between no offsets and insufficient offsets to diminishing returns).

3. Rejecting a possible reason for even greater pessimism in the event of no offsets to diminishing returns.

In the previous illustration, we took it for granted that at a sufficiently low level of output (*e.g.,* at 70 units) no part of the income would be saved. But originally we assumed that in dynamic equilibrium the saved proportion of incomes would always be 20 percent, even though output would be rising all the time. Why should savings disappear at the 70-unit level, if the saved proportion of incomes was assumed to stay uninfluenced by gradual changes in output and income? Why should aggregate savings at the 70-unit level not amount to 14 units? After all, many periods back, when our (now stagnant) economy was still growing, output presumably *was* at the 70-unit level; and since we have assumed that a further growth of output beyond 100 units (which did not actually take place) *would* have been associated with a growth of aggregate savings in the proportion of the output-growth itself, we should presumably visualize the conditions of the distant past, with 70 units of output, as involving 14 units of savings. But now that growth has become interrupted at the 100-unit level of output, we assume that a contraction of output to 70 units eliminates savings altogether, and that a fall below 70 units creates dissaving. Is this not a contradiction?

Not necessarily. It certainly is not inconsistent to assume that when output contracts the saved proportion of income will be low, possibly negative, for some time. The saved proportion of output will decline with the level of output itself. It is true that, when output as a whole gradually rises in the course of the growth process, the saved proportion of incomes does not typically rise. All available statistics indicate that the proportion of the present income which the public saves is no higher, indeed, is probably somewhat lower, than was the proportion which it saved of a very much smaller income several decades ago. At the same time all available statistics indicate that cyclical contraction of output causes the saved proportion of output to fall and that cyclical expansion causes this proportion to rise. The saved proportion does not change much along trend lines, and it presumably would not change much in dynamic equilibrium. But this stability of the saved proportion of income "in the long run" has reasons which do not apply to cyclical movements.

We have seen earlier that the long-run stability of the saved proportion of income is presumably a consequence of the fact that notions concerning a "normal" standard of living change with a gradual rise of national income. The saved proportion of income does not show that the public is gradually getting better off and thus can afford to save a higher percentage of its income. Along trend lines, the average family does not save a rising proportion of its growing income, although, in any one year, a well-to-do family does save a higher proportion than a poor family. A well-to-do family considers itself well-to-do, *in the sense here considered*, because its standard of living is higher than "normal." It saves a comparatively high proportion of its income. But the average family stays "normal" when the over-all growth process raises its income along with the income of other families. It continues to save a "normal" proportion of its income. Therefore, a nation as a whole also continues to do so along its trend lines. However, if output suddenly contracts, the income of the average family becomes "abnormally" low: both consumption and savings are reduced, but consumption shows greater resistance than savings. The statistical evidence proves that it is realistic to assume little long-run change in the saved proportion of national income in the course of the growth process, but that at the same time it *is* realistic to assume that saving will be sharply reduced, or will be turned into dissaving, if output contracts. We were not guilty of inconsistency when we assumed that, after a process of contraction which started at 100 units of output, there was no further saving at the 70-unit level—at least, no further saving for some time.

But don't we have to assume that later, when the public starts considering this low level as "normal," the saved proportion of output will again rise to 20 percent? If so, the permanent disturbance discussed in this Chapter will have even worse consequences than those which were described in the previous Section. The process of contraction might become "bottomless," except for a few occasional swings which now and then might carry the economy back toward the 100-unit level, but which would invariably disappoint those investors who did not get out at the right moment. The contraction might become essentially bottomless because the economy which we are here considering has lost its capacity for long-run growth, and yet it is conceivable that no output level would be low enough to eliminate new saving in the long run.

Fortunately, we have had so far no experience with economies of this sort. Consequently, we can make no categoric statement on the legitimacy of the present argument for greater pessimism. But, on the whole, the sketch contained in Section 2 seems better suited to expressing the essence of the matter than this more pessimistic sketch. At the 70-unit level of output, at which we have arrived in Section 2, there presumably exists a very considerable degree of chronic unemployment. This is a sufficiently "abnormal" feature of the environment to raise serious doubts as to the likelihood of "normal" modes of behavior in relation to saving. Unless the government is running a large deficit all the time—a possibility which will be considered later in this Chapter—the employed fraction of the population will have to contribute continuously and substantially to the livelihood of the unemployed. At a significantly reduced level of ouput and employment new saving would presumably stay eliminated.

4. Rejecting another possible reason why the contraction may become bottomless.

In Section 2 we assumed that output first falls below the 70-unit level, and that, after a period of capital consumption or disinvestment, it rises to the zero-saving level of 70 units. This implies that the aggregate of individual producers acts *as if* they knew that when the capital stock has become reduced to the size corresponding to 70 units of output, it is profitable to produce 70 units for consumption. But at the time when producers have to start acting in this fashion, output is lower, say, 50 units, and at that time the history of the recent past is one of contraction. If producers now believe that output will further contract—to 40, 30, 20 units and so on—then they will try further to reduce the capital stock, with the result that output will never cease contracting.

Logically, this possibility exists regardless of the behavior of the general price level. In the real world prices too are likely to fall while output is contracting. The price deflation which is likely to accompany the contraction of output from 100 units to 50 units *may* provide a further reason for *continued* contraction. For if the price fall is expected to continue, keeping idle money is believed to be less unprofitable than using it for production, and the behavior motivated by these beliefs will result in further contraction, thus justifying the beliefs.

The contraction—instead of landing the economy at the 70-unit level, with a detour over 50 units—may prove to be bottomless, either as a consequence of the reasons discussed in Section 3 or because of the expectational reasons now considered. We gave our initial sketch, the sketch of Section 2, preference over that of a bottomless process in Section 3. We give our initial sketch preference also over the model of expectational pessimism here described. To be sure, expectations are not fully rational: it would be wrong to postulate that if a process *would* work out smoothly, producers will immediately expect those things to happen which will lead them to put the process into effect. But while expectations are erratic, it does seem reasonable to assume that sooner or later processes of many sorts will be tried out. These will usually include the processes which work out according to expectations. If the expectations which would lead firms to produce a 70-unit output lead to results consistent with these expectations, then it seems reasonable to assume that sooner or later the 70 units of output will become produced. In other words, if at the 70-unit of output savings are zero, then a zero-investment economy is likely to "find" this level.

Bottomless contraction is not a *logical* impossibility. But the sketch of Section 2 seems more relevant to the problem of the present Chapter than are sketches of a process of bottomless contraction.

5. A possible reason for smaller pessimism in the event of the cessation of growth.

Instead of adding further pessimism to the tentative conclusions of Section 2, it is possible to supplement the sketch by assumptions which would modify the results in a more favorable direction.

For example, it is likely that the price fall which accompanies the reduction of output will, after some time, not be expected to continue. Instead, after some ups and downs in price expectations, the low price level may be expected to continue. At a sufficiently low price level, the "real" value (value in terms of goods) of the already existing liquid assets of the public (of its money balances and its money claims) becomes very high. This is incompletely offset by the fact that the real value of the money debts, too, is high because the public is a creditor of the commercial banking system to a larger extent than it is its debtor. The debtors of the commercial banks include the government and the central bank. Consequently, the so-called Pigou effect may come into operation: at a sufficiently low price level, the public may feel that it need not save further out of its current income. This may mean that, even at the 100-unit level of real or physical output, there may be no further new saving. In this case, output may settle down at the full-employment level, with the initial capital stock fully utilized. This, too, is a possibility.

Quite aside from the Pigou effect, the stagnant character of the economy which we are considering may influence the saving behavior of the public. Social behavior depends, of course, on the characteristics of the environment in the broad sense. In a nonprogressive environment the outlook of the population might gradually change, and this might result in a gradual cessation of net saving, at all potentially realizable levels of output. This is true especially of corporate savings (undistributed corporate profits), which are largely geared to existing investment opportunities, but the assumption may prove valid also with respect to personal savings. If the assumption is valid, the 100-unit level of output would establish itself, with zero saving and zero investment.

Once more, we suggest that it is preferable to leave the sketch in Section 2 alone, rather than to modify it by the supplementary analysis of any of the subsequent Sections. The present, more optimistic variant implies either a radical deflationary price adjustment or an adjustment in social behavior which would require a very long period of time. The second of these two adjustments would be more likely to take place than the first. But the process would be very time-consuming and, in the event of continued population growth, it would not spare us the hardships of a continued reduction of the average standard of living. Under such a strain the basic characteristics of the societies with which we are here concerned would change in so many respects that not much interest attaches to a theoretical description of the results obtained at the cost of such adjustments.

6. Alternations of expansion and contraction.

The preceding analysis of permanent stoppage possesses merely indirect bearing on the record of industrial societies. We started with an initial disturbance and examined its ultimate consequences, on the hypothesis that the disturbance would persist. But so far these disturbances have always proved temporary. Not all of these disturbances were caused by temporary weaknesses of improvement activity. Progress is inevitably associated with internal shifts in the structure of production. If the required shifts become large and too abrupt, or if the shifts involve resources the mobility of which is particularly small, our second growth corollary, pertaining to specialized resources, becomes violated.[1] These maladjustments may show after inflationary antecedents, and they may even result from these. Yet maladjustments in the strucure of producion do not necessarily imply prior inflationary processes. At the same time we must recognize that our third growth corollary, relating to the proper management of the monetary mechanism, is also not continuously satisfied, and that inflationary or deflationary violations of this corollary also lead to growth interruptions.

Once the growth process is interrupted, part of the pattern described in Section 2 becomes realized—but usually only a small part of it. Regardless of whether the disturbance is initially rooted in violations of the first, the second, or the third corollary, there exists a tendency toward settling down at a lower level of output, with a detour over an even lower level. Yet before this pattern is completed, expansion is usually resumed. The economy starts moving from the 100-unit level of output toward the 70-unit level, with a detour over the 50-unit level (so to

---

[1] See Chapter 9.

speak), but at some stage of this process expansion begins anew and carries the system beyond the 100-unit level. The process described in the preceding Sections is broken at some point by renewed expansion, in which the upward trend of economic activity reflects itself. This is because the rate of overcoming the scarcities, to which the corollaries relate, once more becomes sufficient to induce the necessary amount of desired new investment, given the prevailing real-wage rates and the prevailing appraisal of uncertainty.

When, after a contraction, the economy has expanded to a level of reasonably full resource utilization, a disturbance rooted in the second corollary usually becomes inevitable. At that time, the structure of production —the relative size of the sectors of which the economy consists—is suited to the requirements of rapid cyclical expansion. Whenever the economy is moving *toward* full utilization, the rate of expansion must of course be greater than is the possible rate of growth *in* a condition of full utilization. At the point of full use of any of the required resources, the rate of further expansion must become slower, and the investment-goods industries prove to be oversized in relation to the consumer-goods industries. From here on, the economy can grow only at the rate at which improvements, the mobility of resources, and the expandability of the money supply allow secular growth—provided that the investment induced by these factors is sufficient to match new savings. Even if, given the rate of saving at reasonably stable prices, improvements and the expandability of the money supply are now sufficient to keep the economy on the full-employment growth path, the mobility of resources can scarcely be sufficient for a sudden rearrangement of the structure of production from very rapid cyclical expansion to gradual secular growth. This rearrangement involves some degree of shift from investment-goods industries to consumer-goods industries and a reduction of the rate of further inventory accumulation. Sometimes it involves also a reduction of the size of inventories because the actual size of inventories may reflect the expectation of continued rapid cyclical expansion, rather than merely that of gradual secular growth. These structural rearrangements take time. Contraction is likely to develop in the meantime, as a consequence of temporary scarcities of specialized resources. Only an unusually successful central bank policy could slow the cyclical expansion rate so gradually that it should at the end shade over into the secular growth rate, with practically no discontinuity and hence no cyclical disturbance. But even a moderately successful central bank policy can reduce the discontinuity by cautiously slowing the cyclical expansion in its advanced stages.

In longer periods with favorable characteristics during which the growth tendencies are occasionally interrupted merely by minor cyclical disturbances, many policy decisions center on the problem just considered. This is the problem of reaching an upward-tilted ceiling line with a rate of cyclical expansion that is not too much in excess of the secular upward tilt of the ceiling line itself. The economy does not, of course, move precisely along the full-employment ceiling line, but in periods with favorable characteristics this is mainly a consequence of the fact that structural maladjustments develop whenever the ceiling is hit from below. The ceiling is hit with an expansion rate which must necessarily be greater than is the secular growth rate at a stable general price level (*i.e.,* greater than the upward tilt of the ceiling itself). At this point the rate of expansion must become slower unless the monetary authority makes the mistake of letting the economy temporarily overshoot the ceiling through the inflationary process of "forced saving." It is very difficult to avoid contraction when the rate of growth slows because a slowing of the rate of growth requires changes in the structure of activities. The best way of diminishing the impact of these disturbances is to follow a policy which reduces the rate of cyclical expansion gradually toward the long-run rate of growth before the ceiling is hit. But such a policy cannot be expected to accomplish its objectives with full success.

Contractions caused merely by the necessity of rearranging the structure of activities are likely to be either minor recessions or rather sharp but short depressions. It is not suggested that this is a universally valid rule because some of the rigidities standing in the way of major rearrangements may not be overcome easily. Also, expectational pessimism, feeding on the experience of the recent past, may prolong the contraction beyond the duration which is explainable by scarcities in specialized resources. But there exists a general presumption that contractions caused merely by the need for rearranging the structure of production will usually not be very long. The common characteristic of these disturbances is that there exists a latent demand, at profitable prices, for goods and services the production of which is temporarily blocked by the limited mobility of resources. It was pointed out earlier that a "mere inventory recession" is a special case falling under this heading (see Page 104).

A long-lasting depression is more likely to be caused by the insufficiency of the rate of improvement for overcoming the pressure of diminishing returns; or, more generally expressed, by the smallness of improvement activity as compared to what would be required for inducing, with the existing appraisal of uncertainty, the amount of new investment needed to match full-employment savings. Such insufficiency may last for many years and thus cause a *long and deep* depression. Moreover, during a period of several decades the intervals of vigorous improvement activity may be fewer than during preceding and subsequent periods of similar duration, and hence severe depressions may recur with greater frequency in one longer period than in another, or the average level of activity may fall behind capacity production to a greater extent.

Insufficient expandability of the money supply may also cause long-lasting depressions, and it may cause the recurrence of severe depressions with relatively high frequency in periods extending over several decades. Under metallic currencies a shortage of monetary metals may bring about such conditions. The likelihood of deflationary violations of the third corollary were greater under the gold standard than under present circumstances. On the other hand, the likelihood of inflationary deviations with subsequent contractions is greater now. These contractions result from the necessity of rearranging the structure of production when the inflationary process is stopped.

The conclusions here are essentially identical with those presented at the end of Chapter 3.

7. Compensatory fiscal policy.

Our analysis of the growth corollaries in Chapters 5-9 assumed a balanced government budget. We regarded the equality of net savings with planned net private investment (at positive levels of both these magnitudes and at a reasonably stable general price level) as the basic growth condition, and we subsequently developed the corollaries to it. However, we pointed out on various occasions, first in Section 8 of Chapter 4, that this way of looking at the matter implies the equality of tax payments with government expenditures. If the budget is not balanced, we have to require that net savings *plus tax payments* should equal private net capital formation *plus government expenditures*. The question arises whether the government would not always be capable of preventing an excess of savings *plus tax payments* over private investment *plus government expenditures* (except for the time lag involved in changing tax rates and the rate of government spending). Similarly, we may ask whether, by using a policy of budgetary surpluses, in addition to relying on a central-bank policy of tight credit, the government could not always prevent inflationary deviations.

In the previous discussion of built-in stabilizers we took account of the fact that in expansion tax revenues at given tax rates rise automatically in relation to government expenditures, and that in contraction there is a tendency toward the reverse relationship. In other words, when planned investment increases relatively to savings, planned investment plus government expenditures do not increase *to the same extent* relatively to savings plus tax payments; and when savings increase relatively to planned investment, savings plus tax payments do not increase *to the same extent* relatively to planned investment plus government expenditures. This is part of the mechanism of automatic stabilizers (or built-in stabilizers) which we considered earlier. But the question now raised should carry us further. Can we adjust tax rates and the spending commitments of the government to the requirements of business conditions in such a way as to create, at high levels of employment, *continuous balance* between planned investment plus government expenditures on the one hand, and savings plus tax payments on the other?

We shall argue in Part 5 that in a private enterprise economy compensatory fiscal policy cannot achieve this ambitious objective. But unless the economy is faced with a *significant and chronic* insufficiency of planned investment relative to savings, compensatory fiscal policy can reduce the severity of fluctuations, and it may prove capable of wholly eliminating the special hardships of deep and long-lasting cyclical depressions. Nor is there reason to postulate that fiscal policy would be incapable of correcting a small imbalance, even if this were chronic.

To this problem we shall return in the final Chapter of the volume.

12

Mathematical Models and Looser Frameworks for Guessing at the Future

I. The multiplier-accelerator models.

One of the possibilities discussed in the previous Chapter lends itself particularly well to being illustrated by a mathematical analysis. We refer to the problem discussed at the end of Section 2, Chapter 11 (see Pages 297-298).

Assume that our "first corollary" of continuous growth—the corollary pertaining to the sufficiency and the proper "slanting" of offsets to diminishing returns—tends to be satisfied in the long run only at a level of activity where the resources of the economy are underutilized. This means that in the long run enough planned investment is forthcoming in each successive period to absorb savings in a continuously growing economy *if* the national output or income is all the time at a less than full-employment level, but that investment is insufficient in the long run to match the higher savings on a path which would correspond in each period to a higher national output or income. Each of these paths might be visualized as rising at a rate of, say, 4 percent per year, but in each period the higher path marks, of course, more income and more aggregate saving than does the lower. The higher path is an upward tilted ceiling at the full-employment level.

We have seen that in such circumstances there is always the possibility of cyclical expansion to the full-employment level of output. During such an expansion *toward* the full-employment growth path, the economy moves of course faster than could be the case *along* either of the secular paths which we have described. Such expansion must, however, be followed by contraction, if for no other reason than because on our present assumptions the savings will not be matched by investment along the full-employment path. On the way up to the full-employment path, more investment can be forthcoming because there do not yet exist the scarcities which produce diminishing returns and thus stand in the way of sufficient new investment *on the full-employment path itself.* The subsequent contraction is likely to reduce output below the underemployment growth path on which the economy could be moving continuously, since the expansion raised the capital stock of the economy beyond the requirements of the underemployment growth path. Consequently, output will have to contract sufficiently to bring about dissaving and disinvestment of capital.

It has been proved in the literature that, on these or similar assumptions, fluctuations of the general character of business cycles may result simply from the interaction of the multiplier process with that of acceleration. The multiplier theory, which was originally developed by R. F. Kahn in 1931, says that since investment immediately creates income, and since part of this income will be spent on consumption, income may be viewed as a multiple of investment. The magnitude of the multiplier depends on what percentage of the income which is created by the investments of a period is respent on consumption in successive rounds and thus creates further income in someone else's hands. The acceleration principle says that investment (or at least an important part of investment) may be viewed as being called forth or induced by the growth of output. Coefficients expressing the amount of investment called forth by a unit change in output are called accelerators. In the real world, neither the value of the multiplier nor that of the accelerator stays constant, but mathematical illustrations become simpler if constancy is assumed.

Denote by Y aggregate net income or output; denote by α that fraction of income which, in the subsequent period, the public wishes to spend on consumption; denote by β the coefficient by which a past *change* of income (or of output) must be multiplied in order to get the present net investment in which producers desire to engage as a consequence of the past change; denote by A the amount of "autonomous investment" which is not explained by past changes in income; and indicate the period to which the various magnitudes relate by the appropriate subscripts, so that the subscript n is used for magnitudes relating to period

n, the subscript n-1 for magnitudes relating to period n-1, etc. Then

$$Y_n = \alpha\, Y_{n-1} + \beta\, (Y_{n-1} - Y_{n-2}) + A_n$$

The equation says that net income equals consumption plus net investment.[1] It says this in the multiplier-accelerator form, that is, with the aid of functional relationships which incorporate the principles of the multiplier and of the accelerator.[2] Our assumption that the economy could be moving along an underemployment growth path means that it is possible to describe a continuous growth path of Y such that with a continuous growth of A there should be no undesired accumulation or reduction of inventories, and no inflation which would have to lead to subsequent reversals. If A moves along such a continuous growth path, which here is assumed to be one of less than full employment, the investments which are undertaken in the economy prove profitable without price inflation. Let us start from a condition in which the economy pro-

---

[1] This is a definitionally valid statement if income is defined as the value of output and if the government-acquired final goods and services are included either in consumption or net investment (rather than treated separately). In this case all non-consumed output or income must appear as an addition to the capital stock (net investment).

[2] See Footnote 37, Page 143. In that footnote, we disregarded the income-propagation *lag*, that is, we related total income to simultaneous investment. Disregarding lags is justified only in the analysis of dynamic equilibrium where it is assumed that periods are definable during which all processes work out according to expectations (planned capital formation equals actual capital formation). In the analysis of disturbances, we must trace our processes through the succession of time periods, and hence we must explicitly recognize lags. This is because while certain data of period n will bear the planned relation to specific data of period n-1 (indeed, certain data of period n will be "caused" by specific magnitudes of period n-1), unexpected events will usually prevent the data of any period from bearing the desired relation to other data of the same period.

Aside from the existence of a time-lag in the equation on Page 310, the α factor in that equation equals the term *1-s*, or the term *1-s'* in Footnote 37, Page 143. This is because the α factor stands for the consumed proportion of income, while the s term in Footnote 37, Page 143, stands for saved proportion of income. Hence the multiplier may be written as $\dfrac{1}{1-\alpha}$. The equation on Page 310 implies (in the terminology of Footnote 37, Page 143), that s equals s', because if a constant proportion of income is consumed, regardless of the height of the income, then the same constant proportion of each income-*increment* is consumed. The remainder is saved.

Again, aside from the existence of a time-lag in the equation on Page 310, the β factor in that equation is in the *nature* of $\Delta V / \Delta O$ in Footnote 37, Page 143, and $Y_{n-1} - Y_{n-2}$ is, of course, the $\Delta O / \Delta t$ term. However, the β factor is not *identical* with $\Delta V / \Delta O$ because in the equation on Page 310 part of the investment (part of the ΔV) is treated as autonomous, and only *the other part* is related by β to the change in output (or income), while in Footnote 37, Page 143, all investment was related to changes in output. The β factor in the equation on Page 310 is the $\Delta V / \Delta O$ ratio linking the nonautonomous investment, the so-called induced investment, to output-changes.

ceeds along such an underemployment path of growth, and let us examine the consequences of a small upward deviation from this path.

In the equation a lagged multiplier relation[3] shows in the fact that one constituent of Y_n develops as a consequence of consumption spending out of Y_{n-1}. This constituent of Y_n is αY_{n-1}, where α is smaller than one (because only part of income is spent on consumption, the remainder being saved). It follows from this lagged multiplier relationship that if, in any period, an accidental, once-and-for-all addition to the autonomous investment normally forthcoming generates extra income in the amount of 1, consumption spending will give rise to further extra income in the successive periods, but this further extra income will be flowing at a decreasing rate. Extra income here means "extra" as compared to the income which corresponds to the underemployment growth path. The once-and-for-all initial addition of one unit will give rise to extra incomes of the magnitudes 1, α, α^2, α^3, . . . α^m in the successive periods. Each term is smaller than the previous. The sum total of these terms, over the span beginning with the initial injection, approaches $\frac{1}{1-\alpha}$, considering that α is smaller than one. Consequently, if for one and only one period autonomous investment exceeded the level corresponding to the normal path, the multiplier process, viewed in isolation, would create further additions but income would nevertheless revert toward the normal path. After a while income would be practically back on the initial path.

However, the equation on Page 310 incorporates the acceleration principle as well as the multiplier theory. This shows in the fact that Y_n contains $\beta (Y_{n-1} - Y_{n-2})$, in addition to αY_{n-1}. The income of any period is generated only in part by consumption spending out of the income of the preceding period. In part, it is generated by the investment which is *induced* by past changes in income (or output) via the accelerator; and in part it is viewed here as being generated by autonomous investment, that is, by investment which is not "induced" by past changes in income, but comes about independently of these. The sum total of these three terms may move along a continuously rising path if the rising amount of new investment required for this is profitable.

Whether the rising amount of new investment can prove profitable depends on whether our growth corollaries are satisfied. We now assume that the corollaries are satisfied in the long run—and thus the savings of

---

[3] See Footnote 2, Page 310.

successive periods can profitably be matched by investment—along a growth path of underemployment, but not along a path of full employment. This is because we want to leave room for the economy to shoot temporarily beyond its normal growth path without having to incorporate into the model the consequences of inflationary deviations. Upward deviations could start either from an underemployment or from a full-employment level. The difference is that if an economy deviates upward from a full-employment growth path, then not even in the first approximation can price inflation be disregarded. The assumption of an underemployment growth path simplifies the presentation.

Let us now return to the analysis of an economy which tends to move along an underemployment growth path, but in which autonomous investment exceeds its normal level for one and only one period. Let us take account this time of the acceleration principle as well as of the multiplier. We have seen that the lagged multiplier relation leads to the consequence that the single dose of additional investment and of income which was generated in, say, period $n-1$, gives rise to successive doses of extra income in periods n, $n + 1$, $n + 2$, but that the upward deviation from the normal path will be declining. The successive additions to the normal income will decrease—income will tend to revert to its normal path—because from each period to the next we have to multiply the previous income *surplus* (as compared to the original income) by the real fraction α to obtain the income *surplus* of the next period. Yet now we will recognize that the accelerator relation incorporated in our equation leads to the result that the extra income as compared to the original income stream—in other words, the output-increment—induces extra new investment. The resulting course of events depends on the numerical relationship between the α and the β coefficients.

This relationship can be such that income grows away from its normal path all the time, or that it reverts toward the normal path and then tends to move on it. On the other hand, the relationship can be such that a fluctuating movement, a series of ups and downs, will be called into existence by the single extra injection which took place in period $n-1$. In this case, the amplitude of the successive fluctuations may be increasing or decreasing, or it may stay constant.

One can understand why, with the accelerator as well as the multiplier included in the account, it is possible that a fluctuating movement develops, in other words, that the rise above the normal path will at first become magnified and will then be followed by contraction. The accelerator relationship at first adds to the extra income which is created by the multiplier effect, after the single dose of additional autonomous investment. This is because the output-increment which the initial injection and the multiplier effect bring into existence creates induced investment via the accelerator. But the multiplier relation, taken by itself, creates decreasing doses of income surplus per period—decreasing output-increments—as compared to pre-injection conditions. The accelerator relation, which links the output-increments to induced new investment, may therefore start, after a while, to create decreasing absolute amounts of new investment, and therefore, decreasing absolute amounts of income. The multiplier relation, in itself, pushes the process toward diminishing income surpluses (as compared to the original income path) and if, in this respect, the multiplier relation determines the character of the process,[4] then the accelerator relation will change a pattern of diminishing income surpluses (as compared to the original income path) into a fall below the original level. This is because when, under the influence of the multiplier, income is gradually reverting to its original path, the fall in income as compared to its *immediately preceding* level—that is, the negative output-increment—induces negative investment which further reduces the income level. The multiplier process, viewed in isolation, would let the system fall back toward the initial path the more rapidly the smaller α is.

Even if, as a consequence of induced investment which accrues from the outset, the income surpluses per period (as compared to the original income path) do not initially start diminishing but merely tend to become stabilized, the accelerator mechanism will subsequently produce contraction. From that time on, when there is no further income surplus as compared to the immediately preceding period part of the previous induced investment fails to repeat itself. Even if there is merely a decrease in the accrual of further income surpluses (as compared to the immediately preceding conditions), the induced investment diminishes. Sufficiently marked diminution of induced investment will bring about contraction of output, since the induced investment is one constituent of income and output. On the other hand, the numerical relationship between the accelerator and the multiplier can be such that the accelerator mechanism carries the system away from the outset, with the result that

---

[4] That is to say, if in this regard the consequences of the multiplier relation are not swamped from the outset by those of the accelerator relation and thus the tendency toward reverting to the original path is not suppressed.

in the framework of such a model the movement does not become reversed.

Verbal reasoning is merely capable of suggesting that the nature of the process generated by accidental increases or decreases of autonomous investment. The outcome depends on the numerical relationship between α and β. At this point, mathematical reasoning must take over. The problem was first posed in this fashion by Paul A. Samuelson and he was the first to subject the critical relations between α and β to mathematical analysis.[5] Later, John R. Hicks developed a more comprehensive model and from here on our presentation follows Hicks' in its main outline.

Hicks made a case for the assumption that the numerical relationship between α and β may frequently be such as to generate explosive movements, *i.e.,* either a continuous movement away from the normal path or cycles with increasing amplitudes. He then argued that whenever such explosive movements tend to become generated the economy hits a full-employment ceiling. When this happens, further rise at the previous rate is blocked, and the upward movement could continue only along the upward-tilted ceiling line, that is, on the gradually rising full-employment growth path. But the initial assumption here was that, once full utilization is reached, the induced-plus-autonomous investment in the system is insufficient to match the amount of savings which accrue along the full-employment path of growth. It follows that, at the time when the full-employment growth path is hit, β would have to become smaller (or conceivably A would have to become smaller, or both) than was so during the movement toward the full-employment level, because from then on the amount of investment that can be profitably undertaken is determined by long-run offsets to diminishing returns. This amount of investment falls short of the previous amounts of investment; indeed it falls short of savings along the full-employment growth path.

The model implies that in the long run the conditions of growth (our "growth corollaries") are satisfied merely for an amount of investment which will match savings along a path of less than full employment. On the way from such a lower growth path toward the ceiling, investment could exceed its long-run rate because of the presence of unused resources in the economy. But when the ceiling is reached, the economy

---

[5] P. A. Samuelson, "Interactions Between the Multiplier Analysis and the Principle of Acceleration," *Review of Economic Statistics* (May 1939), reprinted in American Economic Association, *Readings in Business Cycle Theory* (Philadelphia, 1944).

must turn down. The system cannot rise beyond the ceiling because prolonged inflationary developments which could temporarily raise business activity beyond the ceiling are disregarded for the present purpose, and the system cannot move *along* the gradually rising full-employment path or ceiling line because the conditions of growth (our "growth corollaries") are not satisfied for the savings which would develop along the growth path set by the ceiling. We may visualize the economy as "trying" to move along the ceiling path when this is hit, but as not "making it" because in a condition of full utilization the profitable amount of further new investment falls short of savings.

Hence, when the ceiling is reached, the system will turn down. Induced investment will now again be governed by the initially assumed β factor of our equation, or possibly by a smaller β factor, but since $(Y_{n-1} - Y_{n-2})$ now is a negative magnitude, induced investment will also be negative: producers will try to disinvest and thus to adjust their physical capital stock to the falling output level. The system will sink not merely below the ceiling, but even below the underemployment growth path.[6] Sooner or later a floor will be reached, if for no other reason than because net induced investment cannot become a numerically greater negative magnitude than that corresponding to zero maintenance rates on the existing capital stock, and hence to zero gross investment. In no period is it possible to do more toward "disinvesting" (negatively investing) a steel plant than to spend nothing on current replacement.[7] One might perhaps expect stabilization at the floor level which corresponds to zero gross investment. But instead of becoming stabilized at that level, the system will rise again.

In the first place, the desired amount of net disinvestment is smaller if the economy tends to stay at a given level than if it is contracting: indeed, with a tendency toward stabilization at a low level, the desire for further disinvestment soon ceases altogether. This is because negative investment results in this model from an immediately preceding fall in output. If negative net investment (net disinvestment) gives way to zero net investment, then one constitutent of output has already grown. Differently expressed, once the floor is reached output grows because it

---

[6] Indeed, we must remember that the assumed values for α and β give explosive fluctuations (see Page 314).

[7] This implies that at the time when the floor is hit, β must again be smaller than it is during the swings between the floor and the ceiling. For, we are describing here a limit to disinvestment, and β must not determine more disinvestment than is consistent with this limit.

now consists of consumption plus autonomous investment, instead of consisting of these two terms *minus* induced disinvestment. If output grows, induced investment will soon become positive, and output will grow further. Therefore, the multiplier-accelerator mechanism itself now tends to raise output. The system again rises toward the ceiling and tries to shoot beyond it, provided that the numerical relationship between α and β is such as to produce explosive movements.

Hence, what initially was shown to be a potential path of continuous growth has ultimately proved to be merely a line around which the system will fluctuate. By the interaction of the multiplier with the accelerator, small random fluctuations in the rate of autonomous investment become magnified into movements which take place between the ceiling level, set by full use of resources, and a floor level corresponding to the maximum technologically possible rate of net disinvestment per period.

Obviously, there exist factors which can prevent the expansion from reaching the ceiling, and can prevent the contraction from reaching the floor level here described, even if the numerical relationship between α and β *is* explosive. For example, bottlenecks in specific segments of the economy or insufficient flexibility of the money supply may exert a slowing influence, and they may bring about a downturn, before resources as a whole become scarce. Or the expectation of a downturn which would have to come soon may lead to an immediate downturn, before the resources needed for further expansion are exhausted. In the Hicks terminology, this would presumably express itself in reduced "autonomous" investment. In the contraction phase, early expectations of an upturn, by raising the level of "autonomous" investment, may lead to an early upturn. Also, the value of α is likely to rise when output is low, and it is likely to fall when output is high; and the government budget is likely to show a surplus when output is high,[8] and a deficit when output is low.[9] All these are stabilizing influences, but only very much more complex models could give a mathematical description of swings with cyclical changes in α and β and in other variables.

The multiplier-accelerator models here considered are mainly suited to illustrating one important point. They illustrate the proposition that it does not take much to explain why economies fluctuate around their

---

[8] Or the deficit may be smaller when output is high than in times of low output.

[9] Or the surplus may be smaller when output is low than in times of high output.

growth paths instead of moving on them smoothly. Accidental disturbances, in themselves, are very likely to generate fluctuations. To convince oneself of this instability, it is sufficient to assume that the multiplier mechanism and the acceleration principle possess equivalents in the real world.

Indeed, as Lloyd A. Metzler has demonstrated, it is even possible to select simpler assumptions for establishing a tendency toward fluctuations around the long-run path of the economy. Metzler's model describes ups and downs in output which may develop from the interaction of the multiplier principle with an accelerator effect applying to *investment in business inventories*. The investment in business inventories, like Hicks' induced investment, may be made to depend on past income-increments. Such a model can obviously become strictly analogous to the general multiplier-accelerator models just discussed. But Metzler's inventory model may also serve for explaining fluctuations on simpler assumptions.

An unexpected increase in consumer income may be assumed to deplete the stock of business inventories. If the firms subsequently produce an output which is intended to be big enough to satisfy the last period's increased consumer demand [10] *and also* to replenish the depleted inventories to their initial size, then total output, consumer income, and probably consumer demand too, will increase beyond the last period's level.[11] Consumer demand will presumably be greater than was expected, and therefore business inventories will not, for the time being, become fully replenished.[12] This process feeds on itself for several periods, since firms will continue to produce, in each period, an output sufficient to satisfy the last period's demand *plus* an output element intended for inventory replenishment. As a consequence of this latter output element, total output or income is greater all the time than the income implicit in the consumer-demand estimates of producers. But since only part of the income increments are spent on consumption, while part of these increments are saved, the extent to which consumer demand is underestimated will sooner or later start to diminish, that is, the inventories *will* at he

---

[10] This implies the assumption on the part of the producers that last period's demand will continue.

[11] This will be true for consumer demand *unless* without the attempt to replenish the inventories there would be more saving than planned investment, in which case the production for inventory replenishment may not be big enough to outweigh the tendency toward oversaving.

[12] In the initial phases, inventories may even become further depleted.

end become gradually replenished.[13] Once they become replenished, further net investment in business inventories ceases, and hence total income consisting of consumption plus inventory investment, starts contracting. During the contraction phase demand is being overestimated. Producers are now reducing their inventories, and this diminishes output and income below their previous level. The contraction and its ending are analogous to the expansion and its ending.

In the inventory-cycle model just considered we did not assume that output-increments create the desire to hold larger inventories than those which were initially held. If this had been assumed, as it is in some variants of Metzler's analysis, then the problem would have become strictly analogous to that of the general multiplier-accelerator models. But we have just seen that the Metzler model will produce flucuations in output even if the producers merely desire to maintain their aggregate inventories at an initially given fixed level, provided that an unexpected demand increment depletes their inventories temporarily, and provided that from then on they always expect the last period's total demand to continue *without allowing for the fact that their effort to replenish the inventories increases the total demand for goods.*[14]

However, a simple model designed to illustrate the inherent instability of the system with the aid of the general multiplier-accelerator mechanism, or with that of Metzler's inventory mechanism, cannot be expected to give a realistic picture of the course of events in the real economy. We have seen that these illustrations disregard several stabilizing factors and thus may tend to overstate the sensitivity of the system to accidental disturbances.[15] On the other hand, where an inflationary-speculative

---

[13] Assume, for example, that producers expected a consumer demand of 100 units, but were faced with consumer demand amounting to 120 units and thus depleted their inventories by 20 units. If, for the next period, they now expect a consumer demand of 120 units, and, in order to replenish their inventories, produce 140 units, then the attempt to replenish their inventories would be *wholly* abortive only if all the 140 units of income were spent on consumption. If part of the addition to income is saved, and there occurs no corresponding addition to new investment, then the system will be moving gradually toward a replenishment of the depleted inventories.

[14] See Lloyd A. Metzler, "The Nature and Stability of Inventory Cycles," *Review of Economic Statistics* (June 1941); *idem,* "Factors Governing the Length of Inventory Cycles," *Review of Economic Statistics* (February 1947).

[15] This is somewhat less true of Richard M. Goodwin's version of these models, because Goodwin takes into account the slowing influence of specific scarcities in the cyclical expansion. However, many factors must necessarily stay outside these simplified accounts, and some of these factors exert a stabilizing influence (see, for example, Chapter 10, Section 8).

Goodwin's views were developed in several articles, and some of the salient features were summarized in "Secular and Cyclical Aspects of the Multiplier and the Acceler-

attitude takes hold of the public in the upper ranges of the cyclical expansion, or where deflationary price expectations exert an important influence in the lower ranges, there develop in the real world destabilizing forces which are not taken into consideration in the simple models here discussed.

It should also be remembered that the cycle models based on multiplier-accelerator interactions usually drew a sharp distinction between "autonomous" and "induced" investment. As was said in the early part of the present Section, the distinction between autonomous and induced investment is designed to separate those new investments called forth by past increases in output from the new investments otherwise motivated (*e.g.,* from more forward-looking investments). Whether these categories possess much operational meaning in the real world seems questionable. Yet it is essential to the mathematical simplicity or manageability of accelerator models to adopt the working hypothesis that part of the investment is derived from past output-increments with the aid of a *fixed β* coefficient. Since investment in general does not fit this simplifying hypothesis, part of the investment (the *induced* investment) is considered to fit it, while the remainder is termed "autonomous." All this means is that the acceleration principle with a fixed accelerator (fixed β coefficient)[16] does not provide a general theory of investment. The distinction between induced and autonomous investment is largely arbitrary.

The general description of inherent instability in Chapters 10 and 11 avoids much of the arbitrariness which inevitably adheres to the simplified multiplier-accelerator models. But mathematical analysis is far superior to general verbal discussion when it comes to making clear the precise nature of a limited number of specific influences.

The optimistically inclined will feel that this appraisal of the usefulness of mathematical models in dynamic economics is too cautious. To be sure, the simple multiplier-accelerator models are too sketchy to yield directly "realistic" results. These models merely show the consequences of certain influences in pure form, treating as impurities all factors that do not fit neatly into the simple schemes. But why couldn't mathematical models be made sufficiently complex to give a reasonably realistic picture of observable processes?

---

ator," in *Income, Employment and Public Policy* (in honor of A. H. Hansen), and "Econometrics in Business-Cycle Analysis," in *Business Cycles and National Income* (by A. H. Hansen), pp. 417-468.

[16] More precisely expressed: with a fixed accelerator in the entire range *between* a ceiling level and a floor level of output.

2. Toward a closer approximation of reality.

Models claiming greater realism have been constructed, and attempts are being made by econometricians to improve these models. Some dynamic econometric models are exceedingly complex. The pioneering work in this field was undertaken by Jan Tinbergen in Rotterdam, but a more recent example is provided by Lawrence R. Klein's contribution in the United States.[17]

In the "large model" described in Klein's *Economic Fluctuations in the United States, 1921-1941,* sixteen variables are listed as *endogenous.* This means that sixteen variables are included in the functional relationships which describe the movements of the economy, on the assumption that outside information is available on certain *exogenous* variables (thirteen in number). These also influence the outcome of economic processes but they should be capable of being interpreted as not determined *by* the processes described in the model. The variables are "dated." Frequently, one and the same variable is included in the system with an already known value for some preceding period (year), and with an initially unknown value for the period (year) for which the system is being solved. Consequently, there are two sorts of *predetermined* variables in the model: the exogenous variables, about which outside information must be available, and the values of the endogenous variables for preceding years. Given the values of these predetermined variables, the equations *determine* the endogenous variables for any "current" year for which a solution of the system of equations is sought. The claim here is that during the period for which the system was tested the system would have "determined" the correct values of the current endogenous variables, given always the predetermined variables. The current values of the sixteen endogenous variables require for their determination sixteen equations.

To illustrate these concepts, let us assume for a moment that someone claims realism for the simple multiplier-accelerator equation of Page 310:

$$Y_n = \alpha \, Y_{n-1} + \beta \, (Y_{n-1} - Y_{n-2}) + A_n$$

where the subscript n stands for the nth period. Here we have one endogenous variable (income) and one exogenous variable (autonomous investment). The latter is exogenous because we must assume that outside information is available on A, that is, on the amount of investment,

---

[17] See J. Tinbergen, *Business Cycles in the United States of America* (Geneva, 1939); L. R. Klein, *Economic Fluctuations in the United States, 1921-1941* (New York, 1950).

other than that induced by past output-increments. Then the following terms are predetermined: Y_{n-1}, Y_{n-2}, and A_n. We are interested in deriving Y_n from these predetermined terms and from the values of the *structural parameters* α and β. Therefore, using the available data concerning autonomous investment and past incomes, we must obtain best estimates of α and of β. To do this, we must recognize that human behavior is subject to error and that a term u should therefore be added to the right-hand side of our equation, thus making Y_n different from what it ideally "ought to be" by the magnitude of this so-called *error term*. Statistical estimation then consists of finding values for α and β which, when used with the already known values of the predetermined terms Y_{n-1}, Y_{n-2}, and A_n, give for each year the correct Y_n values, *aside from differences which can reasonably be treated as errors*. The behavior of these error terms—*i.e.*, of the difference between the Y_n values computed on the basis of our equation and the actually observed Y_n values—must be such as not to destroy the pragmatic usefulness of the system. Also, any statistical method for obtaining the "best estimates" of the numerical values of α and β implies an assumption concerning the nature and behavior of the error terms in successive periods, and the observed behavior must not contradict this assumption. If no estimates can be found for α and β which would satisfy this condition reasonably well, then the model which we are testing does not describe the behavior of the economy satisfactorily (without informal allowances for variables that have stayed outside the model).

As was said before, the simple multiplier-accelerator models are not intended to satisfy such tests. Even with the modifications introduced by Hicks in his discussion of the "ceiling" and the "floor"—modifications causing changes in the values of the parameters at the top and at the floor of the fluctuations—these models make no claim to realism in the sense of statistical testability. But the problems encountered, for example, in Klein's model with sixteen endogenous variables are *analogous* to those just considered; and econometric models, such as those of Klein, do raise the claim of incorporating statistically testable hypotheses.

Klein's model does not incorporate the acceleration principle, but hypotheses deserving to be tested statistically can be obtained also by further developing and enlarging models that do include some form of the acceleration principle.

Klein's so-called large model for the period 1921-1941 contains the following sixteen endogenous variables:

1. The wage-salary bill in the private sector of the economy (W_1);

2. The price indext of output as a whole (p);

3. Output of the private sector, excluding housing services, in constant prices (X);

4. Net private investment in plant and equipment, in constant prices (I);

5. Stock of business fixed capital, end of year, in constant prices (K);

6. Stock of business inventories, end of year, in constant prices (H);

7. Consumer expenditure, in constant prices (C);

8. Disposable income of individuals, in constant prices (Y);

9. Gross construction expenditures on owner-occupied nonfarm houses, in constant prices (D_1);

10. Index number of rent (r);

11. Gross construction expenditures on rented nonfarm houses, in constant prices (D_2);

12. Average corporate bond yield (i);

13. Percentage of non-farm housing units occupied (v);

14. Demand for "active" money, that is, for working balances (M^D_1);

15. Demand for idle balances (M^D_2);

16. Nonfarm rent payments and nonfarm imputed rents (R_1).

Sixteen equations are formulated, to express hypotheses as to how values of the endogenous variables here listed are related to each other and to the "predetermined" terms in the model. The numerical coefficients of the variables and the constants in the equations are the "structural parameters" which must be estimated. All of these are denoted by Greek letters. The "predetermined" terms consist of values of endogenous variables *for some preceding year* and of the values of all exogenous variables. The list of exogenous variables includes:

1. Excise-tax revenues (E);

2. A variable (T) defined as the difference between net national product and disposable income, that is, a variable consisting of all tax

revenues plus corporate savings minus government transfer payments, in constant prices;

3. The price index of capital goods (q);

4. The price index of construction costs (q_1);

5. The change in the number of nonfarm families (ΔF);

6. The number of nonfarm housing units available at the end of the year (N^s);

7. The excess reserves of the banking system averaged during the year (E_R);

8. Gross construction expenditures on farm residences in constant dollars (D_3);

9. Depreciation on all residential buildings, in constant prices (D'');

10. Government expenditures on goods and services plus net exports plus net investment of nonprofit institutions, in constant prices (G);

11. The wage-salary bill in the government sector (W_2);

12. Rent payments and imputed rents on farm residences (R_2).

Time (t), measured in years from an arbitrary beginning, is also conceived of as an exogenous variable, because the movement of the economy is subject to a trend; by making a decision concerning the year for which the system is being solved, the economist introduces from the outside the value of a variable (in this case of a whole complex of variables symbolized by "time"). Obviously, an improvement could be accomplished by working some of the exogenous variables into the system as endogenous variables. For example, q, q_1, D_3 and the corporate-saving element in T are strong candidates for this, while the other elements in T, or the variable G, are perhaps more inherently exogenous. Klein places great emphasis on the tentativeness and the preliminary character of the "step in model building" which is presented in his book. The method is currently being further developed.

We shall not list here all the sixteen equations which show the relationship among simultaneous endogenous variables, and between these and the predetermined variables, with the structural parameters as the connecting links.[18] The following are merely illustrations. Not only

---

[18] The terms denoted by Greek letters are the structural parameters.

these, but all relations of the system, are assumed to be linear. The subscript -1 means that the term in question is the value of a variable for the preceding year. Where there is no subscript, the term is simultaneous with the variable on the left-hand side. The u terms are error terms.

(1) $C = \delta_0 + \delta_1 Y + \delta_2 t + u_1$

(2) $I = \beta_0 + \beta_1 \left(\dfrac{pX - E}{q}\right) + \beta_2 \left(\dfrac{pX - E}{q}\right)_{-1} + \beta_3 K_{-1} + \beta_4 t + u_2$

(3) $H = \gamma_0 + \gamma_1 (X - \Delta H) + \gamma_2 p + \gamma_3 p_{-1} + \gamma_4 H_{-1} + \gamma_5 t + u_3$

.

.

.

(16) $Y + T = I + \Delta H + C + D_1 + D_2 + D_3 - D'' + G$

The first of these four equations incorporates the hypothesis that consumption is a function of current disposable income and that the relationship between the two is subject to a trend factor. Klein's best estimates for the parameters (by one of the two statistical methods used) are

$$\delta_0 = 11.87, \ \delta_1 = 0.73, \ \delta_2 = 0.04.$$

The second equation gives private plant and equipment expenditure as a function of the value of current output, net of excise taxes paid by business, divided by the price index of capital goods. Last year's value of this same term also is assumed to enter into the determination of current private plant and equipment expenditure. Klein's estimates for the parameters (by the same method which yields the δ estimates of the previous paragraph) are

$$\beta_0 = 2.59, \ \beta_1 = 0.12, \ \beta_2 = 0.04, \ \beta_3 = -0.10.$$

The negative algebraic sign of β_3 indicates that, other things equal, a large capital stock a year ago diminishes present new investment. No estimates are attained for the time parameter (β_4) in this equation or for the corresponding parameter (γ_5) in the third equation, that is to say, the trend terms $\beta_4 t$ and $\gamma_5 t$ are neglected. But, partly as a consequence of the trend term in the first equation here listed, and partly as a consequence of trend terms in other equations not listed here, several constituents of X are treated as subject to trend. Thus X itself is also so treated, and this makes I and H subject to trend.

The hypothesis expressed by the second equation is not identical with the acceleration principle. The equation says that unless the prices of capital goods are high, conditions are favorable for investment in plant and equipment if the capital stock at the end of last year was small, and if last year's output and especially this year's output are high. By an equation not specifically listed in our abridged account of the system, there exists in the model a *linear* relationship which makes the private wage-salary bill move up and down with this year's output as well as last year's output. Therefore, the content of equation (2) bears great similarity to saying that present investment is great or small according as past and present profits (output minus the wage-salary bill) are great or small. Indeed, in Klein's analysis the second equation is deduced from the profit incentive. This is not the same formal relationship as that which is expressed by the acceleration principle. But the acceleration principle also leads, of course, to the conclusion that a large present demand for output and a small capital stock in the recent past jointly create favorable conditions for present investment. A simplified model with a constant accelerator, and with investment derived from past changes in output alone, is certainly very different from a model containing Klein's investment equations. But it might be possible to express the content of the Klein equations—and that of other hypotheses concerning the behavior of investors—in terms of a modified acceleration principle, that is, with flexible accelerators. No one really meant to suggest that the value of the accelerator, by which output-increments induce new investment, is uninfluenced by the wage level, the profit experience of producers, the degree of utilization of plant and equipment, etc.

The third equation on Page 324 represents the demand for business inventories as determined by the level of output,[19] by the level of prices, which affects the speculative demand, and by the previous level of inventories. It is interesting to note that the error term of the inventory equation (u_3) becomes a predetermined variable in the (here unlisted) output-adjustment equation applying to the subsequent year. That is to say, one of Klein's sixteen equations, the output-adjustment equation, gives ΔX as a function of $(u_3)_{-1}$ and of the price change from one period to the next, where $(u_3)_{-1}$ is multiplied by a negative coefficient. Thus the accumulation of excess inventories, due to error, leads to a subsequent negative output-adjustment, while a smaller-than-intended inventory level leads to a subsequent increase in output.

The output-adjustment equation is not listed on Page 324, nor is the interest-rate adjustment equation which makes the change in the

---

[19] Except that that part of output which itself consists of changes in business inventories must be deducted.

interest rate (average corporate bond yield) depend on the size of excess reserves and the interest rate of the preceding year. All these equations contain error terms, while the purely definitional equations, of course, do not. This is exemplified by the last equation which we have listed. The equation contains the definition of the net national product.

Models of this sort would be clearly superior tools of analysis if they were dependable means of forecasting. However, in the present stage of econometrics, it is inadvisable to rely upon them for prediction because no sufficient presumption exists for the applicability to a future period of a set of structural relationships which appear to give a satisfactory explanation for a specific past period. The structural relations *shift;* the environment does not stay unchanged. But this always raises the further question of how adequate the explanation is, even for the specific past period to which the set of structural relations is supposed to apply. Even if the values of the endogenous variables, as determined by the suggested set of structural relations, come close to the empirically observed values of these variables, the results are inconclusive.

At best, it is possible to arrive at the conclusion that the error terms in the various equations are reasonably small relatively to the estimated true values of the variables and that, if the suggested relations *should really be* the "true" relations for a closed period, then the occurrence of errors of the observed magnitude and behavior would not be too surprising. It is almost certain that an equally strong statement could be made in support of an entirely different set of structural relations. Many sets of structural relations, with very different implications, may give error terms (*i.e.,* deviations of the observed from the estimated values of the current endogenous variables) of which it is not possible to say that their characteristics as alleged errors around true values *clearly contradict* the validity of the suggested structural relations themselves.

In principle, the identical statement can be made about any statistical universe, in the natural and the social sciences alike. But if it can be postulated that the true structural relations stay stable, then by testing alternative models with increasingly numerous new data it is possible to discover whether the old explanation should or should not be replaced with a new one, as an explanation of the old as well as of the new observations. For, if the old explanation is clearly inferior, then sooner or later we will find clearly nonfitting new data. This is how an old theory proves inferior to a new theory in the exact sciences. But if when we find clearly nonfitting data, we are prepared to say that at this point the structural relations have changed—*i.e.,* they will be different from now on—then we have done two things at one stroke. We have abandoned the pragmatic claim to usefulness of our tools for prediction; and we have deprived the old explanation, as an explanation of the past, of the chance to prove inferior by the method by which an hypothesis *not immediately and grossly implausible* can nevertheless prove wrong in the exact sciences. By admitting that the dynamic econometric models are not good enough for prediction, we willy-nilly admit at the same time that we know too little about how good they are as explanations of the past. This is true of the dynamic models now in use for the reason that they are incapable of being further tested and reconsidered for the closed period to which they apply with the aid of as yet unexploited data for that same period.

Unless we insist that an ever-increasing quantity of new observations must be in harmony with the old explanation, we can never know more than that a very limited number of observations fits the suggested structural relations for the past reasonably well. This is likely to be true of a great number of alternative structural relations.

It follows from this discussion that at the present stage of their development the econometric business-cycle models cannot be used directly for making up one's mind concerning the probable consequences of events. The economist must ask himself the question whether one or the other of the *past* "structural relations" is or is not likely to prove a reasonable approximation to the true *future* relation, and this means that he must attempt to make informal allowances for changing "environmental" factors. These express themselves not merely in the changing values of exogenous variables but, unfortunately, also in the changing character of the structural relations formulated in these systems. As long as this is the case, much can be said for remaining on the level of the more loosely formulated hypotheses which were discussed in Chapters 10 and 11. To be sure, these hypotheses must be used with heavy reliance on the informal, and partly subjective appraisal of environmental factors, to decide which combination of specific hypotheses seems most applicable to the *ad hoc* conditions with which we happen to be faced.

But with such informal, and partly subjective appraisals the hypotheses of Chapters 10 and 11 are useful. They at least help clarify the question of what legitimate differences in general and informal appraisal may lead one person to one set of conclusions and another person to another set. On the other hand, it is extremely difficult to make informal allowances for vaguely sensed environmental changes in a system with sixteen equations. Any change goes through the whole system of equations, affecting the solution of all variables. The question of *how* the solution is affected does not pose an articulate problem to our faculty of arriving at "general" or "informal" appraisals. Establishing the Tinbergen-Klein type of model as a superior tool of analysis will require finding structural relations which hold for more than the closed periods serving for the *ex post facto* estimation of parameters. To be really useful, the method will have to enable us to dispense, at least in most instances, with informal (quasi-intuitive) allowances for environmental changes. Econometricians are fully aware of this.

And yet the difference between the looser hypotheses and the more highly formalized ones remains, of course, a matter of degree. Sufficiently simplified systems of quasi-mathematical character belong more on our previous level of analysis than on the Tinbergen-Klein level. Looser frameworks, even if they are formulated with the aid of mathematical symbols, must be so strongly supplemented with the kind of appraisal suggested by Chapters 10 and 11. The formal structures of these frameworks perform mainly the function of making specific the points to which the informal appraisals relate.

3. Looser frameworks of quasi-mathematical character.

In this Section we shall describe one of the less formalistic methods of using theory for appraising probable future business conditions. There are few economists who in their own thinking would not use crude and simple methods of this sort. This is understandable, considering the limitations of the more refined techniques. The simplified frameworks need to be heavily supplemented with informal appraisals which are rooted in general reasoning of the type considered in Chapters 10 and 11.

Assume that we possess information concerning the investment plans of business enterprise for a period lying ahead of us, and that we are thus able to estimate the total new private capital formation which will be forthcoming if plans do not change, and if all plans become realized. In the United States such estimates can be based, at least in part, on surveys undertaken by government agencies (the Department of Commerce and the Securities and Exchange Commission).[20] Assume also that we have an estimate of government expenditures on goods and services for the same period lying ahead of us. Thirdly, let us assume that we can estimate in percentage terms the consumed proportion of aggregate income for that same period. This we may do with the proviso that the estimate will be valid only if business conditions are normal, that is, if output rises gradually, at the approximate rate of its trend slope. We base such estimates on observed past relations, with informal allowances for changes which we might anticipate. Having made these assumptions, we can engage in reasoned guesswork as to whether business conditions will or will not be normal.

For if we say that the assumed net private capital formation is $20 billion, the assumed federal, state, and local government expenditure on goods and services is $70 billion and that 75 percent of the net national product is expected to become consumed (in view of the anticipated tax policy and credit policy), then to the $90 billion of investment demand plus government expenditures there will correspond a total demand for a net national product of $360 billion; of an output or income of this size, $270 billion would go into consumption, $20 billion into net private capital formation, and $70 billion into government-acquired goods and services.[21] If we believe that in the period ahead of us reasonably full use of the equipment in our economy will yield an output (a supply) of about $360 billion, with all goods valued in present prices, then our "reasoned guess" is that conditions will be normal, in the sense that growth will not be interrupted and there will be no inflation.[22] If we believe that the full-capacity supply would be appreciably in excess of $360 billion, then we should expect disturbing excess capacities in equipment. Hence we should expect a subsequent sharp reduction of new investment activity, such as must lead to an interruption of the growth process and to deflationary pressure. We can even tell whether the expected pressure will be great or small, although we cannot make a guess at the extent of the output reduction or price reduction without further data which would reflect the changes in the assumed behavior

---

[20] These surveys relate at present merely to planned investment in plant and equipment.

[21] In other words, we must here multiply the investment plus government expenditure by a "multiplier" of four to obtain aggregate income. This multiplier is $\dfrac{1}{1-\alpha}$ where α is the consumed fraction of income (here 0.75).

[22] See, however, Footnote 23, Page 320.

pattern in "abnormal" circumstances. If, on the other hand, we believe that the production capacity of the equipment will be smaller than about $360 billion in present prices, then we are expecting an inflationary pressure (but again we would require further data to make a guess at the extent of the expected price increase).[23]

The production capacity of the equipment during a period lying ahead of us should presumably be estimated by taking the output of a completed period and then asking ourselves the question whether the production capacity of the system is likely to continue to increase at the time rate at which it has been increasing during specific past periods. For example, it may seem reasonable to expect that output per man-hour will continue to rise at an average yearly rate of 2 percent. Then, if the labor force is rising at a yearly rate of 1 percent, and if at present the labor force is fully employed, the productive capacity of the system will be rising at a yearly rate of about 3 percent. If in our previous example the $360-billion output level in the period lying ahead of us corresponds to a 3-percent annual rise from the period just completed, that is, if the present output is about $350 billion, then our method has led us to expect continued growth with full employment of labor. If, on the other hand, an approximately constant percentage of the slowly rising total labor force has recently been unemployed, but the equipment has been sufficiently fully utilized to keep the economy on a growth path, then (assuming the same data in every other respect) our method leads us to expect continued growth of output, with an unchanging percentage of the labor force unemployed. With a present output of, say $380 billion, and a capacity-trend suggesting a 3-percent higher capacity for the period ahead of us, we would be led to the expectation of appreciable excess capacity and of growth-interruption.

An alternative version of this crude method is obtained by using the concept of the accelerator, that is, of the capital requirement per unit of output-increment, instead of relying on direct estimates of planned investment outlays. It is necessary to use this, or some other alternative to the method just described, if the future period with which we are concerned lies further than a few quarters (at most a year) ahead, be-

---

[23] However, even if there exists no inflationary excess-demand of this sort, and the estimates here suggested lead to the expectation of balance at $360 billion, autonomous wage increases might still lead to inflationary price increases. This disturbance will, however, occur only if wages should be raised by more than is compatible with stable prices in view of increasing output per man-hour, and if the credit policy of the central bank should enable the banking system to finance the inflated value of output.

cause direct estimates of planned investment outlays always relate to the near future. Even for the near future, these estimates are incomplete—they do not cover all types of investment—but for the more distant future we have at best very sporadic direct guesses, and these are quite undependable. However, we should remember that the method sketched in the preceding pages implies the expectation of a normal growth rate of output; and if by examining the past relationship between output-increments and capital-increments, and by making informal allowances for changes which we might anticipate, we are willing to commit ourselves to a guess concerning the future relationship between the growth of output and that of capital, then we are able to derive an indirect estimate of the net investment demand which would develop on a normal growth path. The growth of output multiplied by the capital requirement per unit of output-increment[24] gives us the quantity of planned new investment. To return to our previous example, the estimate of $20 billion net private capital formation for the period ahead of us, which in our first illustration was based on direct information concerning the plans of investors, could have resulted alternatively from the indirect method now considered, with the following three assumptions: a present output of 350 billions, a rate of output growth of 3 percent per period, and a new capital requirement of about 2 per unit of output growth.[25] If one or more of these three assumptions were changed, a different estimate of net private investment would result for the period ahead of us.

This latter framework is essentially the same as that described in Chapter 8, Section 3, for tracing processes of dynamic equilibrium (continuous growth).[26] What we are doing in the present context is simply to test whether a set of numerical assumptions is compatible with continuous growth at a reasonably stable general price level, and, if not, to

---

[24] The capital requirement per unit of output-increment is the accelerator. Here, as everywhere except on Pages 310-317, we omit the distinction between autonomous and induced investment. Our position in this regard was explained on Page 319. The capital requirement per unit of output-increment is, of course, the reciprocal of the output-increment per unit of new capital formation.

[25] Precisely 2 would give an investment estimate of $21 billion. However, the method is not quite precisely described in the text, because allowance should be made for the fact that part of the new capital requirement is included in government outlays rather than in private investment outlays.

[26] Except that the balanced-budget assumption of Chapter 7 enabled us to argue that balance between desired private capital formation and savings is necessary and sufficient for dynamic equilibrium. There we did not have to bring the government expenditures explicitly into the framework.

find out the direction and the order of magnitude of the imbalance. While an idea is obtained of the initial size of the imbalance, a model of this sort tells us nothing about the course of secondary (cumulative) disturbances which develop once the impact of the imbalance has made itself felt. For the same reason, models of the type here considered tell us nothing about how the economy comes out of an unbalanced position. For tracing the cyclical path in the course of disturbances, we would need much more complex models (say, of the type used by Klein), and if at the present stage we are not willing to trust these models, we must try to feel our way through the looser sketches of cyclical processes in Chapters 10 and 11. All these sketches describe cumulative disturbances which develop when our growth corollaries, pertaining to the rate of overcoming scarcities, become violated;[27] and all these sketches describe mechanisms by which the system ultimately gets over the disturbances.

On the other hand, if the simple model just sketched leads to the belief that the conditions of balanced growth are approximately satisfied at the $360-billion level, then the proper relationship between the rate of overcoming scarcities and the rate of saving is implied in these expectations. For example, it is implied that *for the amount of new investment required to match savings* the output-increment per unit of new capital formation[28] is not so low as to prevent the investment from being undertaken. This, in turn, implies the proper rate of offsetting the tendency toward diminishing returns by technological and organizational improvements. The avoidance of severe shortages in specialized resources, and the avoidance of an imbalance between the growth of the money supply and the growth of output, are also implied.

It would be unduly pretentious to characterize the mental operations described in the present Section as operations of "predicting" or "forecasting." The guesses resulting from these operations are strongly influenced by informal allowances which we make for expected changes in various statistically observed numerical relationships,[29] and the crude models we have been considering here do not include instructions as to how these allowances should be made. The allowances will, of course,

---

[27] More precisely expressed, the growth corollaries relate to the sufficiency of the rate of overcoming the various scarcities, where "sufficiency" means sufficiency for calling forth the amount of investment required to match savings, in view of existing risk appraisals.

[28] This ratio is the reciprocal of the accelerator.

[29] These are relationships such as the consumed and the saved proportion of output, the capital requirement per unit of output growth (accelerator), etc.

be based on general information and observation, but usually on information and observation which cannot be quantified by any precise procedure and hence must be interpreted in the light of individual judgment and "feel." It follows that different individuals may arrive at very different expectations, even though they use the same framework.

What nevertheless can be claimed for analysis of this sort is that it focuses differences of opinion on specific points. For example, in view of observable developments in monetary policy or tax policy, and in view of what appear to be the general attitudes of the public, is the saved proportion of incomes likely to change appreciably as compared to the past relationships? Is the value of the capital requirement per unit of output-increment likely to change appreciably? Are trends in output per man-hour and in the growth of the labor force likely to be maintained? A person required to make practical decisions has a better understanding of the differences of opinion confronting him if he knows that the disagreement relates to questions of this kind, than if he is simply told that some observers are optimistic while others are pessimistic.

On these same grounds, it is possible to make a case also for the use of the lead-lag propositions of Chapter 3, Section 12, in attempts to discover whether a cyclical turning point is approaching. These relationships, too, must be used with informal allowances for changing environmental factors. But they, too, provide focal points for locating the nature of legitimate disagreement. At least some of these propositions possess sufficient *a priori* plausibility to place the burden of the argument on the person who expects that in the future they will not tend to come true. Considering that use of our looser frameworks can give indications merely of the direction and the crude order of magnitude of initial imbalances, relatively to a path of smooth growth, there is need for consulting further empirical relationships in an attempt to identify at least some stages of a disturbed path. Lead-lag propositions may be useful in this regard.

The operation of "forecasting" differs from that of engaging in "informed guesses" merely in degree; the same can be said about the differences between Tinbergen's or Klein's mathematical model and the frameworks described in the present Section. These differences too, are matters of degree, matters of more or less. The "more or less" here relates to a higher or lower degree of formalization of an analytical system which would possess rigorous validity only if the parameters were unchanging; therefore, the "more or less" relates to smaller or greater reliance on informal allowances which must be made for changes in the parameters. Since the difference is not one of kind but of degree, it must be possible to express the framework described in the present Section as a "mathematical model." To do this is unnecessary, because the models of the present Section are exceedingly simple, and hence answers can be had from them simply by trial and error. But to illustrate the fact that the general character of such frameworks *is* that of mathematical models, we shall end this Section by formulating in simple algebraic terms the conceptual systems which we have just illustrated.

Say that we have reason to believe that planned investment outlays during the next period will be I, that government expenditures on goods and services will be G, that γ times the value of the net national product will reach individual income recipients as disposable income after taxes,[30] and that the fraction ε of the disposable income is consumed. Then, with Y^D standing for the demand for net national product in the next period, the reasoning of this Section took its departure from the equation:

$$Y^D = I + G + \gamma \, \varepsilon \, Y^D$$

or

$$Y^D = \frac{I + G}{1 - \gamma \, \varepsilon} \tag{1}$$

Further, if Y_0 stands for the net national product produced during the period just completed, and ρ for the rate of growth per period of the supply of goods (that is, of the supply of "output") at full capacity and at an unchanging general price level, then avoiding both an interruption of the growth process and inflation requires:

$$Y^D = Y_0(1 + \rho) \tag{2}$$

while inequality between the two sides of Equation 2 creates inflationary or deflationary imbalance.

Consequently, smooth growth requires the following relationship between our predetermined variables and our parameters:

$$\frac{I + G}{1 - \gamma \, \varepsilon} = Y_0(1 + \rho) \tag{3}$$

---

[30] The remainder of the earnings that correspond to the net national product goes into tax payments and corporate savings (undistributed corporate profits). However, if the concepts of the Department of Commerce are used, γ times the net national product exceeds, by the value of the government transfer payments, that part of the net national product which goes neither into taxes nor into corporate savings; and $(1 - \gamma)$ times the net national product is smaller by the value of the government transfer payments than that part of the net national product which does go into taxes and into corporate savings. This is because the disposable income of individuals includes the government transfer payments, while the net national product does not include them.

Equation 3 expresses a relationship between the predetermined variables I, G, and Y_0, and the structural parameters γ, ε, and ρ. This is the relationship between our variables and parameters which must be satisfied along paths of smooth growth. By applying the known values of the variables I, G, and Y_0, and our estimates of the parameters, γ, ε, and ρ, we may discover whether the condition expressed in Equation 3 is likely to be approximately satisfied, and if not, we may arrive at inferences concerning the direction and the initial size of the imbalance.

The statement that we have "estimated" the parameters γ, ε, and ρ, on the basis of observed past values of the parameters, *but with informal allowances* for past and for presumptive future changes in environmental factors, precludes precise formalization of the estimating procedure. Aside from the informal allowances the problem here is that of finding in the available data typical numerical relations between net national product and disposable income, between disposable income and consumption, and between the net national products of successive periods.

The alternative to this loose framework, which was also described above in general verbal terms, treats I in Equation 1 not as a predetermined variable but as resulting from:

$$I = \beta \, (Y^D - Y_0)$$

where the parameter β is the "accelerator," or new capital requirement per unit of output-increment. This factor is again estimated on the basis of past experience, with informal allowances for possible changes.

Hence

$$Y^D = \beta \, (Y^D - Y_0) + G + \gamma \, \varepsilon \, Y^D$$

and we obtain in place of Equation 1:

$$Y^D = \frac{G - \beta \, Y_0}{1 - \gamma \, \varepsilon - \beta} \tag{1a}$$

Equation 2 stays unchanged. It must now be used along with 1a to obtain 3a (instead of being used, as before, along with 1 to obtain 3). Smooth growth requires the following relationship between our predetermined variables and our parameters:

$$\frac{G - \beta Y_0}{1 - \gamma \, \varepsilon - \beta} = Y_0 \, (1 + \rho) \tag{3a}$$

Much of the discussion in the present volume has been concerned with the forces that have produced a long-run tendency toward satisfying a condition of this kind, at high levels of employment, without primary reliance on a deficit-financed G term.

Both versions of the framework here described formulate the condition that, at a stable general price level, private investors and the government should desire to buy that part of the aggregate supply of goods and services which, given their disposable incomes, consumers do not wish to buy. This condition implies that for the required amount of new investment β must not be so high as to make for insufficient profitability. If the condition is satisfied for a range of I magnitudes, then as long as we keep within that range, ρ will be the greater, the greater the saved proportion of output is *and* the greater the output-increment is which is obtainable per unit of new capital formation.

BIBLIOGRAPHY—PART 4

1. List of books and articles from which general supplementary readings may be selected:

Books

Cassel, Gustav. *The Theory of Social Economy*. 2 vols. New York: Harcourt, Brace & Co., 1932 (particularly Bk. IV, Vol. II).

Clark, J. M. *Strategic Factors in Business Cycles*. New York: National Bureau of Economic Research, 1934.

Gordon, R. A. *Business Fluctuations*. New York: Harper & Bros., 1952.

Haberler, Gottfried. *Prosperity and Depression*. Lake Success: United Nations, 1946.

Hansen, A. H. *Business Cycles and National Income*. New York: W. W. Norton & Co., 1951.

Hart, A. G. *Money, Debt, and Economic Activity*. New York: Prentice-Hall, 1953.

Hayek, F. A. von. *Prices and Production*. London: G. Routledge & Sons, 1941.

Hicks, J. R. *A Contribution to the Theory of the Trade Cycle*. Oxford: Clarendon Press, 1950.

Klein, L. R. *Economic Fluctuations in the United States, 1921-1941*. New York: John Wiley & Sons, 1950.

Moore, G. H. *Statistical Indicators of Cyclical Revivals and Recessions* (Occasional Paper No. 31). New York: National Bureau of Economic Research, 1950.

Schumpeter, J. A. *Business Cycles*. 2 vols. New York and London: McGraw-Hill Book Co., 1939.

Wilson, Thomas. *Fluctuations in Income and Employment*. London: I. Pitman & Sons, 1949.

Wright, D. M. *The Economics of Disturbance*. The Macmillan Co., 1947.

Articles

Clark, J. M. "Business Acceleration and the Law of Demand: A Technical Factor in Economic Cycles." *Journal of Political Economy,* March 1917; reprinted in *Readings in Business Cycle Theory* (American Economic Association), Philadelphia: The Blakiston Co., 1944.

Metzler, L. A. "The Nature and Stability of Inventory Cycles." *Review of Economic Statistics,* August 1951.

Samuelson, P. A. "Interactions Between the Multiplier Analysis and the Principle of Acceleration." *Review of Economic Statistics,* May 1939; reprinted in *Readings in Business Cycle Theory* (American Economic Association), Philadelphia: The Blakiston Co., 1944.

Schelling, T. C. "Capital Growth and Equilibrium." *American Economic Review,* December 1947.

2. Further readings relating to topics discussed in Part 4:

Books

Foster, W. T. and W. Catchings. *Profits*. Boston and New York: Houghton Mifflin Co., 1925.

Hobson, J. A. *The Economics of Unemployment*. London: G. Allen & Unwin, 1931.

Kalecki, M. *Essays in the Theory of Economic Fluctuations*. London: G. Allen & Unwin, 1939.

Samuelson, P. A. *Foundations of Economic Analysis*. Cambridge: Harvard University Press, 1947 (particularly Ch. 9).

Tinbergen, Jan. *Business Cycles in the United States of America, 1921-1941*. Geneva: League of Nations, 1939.

Articles

Duesenberry, J. S. "Hicks on the Trade Cycle." *Quarterly Journal of Economics,* August 1950.

Frisch, Ragnar. "Propagation Problems and Impulse Problems in Dynamic Economics," in *Economic Essays in Honor of Gustav Cassel*. London: G. Allen & Unwin, 1933.

Goodwin, R. M. "Econometrics in Business—Cycle Analysis," in *Business Cycles and National Income,* ed. by A. H. Hansen. New York: W. W. Norton & Co., 1951.

———. "Innovations and the Irregularity of Economic Cycles," *Review of Economic Statistics,* 1946.

———. "The Nonlinear Accelerator and the Persistence of Business Cycles." *Econometrica,* January, 1951.

———. "Secular and Cyclical Aspects of the Multiplier and the Accelerator," in *Income, Employment and Public Policy* (in honor of A. H. Hansen). New York: W. W. Norton & Co., 1948.

Kaldor, Nicholas. "A Model of the Trade Cycle." *Economic Journal,* March 1940.

———. "The Relation of Economic Growth and Cyclical Fluctuations." *Economic Journal,* March 1954.

Metzler, L. A. "Factors Governing the Length of Inventory Cycles." *Review of Economic Statistics,* February 1947.

Schumacher, Hermann. "Die Ursachen der Geldkrisis von 1907," in *Weltwirtschaftliche Studien*. Leipzig: Veit and Co., 1911.

Tobin, James. "Asset Holdings and Spending Decisions." *American Economic Review, Papers and Proceedings,* May 1952.

———. "Relative Income, Absolute Income, and Saving," in *Money, Trade, and Economic Growth* (in honor of J. H. Williams). New York: The Macmillan Co., 1951.

PART 5 /

Problems of Policy and the Historical Environment

13

Initial Conditions and the Growth Corollaries in Early Stages of Economic Development

1. The initial stock of resources and administrative unification.

Earlier in this volume,[1] it was noted that an historical point of departure is taken for granted in our statement of the three growth corollaries. The economy needs an initial stock in all factors of production. As a consequence of indivisibilities, the growth process cannot acquire momentum before these stocks reach a reasonable minimum size so that it is possible to exploit the economies of scale, and the complementarities among various types of equipment. In practice, this means that an initial accumulation of physical capital, as well as the administrative unification of areas with sufficient natural resources and with a sufficient population, must precede the historical epoch to which analysis in terms of our growth corollaries becomes directly applicable. The physical composition of the required initial capital stock is, of course, a matter of significance.

Certain major items of physical capital which show particularly strong complementarity with many other individual, specialized items in the capital stock are sometimes called "social overhead." This concept includes transportation facilities, power-producing equipment, educational and training facilities, city housing, etc. The need for social overhead

---

[1] See Chapter 4, Section 9; and particularly Chapter 8, Section 2. The growth corollaries were described in Chapters 8 and 9.

illustrates the proposition that, as a consequence of the interaction of economies of scale with complementarities, it takes a minimum amount of investment to raise returns to a level at which the growth process can be sustained, provided that from there on the system is capable of producing sufficient offsets to diminishing returns.

In Western Europe the acquisition of the initial physical equipment seems to have been an exceedingly slow and gradual process, with occasional spurts. Europe was becoming increasingly more "capitalistic" during the later part of the Middle Ages and in early modern times, but even in the eighteenth century the process was still in its early stages. As seen from the present vantage point, very much the greater part of the development took place in the nineteenth century and in the first half of the twentieth.

All along in history, the expectations of individual producers concerning the roughly simultaneous expansion activities of other producers must have played a part in creating a willingness to accumulate productive capital. But the gradual accumulation of an initial stock which raised the profitability of further investment projects was influenced also by communal decisions. Governmental units owned physical capital in the form of buildings, ships, roads, and in some regions also in the form of canals and even of manufacturing establishments. Governments and communal institutions were also relatively large buyers of certain finished products—of metals for their mints, clothing for their armed forces, of firearms, of luxury products of the courts—and thus they provided an incentive for private capital accumulation. Furthermore, the governments of early modern times, during the era of Mercantilism, usually acted on the assumption that protecting investors from "undue" competition, stimulates private capital formation in early periods of economic growth.[2] The case for import restrictions and for internally administered privileges and subsidies is probably less strong than was believed or pretended at that time, although it is now generally admitted

---

[2] Literature on the problems of this era is very voluminous. We limit ourselves here to reference to the following: E. F. Heckscher, "Mercantilism," in *Encyclopaedia of the Social Sciences* (New York, 1933), X, pp. 333-339, and *Mercantilism* (London, 1935); G. F. Schmoller, *The Mercantile System and Its Historical Significance* (New York and London, 1914); W. Cunningham, *The Growth of English Industry and Commerce in Modern Times, The Mercantile System* (Cambridge, England, 1925); Max Weber, *General Economic History* (New York, 1927); Werner Sombart, *Der Moderne Kapitalismus* (Leipzig, 1902), particularly Volume II.

that the "infant-industry argument" for temporary tariff protection possesses some degree of validity.[3]

The case for "protecting" and subsidizing progressive sectors of the economy in their early stages of development possesses two valid roots, even though pressure groups usually succeed in exaggerating and unduly extending the argument. The case is properly rooted in *risk* considerations, on one hand, and in *external economies* on the other. Prior to the accumulation of an adequate initial stock, investment decisions are particularly risky because the profitability of these decisions depends on the roughly simultaneous emergence of new producers in other sectors of the economy (not, as later, merely on the roughly simultaneous growth of production in other sectors); and also because internal economies of scale may require building ahead of present demand in anticipation of future economic growth. These parts of the infant-industry argument hinge entirely on risk considerations, that is, on imperfections of foresight. They hinge on the fact that producers can only guess about the action of other producers and about future economic growth. But *external* economies of scale could justify protection and subsidization even if the actions of other producers and future growth rates could be foreseen with great precision and confidence.

External economies are said to develop when by increasing its factor-inputs a firm not merely raises its own output but also increases outputs elsewhere in the economic system. The free market provides insufficient rewards for activities involving external economies because part of the social benefit of investment is "given away" by the investor. Among these external economies, an "irreversible" variety, namely the spread of nonpatentable technological and organizational know-how is by far the most important. The significance of this variety of external economy is particularly great under primitive conditions, where starting the growth process requires that progressive sectors of the economy should rise rather suddenly to a much higher level of technological and organizational efficiency. Subsequently the new know-how and the new general attitude can spread to many other sectors. This process is more or less irreversible: knowledge is not lost.

---

[3] The best known early protagonists of the infant-industry argument are Alexander Hamilton in the United States (*Report of the Secretary of the Treasury, on the Subject of Manufactures,* December 5, 1791) and Friedrich List in Germany (*The National System of Political Economy,* London and New York, 1904) .

Even John Stuart Mill, who, of course, was a staunch free trader, admitted that the infant-industry argument possessed validity under certain circumstances. See his *Principles of Political Economy,* edited by W. J. Ashley (London, 1909) , p. 922.

Yet while the infant-industry argument possesses valid roots, it must of course not be overlooked that protecting and subsidizing specific sectors of an economy implies taxing other sectors. The foresight of policy makers and of economists, too, is limited. It is rarely obvious *a priori* which of the many sectors should be treated as potentially progressive and which as presumably incapable of producing large external economies. Much can therefore be said for limiting protective policies to particularly strong cases and to early periods of development. One particular bias that frequently enters into the application of the "infant-industry argument" is an anti-agricultural bias originating in the conception that manufacturing is almost invariably a much more powerful carrier of external economies than is agricultural reorganization. In retrospect, it seems very likely that at least in some countries the Mercantilist policy of early modern times used a substantial overdose of protectionism, in the form not only of export-import restrictions, but also of regulation and supervision of industrial activities. Countries using less of these ingredients were on the whole more successful in rising to a level of sufficient physical stock and sufficient human skills. They were more successful in rising to a level from which technological improvements, adequate mobility of resources, and a developed credit mechanism could carry them further along a steep upward trend.

The accumulation of an initial physical stock, and the unification of sizable areas with a sufficient population and sufficient natural resources, are necessary prerequisites of significant economic growth. However, it is possible to overemphasize the natural-resources requirement because, within rather wide limits, human skills may become substitutes for these. Nations can become prosperous partly through their service industries— trade, finance, tourism, etc.—and partly through the skillful processing of foreign materials.

2. Ideologies and social power relations.

The era of significant economic growth has been an era in which the three corollaries of our analytical Chapters in Part 3 have tended to become satisfied in the long run. As was just noted, all communities that have met this condition have gone through a process of initial, slow accumulation in a "pre-industrial" period, and all have gone through a process of administrative unification. Let us now add that all have shown evidences of the spread of an outlook—of something in the nature of a recognizable "creed"—even before the period of rapid economic development has started. An alternative way of saying this is to state that the relative power of social strata representing the outlook of industrialism has started increasing even prior to the era of rapid economic growth.

The outlook in question is one that measures success largely by the ability to create and to satisfy market demand. It may be unfair to call the outlook narrowly materialistic because the demand which is being created and satisfied through markets is, in part, a demand for products of the arts, for scientific knowledge, for travel, and for more satisfactory family homes. But it remains true that the typical outlook of the age of industrialism is materialistic as compared to other outlooks to which many individuals have become dedicated. The market demand is in large part a demand for material things; and there exist basic impulses or desires which are incapable of being satisfied in organized markets, irrespective of whether material goods or high-grade services are being exchanged in these. In the age of industrialism, "success" is achieved in the main by ability to create and to satisfy market demand. It is measured largely in terms of command over exchangeable goods and services. Some signs have recently been pointing to an increasing degree of impatience with this aspect of industrialism. It is quite possible that a stage of development has now been reached in which greater concern with nonmarket objectives (intelligent use of "leisure") would indirectly raise rather than reduce the level of economic efficiency.

What it takes to "convert" first a small section, and then gradually the major part, of a population to the outlook of market economies is an exceedingly complicated question. It may be suggested that acts of "conversion" to the outlook of industrialism have in some cases been greatly facilitated by the failure of the pre-industrial economies to perform satisfactorily, *even by their own standards.* For example, processes of gradual reorganization in the agricultural sector have tended to reduce the ability of that sector to sustain the existing population, all the more because in some cases gradual improvements in transportation and perhaps also in sanitation have caused the death rate to fall and population to rise. Frequently, there seems to have been an effective push away from old modes of life as well as a pull toward new ones.

The emergence of a substantial sector in which the population is living by the standards of an industrial civilization has, of course, in every case run counter to the interests of established social groups. The change has therefore always required a friendly attitude on the part of governments to the aspirations of newly rising social strata. This friendly attitude has tended to be forthcoming mainly because economic growth enhances the power position of the state. However, in most countries the pure outlook of industrialism has become blended with pre-industrial outlooks of "feudal" character, and at a later stage, with certain varieties of the equalitarian outlook. The pure outlook of industrialism is merely an analytical abstraction. Considering the materialistic traits of the ideology of the market economy, we should not regret that it has come to rule with impurities, that is, with softening admixtures. Yet with an overdose of such admixtures the market economy can obviously not function.

Successful "conversion" to the outlook of industrialism—or to a blend in which this outlook is heavily represented—is always connected with the rapid growth of the relative significance of specific social groups. The ideological changes previously described and the corresponding changes in social power relations are two sides of one and the same process.

Among the strategic social groups of industrial economies (among the carriers of the outlook of industrialism), four deserve emphasis. One is a sizable group of individuals willing to finance risky ventures, that is, to accept the risk of relatively improbable but possible financial loss, for the sake of probable long-run gains. Some of these individuals engage in managerial activities as well as financing, while others engage only in the financing of enterprises which they do not manage. Moreover, especially in the more mature industrial societies, the top managers frequently contribute very little to the funds of the enterprises which they manage. Consequently, we get a second group, consisting of individuals who are making risky business decisions mainly for others. Thirdly, there emerges a considerable group of scientific and technological experts. Last, but not least, it becomes possible to train a large group of disciplined workers who are able to put the methods of advanced technology into effect.

These sociological and ideological shifts have presumably led to an increase in the saved proportion of aggregate income even as a prelude to the phase of rapid economic growth. It was suggested in Chapter 4 that in early stages of rapid economic growth the saved proportion of income increases with rising outputs because notions about the normal standard of living do not yet adjust continuously to rising productivity. But this does not quite explain how the growth process gets started, since accelerated capital accumulation is likely to be a necessary antecedent of accelerated productivity increases. The lag may not be very great, and where a well-developed credit mechanism exists, the prelude might simply be a relatively short period of inflationary pressures, but in general the prelude may also be the increased savings which accompany the emergence of the sociological types required for rapid economic growth. The landlords of classical economic analysis were spendthrifts; the capitalists were savers. Successful starts, of course, always assume that savings in conjunction with technological-organizational improvements should be sufficient to produce an accelerated rate of growth of output. *Per-capita* output will grow only if the growth rate of output exceeds an accelerated rate of population growth, as has been the case wherever the start has been truly successful.

In summary, we conclude that initial accumulation of physical capital, some degree of administrative unification, and rapid spread of the outlook of industrialism[4] are required for creating an environment in which a tendency may develop toward satisfying the three growth corollaries of Part 3. This is the same as saying that the *initial conditions* described in the present Chapter are in the background of analysis such as is based on the three corollaries of Part 3. The historical accounts of early industrialization point clearly to the fact that the significance of our three corollaries, as well as that of the initial conditions, has met the eyes of all competent observers. The accounts of historians pay a good deal of attention to the removal of the initial hindrances by gradual, early capital accumulation, by administrative unification, and by a change in basic attitudes and social power relations. These are our initial conditions. The historical accounts invariably emphasize also the strategic significance for the subsequent growth process of technological improvements of the mobility of resources, and of the supply of money and credit. Our three corollaries relate to these three factors. The analytical framework of Part 3 (growth corollaries), as well as that of the present Chapter (initial conditions) is based on factors of long standing in economic history.

3. Latecomers.

Much arbitrariness is involved in setting precise dates for the attainment of an adequate initial level and for the beginning of the era of significant economic development in any country. One difficulty is caused

---

[4] Instead of the spread of the outlook of industrialism, we may speak of the rising social power of strata that are carriers of this outlook.

by the fact that the "intuitively meaningful" concept of the beginning of the process of significant growth, has to do *not only* with the rapidity of the proportionate rate of growth in the sense proper, but also with the economy's having already grown somewhat beyond the stage of economic unimportance. These ideas are inherently imprecise. However, if the decades surrounding 1800 are regarded as marking the span in which the point of departure for significant economic growth was attained in England, then something can be said for putting the corresponding dates for the other *now* advanced industrial nations well into the nineteenth century. This relates mainly to the advanced nations of Western and Central Europe and of North America. In some countries of Eastern Europe and of Latin America the phase of significant economic development may be said to have started in the present century. Yet the period immediately preceding the "industrial revolution" *in these other countries* was not comparable in any important respect to the period in England before *her* "industrial revolution." Developments in the advanced nations of the Western world have exerted an influence all along on the relatively primitive economies of the same civilization.

What matters from our point of view is that the period in which the three growth corollaries of Part 3 tended to become satisfied in the long run started considerably later in some countries than in others. Have the *prerequisites* for satisfying these corollaries—the *"initial conditions"* of the present Chapter—been the same in the latecomer nations as in England or in the nations that followed relatively early?

A qualified yes seems to be the best answer. However, some differences are important, and they must not be overlooked.

In the first place, one nation can partly satisfy the initial capital-stock requirement for others as well as for itself. To some limited extent, the complementarities among different sorts of specialized resources can be exploited across national borders as well as "intra-nationally." In this respect, the latecomers are at an advantage. More important, perhaps, is the fact that the latecomers can immediately adopt technological and organizational methods which the pioneers had to develop gradually. Some of the significant illustrations of this are, of course, technological in the narrower sense. Others are more properly described as organizational. One important organizational illustration is provided by the achievement of a credit system or "modern" monetary mechanism. Such a mechanism is based, among other things, on the existence of a central bank (bank of issue) and on the widespread use of checks as means of payment. The system has developed very gradually. Its primitivity or virtual nonexistence in the days of Mercantilism may have been one of several reasons for the general reliance of the national states on metal-acquiring policies of aggressively protectionist character. A well-developed credit system is absolutely essential for satisfying the third corollary. The latecomers have had the advantage of starting at a time when this organizational achievement had already been made.

Yet the advantages of the latecomers should not be overstated. The conditions under which "known" technological and organizational methods are put into effect in newly developing countries are sometimes sufficiently different to raise some question as to whether the transplanted methods should typically be regarded as more or less identical with the "known" ones. The necessary degree of adaptation is frequently very substantial. Nor is it obvious that it is always desirable to copy the Western methods as closely as is possible. One illustration is provided by the fact that some Western technological processes may be too labor-saving for those primitive countries which have no unused land for the absorption of a labor surplus. As we have seen, a case can be made for the statement that recently our methods have not been quite laborsaving enough for Western needs. But in circumstances where the ratio of population growth to the growth of capital stock is much higher than in the West, Western technology might nevertheless be too laborsaving. It might increase the population pressure in those primitive countries which have no unused land. The death rate can now be reduced with relatively great rapidity. Hence the relation between growth of the labor supply and growth of the capital stock may become different in some primitive countries, not only from what it now is in the advanced economies of the West, but also from what it was in early stages of Western development.[5] Where initially unemployment exists, actual or "disguised" (Page 239), trends in the relative share of labor are very likely to be less favorable to workers in early than in later stages of development, even if the laborsaving properties of the improvements do not "overshoot." But in this case the initial unemployment at least will become eliminated gradually while if the laborsaving properties of improvements do overshoot, the initial unemployment may even tend to

---

[5] Even if we take a rapid reduction of the death rate for granted, the long-run rate of growth of the labor supply will become great relatively to the rate of growth of the capital stock only if the birth rate stays high for a considerable period (and if investment activity is not so high as to match or outweigh the rate of population growth). See the discussion on Pages 239-244.

become increased. An excess of labor *in general* (of common labor) may very well coexist with an acute shortage of specific varieties of *skilled* labor.

Even where industrialization is not accompanied by the absorption of a labor surplus, it could be argued that the labor surplus increases at a smaller rate under industrialization than it would without technological-organizational change and with the same rate of population growth; and if the high rate of population growth is viewed as a consequence of industrialization, it could be argued that this in itself is a gain, because it results from reduced infant mortality. Still, it seems reasonable to attribute excessively laborsaving character to the improvements if they do not lead to a gradual absorption of such labor surpluses as might initially exist. To be sure, inability to absorb an initial labor surplus, or a tendency to create such a surplus, may in principle also be a consequence of there not being enough improvements (quantitative insufficiency of improvements), or of an insufficiently favorable effect of improvements on the marginal productivity of capital. As we know, the general condition here is that improvements should be sufficiently plentiful *and* should be slanted right toward the various factor-saving effects to assure the required profitability of new investment as well as the avoidance of a labor excess. This the improvements must be able to accomplish in view of the factor supplies actually forthcoming. However, *if* a latecomer country satisfies what we have called "initial conditions," with the result that contemporary Western methods can become transplanted and savings increase, then there still may remain the difficulty of excessively laborsaving effects *even though the other difficulties would then presumably be overcome.*

Furthermore, the reason why the latecomers have not arrived earlier may have quite a bit to do with the greater difficulty of overcoming social rigidities in one nation than in another, that is, with the greater difficulty of converting some nations to a blend of outlooks in which the outlook of industrialism is heavily represented. Given these resistances, belated attempts to meet the initial conditions do not always promise to be highly successful. By the standards of industrial civilization, some latecomer nations are quite likely to remain handicapped.

4. The Soviet latecomers.

Merely a brief comment will be made here to remind the reader that in most countries in which the Soviet system was introduced, this happened before these countries got very far on the path of industrialization, or even before they really got started. In general, the Communist countries are latecomers.

The analytical framework of the present volume relates to private enterprise economies. Adaptation of this framework to a fundamentally different social system would require more than a few comments. However, it may be observed that on the level of the initial conditions Soviet growth, too, is dependent on an initial physical stock and on administrative unification over an area possessing sufficient population and natural resources, and that an ideology oriented to technological-organizational performance for the sake of material things (although not an ideology measuring success by market performance) is necessary for the functioning of the system. This analogy exists on the level of the "initial conditions" which were discussed in the present Chapter.

Furthermore, the Soviet system shares with the Western industrial system the problem of overcoming relative resource scarcities. Therefore, an analogy exists also on the level of the growth corollaries of Part 3. But the reasons why the growth corollaries of Part 3 possess relevance for a Communist country are different from the reasons why these corollaries are significant for private enterprise economies. In other words, *the penalty on not satisfying these corollaries is different.* The *methods* by which the corollaries become satisfied are different, too.

In the Western framework the growth corollaries must be satisfied to keep the profit rate at a level where the desired new capital formation is sufficient to match a flow of net saving big enough to support appreciable growth. This statement implies a balanced budget; in the final Chapter it will be adjusted to the possibility of long-run imbalance in the accounts of the government. However, the adjustment is of no decisive significance. Essentially, a sufficient rate of overcoming relative scarcities in the system is one that keeps the profit rate at a level where the required amount of private investment will be induced. Under the Soviet system private capital formation in the Western sense is unimportant. The economy will grow if the authority finds its possible to enforce the degree of taxation and of saving required for new investment, and if structural maladjustments do not block the process. There is no reason why there should ever be more taxation plus saving than the equivalent of the rate of public expenditure, including the net capital formation. Net capital formation does not depend on profit rates.

But in spite of this difference, the objective in a Sovietized economy is to overcome resource scarcities at least to the same extent as that in which they are overcome by the Western response mechanisms. Obviously, if a comparison is made between rates of growth, the present high rates of the Soviet world should be compared not with the present Western rates but with the Western rates of the early era of rapid industrialization. But the growth rates on the other side of the Iron Curtain seem to be high by any reasonable standard. With an insufficient rate of technological and organizational improvement, and with insufficiently mobile resources, these growth rates would be accompanied by diminishing output-increments per unit of new investment. Furthermore, these growth rates would presumably not be sustainable under constant monetary disorder. The reason why the growth corollaries must be satisfied in the Soviet system is that otherwise the maintenance of high growth rates would require an ever-increasing degree of taxation (or compulsory saving). A significant reduction of the rate of growth would, of course, be undesirable politically as well as economically; and, given the present standard of living in the Soviet world, an ever-increasing degree of taxation would not be feasible.

In conclusion, we may say that in the Soviet world the growth corollaries of Part 3 are important, not because the profit rate must be kept at a level where it will induce a sufficient amount of investment, but because the better the corollaries are satisfied, the lower is the degree of taxation and of compulsory saving required for given rates of growth.

An even more important difference meets the eye when we turn to the question of what methods are used for satisfying the corollaries. Ultimately, the state is the only significant employer in the Soviet economies. The state is not led by the profit motive, and it is under no compulsion to adjust the composition of the output to buyers' preferences. This should be somewhat qualified by the statement that an extremely malcontent population may become politically unmanageable. But this qualification merely sets vague upper limits to the permissible discrepancy between preferences on the one hand and the structure of the output of consumer goods on the other. Also, it is doubtful whether a population richly endowed with consumer goods of its own choosing is the best material for totalitarian management. In general, in the Soviet economies, the corollaries need not be satisfied for a composition of output that is well adjusted to consumer preferences. The composition of output is very much more "arbitrary" under a Soviet system than in a private enterprise economy. This is because the Soviet state possesses a monopoly and monopsony position which is not comparable to the position of any large economic unit in the Western world.

To say that the Soviet state uses no income incentives for satisfying the corollaries, and that it entirely disregards buyers' preferences, would of course, be an overstatement. But as compared to Western economies, the Soviet system relies very heavily on direct political power and compulsion, and less heavily on income and consumption incentives.

5. Summary.

In early phases of economic development the policy problems of private enterprise economies are centered on creating a specific sort of environment. This is an environment in which the growth corollaries of Part 3 tend to become satisfied, in the long run, by responses of individuals acting very largely under the income incentive. To create such an environment, the accumulation of an initial stock is required so that economies of scale and complementarities can be exploited; a reasonable degree of administrative unification must be achieved over an area with sufficient population and natural resources; and the government must support the spread of an outlook which measures success in life by performance in the market. However, in all actually observable cases this ideology has become blended with others to a greater or lesser extent. The ideological requirement in question has a counterpart in shifting social power relations.

Industrializing governments of the Soviet variety must, of course, also be able to build on an initial stock, without which the phase of rapid growth cannot be entered. They, too, must achieve administrative unification. Furthermore, they must spread an outlook which measures success very largely by economic performance, although not by performance in free markets. Given these conditions, Soviet governments become concerned with satisfying the three corollaries in order to maintain high growth rates. In this attempt, they rely on market preferences and the income incentive to a smaller degree than do private enterprise economies. The growth pattern is very largely predetermined by decisions of the central authority. Behind these decisions there is the unparalleled power of the totalitarian state.

14

The Initial Conditions and the Growth Corollaries at a Later Date

1. Three questions.

Let us now consider the contemporary scene in advanced private enterprise economies. Do these economies continue to meet the "initial conditions" of Chapter 13 which had to be met before our three growth corollaries could become satisfied? If certain changes are noticeable in this regard, how will these changes affect the tendency to satisfy the growth corollaries of Part 3? Do there exist other reasons, unconnected with the initial conditions, for believing that the tendency to satisfy the growth corollaries might not continue?

2. The initial capital stock as a requirement for exploiting economies of scale and complementarities.

The contemporary Western world meets this requirement with much less difficulty than did the early Western environment. However, it would be wrong to say that there exists *no* contemporary problem under this heading. As was said before, industrial growth is always associated with change in the composition of output: there develops a sequence of leading industries, and of leading sectors in the economy. In discussing Schumpeter's theory we encountered one sequence which seems to possess some degree of validity for several countries. This is the famous sequence moving from textiles and iron to railroads and steel and then to chemicals and electricity and to automobiles and the light metals. Arbitrariness cannot be avoided in selecting a small number of industries for characterizing a long historical process, and to some of the latecomer countries this particular sequence does not apply at all well. But there have existed everywhere gradual shifts in the composition of output, with a succession of leading sectors in the broad sense. In all economically advanced countries, manufacturing as a whole gained in relative significance for many decades. From a later stage on, the utilities, trade, and the service industries (including finance, personal services, and the government) have been growing to greater relative weight. Initial capital stocks are needed for exploiting economies of scale and complementarities in *any* new sector, even in advanced economies. One subsegment of a new sector depends on another.

Yet in a fairly advanced industrial economy it is frequently possible to rely on the willingness of many investors to proceed more or less simultaneously. Also, not all physical capital and labor are so narrowly specialized as to preclude their use, outside their proper field of specialization, for bridging initial time intervals. The problem of satisfying the initial conditions for the development of new sectors is much less serious in advanced than in primitive economies.

3. Administrative unification as an initial condition for satisfying the corollaries.

This problem is supposed to be "solved" by the time the economy of a nation becomes highly developed. Of course, problems of this sort are never really solved in the sense of giving rise to no further institutional evolution. But if we take the present characteristics of the world community for granted, we may perhaps say that in few advanced Western nations will economic growth be impeded by insufficient *national* administrative unification. The present state of the world community, however, can scarcely be regarded as stable. This may ultimately lead into international administrative problems of unparalleled size, with detours that are not enjoyable to contemplate.

4. The outlook of industrialism.

In this regard, a specific difficulty does develop in advanced industrial communities.

In the early period the problem in most countries was that of letting the outlook of the market economy gain its victory over some variety of feudalism. In the end a blending of these outlooks frequently took place, but the new element became very heavily represented in the blend. The social groups rooted in the feudal type of economy were significantly weakened and those spreading the values of the market greatly strengthened.

In the contemporary Western world the outlook of the market economy becomes blended with the equalitarian outlook. The outlook of the market economy measures success by performance in markets which register buyers' preferences. Equality-mindedness, in its pure form, would treat individuals according to their needs rather than according to their ability to perform by market standards; and the pure outlook of equalitarianism would accept differences in needs only when, on grounds of equity, a strong case can be established for them. The strengthening of the political power position of relatively low-income groups and of their representatives is the main reason for the growth of equalitarianism in the sense of *predetermined "fair shares" (rather than of equal opportunities to earn differential incomes)*. This change in the political power structure is, in turn, mainly a consequence of urbanization, or geographical concentration, coupled with increased literacy and schooling of the relative low-income groups. The equality-minded groups have become powerful enough to force a blending of the market-economy outlook with theirs. Will the tendency to satisfy our three "corollaries" continue under the contemporary blend?

Before turning to a discussion of this question, we should add that the equalitarian orientation with which the outlook of the market economy has become blended carries a considerable degree of security-mindedness with it. This is to be expected because the insecurity of employment in a market economy—the risk of unemployment—obviously violates equalitarian principles. However, in part, the increased security-mindedness may well have different roots. For example, hired managers of large corporations may be more security-minded than were the old-style owner-managers. Also, increased security-mindedness among businessmen is one of the reactions which may develop to the equalitarian policies pressed by other groups. What really has become blended with the outlook of the market economy is increased equality-security-mindedness. Equality and security tendencies overlap to a large extent, but some of their roots may well be distinct.

A sufficiently large dose of the equality-security outlook could undoubtedly strangle the growth process. However, this in itself should not lead one to the conclusion that the actual admixture of this outlook to the attitudes of the market economy must necessarily weaken the process of growth. Some degree of blending may have a stimulating effect. For example, in most of the advanced European nations of the nineteenth century the pre-industrial ("feudal") admixture was quite noticeable. This expressed itself clearly in the workings and the ideals of the educational system, and thus in the type of conditioning to which the leading strata became exposed. The majority of people eligible for leading positions—especially in politics, but to some extent also in business—had to qualify in more ways than one. How much of this blending was conducive to growth is not an easy question to answer. To be sure, an overdose of the outlook of the pre-industrial era would have been incompatible with rapid industrialization. But without some admixture of that outlook the European educational system and the European political system of the nineteenth century would have been different. Who can tell how well the economies of Europe would have functioned under a different educational or political system?

Something similar may well hold true of the equality-security admixtures. Fortunately, it would be quite wrong to postulate that an industrialized economy can function effectively only under a textbook version of the pure industrial "creed." When does an admixture become an overdose? What happens to the corollaries of Part 3 under various blends of the market-economy outlook with the equality-security outlook? No one can suggest precise answers to these questions. But we shall attempt to illustrate the nature of the problem with observations relating to major policy issues of the present epoch.

5. Fiscal policies for full employment.

Probably the most uncontroversial statement that can be made about the consequences of the new ideological admixture is that extended periods of substantial unemployment have become intolerable. If periods of this sort should recur, the private enterprise system would be very unlikely to survive. The fateful consequences of the nineteen-thirties tell a very convincing story. It is true, of course, that that depression was quite exceptionally severe. But in the present circumstances less than what happened at that time would be sufficient to bring about radical changes in the social and institutional environment. Is government policy likely to succeed in its efforts to prevent, within the framework of a market economy, the recurrence of extended periods with mass unemployment?

The so-called automatic stabilizers have almost certainly reduced the tendency to deviate from the long-run path of the economy, and thus they have reduced the tendency toward the *cyclical* recurrence of large-scale unemployment. But many of these stabilizers stem from equality-security-oriented policies, and their character is such that they might conceivably have a lowering effect on the long-run path itself. Graduated individual income taxes and high corporate profit taxes provide an example, even if they are coupled with high government expenditures. Another example is provided by increasing reliance on internal funds, that is, on corporate savings, for the financing of investment. The two sides of this problem were pointed out earlier in this volume.[1] We are unable to gauge precisely the effect of these and of other institutional changes on the long-run path. Some of these stabilizers might tie the economy more closely to a trend path, the slope of which is small; and if these stabilizers do not act at the same time sufficiently to reduce savings at the full-employment level of output, they may even produce chronic unemployment. The experience of the recent past suggests that these consequences need not show. Policies oriented toward equality and security are capable of producing these consequences, but the "automatic stabilizing effect" of some of these policies illustrates the proposition that we are faced here with a matter of degree.

The mere fact that deviations from the trend path are reduced, should be expected to raise the trend path because the waste caused by abrupt and unpredictable fluctuations is diminished. Other effects of the tax structure, and of built-in stabilizers in general, must outweigh the favorable consequences of reduced instability before there will be a *net* adverse effect on long-run growth-rates, and especially before there will be a net adverse effect on employment.[2] Let us assume, for the time being, that the equality-security policies expressing themselves in the existence of automatic stabilizers will not be carried to the point where appreciable net adverse consequences would develop for the long-run rate of growth. Whether or not this optimistic assumption is justified is a question to which we shall return later. On balance, we are inclined to optimism in this regard. The assumption implies that the automatic stabilizers will reduce the tendency toward cyclical unemployment (and

---

[1] See Chapter 3, Pages 94-96, and Chapter 10, Section 7.

[2] A net adverse effect on growth rates will develop if the discouraging effect of the tax structure reduces capital formation in the long run in spite of the lessening of cyclical instability. A net adverse effect on the level of employment requires that the adverse effect of the tax structure on consumption plus private investment should be greater than the positive employment effect of government expenditures in the government sector.

also toward recurrent inflation) without possessing appreciable long-run disadvantages. But if the policies resulting in these automatic stabilizers are not carried to extremes—that is, if long-run disadvantages *are* avoided—cyclical swings of some significance are likely to recur, and the question remains whether *ad hoc* fiscal policies or other deliberate stabilizing measures will prove capable of coping with these disturbances when they arise. Furthermore, even if the policies resulting in the automatic stabilizers are not carried to extremes, this does not in itself exclude the possibility that tendencies toward *chronic* unemployment may develop from the laborsaving character of improvements. The problem of deliberate (or *ad hoc*) compensatory policies remains important at any event.

In periods of unemployment the government is capable of deliberately reducing the budgetary surplus or of increasing the budgetary deficit, and of thus reducing the existing unemployment. It can do this by lowering tax rates and by speeding up central and local budgetary expenditures. This must be distinguished from the workings of the automatic stabilizers. The "automatic" stabilizing effect of the budget expresses itself in tax revenues which, at given tax rates, increase and decrease in a higher proportion than the fluctuating national income; and it expresses itself also in various public expenditures that move countercyclically, on the basis of past commitments (*e.g.*, unemployment insurance). But in periods of unemployment governments can also reduce tax rates, and they can deliberately enter new spending commitments. Thus, aside from the lag involved in adjusting fiscal policy to business conditions, is it not always possible to ensure that at the full-employment level of output, and with a reasonably stable price level, private investment *plus government expenditures* should balance with savings *plus tax payments*? If the conditions of dynamic equilibrium (continuous growth) are not satisfied with a balanced budget, can they not always be put into effect by compensatory fiscal operations? Or if these conditions tend to become satisfied at a level of less than full employment, can deficit-financing operations not always raise the growth path to the full-employment level? What are the limitations of compensatory fiscal policy in the framework of a market economy? Several previous passages in this volume lead up to this question, but the answer has always been postponed. We shall now attempt to give a concise answer.

The main limitations of deficit-financing policies are the following:

(*a*) Deficit-financing is incapable of reducing the kind of unemployment which may exist in spite of the fact that, at the full-employment level, desired investment would not fall short of saving. We saw in Chapter 4, Section 7, and in Chapter 8, Section 5, that unemployment of this sort, when it is not limited to specific religions or occupations, is the consequence of the insufficiency of the physical capital stock that can be constructed without inflation. Such relative capital scarcity may develop either because the labor supply is growing at a faster rate than the capital stock, or (if labor is the less rapidly growing factor) because the labor-saving character of the improvements has overshot the mark set by the relative labor scarcity. In such circumstances deficit financing is not the appropriate policy. With sufficiently easy credit the required additional capital formation would be forthcoming at any event, although this would occur under inflationary conditions. Only increased savings, increased taxation of consumers, or wage reductions can enable the economy to engage in the required additional capital formation without inflation. Increased taxation of consumers, too, is a "fiscal policy," but obviously not a policy of "deficit-financing." A policy of "deficit-financing" is inappropriate here.

Cyclical unemployment (depression-caused unemployment) is not of this variety. In depressions there exists no over-all shortage of equipment.

(b) Unemployment in one region or occupation, coupled with a sellers' market (vigorous demand) in the other segments of the economy, cannot be remedied by compensatory fiscal policy. Deficit financing would create inflationary pressures in at least some important segments of the economy, and it could scarcely be directed in such a fashion as to favor the proper reallocation of resources. However, unemployment that initially has these characteristics of "wrong specialization" or "wrong location" may tend to spread over the economy as a whole. We are faced here with violations of the second growth corollary of Part 3, and we know that the effects of such violations need not *stay* localized. Localized or specific shortages may block expansion in otherwise promising areas of activity, and hence the localized expansion which should offset the consequences of initially localized contraction in specific areas does not materialize promptly enough. Excess capacity may become generalized, and in this event temporary deficit financing can be helpful. After the required readjustments in the structure of production the unemployment will become absorbed, even without further deficit financing.

(c) When we are faced with the first of the two types of unemployment described in Chapter 4, Section 7,[3] then neither of the two difficulties so far considered needs to be taken into account. In this case, the unemployment is a consequence of insufficient rates of return on further capital formation, in view of the relative scarcity of factors of production cooperating with capital. A higher level of output and of employment cannot materialize because at a higher level of output and employment *saving plus tax payments* would outrun *private investment plus government expenditures,* and hence a deflationary pressure would develop. Unemployment of this sort can be cyclical or long-lasting. *Deficit financing can help here because deficit financing means reduction of tax payments relative to government expenditures.*

Yet compensatory fiscal policy has certain limitations even in this case. A *de facto* guarantee of full employment, by means of fiscal policy, would presumably lead to a constant pressure toward higher money wages, and it would be exceedingly difficult to keep wage rates from rising more rapidly than output per man-hour. Partly for this reason, and partly because the risk of deflationary interludes would become eliminated, firms, too, would be making commitments in view of the likelihood of continuous price increases. It is very difficult to imagine that chronic inflation could be avoided in such circumstances, except perhaps by comprehensive price controls and rationing, which are incompatible with the principles of a market economy. The inflationary trend would presumably express itself partly in rising prices and partly in the deterioration of the quality of performance. These considerations, too, speak for not engaging in deficit financing before contraction has reached a stage of noticeable "general" underutilization of physical capital as well as of labor. It is necessary to gear fiscal policy to wage-price movements as well as to movements in employment.

(*d*) The objective of maintaining foreign trade relations with other countries at reasonably stable exchange rates makes it very difficult to prevent major economic fluctuations in the outside world from spreading into the domestic economy. A prosperous economy in a depressed world would be one that could export very little and yet would want to import much. The international gold standard gave priority over other objectives to automatic exchange-rate stability, aside from movements within the so-called gold points. The world is not at present willing to accept such a scale of preferences. Yet exclusive concern with domestic economic conditions would have to result in highly disorganized international

---

[3] See also Chapter 8, Section 5.

economic relations. Fiscal policy must take account of the requirements of international trade and finance as well as of domestic employment objectives. Within certain limits, it may be necessary to go along with deflationary developments that take place in the outside world.

This list of limitations may look formidable at first sight. However, its appearance is much more formidable than its essential content, unless we should become faced with a chronic and increasing insufficiency of private investment. The conclusion can be summarized in the following propositions, taking it for granted from the outset that localized unemployment, coupled with localized labor shortages, cannot be remedied by over-all fiscal measures. (1) Deficit financing is inappropriate for combating the type of general unemployment which may exist even though, at the full-employment level of output, saving would not outrun desired investment. This sort of unemployment is attributable to a shortage of factors cooperating with labor, notably to the insufficiency of the capital stock for tooling the available labor force. When unemployment is of this kind, the inducement to invest is usually high, the equipment of the economy is fully utilized and restrictive monetary policies are required to prevent desired investment from running ahead of savings. Increased savings, consumption taxes, or wage reductions are needed for gradually raising the capital stock to the level where the labor force is fully employed, or for gradually transforming the character of equipment in the direction of greater labor intensity. (2) Deficit financing—a reduction of tax rates and/or increase of the spending commitments of the government—is an appropriate policy for combating the kind of unemployment which may exist for the reason that increased employment would make savings exceed desired investment. This sort of unemployment is usually recognizable by the fact that the inducement to invest is low, even without restrictive monetary measures. But while deficit financing *is* appropriate for reducing such unemployment, the policy cannot be used successfully to prevent minor fluctuations in employment (minor recessions) without sacrificing other essential objectives.[4] The policy can be applied in stages where contraction has spread more or less over the economy as a whole, *and it may be relied upon to stop a cumulative downward tendency toward a condition of mass unemployment.* Some degree of coordination of policies on the international level is necessary for success.

---

[4] Chronic inflationary pressure would express itself in steadily rising prices, unless it were suppressed by comprehensive direct controls. Consequently, producing such pressure means sacrificing essential objectives.

Furthermore, if the policy relies on increased public spending as well as on tax reduction, then the public projects should be noncompetitive with private investment. Road building, the construction of educational and medical facilities and flood regulation are examples.

These conclusions contain a very strong positive element. The positive content stays significant even though, on a somewhat different level, it is necessary to add a further qualification. The type of unemployment which can be reduced by deficit financing may be either cyclical or chronic. No further qualification is needed if the unemployment in question is cyclical (*i.e.,* occasionally recurring or intermittent). In this case, the essential qualification is merely that the policy must not become so ambitious as to create chronic inflationary pressure. With this qualification deficit financing is an appropriate policy for reducing cyclical unemployment in private enterprise systems. But if a *significant* deficiency of private investment relative to full-employment savings were to become *chronic,* and the deficiency were made up by budgetary deficits, then this would presumably result in thoroughgoing institutional change.

The deficit-spending could not in such circumstances express itself mainly in government *investment* (capital formation) without further reducing, or completely suppressing, investment activity in the private sector. A very large volume of public investment cannot help becoming competitive with private investment. In an economy in which the bulk of the new investment activity is undertaken all the time by government agencies, the entrepreneurial function loses its essential content. This particular form or variant of the difficulty could be avoided if the government offset the savings of the private sector by *consumer subsidies* (large deficit-financed transfer payments) rather than by public *investment.* Thus a static or near-static economy could be created with sufficient consumer demand to maintain full employment. But even in this case the entrepreneurial function would have lost its substance. The essentially routinized economic activities of a static system do not require private initiative, and they do not call for the social organization of Western capitalism. This is the reason why it would be difficult to visualize the survival of the contemporary institutional setting in the stationary state (*even* in the "classical" stationary state where both net private investment and net saving were supposed to cease at the full-employment level of output and without government deficits) .

These conclusions suggest that by means of fiscal policy it is possible greatly to diminish, although not wholly to eliminate, the kind of *cyclical* unemployment which tends to develop in major depressions. This might require appreciable deficits in some stages and appreciable surpluses in others. At the same time, these conclusions suggest that it would scarcely be possible to prevent, by methods of fiscal policy, the establishment of a centralized economic and social system if we were faced with a significant *chronic* insufficiency of private capital formation. A minor chronic insufficiency does not, however, deserve to be sharply distinguished from recurring cyclical difficulties because there is no need to require that the weight of the periods in which budgetary deficits develop should bear precisely the one-to-one ratio to the weight of the periods with a budgetary surplus. What is important here is not the arbitrary concept of long-run "budgetary balance," or prevention of a rise in the public debt. What matters is our ability to maintain appreciable and reasonably steady growth rates with primary reliance on private investment activity.

An internally held public debt is a claim of part of the national population against another part, and it does not create the dangers of national bankruptcy. This is not to say that the public debt problem needs to be watched *only* because deficit financing can be carried to the point of inflationary pressures. Paying interest on a public debt which is large relatively to the national income gives rise to a potentially harmful transfer problem by making it necessary to arrange a transfer of funds from taxpayers to the claimants of interest. This is true quite aside from inflationary dangers. But a growing economy with a growing national income, and thus with a growing tax base, can stand a gradually increasing public debt, especially if the interest is received by domestic individuals and institutions.[5] The essential objective of *maintaining appreciable rates of output growth, with primary reliance on private capital formation,* requires that in the long run government expenditures should *not largely replace* private capital formation, and that they should not create an unmanageable inflation problem or an unmanageable transfer problem. This sets limits to what can be accomplished by fiscal policy in the long run. But precise balancing of the budget, in the short run or in the long run, is not a meaningful objective. Essential objectives must not be subordinated to an accounting formula.

The only rational objection that could be raised against this last state-

---

[5] In this context it may be pointed out that while the "administrative budget" of the United States shows a cumulated deficit from the end of World War II to the present (see Footnote 18, Page 93), the public debt has been declining substantially in relation to the national income. Only in part is this a consequence of price inflation. Much of it is a consequence of a rise in real output.

ment is that the vagaries of politics (to use a Schumpeterian phrase) may exceed even the vagaries of a rule of thumb of accounting. However, the dangers of a rule of thumb, such as that of precise budgetary balance, are extremely grave in this case. This, for all practical purposes, compels us to place our trust in discretionary policies to prevent major cyclical depressions and mass unemployment. It seems to the present writer that the gradual recognition of this truth by fundamentally conservative groups is a political fact of great importance. The likelihood has become reduced that policies required for sustained growth will always appear in one "package" with reformism of a very different kind which must be appraised by different criteria.

The arbitrariness of budgetary balance as an ultimate criterion becomes particularly apparent if we ask ourselves the question whether large *tax-financed* government production could cope with chronic unemployment tendencies. Let us assume that the unemployment is a result of savings exceeding planned investment at the full-employment level of output. Only this kind of unemployment can be reduced by government production, deficit-financed or other. Yet if the unemployment is of this type, not merely deficit-financed but also tax-financed, government output would dependably reduce or eliminate the unemployment, provided that the character of the tax structure were such that the willingness to accept the risks of production would not be appreciably reduced by taxation.[6] This follows from the balanced-budget multiplier analysis

---

[6] This is because output would be increased in the government sector, and there would occur no increase in *aggregate saving* and no diminution in *aggregate planned investment* that would throw these two magnitudes out of balance at the higher output. Instead of increased savings, we would merely get increased tax revenues at the higher output levels and these would be matched by increased government expenditures for goods and services. The demand for the *goods produced in the private sector* remains unchanged because, while the tax payments constitute a deduction from disposable income, the new income in the government sector constitutes an equal addition. The government-produced output is a *net* addition to total output.

This proposition assumes that the distribution of income, and thus the propensity to save out of disposable income is the same, when tax revenues are raised and used for income payments in the government sector as when the equivalents of these tax revenues remain in the hands of the original income recipients. The unemployment-reducing effect of tax-financed government production would, even in this case, be smaller *per unit of expenditure* than is the effect of deficit-financed spending because the recipients of the income surplus which is attributable to government production could not respend their income surplus on privately produced goods. The surplus would be taxed away to finance the government production. The government induced initial output-increment would not become further propagated. But unemployment would be reduced, and with sufficiently high government spending it could even be eliminated.

This is another way of saying that the multiplier by which we must multiply the

which, along with its essential qualifications, was first developed by H. C. Wallich.[7] The employment-raising effect of deficit-financing government expenditure would be greater, per unit of spending, than the effect of tax-financed expenditure, but both would raise the level of output. Yet if the point of departure were one of negligible private investment, and if in the long run the system were kept going by the superimposition upon the private sector of large tax-financed government investment, then the institutions of a private enterprise economy would have lost their functions just as completely as if the public investment had been deficit-financed. Budgetary balance is of no help here.

If, on the other hand, the long-run inducement to engage in private capital formation is sufficient to carry the growth process, then the performance of a private enterprise economy can be improved by flexible regulation of the relationship between tax revenues and government expenditures. No one can predict whether the objective of preventing the cyclical recurrence of large-scale unemployment, on the one hand, and of inflation on the other, will in the long run require budgetary deficits, budgetary surpluses, or an approximately balanced budget. What we can say empirically is that so far in the Western world private capital formation *has* remained the primary carrier of the growth process. In the United States, for example, private investment now accounts for a proportion of total output similar to that in the nineteen-twenties, even though government expenditures account for a higher proportion (and consumption, of course, for a lower proportion.) The increased need for defense expenditures is, at present, the main cause of increased government spending.

It is sometimes maintained that our imperfect foresight of future

---

tax-financed government output to obtain the total effect on aggregate output is *one,* while the multiplier applying to a deficit-financed government output is greater than one. But it must be remembered that the theorem which says that the "balanced-budget multiplier" is one assumes a tax structure and a type of government production which have no adverse effects on the willingness to engage in private investment. On realistic assumptions, this multiplier can be much smaller than one and even negative. See Footnote 19, Page 93.

On the other hand, if the tax structure is progressive the propensity to save out of disposable income may be reduced (the propensity to consume may be increased) and this tends to raise the value of the balanced-budget multiplier. However, it follows from the estimates in Appendix I to Part 2, and from the discussion on Page 284, that this effect (which hinges on the marginal propensity to save) is smaller than would be suggested by a comparison of the average propensities to save for the various income groups.

[7] See H. C. Wallich, "The Income Generating Effects of a Balanced Budget," *Quarterly Journal of Economics* (November 1944).

movements in the economy will prevent intelligent use of flexible fiscal policies. We may decide to compensate a deflationary movement, yet by the time our anti-deflationary measures take effect conditions may be inflationary; or we may decide to compensate an inflationary movement and end up by reinforcing deflation. But this point would be of decisive significance only if, aside from the imperfections of foresight, it were advisable to aim at suppressing all fluctuations in employment. In reality, it is not advisable to use powerful methods of policy before general contraction is noticeable and before it threatens to become a serious problem. When this stage is reached, it is more important to find a method that prevents further aggravation than to avoid the risk of overstimulating business in the event of an unexpected sudden reversal. For analogous reasons, it seems safe to exert an anti-inflationary fiscal influence if inflationary pressures have already become disturbing. This can be done by raising tax rates and reducing government expenditures.

Yet it must be recognized that the lag between fiscal decisions and their consequences is big enough to create the possibility of perverse impacts. Compensatory central-bank policies are subject to less delay, mainly because they do not require new legislation. These policies are sometimes called "monetary policies," in contrast to the "fiscal policies" just considered. It will be seen presently that central-bank policies can be made reasonably effective against inflation, unless other policy objectives interfere with the activities of the central bank. Compensatory monetary policies serve well also in moderate contractions, but they are insufficient to cope with major depressions.

6. Central-bank policy.

The purely "monetary" policy of making central-bank credit tighter in boom periods and more readily available in periods of contraction has been increasingly used even in the past. It is true that until recently the managements of central banks would not have subscribed to the general principle that one of their significant functions is to counteract cyclical swings in business activity. But they have increasingly interpreted their regulatory principles and "rules of thumb" in such a way that these have had at least something in common with the principle of counteracting inflationary and deflationary swings.

For example, we saw earlier that in England the Peel Act of the mid-nineteenth century was devised mainly to make the actual currency function *as if* it were a purely metallic currency. From the outset this ill-defined objective had something in common with the objective of not letting inflation develop, and very soon the Bank also started deliberately to alleviate the consquences of credit stringency in periods of crisis. The Federal Reserve, too, had tended to counteract cyclical swings, although the avowed objective of the System—that of satisfying the legitimate need for productive short-run credit—was not a well-defined objective in terms of economic principles. There are at least two reasons why the depression-mitigating activity of central-bank policy has not gone as far as it might have. One reason is that under the gold standard the gold-backing requirements set definite and inflexible limits to credit expansion. The other reason is that the avowed objective of most central banks —that of satisfying the need for certain types of productive credit—was only indirectly connected with the objective of counteracting cyclical swings, and hence whatever they have accomplished along these lines had to be done by *stretching* some other "principle" or formula. Analogous reasons have also impeded the *anti-inflationary* activities of central banks. However, let us first complete our brief discussion of the potentialities and the limitations of central-bank policy in periods of deflationary pressure.

Central banks have increasingly attempted to reduce the deflationary impact of depressions, and in the future they are likely to go further in this direction than they have in the past. They have become less willing to subordinate domestic economic objectives to international exchange-rate stability, and they have become inclined to consider the avoidance of large economic swings as one of their primary objectives. What can central banks accomplish in periods of depression if they are unimpeded by other objectives?

The usual means employed by central-bank policy to mitigate depressions is that of discounting, with government securities as collateral, the acceptances of commercial banks on more liberal terms; of rediscounting at lower interest rates short-term commercial securities which bear the signature of a commercial bank along with that of a customer of the bank; and of buying government securities (usually short-term securities) from the public in general, as well as from the commercial banks. Thus the cash balances of the public and the reserve balances of the commercial banks in the central bank, are increased, and interest rates are lowered by cheaper central-bank credit. In countries where commercial banks must observe legal reserve requirements in the form of reserve balances held in the central bank, the required ratio of reserves to the liabilities of the commercial banks may also be lowered. This increases their lending potential, just as an ampler supply of reserve balances does.

Recession tendencies can be effectively mitigated by these means alone, provided that the deflationary forces are not very strong. A tendency toward major depression will not become eliminated by central-bank policies alone because greater liquidity of the public and greater lending potential of commercial banks can provide only a limited incentive to invest more than would otherwise be planned.

Not even the interest rates on government securities can be lowered quite to the zero level: at the zero rate there would be a clear-cut preference for holding cash rather than government securities. This means that the rates on government securities must stay somewhat above the zero level and that the rates on most types of business loans must stay considerably above it. Only if the central bank purchased, in the open market, long-term business securities as well as government securities could the rates on business loans in general also be brought near zero. Such a policy would, however, involve highly arbitrary subsidization of specific industries and private firms. The risk premium on the specific securities so purchased would become reduced. The arbitrariness involved in such subsidization would be considered very objectionable. Even if by such a policy the rates on business loans were reduced to very low levels, this in itself would still be insufficient to induce a high volume of private investment, provided that, in the cyclical phase under consideration, the economy fell *far* short of satisfying the first two growth corollaries of Part 3. In other words, a significant and uncompensated tendency toward diminishing returns cannot be cushioned by this mechanism alone; nor can this mechanism in itself prevent the general deflationary consequences of significant readjustments in the structure of production.

Severe depression calls for a combination of expansionary central-bank policies (easy-credit policies) with fiscal measures (deficit financing). How frequently such tendencies will show in systems with strengthened "automatic stabilizers" is a question which only future experience can answer. The recent past supports some degree of optimism in this regard. On the other hand, the increased significance of durable consumer goods may have to be weighed against the built-in stabilizers. Purchases of durable consumer goods tend to become bunched. These goods bring the cyclical "acceleration" effect into play. A diminished rate of increase in the demand for the services of these goods (say, a diminished rate of increase of passenger miles driven) brings an absolute decrease in the demand for the goods themselves (say, of automobiles). But it may not be too optimistic to believe that the greater significance of automatic stabilizers contributes more to stability than does the greater weight of durable goods to instability.

Let us now turn to the problems with which central-bank policy is faced in inflationary periods.

If anti-depression policies are carried merely to the point where they are compatible with the avoidance of chronic inflationary pressure in the absence of direct controls, then, of course, there will by definition be no "chronic inflationary pressure." But it is difficult to imagine that it should be possible to carry out such a policy without *somewhat* weakening the hand of the monetary authority in times when the cyclical tendency is inflationary. The easy-money policies and deficit-financing operations of recession periods create additional cash balances and government securities. When there is renewed expansion, the cash balances tend to become spent. Also, attempts are made to unload the government securities on the central bank and thus to obtain spendable cash for them. How effectively can a well-managed central bank counteract these inflationary pressures in the contemporary environment?

In periods with inflationary tendencies, the anti-inflationary objectives of central banks "ideally" call for refraining from the purchase or the "support" of government securities, and for letting their prices fall. This would not only block the way of the public and of the commercial banks from government securities to spendable cash, but it would also provide an incentive for putting further cash into low-priced (high yielding) government securities. The inflation potential created by the easy-money policies and by the deficit-financing operations of recession periods as well as of war periods can thus be reduced or eliminated. The main effect of such a policy is to reduce the size of the funds that can be made available to investors, directly or via the commercial banks. By raising interest rates, the amount of credit *demanded* by investors is also reduced. It is usually necessary to raise discount rates at the same time, and thus to prevent the commercial banks from acquiring lendable funds by rediscounting large quantities of their commercial paper or by selling their acceptances to the central bank. It is possible to describe an anti-inflationary policy of this sort which would wholly suppress the inflation potential of boom periods, even though the inflation potential were substantially increased by preceding anti-depression policies. But it is unlikely that in the long run the monetary authority should find it possible to carry out these anti-inflationary measures with *full* success.

There is always the danger that if, in inflationary periods, the prices of government securities are allowed to drop, the public and the commercial banks will at first react not by regarding these securities as *cheap* and hence as desirable, but by regarding them as *being in the process of falling in value* and hence as being undesirable. Banks and other institutions, nevertheless, seem to feel compelled to hold on to long- and medium-term government securities when the prices of these fall below par because they are reluctant to sell at a loss. However, a substantial fall in the prices of government securities is very likely to interfere with the treasury's "refinancing" operations, that is, with issuing new government securities when old securities mature. The difficulties of refinancing apply especially to long-term securities. The replacement of matured securities with new ones is very likely to be made difficult by substantial instability of the price of government securities because long-term investors are likely to become discouraged by the fact that these securities are allowed to fluctuate greatly. It is true, on the other hand, that a low "present" price should provide an encouragement to buy the securities, but the purchase of government securities is not intended to be a primarily speculative transaction. *Great* instability of the price would make the market behavior of these securities too unpredictable for many buyers on whom the government is forced to rely in its refinancing operations.

Therefore, given a large public debt, central banks and treasuries may be expected to follow a line of compromise in meeting periodic inflationary pressures. The unloading of government securities on the central bank will not be made literally impossible in all circumstances. Instead, the central bank is likely to start supporting the market only if and when bond prices have fallen to some "abnormally" low level. Until this happens, central banks can afford not to buy additional government securities (and thus not to increase the money supply) in inflationary periods. This makes it more difficult and more expensive for owners to unload securities on the central bank for the sake of acquiring additional spendable funds. But central banks will presumably not be willing to let the prices of government securities fall and fluctuate to such an extent that the market for these securities would scare away conservative buyers when the treasury engages in refinancing operations.

During the inflationary years of World War II and of the early postwar period the Federal Reserve policy in the United States was one of sacrificing anti-inflationary objectives for the stability of the market for government securities. The Federal Reserve was always willing to buy bonds at par, for fear of a disorganization of the market for government securities. There could occur no general tightening of credit: owners of government securities could always exchange these for money. During the war, there existed, of course, a comprehensive system of direct economic controls extending over prices, over the use of scarce goods, and over new investments. The Federal Reserve relied on certain "selective credit controls" also in the early postwar period. By these selective credit controls minimum down-payment requirements were introduced for installment credit and for real estate credit, the duration of these two types of loan was legally limited, and the maximum amount of credit obtainable on stock purchases was fixed at a definite percentage of the purchase price of the stocks. At the present time, only stock exchange purchases are subject to selective credit control by the Federal Reserve; consumer credit and real estate credit are not. The emphasis has been shifting back to general credit control. This involves reducing required reserve ratios and supplying the commercial banks with more reserves (by central-bank purchases of short-term government securities) in periods of recession. It also involves reversing these policies and tightening credit gradually when an inflationary situation seems to be approaching, even before price-inflation actually shows. The policy requires refraining from the support of the market of government securities (refraining from the purchase of securities) when the objective is that of gradually slowing cyclical growth rates which are not sustainable in the long run.

In the advanced stages of the cyclical expansion which preceded the peak of 1953, the Federal Reserve did not find it necessary to support the bond market at all, and the prices of long-term bonds were allowed to fall ten points or more below par. Credit was tightened and the Federal Reserve was unwilling to exchange government securities for money. But at that time the refinancing operations of the Treasury did meet with appreciable difficulties. It is not clear how sharply and for what length of time the Federal Reserve will let bond prices fall, or up to what point it will persist in its reluctance to supply the commercial banks with additional reserves, if in future periods of cyclical expansion the desire of banks to turn away from government securities toward business and consumer loans should become strong and prolonged.

Yet these dangers must not be overrated. Over most of the Western world there is a shift back toward flexible general credit policies. These should be capable of preventing violent inflationary outbursts. In periods of advanced expansion, the monetary authority should find it possible effectively to tighten credit and, in most cases, to prevent the public and the commercial banks from exchanging government securities for spendable cash and reserve balances. The fact that, given the size of the public debt, there are limits to the "tolerable" extent and duration of a fall in bond prices *reduces somewhat* the anti-inflationary freedom of action of central banks. Moreover, as was seen earlier, the general tendency to play safe against the recurrence of major depressions is in itself likely to render the long-run trend in prices *somewhat more* inflationary than used to be the case in an epoch during which severely deflationary phases stayed uncompensated. But this need not imply that the limits of tolerance of the system to inflationary tendencies will be overstepped. We do not know what the future will bring, but it may be repeated here that the American general price level has been kept fairly stable since 1951. This is true even though the debt of the federal government now comes close to $280 billion,[8] much the greater part of which was contracted during World War II.

So far, we have had little practical experience with the aftermath of systematic anti-depression policies. But we have had quite a bit of experience with the aftermath of major wars, and this experience supports the conclusions which were here presented. Postwar periods, too, are characterized by the preceding accumulation of idle funds and of government securities in the hands of the public. The reasons are, of course, different from those which would lead to this result in the event of consistent anti-deflationary policies in times of contraction. The inflation potential of postwar periods is very largely a consequence of the inability of governments to impose, in times of war, a degree of taxation which would be sufficient to cover military expenditures. Experience shows that the accumulation of idle funds and of a significant quantity of outstanding government securities creates a subsequent inflation problem which requires careful handling, and which probably cannot be man-

---

[8] This figure includes, however, about $40 billion which the government owes in a sense to "itself," mainly to the Social Security trust account that invests its surpluses in government securities.

The $280-billion figure corresponds to slightly more than twice the American money supply (currency plus check deposits) . It amounts to 0.75 times the figure at which the Department of Commerce estimates the present yearly gross national product. See also Footnote 5, Page 364.

aged with *full* success. Yet we know also that a combination of fiscal and monetary policies is capable of preventing runaway inflation in postwar periods, except in countries where the war has disorganized the existing productive apparatus and the administrative machinery. Moreover, the size of postwar inflation problems considerably exceeds the size of the presumptive postdepression problems, unless governments are pressed into following a rigid line of full-employment guarantee.

These conclusions are distinctly optimistic for a monetary and fiscal policy that uses easy-money measures, tax reductions, and increased government expenditures to offset severe depression tendencies, but does *not* attempt to eliminate even minor cyclical setbacks and thus to guarantee full employment. In other words, the conclusions are optimistic for a depression-reducing monetary and fiscal policy that deliberately stops short of the degree of thoroughness which (in the absence of comprehensive direct controls) would create chronic inflationary pressure. We see no good reason for assuming that such a policy would weaken the long-run tendency in our economies to satisfy the three corollaries of economic growth. On the contrary, such a policy is very likely to strengthen this tendency by reducing the wastes of fluctuations.

However, these optimistic conclusions are based on the premise that depression tendencies come merely periodically. In other words, the premise was that none of the equality-security characteristics or other properties of our age lead to a chronic weakening of the growth process. We do not maintain that compensatory monetary or fiscal policies could be successfully used to offset a chronic stagnation tendency in the private enterprise framework (see Pages 363-364). Is it likely that equality-security characteristics or other environmental properties of our time will produce such tendencies?

One brand of pessimism in this regard stresses the discouraging effect of equality-security oriented behavior, quite aside from the full-employment policies which we have already discussed. We shall consider this problem in Sections 7 and 8. A second brand of pessimism is based on the fear that smaller population growth and the cessation of territorial expansion will make it very much more difficult to find the necessary offsets to diminishing returns. This problem will be considered in Section 9.

7. Unionism and graduated taxation.

Urbanization results in the geographical concentration of large masses of people belonging to the low-income groups. These masses lend themselves well to being organized. This is true especially of people who during their working hours operate as members of large groups. Widespread schooling, also a by-product of urbanization, contributes to making the members of these groups politically articulate. The influence of these equality-minded and security-minded groups has lifted the proposition that mass unemployment is intolerable from the status of a subjective value judgment to that of a statement of fact. At the same time, the increased influence of the groups in question has altered the method by which wage rates are established.

Collective bargaining between employers and tightly organized labor unions is a comparatively recent feature of Western economic development, even though in most countries the gradual tendency in this direction has been gaining strength since the later part of the nineteenth century.

In spite of the increased bargaining power of labor groups, the evidence does not support the claim that unionization and collective bargaining have increased the share of labor in national income *before taxes*. The long-run trends observable in employee compensation as a percentage of national income suggest no appreciable difference between earlier periods during which unions were weak and few and more recent periods during which they were strong and many.[9] For example, if correction is made for the increasing weight of "employees" in the total population, the relative share of employees in the American privately produced output does not seem to have changed greatly from 1920 to the present. We have seen that in the United States the period 1920-1929 brought practically no change in relative shares, aside from cyclical variations. This was a period during which union power was small. The subsequent period, 1929-1950, brought a very significant growth of union strength. But it brought very little long-run change in the relative share of labor income, practically none if we disregard changes caused by shifts in the composition of output. On the other hand, the relative share of labor does seem to have increased more appreciably in the decades immediately preceding that of the 'twenties, even though at that time union strength was very small. These negative conclusions concerning the distributional effect of unionism are confirmed by the fact that a comparison of trends in union wage rates with trends in nonunion rates

---

[9] See D. G. Johnson, "The Functional Distribution of Income in the United States, 1850-1952," *Review of Economics and Statistics* (May 1954), pp. 175-183. See also our detailed discussion in the Appendix to Part 3.

for given types ("specifications") of labor points to no appreciable differentials.[10] The impact of union wage increases on prices does not seem to be significantly tempered by competition coming from nonunionized sectors in the economy. When the price of labor services in general is raised, a rise in commodity prices and the added incentive toward labor-saving improvement seem to reduce or to neutralize the effect on the share of labor. These consequences do not show instantaneously but the lags are more significant for a discussion of short-run disturbances than for trend analysis.

It seems unlikely, therefore, that unionism should weaken the improvement mechanism by diminishing the share of investors in *income before taxes*. Direct pressure from unions to prevent the introduction of new techniques may, however, in some cases weaken the tendency to satisfy the first as well as the second of our three growth corollaries. The same is true of job-allocation clauses, by which assignments may be prevented from going to the most efficient workers. In general, unionism is perhaps more likely to interfere with the tendency toward satisfying the second than the first of our corollaries. This is because the mobility of labor is reduced. Strong unions can prevent the reduction of wage rates and of prices in relatively oversupplied fields of specialization and relatively overproducing industries. They can slow the transfer of resources to more productive uses. Also, they are likely to contribute to making upward deviations from the third corollary more common than downward deviations, and thus to tilting price trends upward. We have seen that anti-deflationary policies must, in general, be expected to place some obstacles in the way of fully successful anti-inflation policies. The effect of this on price trends may become accentuated by union influence, which lessens the degree of price decline in periods of output contraction. Union influence may also increase the degree of price rise in periods of economic expansion.

The present writer finds it difficult to believe that these various direct effects of unionism should decisively interfere with the long-run tendency toward satisfying the growth corollaries. A serious threat to the institutional framework does develop where unions become aligned with radical political parties. On the other hand, in several countries, of which the United States is an outstanding example, the union movement has offered an alternative to radical political organization. Once geographical

---

[10] As was argued on Page 269, this does not necessarily exclude an appreciable effect of unionism on the wage-salary structure.

concentration, expressing itself in urbanization and in plants with thousands of workers, is taken for granted, the organization of workers should also be. In some countries unionism has become the alternative to forms of organization which would have had a much more profound effect on the essential institutional features of the economic system. In this sense, unionism has been a distinctly conservative force in some countries.

Even in these countries, unionism has, however, exerted a significant equalitarian influence through political channels. Perhaps this may be regarded as an indirect effect of the organization of labor, but its importance must not be underrated. Highly graduated taxation is an outstanding characteristic of the contemporary Western environment, and the pressure toward redistribution through taxation springs in large part from organized labor groups. Unions do not have to favor radical institutional change to make it appear likely that political candidates favoring highly graduated taxation will capture large blocks of labor vote. To this extent, unionism is almost inevitably political.

Sufficiently highly graduated taxation would undoubtedly weaken the performance of industrial nations. Monetary incentives to efficient performance would become eliminated, and there would be nothing to take their place. Under a system operating in this fashion, even the "pure prestige value" of industrial success would be significantly diminished. However, it is impossible to make categoric statements about the degree of tax graduation at which the effects become truly threatening. For it is the impact on the margin of earnings—the so-called marginal tax rate —which damages incentives.[11] A lump-sum tax, which would be levied on taxpayers in an amount unaffected by the size of income, would be highly inequitable, but it would probably increase the incentive to work and perhaps also to invest (unless it destroyed the health or the morale of the taxpayer). This is because an incentive would be created to work more and to assume additional risks in order to offset the burden of the lump-sum tax. The marginal tax rate for such a tax would be zero. A flat-rate tax has, of course, the same marginal as average rate throughout the range of incomes, and for a graduated tax the marginal rate is higher than the average rate for any given income class.

---

[11] If, for example, the average tax rate (so-called effective tax rate) on a $5,000 income is 4 percent, and on a $10,000 income 12 percent, then the marginal rate on the rise from $5,000 to $10,000 is 20 percent because, of the $5,000 increase, $1,000 go to the treasury.

While the marginal rate *per se* is damaging to incentives, the tax as a whole combines the effect of a hypothetical lump-sum burden with the effect of a hypothetical burden that would fall exclusively on the margin. On balance, a graduated tax need not, therefore, always reduce incentives. The more graduated it is, the more likely it is to damage incentives because the more likely is it that the incentive-weakening effect will outweigh the incentive-strengthening effect. In some countries, for example in England, taxes are so highly graduated that it is difficult to imagine that they do not damage incentives. In most other countries the degree of graduation is less severe. In the United States this is partly because each spouse may pay income tax on one half of the joint income. But the shift toward high graduation has been marked everywhere, and it has been associated with high taxation of corporate profits, that is, with the double taxation of corporate ownership-income,[12] as well as with high inheritance taxes which reduce the incentive to accumulate wealth for later generations.

The quantitative appraisals which are required for forming judgments in these matters cannot be undertaken with scientific accuracy. It is impossible to tell how much private investment is suppressed, and whether in specific instances of tax-financed public spending the government-provided employment is smaller or greater than the tax-suppressed private employment.[13] That it is possible to increase tax graduation to a point where it would put an end to the long-run tendency toward satisfying the growth corollaries in the private enterprise framework is beyond reasonable doubt. Moreover, it is beyond reasonable doubt that an appreciable reduction of growth rates, as a consequence of high graduation, would be disadvantageous to the low-income as well as to the high-income groups. Consider, for example, economies in which there has occurred a rise in output per man-hour at an average annual rate of about 2 percent,[14] with an approximately stable or rising relative share of labor before taxes. We need not extend our horizon beyond ten or twenty years to reach the conclusion that in such economies a significant reduction of the rate of productivity increase damages the low-income groups by more than the equivalent of their possible gains through redis-

---

[12] The corporation pays corporate income tax (profit tax), and the dividend recipient pays personal income tax.

[13] See in this context Pages 357-358, and Footnote 6 on Page 365.

[14] For "Western economies in general," *although not for the United States,* this seems to be somewhat more than the "typical" long-run rate of increase. But the argument that follows includes quite a bit of safety margin (it plays very safe).

tribution. This is because continuation of the past trend gives the average worker a very good prospect of roughly a 50-percent increase in his real-wage rates within twenty years, while redistribution in itself does not hold anything like this prospect. For longer periods, the case is, of course, even more obvious. Indeed, the case is sufficiently convincing for yearly productivity increase of 1 percent, which seems untypically low for Western economies in general. But for the reasons here discussed it cannot be taken for granted that a moderate degree of redistribution through tax graduation reduces the upward trend in productivity; and it is not obvious where, precisely, the dividing line between "moderate" and "damagingly high" lies.

.The argument should take into account also the *cyclical stabilizing effect* of graduated taxation, and of fiscal commitments to help the unemployed [15] or other recipients of substandard incomes. If the incentive-damaging effect is small enough when we *abstract* from the cyclical stabilizing effect, then in reality a net incentive-stimulating effect may result from the redistributive elements of the tax structure. This is because the cyclical stabilizing effect in itself presumably exerts a favorable long-run influence on incentives. It is very likely that reduction of the fluctuations around trend lines raises the trend lines themselves. But if, aside from the cyclical stabilizing effect, the incentive-damaging consequences of the tax structure are substantial, then the adverse consequences will, of course, predominate. Ultimately, incomes after taxes must be sufficient to provide the required incentives *in view of whatever degree of instability and uncertainty there remains in the economy.* It is extremely unlikely, for example, that a 52-percent corporate profit tax should have stimulating consequences. For while such a tax (which happens to be in effect at present in the United States) is an "automatic stabilizer," it takes a great deal of stabilizing and risk reducing to change $48 into the investment stimulant that $100 used to be.

As for the corporate income tax, it is sometimes maintained that this is shifted to the buyers and thus does not fall on profits. Businessmen frequently have an interest in saying this when they argue against the imposition of such a tax, and the critics of business frequently say the same thing when arguing that business does not carry the burden which it

---

[15] The cyclical stabilizing effect of tax policies and of fiscal expenditure results from the fact that in periods of expansion they increase tax revenues relatively to aggregate income, and, even more, relatively to fiscal expenditures. In periods of contraction, on the other hand, they increase fiscal expenditures relatively to aggregate income, and, even more, relatively to tax revenues.

appears to carry. But it is unlikely that the corporate income tax should be "shifted" in any usual sense of the word. This is because the prices which seem most profitable to an enterprise when it can keep 100 percent of the profits cannot in general be different from the prices that seem most profitable to the enterprise when it can keep 48 percent of the profits. Any "shifting" in the usual sense would imply the setting of different prices in these two sets of circumstances. The corporate income tax is likely to keep firms from carrying out some of the risky projects which otherwise would seem sufficiently promising. But this is a different question, even though changes in the volume of investment have an effect on the price level.

One analytical statement may be added here about which a fair degree of agreement exists. The incentive-damaging consequences of taxation can be reduced by loss-deduction ("carry-over") provisions.[16] Loss deduction makes the treasury a partner in losses as well as in gains, at least if the gains of a longer period outweigh the losses. Essentially, these provisions are income-averaging devices for a longer period. They are devices recognizing the arbitrariness of the year as a unit of time for fiscal purposes.

The most adequate formulation of these various conclusions is perhaps that modern nations are very likely to weaken their ability to satisfy the growth corollaries if in their ideology high tax graduation becomes the dominant ethical postulate, to which the objectives of performance and efficiency become subordinated. This is another way of saying that the system will not function if the equalitarian creed displaces the outlook of the market economy instead of becoming admixed with it in moderate doses. If this happens, the growth process can scarcely be expected to continue in the private enterprise framework. Growth will cease, or, what is more likely, the profit-incentive economy will be replaced by an economy of government ownership and government operation. Where there exists the inclination to experiment with workable blends of the ideology of the market economy with that of equalitarianism, this expresses a strong disinclination, in the lower income groups and in their representatives, to run the risk of placing themselves under a centralized authoritarian system of comprehensive government ownership. For if private enterprise is left with no incentive to perform the strategic economic functions efficiently, then only the state can. The government

---

[16] This is true particularly if the provisions in question are drafted and administered in such a way as not to reduce the cyclical stabilizing effect of the tax structure.

of such a state would inevitably become a formidable power group. It is utopian to believe that governments will be voted out of office periodically in countries in which the state is the only significant employer. Meaningful electoral campaigns cannot be organized by persons entirely dependent on the state for their jobs. Nor can they be conducted before an electorate practically all of which is in the identical status of dependency.

On the whole, it does not seem likely that in economies with satisfactory productivity and wage trends, and a reasonable degree of cyclical stability, large blocks of the population would have a preference for a radical redistribution of incomes *over continuation of the trend,* or even that large blocks of the population would genuinely press for policies involving appreciable risks in this regard. Nor does it seem likely that the leadership of labor unions should be unaware of what comprehensive government ownership would do to the institutions which they represent. Severe and long-lasting depressions must, of course, be expected to breed radicalism because they very greatly increase the number of people who have little to lose. This lesson has now probably been learned. But it is difficult to imagine that in an economy with appreciable upward trends *and with properly managed cycle-compensating policies* there should develop or persist a strong sentiment for carrying equality-security measures to extremes. Radicalism of this sort has originated in long and severe depressions, and it is not likely to carry much weight in periods of reasonably stable growth. To keep the equality-security admixtures within reasonable limits remains one of the essential problems of all Western nations. But in economies with satisfactory long-run growth rates reduced cyclical instability is quite likely to diminish redistributional pressures.

8. Security-mindedness in business.

It is probably correct to assume that in the advanced industrial societies businessmen, too, become more security-minded. This may be in part a reaction to the equalitarian policies of advanced industrialism. But the phenomenon may be connected also with the increased significance of the corporate form of enterprise, and particularly with the increased significance of corporations in which ownership is sufficiently diffused to leave hired managers with a great deal of influence. A person violates the trust of others if, at their expense, he engages in very risky ventures which miscarry; he does not violate the trust of others by failure to engage in very risky ventures, even if these would have turned out successfully and would have proved capable of yielding large "speculative" profits.

The speculative characteristics of some former booms—for example, those of the late nineteen-twenties—undoubtedly contributed to the aggravation of conditions during the subsequent depressions. It is quite possible that some increase in the security-mindedness of businessmen tends to improve the long-run performance of a market economy—especially in the United States, which has habitually been a country with a high propensity to bear risks. Here, too, an overdose of security-mindedness would, of course, destroy the long-run tendency to satisfy the corollaries of the growth condition. An overdose of security-mindedness in business could develop in reaction to an overdose of the equalitarian admixture. Aside from this, it could develop as a consequence of the growth of oligopoly.

Oligopoly is said to exist in an industry if the number of firms jointly accounting for a high proportion of the industry-output is small enough to make each of these large sellers aware of the fact that his individual actions affect the other sellers appreciably. In oligopoly the proper course of action of each firm depends on the expected reaction of the others, and each firm knows that the reaction of its rivals depends in turn on what they think *its* reaction will be to their actions. This gives rise to a process which may be characterized as "implicit bargaining," that is, to a process in which each party reads from the behavior and reactions of others what its own most profitable behavior is, given all the responses. Implicit bargaining tends to lead to the gradual establishment of mutually accepted standards of behavior, which we may call implicit agreements or "quasi-agreements." However, these *quasi-agreements usually relate primarily to price policy.* They fall short of a truly monopolistic maximization of the joint profit; indeed, they usually fall far short of it. The reason for this is that unlimited joint maximization—that is, monopolistic maximization—would require full agreement on the proper way of distributing the maximized joint gain among the participants. True maximization is maximization of present and future gains, that is, maximization of present capitalized values. While firms in an industry with known "present" characteristics may have mutually compatible appraisals of their "present" relative strengths, they are usually unwilling to discount and to sign away their ability to acquire skills more rapidly in the future and thereby to improve their relative strength in the group. Thus, oligopolistic quasi-agreements usually fall short of monopolistic profit maximization, by leaving outlets for the competitive introduction of technological and organizational improvements, for product variation, and for new modes of advertising. At least within certain limits, these methods of *nonprice competition* are accepted as part of the approved pattern of behavior, and hence they do not give rise to retaliation by cut-throat price retaliation. Therefore, technological advance belongs among the less "regulated" processes even in oligopolistic structures. Nevertheless, risk-aversion may lead to a small rate of technological and organizational progress under oligopoly, in addition to weakening the price-adjustment mechanism.

The main reason why risk-aversion (security-mindedness) is likely to be greater in oligopolistic industries than in highly competitive ones is that oligopolists are more likely to be able to earn adequate profits even if they keep to relatively safe projects. New entry into the oligopolistic group may be limited by real economies of scale, that is, by the fact that smaller firms woud be producing at higher real cost; or it may be limited by discriminatory arrangements with those who sell to the industry or with those who buy from the industry, that is, by the inability of potential entrants to operate under the same conditions as those under which the existing oligopolists do. But in either event entry is limited, "naturally" or "artificially." This is why the industry is oligopolistic. Conservative appraisal of investment projects is more likely to exist in such a closed environment than in one of very keen competition. Risk-aversion within an oligopolistic group can, of course, not prevent outsiders from establishing themselves in new areas, which are opened up by technological progress and from which it is frequently possible to compete with an oligopolistic group. This at the same time reduces the risk-aversion which the old firms can afford. Still, the pressure to explore all profitable lines of development is reduced if a market becomes oligopolistic.

The tendency to satisfy the first growth corollary of Part 3 may be weakened: a reluctance may develop to introduce improvements which would inevitably involve more risk than do routine operations in the narrower sense. Oligopolistic rigidities may also weaken the tendency to satisfy the second corollary: relative price adjustments which should encourage the flow of resources from one sector to the other may become retarded. These price adjustments, unless they are adopted by "quasi-agreement," may give rise to retaliation by rivals. Moves aimed at feeling out the reactions of the rivals to tentative price reductions are risky because they can be misinterpreted as aggressive moves.[17] Oligopoly tends to slow adjustments in the relative price and cost structure.

On the other hand, it should be admitted that the very high mobility and very prompt price adjustments, into which the producers of a "purely" competitive industry would be pressed by extreme ease of entry would, in all probability, create an exceedingly high degree of uncertainty. This might after some time strongly discourage investment, and it might weaken growth tendencies. Periods with very vigorous investment activity and with large losses might be expected to alternate with relatively stagnant periods. Consequently, in dynamic analysis, which must recognize the significance of uncertainty and of attitudes to business risk, the case against oligopoly is not so sweeping or unqualified as in the conventional static analysis. Atomistic competition here ceases to be an ideal. But the degree of oligopoly which seems desirable from the point of view of the individual oligopolist is, of course, out of line with the deviations from atomistic competition which are justifiable on the basis of general economic considerations. There exists a strong presumption that the performance of contemporary economies could be improved by policies aimed at reducing the attainable degree of oligopoly, and that further growth of oligopoly would expose all Western nations to a substantial danger. The insufficiently competitive character of economic relations provides one of the most plausible explanations of the relatively weak contemporary economic performance of some countries.

The problems arising from this are not the same in the various countries of the Western world. As for the United States, there is not much reason to assume that oligopolistic concentration has increased here in recent decades. What has increased is the deliberate limitation of competition in atomistic groups of workers, farmers, and retailers with the aid of government regulation. These limitations undoubtedly reduce the mobility of resources. The oligopolistic concentration of firms does not seem to have increased. But while it does not seem to have increased, it is nevertheless quite substantial, especially in manufacturing and mining (and also in transportation and the utilities where, however, there exists government supervision). The problem is to prevent the degree of concentration from rising further and to reduce it where this can be done without sacrificing important economies of scale. In the United

---

[17] This additional rigidity, caused by the risk of feeling out the reactions of rivals, is reduced in cases where one firm is accepted by the others as the "price leader."

States relatively the most promising method for achieving this is to increase the ease of entry where entry is blocked by discriminatory practices. The anti-trust acts enable the government to make an effort in this direction.

As we have seen, oligopoly may lower the rate of improvement because improvement is risky, and firms with appreciable profits may be able to afford a more cautious attitude. The possibility of reduced rates of progress under oligopoly is generally noted in the literature, but the discussion is not always properly linked to the problem of foresight and risk aversion. The conventional argument is based on the idea that in monopolistic and oligopolistic circumstances a given new method of production will be introduced and prices will be lowered only if the *total cost of production with the new method* is smaller than the *variable cost with the old method* (because the fixed or sunk costs of the old method are bygones which do not enter into the comparison of the two expenditure plans for producing a future output stream).[18] On the other hand, in a purely competitive industry with completely free entry, new firms will enter with a given new method even if the *total cost of production with the new method* is merely lower than the *total cost with the old* (but possibly higher than the variable cost with the old). These entrants will then force the old firms to price their output at a loss, namely, at the new total cost, *as if* they, too, were producing with the new method. Hence, according to this argument, the more competitive the industry is, the more rapidly will given inventions be introduced to the benefit of the consumer. This has by now become the "conventional argument" concerning differences in the rate of progress between competitive industries with free entry and monopolistic or oligopolistic industries with limited entry.

The argument implies that the competitive firms are always excessively optimistic—they have an unjustifiably low appraisal of the risk involved in sinking costs into any given method of production—and thus they suffer losses whenever a new method becomes applicable. When improved methods become known, new entrants force the existing producers to price their products at a loss. If the firms had correct foresight, the number of firms in the competitive industry would be smaller in each period and the aggregate output of the competitive industry would be smaller

---

[18] Complete statement of the argument requires taking account also of demand-elasticity, to compare the size of the demand when the old method is used with the size of the demand when the firm changes to the new method and to a different price.

too. Thus prices would be kept higher, on the average, during the successive periods, and in each period the individual firms could amortize their fixed costs in spite of the gradual introduction of new methods by new firms. In other words, with correct foresight the competitive as well as the monopolistic or oligopolistic firms would be able to write off their sunk costs during the lifetime of their equipment. Under no market conditions will the rate of progress be greater than that which is compatible with this result, *as long as foresight is correct*. With correct foresight the conventional argument would be wholly wrong.

If foresight is limited, as is always the case in the real world, a difference will develop between the rates of progress under alternative market conditions, provided that the propensity to engage in risky ventures is different in different market environments. On the other hand, there exists also the difference that the research efficiency of large-firm laboratories is presumably greater than the inventive efficiency of small producers, although it is not necessarily true that the largest firms of each industry are the most efficient in this regard. But once the rate of making new inventions is given, the rate of their industrial introduction depends mainly on the quality of foresight and the attitude to uncertainty. Consequently, the conventional argument about the allegedly higher rate of industrial innovation under pure than under limited competition leads back to the question of foresight and the appraisal of risk. If there existed no difference in these regards, the conventional argument would be incorrect. However, it is likely that the safety-preference of well-established oligopolists is relatively high, and that their propensity to introduce known new inventions is therefore smaller than that of firms operating under more competitive conditions. This is what makes the conventional conclusions more valid than wrong, for reasons that are identical with those previously discussed under the heading of oligopolistic risk-aversion or security-mindedness.

Where oligopoly interferes with the growth process, it does so mainly by creating excessive safety preference (unwillingness to experiment with improvements) and by slowing the process of price and cost adjustments to the changing structural requirements of the economy.

It is conceivable that the various manifestations of the equalitarian outlook, and of security-mindedness in labor and in business, will result in a fatal weakening of the long-run tendency to satisfy the growth corollaries in the framework of private enterprise systems. However, there is very little to support such a pessimistic forecast for the United States, for other American economies, and for several important countries of the European continent. Their recent record does not point in this direction, even though all these economies combine competitive features with monopolistic as well as with equalitarian traits. The relative inefficiency of a few among many economically interrelated nations does not usually lead to fundamental change throughout the area, although it does, of course, lead to important shifts in the power hierarchy of nations. The losers in this reordering are likely to be the countries with a particularly high degree of security-mindedness or of economic equality-mindedness, or of both.

9. The Keynes-Hansen stagnation thesis.

The doctrine known in the nineteen-thirties as the stagnation thesis is not based on the hypothesis that the equalitarian characteristics of the twentieth century, or its security-mindedness, will destroy the long-run tendency to satisfy the growth corollaries in private enterprise economies. The stagnation doctrine is based on the assumption that the scarcities in the factors of production which cooperate with capital have become too great to be offset by technological and organizational improvements. According to the stagnation thesis, the slackening of the rate of increase of the cooperating factor supplies makes it improbable that the sharper tendency toward diminishing returns will be overcome. More precisely expressed, in such an environment improvements will be insufficient to offset the tendency toward diminishing returns *for the amount of new investment which will be required to match savings when the economy grows* at high levels of employment. Consequently, the economies in question will cease to grow; output will contract to the level where a diminution of savings eliminates further deflationary pressure. This is a level at which there exists appreciable unemployment of labor. Such a condition will become typical of mature capitalism, although there may occur occasional booms, which temporarily lift the economy to higher levels and occasional depressions which press it to even lower rates of activity. However, the tendency toward underemployment equilibrium can be counteracted by the proper fiscal policies, essentially by deficit-financing.

Earlier in this volume, the opinion was expressed that a chronic weakness of the improvement mechanism *would* lead to the result predicted by the stagnation thesis, or, at least, that the possible automatic adjustment of saving habits would be so slow that our social systems could not survive the interval. Disagreement was expressed with the proposition that a *chronic* situation of this sort would be curable by deficit financing. Indeed, we believe that the essential characteristics of the Western institutional framework would become destroyed by a transition into the stationary state, even if Say's Law proved valid and saving automatically ceased at the full-employment level. However, what is mainly of interest here is the question of the validity of the prognosis that in the future the improvement mechanism will be incapable of inducing a sufficient rate of private investment.

It is impossible to arrive at categoric conclusions with respect to the future functioning of the mechanism of induced improvements. The supply of factors cooperating with capital may grow less rapidly in the future than was the case in the nineteenth century. This is true even of the labor supply, although the present predictions concerning the future population growth of the West are considerably higher than those of ten or twenty years ago. Some of the past estimates have been proved much too low in recent years. However, in the United States, while population may continue to increase more rapidly than was believed to be possible a short while ago, the population growth of the nineteenth century will certainly not repeat itself. As for the rate of increase of the stock of natural resources available for economic development, this will undoubtedly become smaller *in one sense*. Colonization of the nineteenth-century type is a matter of the past, and there exists nothing that is strictly analogous to the empty spaces of the North American continent which have become populated by millions of European emigrants and their descendants. But what is really essential about the Western acquisitions of new natural resources is that they constitute a specific type of *social-organizational improvement* or innovation, one that renders exploitable a stock of resources that has existed all along. It is uncertain whether the present century and the next will turn out to have brought less resource acquisition *so defined* than did the nineteenth. This is partly a question of how much international political integration will occur in the coming epoch. Also, stocks of natural resources may become more easily exploitable by technological discovery, rather than primarily by social-organizational change, and this process is continuing very forcefully indeed. In this volume we have repeatedly pointed to indicators of an accelerated rate of technological-organizational progress.

In what sense the scarcity of factors cooperating with capital will in the future be greater is therefore not entirely clear. It must not be overlooked that important changes in the rate of increase in factor supplies cooperating with capital have occurred in the past. The United States has seen many decades of declining proportionate population growth during which economic trends were distinctly satisfactory, and it is not yesterday that the frontier disappeared. The improvement mechanism has tended to adjust to such changes in the long run. This mechanism has so far shown a considerable degree of adjustability to the relative resource position of Western economies.

The stagnation thesis, in the form here discussed, is based on ideas which were expressed by Lord Keynes in England and further developed by Alvin H. Hansen at Harvard University.[19] This happened during the depressed years of the 'thirties. The thesis suggested that the world was at that time faced not with a long and deep depression—not with a phase of the cycle—but with the beginning of a new era. The new era was supposed to show a tendency toward chronic stagnation and chronic un-employment, a tendency which according to Keynes and Hansen could have been offset by chronic deficit financing. In each of the two decades that have followed a sufficient number of "abnormal" or "exceptional" things have happened to render us unable to confirm or to refute the long-range prediction of the Keynes-Hansen school. But so far stagna-tion has not come and it surely does not seem to be around the corner, even though in the United States, to take the most important example, the large budgets of the first postwar decade[20] were financed by taxes rather than by cash deficits, and even though some of these taxes are very likely to have an appreciable disincentive effect. We may be living on borrowed time. But so many significant writers of the past have greatly underestimated the amount of time which we have borrowed that we may suspect some of our contemporaries of the same tempera-mental bias.

If it were possible to disregard the relations between the two camps into which the world has become divided, we would conclude that the future of our social systems depends ultimately on their ability to tame and to assimilate the security-equality currents of the century. The ma-jority of the Western nations seems to be getting on fairly successfully with this task. They will inevitably lose some cultural values of an earlier epoch, but they are gaining others, and over most of the area of Western civilization there is no lack of vitality. Signs are observable of greater

---

[19] See Pages 136-137.
[20] We mean here the decade as a whole.

concern with noneconomic objectives, that is, with values to which the goods of the market are merely instrumental. At the present stage of development, this does not seem to diminish the efficiency of our market-oriented, instrumental activities. Economics, which threatened to become a dismal science on at least three occasions—with Ricardo, with Marx, and with Keynes—is once more a distinctly hopeful science. But, as matters stand, the future depends most of all on whether systems of mild coercion, based on Western methods of rewarding and penalizing, will prove capable of holding their own against growing and expanding systems of violent coercion. Here there exists no middle ground between confidence and despair.

BIBLIOGRAPHY—PART 5

1. List of books and articles from which general supplementary readings may be selected:

Books

Ashton, T. S. *The Industrial Revolution, 1760-1830.* London and New York: Oxford University Press, 1948.

Cunningham, W. *The Growth of English Industry and Commerce.* Cambridge, England: University Press, 1927.

Day, Clive. *Economic Development in Europe.* New York: The Macmillan Co., 1942.

Gordon, R. A. *Business Fluctuations.* New York: Harper & Bros., 1952.

Hansen, A. H. *Full Recovery or Stagnation?* New York: W. W. Norton & Co., 1938.

———. *Monetary Theory and Fiscal Policy.* New York: McGraw-Hill Book Co., 1949.

Keynes, J. M. *The General Theory of Employment, Interest, and Money.* New York: Harcourt, Brace & Co., 1936.

Nurkse, Ragnar. *Problems of Capital Formation in Underdeveloped Countries.* New York: Oxford University Press, 1953.

Rostow, W. W. *British Economy of the Nineteenth Century.* Oxford: Clarendon Press, 1948.

Schmoller, G. F. *The Mercantile System and Its Historical Significance.* New York and London: Macmillan & Co., 1914.

Terborgh, G. W. *The Bogey of Economic Maturity.* Chicago: Machinery and Allied Products Institute, 1945.

United Nations Secretariat, Department of Economic Affairs. *Measures for the Economic Development of Under-developed Countries.* New York: United Nations, 1951.

Williams, J. H. *Postwar Monetary Plans, and Other Essays.* New York: A. A. Knopf, 1947.

Articles

Heckscher, E. F. "Mercantilism," in *Encyclopaedia of the Social Sciences.* New York: The Macmillan Co., 1933.

Lewis, W. Arthur. "Economic Development With Unlimited Supplies of Labour." *The Manchester School,* May 1954.

Rosenstein-Rodan, P. N. "Problems of Industrialization of Eastern and South-Eastern Europe." *Economic Journal,* June 1943.

Spengler, J. J. "Population Theory," in *Survey of Contemporary Economics,* Vol. II, ed. by B. F. Haley. Homewood, Ill.: Richard D. Irwin, 1952.

2. Further readings relating to topics discussed in Part 5:

Books

Hayek, F. A. von, ed. *Capitalism and the Historians.* Chicago: University of Chicago Press, 1954.

Heckscher, E. F. *Mercantilism.* 2 vols. London: G. Allen & Unwin, 1935.

List, Friedrich. *The National System of Political Economy.* London and New York: Longmans, Green & Co., 1904.

Sombart, Werner. *Der Moderne Kapitalismus.* 2 vols. Leipzig: Duncker & Humblot, 1902. Vol. II.

Usher, A. P. *An Introduction to the Industrial History of England.* New York: Houghton Mifflin Co., 1920.

U. S. Treasury. *Report of the Secretary of the Treasury* [Alexander Hamilton] *on the Subject of Manufactures Made the Fifth of December, 1791.* Washington: R. C. Weightman, 1809.

Weber, Max. *General Economic History,* trans. by F. H. Knight. New York: Greenberg, 1927.

Articles

Goldsmith, Selma, G. Jaszi, H. Kaitz, and M. Liebenberg. "Size Distribution of Income Since the Mid-Thirties." *Review of Economics and Statistics,* February 1954.

Johnson, D. G. "The Functional Distribution of Income in the United States, 1850-1952." *Review of Economics and Statistics,* May 1954.

Sultan, P. E. "Unionism and Wage-Income Ratios: 1929-51." *Review of Economics and Statistics,* February 1954.

Wright, D. M. "The Great Guessing Game." *Review of Economic Statistics,* February 1946.

Tables for Graphs

TABLE I—Wholesale Price Index (All Commodities), Bureau of Labor Statistics

(1926 = 100)

Year		Year		Year		Year		Year		Year	
1801	111.8	1826	71.1	1851	64.5	1876	72.0	1901	55.3	1926	100.0
1802	91.8	1827	71.8	1852	62.5	1877	67.5	1902	58.9	1927	95.4
1803	93.9	1828	68.3	1853	66.4	1878	61.7	1903	59.6	1928	96.7
1804	101.5	1829	67.6	1854	68.8	1879	58.8	1904	59.7	1929	95.3
1805	104.2	1830	65.6	1855	68.9	1880	65.1	1905	60.1	1930	86.4
1806	102.2	1831	70.4	1856	68.9	1881	64.4	1906	61.8	1931	73.0
1807	96.0	1832	71.1	1857	68.5	1882	66.1	1907	65.2	1932	64.8
1808	93.9	1833	70.4	1858	62.0	1883	64.6	1908	62.9	1933	65.9
1809	98.7	1834	65.6	1859	61.0	1884	60.5	1909	67.6	1934	74.9
1810	107.7	1835	74.6	1860	60.9	1885	56.6	1910	70.4	1935	80.0
1811	104.9	1836	83.5	1861	61.3	1886	56.0	1911	64.9	1936	80.8
1812	106.3	1837	82.8	1862	71.7	1887	56.4	1912	69.1	1937	86.3
1813	123.6	1838	79.4	1863	90.5	1888	57.4	1913	69.8	1938	78.6
1814	154.6	1839	83.5	1864	116.0	1889	57.4	1914	68.1	1939	77.1
1815	121.5	1840	71.1	1865	132.0	1890	56.2	1915	69.5	1940	78.6
1816	103.5	1841	70.5	1866	116.3	1891	55.8	1916	85.5	1941	87.3
1817	104.2	1842	65.7	1867	104.9	1892	52.2	1917	117.5	1942	98.8
1818	102.2	1843	61.8	1868	97.7	1893	53.4	1918	131.3	1943	103.1
1819	89.7	1844	62.1	1869	93.5	1894	47.9	1919	138.6	1944	104.0
1820	76.6	1845	62.6	1870	86.7	1895	48.8	1920	154.4	1945	105.8
1821	73.2	1846	64.8	1871	82.8	1896	46.5	1921	97.6	1946	121.1
1822	75.2	1847	64.9	1872	84.5	1897	46.6	1922	96.7	1947	152.1
1823	71.8	1848	61.8	1873	83.7	1898	48.5	1923	100.6	1948	165.1
1824	71.1	1849	60.1	1874	81.0	1899	52.2	1924	98.1	1949	155.0
1825	71.8	1850	62.3	1875	77.7	1900	56.1	1925	103.5	1950	161.5
										1951	180.4

Source: 1801-1945, *Historical Statistics of the United States, 1789-1945,* L-15.
1946-1951, *Statistical Abstract of the United States, 1952,* p. 273.

Table 2—British Wholesale Price Index 1779-1953

(1867-77 = 100)

Year		Year		Year		Year		Year		Year		Year	
1779	106	1804	153	1829	94	1854	102	1879	83	1904	70	1929	114
1780	108	1805	160	1830	93	1855	101	1880	88	1905	72	1930	96
1781	117	1806	157	1831	95	1856	101	1881	85	1906	77	1931	82
1782	118	1807	152	1832	94	1857	105	1882	84	1907	80	1932	79
1783	103	1808	166	1833	97	1858	91	1883	82	1908	73	1933	78
1784	99	1809	176	1834	97	1859	94	1884	76	1909	74	1934	81
1785	96	1810	176	1835	100	1860	99	1885	72	1910	78	1935	83
1786	98	1811	158	1836	112	1861	98	1886	69	1911	80	1936	88
1787	102	1812	163	1837	102	1862	101	1887	68	1912	85	1937	102
1788	98	1813	185	1838	104	1863	103	1888	70	1913	85	1938	90
1789	95	1814	198	1839	111	1864	105	1889	72	1914	85	1939	94
1790	100	1815	166	1840	108	1865	101	1890	72	1915	108	1940	128
1791	99	1816	135	1841	103	1866	102	1891	72	1916	136	1941	142
1792	102	1817	143	1842	94	1867	100	1892	68	1917	175	1942	151
1793	109	1818	150	1843	86	1868	99	1893	68	1918	192	1943	155
1794	107	1819	136	1844	87	1869	98	1894	63	1919	206	1944	160
1795	126	1820	124	1845	88	1870	96	1895	62	1920	251	1945	164
1796	136	1821	117	1846	89	1871	100	1896	61	1921	155	1946	186
1797	141	1822	114	1847	95	1872	109	1897	62	1922	131	1947	230
1798	149	1823	113	1848	78	1873	111	1898	64	1923	129	1948	260
1799	156	1824	106	1849	74	1874	102	1899	68	1924	139	1949	274
1800	159	1825	118	1850	77	1875	96	1900	75	1925	136	1950	324
1801	166	1826	103	1851	75	1876	95	1901	70	1926	126	1951	402
1802	143	1827	101	1852	78	1877	94	1902	69	1927	122	1952	380
1803	156	1828	97	1853	95	1878	87	1903	69	1928	119	1953	366

Source: 1779-1845, N. J. Silberling, "British Prices and Business Cycles, 1779-1850," Review of Economic Statistics (October 1923), pp. 232-233. 1846-1907, A. Sauerbeck, The Course of Average Prices of General Commodities in England (London, 1908). 1908-1953, Continuation of Sauerbeck's index in The Statist (July 3, 1954), p. 78.

Table 3—British Consol Yields, 1849-1954

Year		Year		Year		Year		Year	
1849	3.25	1870	3.28	1891	2.67	1912	3.30	1933	3.40
1850	3.11	1871	3.27	1892	2.65	1913	3.41	1934	3.11
1851	3.09	1872	3.28	1893	2.59	1914	3.35	1935	2.90
1852	3.02	1873	3.28	1894	2.52	1915	3.83	1936	2.96
1853	3.07	1874	3.28	1895	2.39	1916	4.32	1937	3.28
1854	3.27	1875	3.24	1896	2.29	1917	4.63	1938	3.38
1855	3.32	1876	3.16	1897	2.25	1918	4.41	1939	3.72
1856	3.22	1877	3.14	1898	2.28	1919	4.64	1940	3.40
1857	3.27	1878	3.15	1899	2.36	1920	5.34	1941	3.13
1858	3.10	1879	3.08	1900	2.53	1921	5.23	1942	3.03
1859	3.15	1880	3.05	1901	2.67	1922	4.44	1943	3.10
1860	3.19	1881	3.00	1902	2.65	1923	4.33	1944	3.14
1861	3.28	1882	2.99	1903	2.75	1924	4.40	1945	2.92
1862	3.23	1883	2.96	1904	2.84	1925	4.46	1946	2.60
1863	3.24	1884	2.97	1905	2.78	1926	4.57	1947	2.76
1864	3.33	1885	3.02	1906	2.83	1927	4.63	1948	3.21
1865	3.35	1886	2.98	1907	2.97	1928	4.49	1949	3.30
1866	3.41	1887	2.95	1908	2.91	1929	4.62	1950	3.54
1867	3.23	1888	2.61	1909	2.98	1930	4.50	1951	3.78
1868	3.20	1889	2.63	1910	3.09	1931	4.41	1952	4.23
1869	3.26	1890	2.64	1911	3.19	1932	3.76	1953	4.10
								1954	3.90*

1849-1936 from J. Stafford, "The Future of the Rate of Interest," *The Manchester School*, No. 2, 1937, p. 137. Some of Stafford's figures are taken from T. T. Williams, "The Rate of Discount and the Price of Consols," *Journal of the Royal Statistical Society*, March 1912.

1937-1952 Great Britain, Central Statistical Office, *Annual Abstract of Statistics*, Vol. 85, Table 267 and Vol. 90, Table 301. From Bank of England and Actuaries Investment Index.

1953-1954 *Lloyds Bank Review*, July, 1954, p. 49.

* (First half).

Table 4—Yields of Best Five American Railroad Bonds
(Lowest Yielding) each January, 1857-1936

Year		Year		Year	
1857	7.63	1883	4.53	1909	3.82
1858	7.98	1884	4.41	1910	3.91
1859	7.14	1885	4.29	1911	3.97
1860	6.94	1886	3.94	1912	3.99
1861	6.86	1887	3.92	1913	4.07
1862	6.82	1888	4.01	1914	4.20
1863	5.12	1889	3.82	1915	4.27
1864	5.73	1890	3.87	1916	4.18
1865	5.76	1891	4.05	1917	4.09
1866	7.13	1892	3.98	1918	4.80
1867	6.83	1893	3.94	1919	4.81
1868	6.92	1894	3.94	1920	5.10
1869	6.95	1895	3.74	1921	5.19
1870	7.05	1896	3.71	1922	4.66
1871	6.90	1897	3.64	1923	4.59
1872	6.66	1898	3.46	1924	4.68
1873	6.79	1899	3.29	1925	4.62
1874	6.71	1900	3.29	1926	4.53
1875	6.22	1901	3.28	1927	4.39
1876	5.78	1902	3.28	1928	4.15
1877	5.52	1903	3.47	1929	4.46
1878	5.55	1904	3.64	1930	4.45
1879	5.30	1905	3.57	1931	4.18
1880	5.02	1906	3.61	1932	4.85
1881	4.48	1907	3.77	1933	4.25
1882	4.45	1908	3.97	1934	4.15
				1935	3.57
				1936	3.42

Source: F. R. Macaulay, *The Movements of Interest Rates, Bond Yields and Stock Prices in the United States Since 1856* (New York, 1936), pp. A 111-A 112.

Table 5—American Railroad Bond Yields, 1919-1952

Year		Year		Year	
1919	6.42	1930	4.96	1941	3.95
1920	7.12	1931	6.09	1942	3.96
1921	6.91	1932	7.61	1943	3.64
1922	5.89	1933	6.09	1944	3.39
1923	6.24	1934	4.96	1945	3.06
1924	5.90	1935	4.95	1946	2.91
1925	5.51	1936	4.24	1947	3.11
1926	5.13	1937	4.34	1948	3.34
1927	4.83	1938	5.21	1949	3.24
1928	4.85	1939	4.53	1950	3.10
1929	5.18	1940	4.30	1951	3.26
				1952	3.36

Source: U. S. Department of Commerce, *Survey of Current Business,* 1938 Supplement, p. 75. From Moody's.

Table 6—Yields, 20-Year American Highest-Grade Corporate Bonds, 1900-1945

Year		Year		Year	
1900	3.30	1915	4.20	1930	4.40
1901	3.25	1916	4.05	1931	4.10
1902	3.30	1917	4.05	1932	4.70
1903	3.45	1918	4.82	1933	4.11
1904	3.60	1919	4.81	1934	3.91
1905	3.50	1920	5.17	1935	3.37
1906	3.55	1921	5.31	1936	3.04
1907	3.80	1922	4.85	1937	2.90
1908	3.95	1923	4.68	1938	2.91
1909	3.82	1924	4.69	1939	2.65
1910	3.87	1925	4.50	1940	2.55
1911	3.94	1926	4.40	1941	2.50
1912	3.91	1927	4.30	1942	2.61
1913	4.02	1928	4.05	1943	2.61
1914	4.16	1929	4.45	1944	2.60
				1945	2.55

Source: Historical Statistics of the United States, 1789-1945, N 199. From Board of Governors of the Federal Reserve System.

Table 7—American Stock Yields, 1871-1937

ALL STOCKS

Year		Year		Year	
1871	5.26	1893	4.98	1915	4.96
1872	5.70	1894	4.58	1916	5.62
1873	6.54	1895	3.93	1917	7.90
1874	6.89	1896	4.12	1918	7.24
1875	6.49	1897	3.88	1919	5.75
1876	7.02	1898	3.74	1920	6.13
1877	5.70	1899	3.21	1921	6.49
1878	5.12	1900	4.28	1922	5.80
1879	4.70	1901	3.78	1923	5.94
1880	4.78	1902	3.71	1924	5.87
1881	4.85	1903	4.66	1925	5.19
1882	5.16	1904	4.20	1926	5.32
1883	5.69	1905	3.53	1927	4.77
1884	6.31	1906	3.83	1928	3.98
1885	5.09	1907	5.38	1929	3.48
1886	3.85	1908	4.94	1930	4.26
1887	4.24	1909	4.31	1931	5.58
1888	4.18	1910	4.80	1932	6.69
1889	3.88	1911	4.92	1933	4.05
1890	4.01	1912	4.85	1934	3.92
1891	4.28	1913	5.37	1935	3.88
1892	4.16	1914	5.01	1936	4.35
				1937	4.87

INDUSTRIAL STOCKS

Year		Year		Year	
1871	4.80	1893	8.12	1915	4.14
1872	5.10	1894	6.05	1916	6.16
1873	6.49	1895	5.46	1917	9.78
1874	6.72	1896	5.56	1918	7.71
1875	6.06	1897	5.32	1919	5.18
1876	6.99	1898	5.04	1920	5.54
1877	4.21	1899	3.62	1921	5.84
1878	5.34	1900	4.77	1922	5.37
1879	4.76	1901	5.25	1923	5.40
1880	6.85	1902	4.83	1924	5.25
1881	5.06	1903	6.77	1925	4.75
1882	5.23	1904	4.83	1926	5.24
1883	6.26	1905	3.76	1927	4.72
1884	6.25	1906	4.18	1928	3.82
1885	6.02	1907	6.16	1929	3.65
1886	5.46	1908	4.81	1930	4.45
1887	5.13	1909	3.65	1931	5.82
1888	4.29	1910	5.14	1932	6.58
1889	4.41	1911	5.36	1933	3.56
1890	5.07	1912	4.98	1934	3.45
1891	5.96	1913	5.71	1935	3.51
1892	5.61	1914	5.31	1936	4.27
				1937	4.91

Source: *Historical Statistics of the United States, 1789-1945*, N 206-207. From Alfred Cowles 3rd and Associates, *Common Stock Indexes, 1871-1937* (Bloomington, Ind., 1938).

Table 8—American Stock Yields 1935-1952

ALL STOCKS (200)

Year		Year	
1935	4.06	1944	4.81
1936	3.50	1945	4.19
1937	4.77	1946	3.97
1938	4.38	1947	5.13
1939	4.15	1948	5.78
1940	5.31	1949	6.63
1941	6.25	1950	6.27
1942	6.60	1951	6.12
1943	4.89	1952	5.50

INDUSTRIAL STOCKS (125)

Year		Year	
1935	3.52	1944	4.56
1936	3.36	1945	3.99
1937	4.79	1946	3.75
1938	3.86	1947	5.06
1939	3.85	1948	5.87
1940	5.30	1949	6.82
1941	6.33	1950	6.51
1942	6.44	1951	6.29
1943	4.54	1952	5.55

Source: United States Dept. of Commerce, *Survey of Current Business,* 1953 Supplement, p. 101. From Moody's.

Indexes

Index of Authors

Index of Subjects